Organized workers and socialist politics
in interwar Japan

Organized workers and socialist politics in interwar Japan

STEPHEN S. LARGE

Senior Lecturer, Department of History
University of Adelaide

WITHDRAWN

CAMBRIDGE UNIVERSITY PRESS

CAMBRIDGE

LONDON   NEW YORK   NEW ROCHELLE
MELBOURNE   SYDNEY

Published by the Press Syndicate of the University of Cambridge
The Pitt Building, Trumpington Street, Cambridge CB2 1RP
32 East 57th Street, New York, NY 10022, USA
296 Beaconsfield Parade, Middle Park, Melbourne 3206, Australia

First published 1981

Printed in Great Britain by
Western Printing Services Ltd, Bristol

British Library Cataloguing in Publication Data
Large, Stephen S.
Organized workers and socialist politics in
interwar Japan.
1. Labor and laboring classes – Japan – History
2. Socialism – Japan – History
I. Title
335′.00952   HD8726   80–42158
ISBN 0 521 23675 4

Contents

To my parents
Dwight and Frances Large

Acknowledgments

It is a genuine pleasure to be able to thank the many people who assisted me while this work was in progress. Professor Solomon Levine of the University of Wisconsin and Professor Gary Allinson of the University of Pittsburgh read the manuscript in its entirety and offered valuable comments. Professor Royden Harrison of the University of Warwick was equally generous with his time in this respect. I am grateful for his insights from the perspective of Western labor history and for his hospitality while I was a Visiting Fellow at the Centre for the Study of Social History at Warwick in 1978. Another gracious host was William Currie, S.J., Dean of the Graduate School, International College, at Sophia University, during one of my research trips to Japan.

I have benefited a great deal over the years from testing my ideas in discussions with Professor Komatsu Ryūji of Keiō University, Professor Ikeda Makoto of Saitama University, Professor Ishida Takeshi of Tokyo University, and Mr David Levin of the University of Hong Kong. Dr J. A. A. Stockwin, Professor E. Sydney Crawcour, and Dr John Caiger of the Australian National University, Dr Yoshio Sugimoto of La Trobe University, and Dr Ross Mouer of Griffith University have added to my general understanding of Japanese society, past and present. Mr Watanabe Etsuji opened many archival doors to me in Japan but his great enthusiasm for research in Japanese labor history has meant just as much in stimulating my own interest in the subject.

Several participants in the Japanese labor and socialist party movements were kind enough to share with me their memories of the past. I owe a special word of thanks to Okada Sōji, Uchida Sakurō, Tanahashi Kotora, Iwauchi Zensaku, and Matsuo Nobuyuki.

I am indebted to the University of Iowa, the Joint Committee on Japanese Studies of the American Council of Learned Societies and the Social Science Research Council, the Hill Family Foundation, the Leverhulme Foundation, and the University of Adelaide for the financial assistance that enabled me to do research in Japan, England, and the United States. I also appreciate the assistance of the staffs of the Ōhara Social Problems Research Institute, the Institute of Management and Labor Studies at Keiō University, the Asia Library of the University of Michigan, and the Menzies Library of the Australian National University. Mrs Susan Day and Mrs Anita Taylor of the University of Adelaide have my gratitude for their efficient typing of the manuscript. The editorial staff of Cambridge University Press have made the completion of the manuscript a pleasant task.

Finally, I will always be grateful to Kerstin, my wife, and to the children, Timothy and Laura, for their many sacrifices while I researched and wrote this book. I can never hope to express adequately my appreciation to my parents, to whom the book is dedicated, for their love and support.

Any errors of fact and judgment are my responsibility alone.

CONVENTIONS

In this book Japanese names are given in their proper order, with the surname preceding the given name. However, in the case of Japanese authors writing in English, the order natural to English is preserved.

Introduction

Western scholars have only just begun to build up an understanding of what went on in Japanese history in the period between the two World Wars. Much of our knowledge of Japan in this period concerns elites in power, their domestic and foreign policies, and the emergence of Japan as an important force in Asian and world affairs. By contrast, we know little about the origins of the ferment at the lower depths of Japanese society which prompted a broad array of social protest movements in the interwar decades. In particular, we have yet to inquire what it was about the nature of Japanese society and politics that allowed these movements to begin this period with promising vitality, only to sputter and die out in the 1930s. This is the central question of this book which is a study of the political role of organized labor in Japan from 1919 to 1940.

The proliferation of popular social protest movements, including organized labor, in Taishō (1912–1926) and early Shōwa (1926–1940) Japan reflected the growing complexity of a society undergoing rapid modernization following the Meiji Restoration of 1868. As in other developing countries, industrialization and the concurrent process of social differentiation led to the formation of interest groups in all classes.[1] This impetus, which stimulated workers, farmers, students, women and other groups deprived of a fair share in the distribution of wealth and power in Japan, to organize themselves into social movements for the expression of their grievances, soon made the social movement – defined here as a 'purposive and collective attempt by a number of people to change individuals or societal institutions and structures'[2] – a conspicuous phenomenon on the Japanese scene.

However, unlike most other major industrializing societies, the dynamics of rapid change did not produce social movements in Japan which developed significant political influence in pursuing their objectives. Although Japanese social movements attempted to engage in political action to improve the lot of their members, whose deprivations

1

were seen to be largely political in origin, they remained on the periphery of society and the political process until the eve of World War II when they were dissolved into a New Order which, in its overwhelming emphasis on collectivist nationalism, brooked no tolerance of their pluralist existence. This fate was shared by the Japanese labor movement.

Japanese writers have been more intrigued than have Western historians with the problem of explaining the pattern of futility which characterized the history of social protest movements in their own country. There exists a large and growing body of literature in Japanese dealing, for example, with why the first attempts to form labor unions in Japan in the 1890s did not meet with success and why the revival of unions during World War I did not lead to a strong and politically effective labor movement in the 1920s and 1930s.

In general, two explanations are offered in this literature, the first by scholars who stress a labor relations approach to labor history. They suggest that the political ineffectiveness of labor in realizing its goals on behalf of the factory workers was a result of the persistent weakness of the institutions of organized labor, rejected in Japan as being incompatible with the evolving system of industrial relations that incorporated traditional values and practices inherited from the feudal past. The concept, structure, function, and political ideology and programs of the labor movement – all of which were derived chiefly from Western models – were considered to be inappropriate to Japanese conditions and unnecessary to the success of Japan's quest for national wealth and power.[3]

The problem of gaining acceptance in society for their existence and activities is common to labor movements everywhere. As one Western writer notes,

> The effectiveness of a protest movement, such as trade unionism, depends on its ability to overcome the disapproval and opposition it engenders. The workers' demands and their means of enforcing them must somehow become legitimate in the eyes of the employers, the government, the public, and the workers themselves.[4]

Specialists in the history of Japanese labor relations argue that the effectiveness of the labor movement in acquiring legitimacy during the interwar period was precluded by the fact that the institutions and goals of organized labor were seen to be irrelevant to the Japanese model of industrial development which evolved under the sponsorship of the government and business, with the general support of the public as well as the vast majority of factory workers.

This perspective helps to explain the inability of the labor movement to organize more than 8 per cent of the factory workers, even in its strongest moments during the interwar period. Such a weak base in the factories limited the capacity of the unions to exert political leverage of any sort. However, because of its narrowness, the labor relations approach to labor history is not by itself sufficient to explain the political failure of the Japanese labor movement. Consequently, the second explanation for the vicissitudes of organized labor, which may be referred to as the 'Taishō democracy' interpretation, is of much interest.

Stated briefly, this interpretation contends that the labor movement and many others associated with the popular impulse of 'Taishō democracy' were suppressed from above by an authoritarian State backed up by a conservative capitalist order.[5] This suppression was pervasive: it included political, social, economic, and cultural constraints imposed on Taishō democracy by the established centers of power in Japan who wished to preserve their grip on the monopoly of wealth and power in the country and their general control of its affairs.

This interpretation is attractive on several counts. It assigns to the labor movement, and to Taishō democracy in general, a political significance which concurs with the view of many of the participants in the Japanese social protest movements of the 1920s and 1930s. It provides a martyr's image for Taishō democracy by ascribing its demise to repression by a hostile environment rather than to internal weaknesses. And, it places the history of political struggle between popular democracy and authoritarianism in this period within the broader history of modern Japan. Proponents of this view believe that this struggle had its antecedents in the conflict between the *jiyū minken undō* (movement for popular rights)[6] and the State in the Meiji period, and that the same struggle between the progressive forces of the left and the ruling partnership of big business and the Liberal Democratic Party has raged in Japan since 1955. Seen in the perspective of this last point, the massive revival of the Japanese labor movement after World War II suggests that the travails of the interwar period were not in vain and that organized labor has successfully overcome the debacle of the past.

Yet, there is reason to question whether the Taishō democracy interpretation is altogether valid where it concerns Japanese labor history. This book agrees that the dynamics behind the importance of the labor movement and its ultimate demise prior to World War II were mainly political. But it suggests that the political significance of the labor movement lay in its reinforcement of, not its challenge to, the existing order of Japanese capitalism, nationalism, and imperialism. Further, it is argued that organized labor bolstered the establishment not only because the environment excluded alternatives but also because labor leaders, and the majority of workers in the unions, wanted to accommodate the unions to the status quo.

Whereas the Taishō democracy interpretation rests on the assumption that social protest movements are locked into a conflict relationship with their environment, this book proposes that because they are also an organic part of the context within which they operate, their political behavior invariably reflects, and is conditioned by, the general values and practices in the society around them. Accordingly, the study of labor politics in interwar Japan yields fruitful insights into the general nature of society and politics in this critical phase of modern Japanese history.

These themes are pursued in this book with special reference to the history of one organization in the highly ramified Japanese labor movement, the Nihon Rōdō Sōdōmei (Japan General Federation of Labor). It was decided to study the politics of the labor movement through the Sōdōmei for three reasons, two of which arise from convenience, the third from necessity.

First, the Sōdōmei was the only labor organization in Japan whose history spanned the entire interwar period. Founded in 1919 as an outgrowth of the Yūaikai (Friendly Society) begun seven years earlier, and extinguished in 1940, the Sōdōmei provides a convenient benchmark for the study of labor politics in these decades.

Second, the documentary evidence for the Sōdōmei is more substantial than that pertaining to other labor organizations in this period. It includes a wide range of primary sources such as *Rōdō* [Labor], the official organ of the General Federation published continuously from 1919 to 1940, various union publications within the Sōdōmei, public speeches by Sōdōmei officials, press accounts of the Federation, autobiographies of key Sōdōmei leaders, statistical surveys published by the government and private sources, and the primary materials of the proletarian parties with which the Sōdōmei was associated.

In addition, this book uses contemporary journals such as *Kaizō* [Reconstruction], *Kaihō* [Liberation], *Chūō Kōron* [Central Review], all of which regularly carried commentaries, some critical, some apologetic, on the Sōdōmei and other labor organizations; the primary documents relating to other sections of the labor movement, the Japanese Communist Party, and other leftist parties; governmental proceedings affecting labor; and materials relating to organized business. All of these sources are supplemented with extensive secondary works, including institutional histories of the labor movement, biographies of important labor and political party leaders, and so forth.

The third and most compelling reason for focusing on this organization arises from its strategic position in the evolution of labor politics during this period. The following chapters will show that by adhering rigidly to a reform oriented socialist formula of working for progressive change from within the established order rather than mounting a revolutionary attack against it, the Sōdōmei played a significant role in setting the political pace for the labor movement as a whole.

However, once the Sōdōmei and other labor organizations in the mainstream of the labor movement that took their cue politically from the General Federation adopted this strategy, they soon ran up against a dilemma of political choice which confronts and often overtakes any social movement rejecting violent confrontation with its environment in favor of reformist strategies for change. A perceptive statement of this dilemma is given by Peter Gay in his study of Eduard Bernstein: 'A democratic Socialist movement that attempts to transform a capitalist into a Socialist order is necessarily faced with a choice between two incompatibles – principles and power.'[7] An emphasis on the purity of principles may sustain the identity of a movement. But it may also expose the movement, particularly if it is in a weak position, to repression by governments who, in an attempt to defend certain values, seek to control dissent and insist on conformity in society. On the other hand, compromise with the established order, however justifiable it may seem as a means of working for change from within the existing institutions of society, runs the risk of subjecting reform movements to the danger of co-optation and absorption by that order, particularly if they are weak initially or if the pressures upon them to sacrifice their principles for the national good become irresistible.

Ultimately the Sōdōmei, and the labor movement in general, succumbed to this dilemma of political choice and sacrificed their commitment to social democracy in a futile endeavor to preserve the institutions of the labor movement amidst a political and economic environment that became increasingly intolerant of their existence. This becalming of political purpose was not, however, confined to the labor movement. The same surrender of socialist ideals occurred sooner or later throughout the Taishō democracy movement.

Moreover, a similar becalming of social protest in this period is discernible in the history of social movements in other countries, notably Germany. The strong parallels between the history of Japanese and German labor politics in the 1920s and 1930s raise a question which is considered in the Conclusion of this book, not with the intention of making a final statement, but rather to identify an important area for future research in the comparative study of social movements: in what ways was the political behavior of the socialist parties in both countries influenced by their mass-based organizations in the labor movement?

Historians of German socialism have found that it is impossible to analyze the political ideology and policies of the German Social Democratic Party without considering the influence of the German labor movement upon the Party. In the case of Japan, most studies of Japanese socialism have, to date, emphasized the top-down perspective of the socialist parties themselves. It is hoped that this book will help meet the need for a bottom-up perspective and clarify the impact of labor politics on the socialist party movement in Japan. Similar studies of other movements, particularly the agrarian union movement, in the history of Japanese socialism are also needed before a fully rounded picture of the interaction between the parties and their mass-based organizations can be attained.

It remains to mention briefly the specific problem-areas analyzed in this study of Japanese labor politics.

First, the book examines the institutional arrangements which existed in the Nihon Rōdō Sōdōmei for the legitimation of authority, the allocation of power, the definition of goals and the means to achieve them, and the recruitment and politicization of the rank and file members. It is necessary to distinguish between the formal and informal aspects of these arrangements. The former included a decision-making machinery which came into play principally during the annual national conventions of the Federation and which was designed to maximize the participation of the rank and file, through the elected representatives of the unions, in the making of policy. To the extent that the machinery served this purpose, the internal political dynamics of the Federation were consistent with the organization's image as a democratic movement.

However, it will be seen that formal procedures, essentially democratic in nature, were more often than not superseded by the informal institutions of personal factionalism. Through these the elites of the Sōdōmei manipulated the organization for the sake of preserving their own power and imposing their policies on the rank and file. The presence of factionalism, in the form of vertical cliques controlled by the leadership, led to authoritarian practices in the Sōdōmei which, in the long run, inevitably colored the political performance of the Federation in coping with its environment.

Second, attention is given to the ways in which the political expectations and actions of the elites and of the rank and file coincided and diverged during the history of the Sōdōmei. It is suggested that while the former often imposed their political goals and programs on the latter, it is also true that the elites framed their policies in response to what the rank and file expected of the labor movement in the realm of political action. On several occasions, however, the interests of the elites and of minority elements within the rank and file clashed so that the Federation experienced great strain from within which exacerbated the tension between the labor movement and its environment. This resulted in splits within the Federation which fragmented the labor movement and led to divisions within the socialist party movement as well. The impact of these successive splits on the political behavior of the Sōdōmei is analyzed at length in order to clarify the way in which they resulted in an increasing political conservatism among labor leaders and their followers in the interwar period.

It should be emphasized at this point that a serious methodological problem exists in studying the two levels of leaders and followers in social movements. It is relatively easy to determine the thoughts and actions of the elites, because they were, despite the presence of factionalism – particularly between worker–leaders and intellectuals – more homogeneous in terms of composition and political orientation than the rank and file, and therefore more readily distinguishable as a discrete group for analysis. Also, they left behind documents which reveal their attitude and behavior.

By contrast, it is difficult to be certain of what the rank and file wanted from the labor movement, or indeed what they did. In generalizing about their collective behavior, it has been necessary in this book to distinguish between the heterogeneous elements of the rank and file: workers in different trades and industries, skilled and unskilled workers, workers in different positions in the formal ranking system of the factory hierarchy, workers in different regions, and so on. It has also been necessary to exercise caution in the interpretation of the data of their strike demands, as these constitute an important indicator of their aspirations.

Third, this study investigates the process whereby the leaders of the Sōdōmei became progressively more bureaucratic and oligarchic in their exercise of power in response to protracted conflict with their environment, to episodic rebellion on the part of a minority of radical workers against their policies, and to widespread passivity and apathy among the majority of the workers toward the political goals and programs advocated by the elites. This is an important area of inquiry because these developments predisposed the Sōdōmei elites to emphasize system-maintenance – both in the sense of preserving their own power in the movement and in the sense of protecting the unions from hostility from without – over goal-achievement, or the realization of political objectives defined by their socialist ideology.[8]

Fourth, it is necessary in this study to consider the political history of the Sōdōmei in the light of theories which emphasize that social movements are inevitably bearers of class struggle. The theme of class struggle lies at the heart of the Taishō democracy interpretation of Japanese labor history. But it also pervades the theoretical literature on social movements in general. For example, Rudolf Heberle, who defines class as a 'collectivity of people in a like economic position', asserts that the 'causal relation of social class to political parties and social movements can be best understood if one considers that all social movements aim directly or indirectly at change in the distribution of power or in the distribution of wealth' and that 'conflicts between political parties which are apparently caused by disagreement on problems of constitutional law or on political theory are most likely conflicts over the redistribution of political power between social classes'.[9]

A similar emphasis on class conflict as the keystone of political behavior in social movements is inherent in theories of relative deprivation intended to explain the psychology of collective dissent. Relative deprivation is defined by Ted Gurr as the 'actors' perception of discrepancy between their value expectations and their value capabilities. Value expectations are the goods and conditions to which people believe they are entitled. Value capabilities are the goods and conditions they think they are capable of getting and keeping.'[10] Or, as James Geschwender expresses it, relative deprivation occurs when people experience discontent after comparing their circumstances with those of another group apparently undergoing a higher level of need satisfaction.[11] The implication here is that the other group in question is usually a social class.

Recent quantified studies of labor unrest in Japan in the interwar period support the view that worker protest was motivated by a widespread sense of deprivation which the participants felt in relation to the fledgling middle class, which in the course of industrialization had emerged above them on the social ladder.[12] Whether the middle class as a whole was all that much better off than the proletariat in Japan is perhaps open to question. But some workers believed this to be true. As Arthur Kornhauser cautions, 'Not what is, but what men believe to be the case, counts in action and what men believe turns not only on changing conditions of the world itself but most significantly also upon the meaning ascribed to these conditions.'[13]

However, although the proposition that social movements are institutions for the waging of class struggle may explain why they arise in the first place, it does not necessarily provide the conceptual key to understanding their subsequent political behavior. The history of the Sōdōmei reveals that despite the rhetoric of class conflict in the labor movement, in reality there existed very little class consciousness on the part of most labor leaders and rank and file unionists. Why this was so, and what the implications of a shallow class consciousness were for labor politics, are other topics considered in this book.

Fifth, attention will be given to international influences upon the politics of the labor movement as well as to labor's immediate political and economic context in Japan, for the 'international migration of ideas'[14] often determined how participants in the labor movement interpreted the so-called 'trends of the times' (*jisei*) in mapping out their strategies for the movement.

In concluding this Introduction, several further problems must be cited. First, the primary and secondary sources used in this study, most of which are in Japanese, contain considerable bias in the presentation and interpretation of material. The study of Japanese labor history in Japan has always been, and remains today, studded with controversy. This situation challenges the ability of the historian to maintain his own objectivity in handling these works upon which he is largely dependent.

Second, there is the problem of coping with the terminology used in this literature. Words such as *shakaishugi* (socialism), *anākizumu* (anarchism), *kaizō* (reconstruction), *kaihō* (liberation), *musan kaikyū* (proletariat, literally, 'propertyless classes'), *fashizumu* (fascism), *uyoku* (right wing), *sayoku* (left wing), *chūritsuteki* (centrist), and many others meant different things to different people in the labor movement and have been variously interpreted by scholars of the period. It is necessary to give their meaning as it was understood by the persons who employed this vocabulary rather than by the researcher.

Finally, the historian is confronted by the bewildering complexity of events in Japan during this period, especially the complexity of a very checkered array of organizations in the labor and proletarian party movements. This complexity poses the problem of how to arrive at a synthesis of specificity and generality which portrays accurately the drama of the labor movement in all of its vivid and fascinating detail while at the same time elucidating broad trends and their meaning. A wide-angled lens is required. Accordingly, this book takes its cue from Eric Hobsbawm's definition of labor history:

> The history of labor is a multilayered affair, though the levels of analysis form a whole: workers and movements, rank and file and leaders, socio-economic, political, cultural, ideological, and 'historical' both in the sense that they operate within a context given by the past and in the sense that they change over time in certain specifiable ways.[15]

If this book achieves a balanced synthesis with this approach, its purpose of stimulating further research on this important and lively period in Japanese history will have been at least partially fulfilled.

I

Labor's image of the past in 1919–1920

If one considers Japanese labor history in the light of Daniel Bell's suggestion that labor union movements usually pass through three successive stages in their development – 'eruption', 'expansion', and 'enforcement'[1] – then it is apparent that organized labor in prewar Japan erupted several times, expanded very little, and made practically no progress at all in the imposition of its objectives.

The history of organized labor was particularly choppy in the Meiji and early Taishō periods. Despite attempts to form labor movements in the late 1890s, the 187 unions operative in Japan in 1919 were the direct result of efforts to organize the workers initiated in 1912. After World War I, therefore, the movement had to contend with its own immaturity in addition to a generally negative environment. It also meant that 'labor's image of the past',[2] which shaped expectations of the future in 1919 and 1920, would be framed in memories of past frustration. Yet, in the immediate aftermath of World War I, there was reason to hope that the labor movement had finally 'erupted' with sufficient force to make the unions a permanent presence in the factories and that a time of expansion and enforcement lay ahead. To place this optimism in perspective, it is right to begin this study with a brief survey of Japanese labor history from 1897 to 1920.

When Japanese labor unions were first organized in 1897, they constituted an important aspect of what was then known as the 'labor question' in contemporary society. In its broadest sense, the labor question signified the emergence of an industrial proletariat and the outbreak of industrial unrest in the factories during Japan's accelerating industrial revolution in the 1890s. From the perspective of employers and the Meiji government, the labor question was an object of grave concern, for it was feared that Japan might succumb to the same social strains and divisive tensions that had attended the industrial revolution in the West. The problem was how to contain the labor question before it became an unmanageable obstacle to the successful pursuit of national wealth and power.

The dimensions of the labor question, while not great by recent standards, were nonetheless considerable in the context of the period. As the number of factories multiplied, from 778 with a combined capitalization of 44,590,000 yen in 1894 to 1,881 factories with a combined capitalization of 105,380,000 yen by 1897, so too did the industrial work force begin to assume large proportions.[3] For instance, in 1892, there were 294,425 factory workers in Japan; by 1897, this number had reached 439,549.[4] In the last six months of 1897, the year in which the first unions arose, there were thirty-two strikes encompassing 3,517 workers; in 1898, forty-three strikes occurred, involving 6,293 participants.[5] Observing that these strikes coincided with the appearance of labor unionism, many contemporary analysts assumed that the unions were responsible for whipping up worker protest and that, therefore, unions had to be watched closely and if necessary destroyed in order to establish peace in the factories.

In retrospect, this assessment of the new labor movement was exaggerated. The first labor organization in Japan, the Shokkō Giyūkai (Knights of Labor), which became the Rōdō Kumiai Kiseikai (Association for the Formation of Labor Unions) shortly after it was founded in April 1897 in Tokyo, was actually a rather benign institution oriented toward business unionism on the model of the conservative and nonpolitical American Federation of Labor.[6] Led by Takano Fusatarō and Katayama Sen, two Christian intellectuals motivated by a humanitarian concern for the welfare of Japanese workers, the Kiseikai and a small number of unions it had organized among the iron workers, printers, and railroad employees of Tokyo[7] endeavored to raise worker wages and improve working conditions. However, it rarely engaged in strikes and was hardly responsible for triggering the wave of labor unrest that swept over Japan late in the decade. The origins of worker deprivation ran deep in Japan and the growing number of workers who resorted to industrial action in order to express their grievances did not need the prodding of a tiny moderate labor movement to do so. The Kiseikai's unions may have symbolized the emergent labor question but the labor question itself reached far beyond the labor movement in scope.

The harsh plight of Japan's factory workers in the Meiji period has been fully documented elsewhere.[8] A large part of the work force in urban factories was drawn from an abundant supply of cheap labor in the countryside. Most factories were located in the Tokyo–Yokohama and Osaka–Kobe–Kyoto industrial belts. More than half of these workers were young females who entered the textile factories on short-term labor contracts.[9] In general, all of the workers were subjected to poor physical conditions, long hours of labor, and very low wages which were eaten away by increased taxes and rising inflation, especially during the Sino-Japanese War (1894–1895).

They had to endure poor lighting, inadequate heating, and deficient ventilation while they remained at the work place for as long as twelve, and sometimes even sixteen, hours at a stretch. Their lungs were assaulted by phosphorus fumes (in match factories), cotton dust (in cotton spinning factories), or lead dust (in machine industries). Their bodies were racked by fatigue, for they were given no time to rest during the work day and had to work every day of the week. Sanitary conditions were poor, obliging the workers to eat hurried and inadequate meals in squalid surroundings. Night work was common-place and child labor, particularly in the cotton spinning, glass, match, and tobacco industries, was an important feature of the factory system. No relief was afforded the workers at the end of the gruelling work day as they returned to crowded conditions in factory-run dormitories or their own homes where rest was impossible and poverty was the norm.[10]

In the textile, machine tool, shipyard, match, chemical, electrical, and mining industries, the workers were treated more like animals than human beings by a brutalizing and predatory factory system which contained many of the same evils that had blighted the industrial revolution in the West. Bad as their physical conditions were, their psychological deprivations were even more deplorable because they experienced acute alienation in the strange and impersonal environment of the factories, in great contrast to the familiarity of their former rural villages. As mere cogs in the Japanese factory machine, they could feel no self-respect and had no sense of control over their lives. In the absence of protective factory legislation they were open to the exploitation of employers who cared more about profits than about the welfare of the workers. Their only recourse was to protest by desperate labor strikes, which rarely resulted in any gains and often cost them their jobs. Surveying the scene in 1897, Takano Fusatarō remarked,

> In this country a man as a worker is socially a doomed being, whether he is a skilled mechanic or a waste paper picker. When we look at the life conditions of the workers, the demarcation line of their trades is completely blotted out, for they lead, one and all, a life of hopelessness.[11]

Takano's observation poignantly illustrates the misery of most Japanese workers in the Meiji period. But it needs qualification. Life was not always so hopeless for the skilled male worker who knew his way around the machinery of the heavy industries. His skills were urgently needed by factory management for production. In contrast to the abundance of cheap unskilled labor, there were not enough skilled workers to serve a rapidly expanding heavy industrial sector in this period.[12] Some of them could regularly sell their skills for higher wages from one factory to another.[13]

Moreover, an important function gave them a strategic place in the factory system. As *oyakata* labor bosses, they recruited and trained under their personal supervision unskilled workers who were attached to them, through personal ties, as *kokata*.[14] To ensure their continued services, employers were generally obliged to grant them concessions. As a result, their wages tended to be higher than those of the unskilled workers and they possessed a degree of prestige in the factories which made them, in the eyes of some critics, the *rōdō kizoku*, or 'labor aristocracy', of the work force.[15]

This discrepancy between the positions of the skilled and unskilled workers might suggest that the skilled workers would have less to gain than the unskilled workers from participation in an untried and very small labor movement. But, as in other countries, the skilled workers played a strategic role in the new unions, as they did in the factory system as a whole. The unions established by the Kiseikai appealed predominantly to the *rōdō kizoku*, and union officers came mainly from this stratum. In large part, the early labor movement revolved around the close cooperation between these workers and involved intellectuals.

The interest of the skilled workers in unionism can be explained by the advantages the *rōdō kizoku* enjoyed in terms of wages and working conditions by ad hoc arrangements with management. These were the results of special and transitory circumstances of a fluid labor market at an early point in Japanese industrialization and there was no guarantee that these arrangements would last in perpetuity. Indeed, certain government-run industries, such as the Yokosuka Shipyards, were already experimenting with new labor relations policies with the aim of recruiting and training workers in specialized skills without relying on the mobile *oyakata* skilled craftsman.

These policies were designed to attach the work force more firmly to the factory, through various incentives rewarding seniority and long-term service. The subsequent spread of these measures will be discussed later in this book.[16] They prompted some skilled workers to join the movement in the hope that it would assist them in formalizing their advantages in the factories through collective bargaining with management. In sum, they turned to the labor movement to protect gains already achieved. Not surprisingly, employers were all the more wary of the labor movement because it seemed to attract the very skilled worker stratum which, by virtue of its mobility and assertiveness, they sought to bring under their control.

However, employer resistance to unions was philosophical as well as practical in origin. The prevailing ideal of industrial relations in Meiji Japan was *onjōshugi* (paternalism) which referred to a factory system based on hierarchical relations (*shūjū kankei*) between workers and employers who were obligated to fulfill reciprocal obligations in accordance with their positions in the hierarchy. One prominent financier summed up the system this way: 'The master – the capitalist – is loving toward those below, and takes tender care of them, while the employee – the worker – respects those above and will sacrifice himself to his work. The spirit of loyalty and love of country...is by no means limited to the relationship between sovereign and subject.'[17]

Honored more in the breach than in practice, *onjōshugi* nonetheless grew in stature as a normative vision of labor relations in the minds of employers as the number of labor disputes that they saw around them rose. Indeed, *onjōshugi* appealed to them as a uniquely Japanese way to avoid labor unrest. As one advocate of paternalism said, 'The evils of foreign countries can be avoided and the merits peculiar to our own country can be fostered. By these means we shall see for the first time a solution to the problem of capital and labor – a solution unique to our own country.'[18]

Admittedly, a few 'management modernizers' tried to prove the validity of *onjōshugi* by improving factory conditions in the hope that the workers would accept this ideal relationship with their employers.[19] But rarely did these innovations include toleration for unions in Meiji Japan. On the contrary, most employers opposed the legalization of unions from the belief that unions were objectionable as 'foreign' institutions incompatible with Japanese capitalism and nationalism.[20] Many public officials agreed. Accordingly, several articles intended to contain the labor movement were included in the famous Peace Police Law of 1900, although the Law as a whole was mainly designed to suppress all allegedly subversive political activities. Article Seventeen made it virtually impossible to legally organize unions; Article Thirty supplied harsh penalties for violators of Article Seventeen.[21]

The Peace Police Law was not formally invoked against the unions as often as some accounts suggest. But its presence intimidated the labor movement and made it harder for the Kiseikai to expand its influence among the workers, many of whom thought twice before associating with a movement which might become the object of police surveillance and repression. Even without this Law, however, the movement faced a formidable task in recruiting new members. It was practically impossible to mobilize the large mass of female workers in the textile plants because these women, kept virtually under lock and key by their employers in large, dismal factory dormitories and sweatshops, were physically out of the reach of labor organizers. They were psychologically out of reach as well, because they longed to return home to their families in the villages once their labor contracts were completed. They were therefore an unreliable source of support even when they were organized, which was rare.

Difficulties were encountered in recruiting unskilled male workers, who also tended to drift back to their villages. In these unfavorable circumstances, it proved difficult to rally workers to unions, particularly when it became obvious that employers would resort to blacklisting labor organizers and dismissing those workers who did join unions. Consequently, the Kiseikai and its unions soon withered and died, so that by 1902 the Meiji labor movement had disappeared altogether.[22]

It is significant that before it faded out, the originally nonpolitical Meiji labor movement became involved in political action to assist the workers. The Kiseikai realized that labor's 'act of revolt'[23] against existing inequities in the factories would be meaningless unless the movement achieved legislation which legalized unions and ameliorated labor's lot. Therefore, representatives of the Kiseikai participated in the Shakaishugi Kenkyūkai (Society for the Study of Socialism), founded in 1898, and in 1901 they took part in establishing the first socialist party in Japan, the Shakai Minshutō (Social Democratic Party).[24]

This Party was more democratic than socialist, more pacifist than militant. However, the name of the organization, reflecting a Western, socialist orientation, aroused the government to close down the Shakai Minshutō almost as soon as it was formed. Katayama Sen and others in the then-defunct labor movement later assisted in the formation of a second socialist party, the Nihon Shakaitō (Japan Socialist Party) in 1906. The new Party soon became polarized between a radical anarchist faction led by Kōtoku Shūsui and a moderate socialist wing led by Katayama and the Christian socialist Abe Isoo. Kōtoku's group advocated militant 'direct action' in opposition to the emphasis on legal, parliamentarian initiatives by Katayama and Abe. Alarmed by the radical wing of the Party, the government prohibited the Nihon Shakaitō in 1907. Finally, the Meiji proletarian movement ground to an abrupt halt with the trial and execution of Kōtoku and some of his followers for allegedly plotting to slay Emperor Meiji in 1911.[25]

The involvement in the Meiji socialist movement of men once active in the labor movement meant that when the labor movement 'erupted' again, in early Taishō, it would have to be politically cautious lest it fall prey to accusations of subversion. Such circumspection was especially discernible in the first labor organization to emerge in the Taisho period, the Yūaikai (Friendly Society), founded by a Christian intellectual, Suzuki Bunji, in Tokyo in August 1912. The Yūaikai, originally comprising intellectuals and workers from a variety of trades, embraced such mild goals as 'mutual aid in friendship and cooperation', the cultivation of enlightenment, virtue, and labor skills among the workers, and raising their status through 'sound programs depending upon the strength of cooperation'. But beneath this rather bland exterior, the Friendly Society made the development and promotion of labor unions its primary mission.[26]

In its first years, the Yūaikai resembled the earlier Kiseikai by making business unionism, cut from the pattern of the American Federation of Labor, its main approach to the labor movement. Unlike the Kiseikai, however, the Yūaikai experienced a relatively spectacular growth in its evolution. By June 1913 it had expanded from a fifteen-man organization in Tokyo into one claiming 1,295 members in a growing network of branches throughout Japan. By the end of 1915, the membership was 7,000 and by April 1917, it had climbed to over 20,000. In 1919, the Yūaikai rolls numbered around 30,000 workers.[27] Clearly, the Yūaikai had far surpassed the Meiji labor movement in gaining a foothold in the factories. How is this growth of the Friendly Society, and other Taishō labor organizations, to be explained?

One reason for this growth, in the case of the Yūaikai, was the resourcefulness of its leader, Suzuki. A graduate of the law faculty of Tokyo Imperial University, he proved to be very adept at building up the Yūaikai and at arguing the cause of unionism as he attacked paternalism in the factories. Suzuki mixed freely with ordinary workers and important business and political leaders alike. A huge and imposing figure in a business suit with a gold watch chain, he commanded considerable respect as the 'father of the labor movement' in early Taishō Japan.

But Suzuki and the Yūaikai would not have gone very far had it not been for the growing flexibility in the attitude of the establishment toward Japanese labor relations in this period. This was a second reason for the proliferation of unions after 1912. Paternalism remained the predominant approach of most employers to the labor question. But an increasing number of them were prepared to innovate with new policies in the factories, even to the point of granting the workers concessions such as the right to form unions, for the sake of harmony with the work force. In this, they received considerable support from such semi-official organizations as the Shakai Seisaku Gakkai (Social Policy Association), a blue-ribbon circle of industrialists, financiers, academics and public servants who proferred advice to the business community and the government concerning major social problems in Japan. As has been shown elsewhere,[28] the Gakkai, founded in 1896, lent considerable support to the Taishō labor movement by advocating legalization of unions to stabilize labor relations. The Gakkai was likewise active in persuading the government to legislate the Factory Law of 1911 which protected some workers at least from the exploitation of employers. Links between the Gakkai and the Yūaikai were particularly strong; men of the Gakkai served as advisers to the Yūaikai and Suzuki was a respected member of the Association.

Third, the growth of the Taishō labor movement was facilitated by the special conditions of World War I in Japan. Japan became an Asian arsenal for war-related materials and munitions which were sent to her allies in the West. Industrial production boomed accordingly, so that the real net domestic product rose by 61.5 per cent over the 1910–1920 period, particularly during the war.[29] Indeed, Japan shifted from being a debtor nation of 1.1 billion yen as of the end of 1914 to a creditor nation of 2.77 billion yen by early 1920.[30] During the wartime industrial boom, the work force expanded dramatically from 853,964 factory workers employed in 17,062 enterprises in 1914 to 1,777,171 workers in 44,087 factories in 1919, the year after the war ended.[31]

Japan's prosperity during the war did not, however, benefit the workers very much. Statistics on wages during this period are not reliable. But it is certain that while the money wages of the workers rose in the war years, their real wages dropped due to an upward escalation of prices of urban commodity goods, notably rice.[32] As Kozo Yamamura notes, 'One source puts the index of real wages of factory workers at ninety-five in 1916, eighty-three in 1917, seventy-eight in 1918, ninety-four in 1919, with 1912 equal to 100.'[33]

The perceived gap between their real wages and the nation's prosperity was clear in the remark of one labor activist, 'While the capitalists have the right to play and eat wrapped in silk kimonos, the workers who toil naked should have the same right.'[34] Such sentiments of relative deprivation lay behind the unprecedented tide of labor strikes in World War I Japan, most of which concerned wages. There were fifty labor disputes involving 7,904 workers in 1914, 108 disputes involving 8,413 workers in 1916, 398 disputes encompassing 57,309 participants in 1917, 417 in which 66,457 workers took part in 1918, and a total of 497 disputes with 63,137 participants in 1919.[35]

Even though, under Suzuki's cautious leadership, the Yūaikai did not officially encourage its members to engage in industrial disputes, the Friendly Society benefited from this upsurge of worker protest by recruiting a number of workers who joined because they regarded it as a promising organizational vehicle for the articulation and advancement of their interests. This was also true of other labor organizations. Accordingly, the number of unions in Japan grew from forty-nine in 1914 to 187 in 1919, including about 100,000 workers.[36] In the case of the Yūaikai, it appealed to the workers through the implementation of consumer cooperatives, medical clinics, various other welfare programs and recreational services, and educational classes conducted in Yūaikai locals (local branches).[37]

Moderate labor organizations like the Yūaikai benefited from labor unrest in this period in other important respects. The spontaneous development of unions during the war included the rise of anarchist organizations such as the Shin'yūkai (Faithful Friends' Society) and Seishinkai (True Progress Association) which employers sought to combat by using the Yūaikai as a moderate buffer in their factories.[38] Some employers allowed the Yūaikai to organize unions in their enterprises in order to lock the skilled workers and their *kokata* to the firm, a goal which, ironically, both the employers and the Yūaikai shared, albeit for different reasons. Employers sought a stable work force to increase production amidst the continuing fluidity of the labor market; the Yūaikai sought a stable membership for the purpose of building up its locals.

As in the Meiji period, then, the principal target of employer labor relations strategies and of the labor movement was the skilled worker. Employers held him in contempt. He was called, pejoratively, a 'man of moods' and a 'wanderer'.[39] He offended management because, 'Mentally, the workers' pride and independent spirit as skilled craftsmen continued to reinforce their feelings of equality with employers.'[40] True believers of *onjōshugi* among the employers were loath to accept this sense of worker equality. Yet, some accommodation with the aspirations of the skilled workers was necessary, for the time being at least, because of their indispensability in wartime production.

By contrast, labor leaders depended upon the skilled workers in developing the unions because they realized that if they could recruit *oyakata* into unions, they would also be able to recruit the *kokata* under their control. Suzuki went to great lengths to personally recruit Matsuoka Komakichi into the Yūaikai for this reason. Matsuoka was a skilled lathe worker at the Muroran Steel Works in Hokkaidō where he had gained a reputation for leading worker protest over wages. When Matsuoka entered the Yūaikai, he was given much authority in administrative affairs; similar posts were offered many of his *kokata*, including Miki Jirō, who had joined with him. Yūaikai leaders also tried to recruit skilled workers who had already formed their own unions. This was true of Nishio Suehiro, another lathe operator in an Osaka plant who had founded the Shokkō Kumiai Kisei Dōshikai (Society for the Establishment of Factory Workers' Unions) there in 1916. When Nishio entered the Yūaikai, most of his followers in the Dōshikai joined him, thus providing the Friendly Society with a ready-made union network in Osaka.[41]

A fourth factor aiding the rise of organized labor in the early Taishō period was the existence of a political climate more favorable to interest group particularism than in the Meiji era. There is little doubt that the labor movement benefited enormously from contemporary perceptions of Japan's role in a changing world after the Great War. For instance, Japan's alliance with the victorious democracies in the war fostered liberal expectations that the country stood at the dawn (*reimei*) of a new democratic age in its modern development.

The most famous advocate of this vision was Professor Yoshino Sakuzō of Tokyo Imperial University. Yoshino argued, in countless writings during the war, that liberalism could be made compatible with the Meiji Constitution. He called for a greater devolution of political power to the lower house of the Diet and an end to the elitist rule of the *genrō* (elder statesmen), the bureaucracy, the Peers, and the military. He also demanded universal suffrage to involve the people in the political process. Most importantly, Yoshino advocated the formation of trade unions as a means of realizing basic human rights. He asserted that these democratic changes were consistent with similar trends in other countries and that they would assist Japan in its continued modernization.[42]

The impact of Yoshino's ideas and those of other liberal theorists should not be overstated. Yet, as the war came to an end, it seemed as if the 'trends of the times' toward democracy in Japanese politics were about to be fulfilled. To many observers, the growing strength of the so-called 'bourgeois' political parties, culminating in the formation of the Rikken Seiyūkai (Constitutional Political Fraternal Association) Party cabinet under Prime Minister Hara Kei in 1918, indicated the imminent end of Japan's domination by the conservative centers of power which had ruled the country since 1868.[43] In this context, the rise of labor was not an isolated phenomenon based on the idealism of a handful of visionaries, but the stirring of democratic consciousness at the lower rungs of society matching increased democratic pluralism in government.

But liberalism was only one democratic expectation of wartime Japan. Another was political radicalism following the Russian Revolution of 1917. The triumph of the workers and peasants over the Tsar in that year inspired some Japanese to believe that the democratic 'trends of the times' would be carried forward by the revolutionary potential of the *musan kaikyū* ('propertyless classes'), not by liberalism. That the awakening of this revolutionary potential had already begun seemed apparent in the Rice Riots of 1918 in which thousands of farmers and their families demonstrated throughout the country, sometimes violently, against the rising price of rice. Alongside the dramatic escalation of worker protest near the end of the war, the Rice Riots were interpreted as evidence that what had been accomplished in 1917 in Russia could also be accomplished in Imperial Japan. The repression of the Riots, in some instances using the Japanese army, was seen as the desperate act of a dying ancien régime.[44]

Against this background of rising liberal and radical expectations for democracy, men and women in and outside of the Japanese labor movement increasingly believed that labor's problems required political solutions. These would necessarily involve the movement in political action, and labor's political struggles would transcend class interests while promoting democratic change in Japan. Consequently, during the war the Yūaikai turned sharply away from its cautious business unionism to political initiatives previously undreamed of.

One impetus for the political involvement of the labor movement came from workers themselves. For example, even before he joined the

Yūaikai, Nishio Suehiro committed his Dōshikai union in Osaka to several campaigns for the election of pro-labor candidates to the municipal assembly.[45] Moreover, worker enthusiasm for political action manifested itself in many demonstrations on behalf of universal suffrage held by Yūaikai organizations in Kobe, Osaka, and Kyoto toward the end of the war. Typically, these demonstrations consisted of marches in the streets and public rallies addressed by such famous pro-suffrage spokesmen as Ozaki Yukio.[46]

Worker interest in politics was also expressed in a growing desire for a greater share of power in the Yūaikai, which up to this point had been managed largely by Suzuki and his small coterie of intellectuals. These demands were revealed, for instance, in the creation of the Kansai Rōdō Dōmeikai (Kansai Labor Federation) in 1919. This was a coalition of Yūaikai unions in Western Japan which emphasized the principle of collective leadership including primarily workers who were elected by their unions to serve on the Dōmeikai governing council. The Dōmeikai also called upon the Yūaikai national leadership to commit the Friendly Society to mass political campaigns for universal suffrage, progressive amendments to the 1911 Factory Law, the enactment of a labor union law, and the repeal of the loathed Peace Police Law.[47] Before long, similar demands were made from Yūaikai locals in the Kantō region of Eastern Japan.

Another impetus for labor's political awakening came from intellectuals who had joined organizations like the Yūaikai in the war years. The political activism of the workers in Western Japan, for instance, was strongly encouraged by Kagawa Toyohiko, the well-known Japanese Christian who had earlier earned a reputation for his relief work among the slum-dwellers of Kobe. Professor Kawakami Hajime of Kyoto Imperial University was another intellectual who tried to stimulate worker interest in the politics of social protest in this period, but it was Kagawa in particular who exercised the most influence in the Yūaikai's Kansai organizations, holding positions of power in the Kobe labor movement and in the Kansai Rōdō Dōmeikai which he had helped to establish.[48]

Intellectuals also entered the labor movement in Eastern Japan. Many of them were young university graduates who belonged to such organizations as the Shinjinkai (New Man Society) formed in the universities during the War for the study of Western democratic thought and its application to Japan. The Shinjinkai, for example, was based at Tokyo Imperial University, and its patron Professor Yoshino

Sakuzō encouraged the Shinjinkai members to join the Yūaikai and help awaken the workers' political consciousness. This they did, carrying out their slogan of 'To the Masses!' Among them were men who were to play a significant role in the labor and socialist party movements over the ensuing decades: Asō Hisashi, Tanahashi Kotora, Yamana Yoshitsuru, and Akamatsu Katsumaro.[49] Other intellectuals who joined the Yūaikai out of political motivations included Nozaka Sanzō, inspired to help the workers by his professor at Keiō University, Horie Kiichi, and Kamijō Aiichi who entered the labor movement from Waseda University. Nozaka subsequently became a key figure in the Japanese communist movement, Kamijō in the socialist cause.

The precise political ideology of these young intellectuals is hard to define because their thought at this time contained a nebulous amalgam of ideas. The Shinjinkai circle was undoubtedly influenced by Yoshino's liberalism. At the same time these men were interested in other ideologies, including English guild socialism, anarchism, and later communism. In contrast to Yoshino, their enthusiasm for the Russian Revolution led them to believe in the necessity of class conflict. But, as later chapters will make clear, they were strongly attracted to the scientific and rational dimensions of guild socialism, as was Kagawa Toyohiko in Western Japan.

For example, Asō Hisashi wrote in 1919,

> The real solution of labor's problems does not lie in disputes with factory owners, or in social policies, or in social-reformist policies, or reduced work time. It lies in changing from the present-day *irrational* social systems around the world to *rational* social systems [my italics].[50]

Despite the eclectic nature of their ideas, the Shinjinkai members were united by the conviction that their mission was the democratic reconstruction (*kaizō*) of Japan and the liberation (*kaihō*) of the proletariat. How this was to be done was yet to be defined. However, they believed that the first step was to mobilize the workers and raise their political consciousness so that they could struggle together against an exploitative capitalist system and attain their human rights. These sentiments led these men, once they had assumed positions of authority in the Yūaikai, to plunge the Eastern wing of the Friendly Society into the same political demonstrations which characterized labor's new assertiveness in Western Japan. In 1919 especially, the Yūaikai workers of Tokyo and Yokohama took to the streets with increasing frequency to march behind banners calling for universal suffrage, legalization of unions, and the abolition of the Peace Police Law.

Anarchism was another powerful political current of the labor movement in the later wartime period. The revival of anarchism in the early Taishō period was due to the efforts of Ōsugi Sakae, Arahata Kanson, Sakai Toshihiko, and Yamakawa Hitoshi, all of whom had been linked with its first appearance in the radical wing of the Meiji socialist movement. Once more, they proclaimed the imperative of direct-action confrontation with capitalism which they hoped would ignite spontaneous class conflict between a politically awakened industrial proletariat and the capitalist order. Ōsugi and other anarchists rejected the cause of universal suffrage and parliamentary politics in general, arguing that these were reformist opiates that fell short of what was really required to end the exploitation of the proletariat: revolutionary overthrow of the entire social and political order.[51]

Amidst the rising worker unrest of the wartime years, these ideas appealed strongly to many workers in Japan. Although they remained small in size, such organizations as the Shin'yūkai and the Seishinkai developed a politically committed membership. A small but cohesive group of anarchist unions also sprang up in the Yūaikai, principally among the iron workers of Tokyo and Yokohama. Their leaders included workers such as Takata Waitsu and Yamamoto Kenzō, both of whom had been introduced to anarchism through the works of Kropotkin by members of the Shinjinkai.[52] Another anarchist worker initially introduced to both the labor movement and radical politics by the Shinjinkai was Watanabe Masanosuke, its first member from the workers. His close ties with the New Man Society are shown by the title of a labor union which he founded in 1919 at the Nagamine Celluloid Company where he worked, the Shinjinkai Nagamine Celluloid Union.[53] It is doubtful whether any of these workers possessed a deep understanding of anarchist philosophy, but their commitment to radical politics was nonetheless real. The next chapter discusses the role they played in the Japanese labor movement during the early 1920s.

The significant trend across the whole labor movement as it emerged from the World War I period was, then, the political awakening of at least a small number of organized workers. In 1919 it was difficult to predict where this trend would take the labor movement in the future since the movement contained many conflicting political impulses. But generally there was agreement that the issue was not whether labor should be political but rather what political action the unions should undertake.

It was in this context that the Yūaikai was transformed into the Dai

Nihon Rōdō Sōdōmei-Yūaikai, or Friendly Society Greater Japan General Federation of Labor, in the August convention of the Yūaikai, 1919. The decision to transform the Yūaikai was a political one by a small group of worker–leaders and intellectuals in the Friendly Society who wanted the labor movement to abandon unequivocally the former business unionism of the Yūaikai. In its stead they wanted the movement to take on a distinctly political identity.[54]

So strong was this determination that Suzuki Bunji, who had previously avoided political priorities for fear of exposing the Yūaikai to police repression, felt compelled in 1919 to announce his personal conversion to socialism. Suzuki's new-found commitment to political struggle also prompted him to reject an invitation from the Kyōchōkai (Harmonization Society, founded in 1919), a government-backed association for the promotion of industrial peace, to represent the labor movement on its board of directors.[55]

Once Suzuki's cooperation was assured, the coalition of worker–leaders, led by Matsuoka Komakichi, and Shinjinkai intellectuals, led by Asō Hisashi, proceeded without difficulty to recast the principles and programs of the Yūaikai in order to realize their goal of making the Yūaikai more political in its orientation and more democratic in its governance. These changes were enthusiastically ratified by the 1919 convention of the Friendly Society.[56]

Specifically, this convention affirmed the principles of collective leadership by replacing Suzuki's 'autocratic' rule with an executive committee and a central executive committee which were charged with administering the Yūaikai on the national level from headquarters in Tokyo. The executive committee consisted of twenty-five members, elected annually to their posts by a formula of regional distribution which guaranteed the inclusion of representatives from the Kansai Rōdō Dōmeikai, and a similar body to be established in the Kantō area. But real power in the Yūaikai lay with the central executive committee whose members were drawn from the larger organ. Suzuki, who was re-elected chairman of the Yūaikai, nominally presided over both committees but Matsuoka Komakichi, who had been given the post of director (*shuji*) was more powerful. He, Nishio Suehiro, and Asō Hisashi held the balance of power in the reorganized leadership by virtue of having successfully placed their personal followers in the majority of posts on the two committees in Yūaikai headquarters.

These administrative changes in Yūaikai headquarters made the national executive of the organization more responsive to the will of the rank and file unions. The workers in the Yūaikai could now believe that this was their labor movement. The new declaration of principles adopted by the 1919 convention, which replaced the earlier, very mild statements of the Yūaikai, was likewise intended to deepen the enthusiasm of the workers for the transformed Friendly Society. Beginning with the words, 'Man is by nature free', the declaration stated, in part:

> Workers are people with personalities. They are not to be bought and sold with wages on the labor market. They must therefore have the right to form unions...We are not machines. In order to ensure the development of individual character and a society of human beings, we demand an organization of society in which the producers can attain perfect culture, stability of livelihood, and the right to control our environment.[57]

Elsewhere the declaration, written by Kagawa Toyohiko, proclaimed the goal of labor to 'rid the world of the evils of capitalism', and stated: 'We workers declare to the world that the workers of Japan, with the League of Nations, will struggle like martyrs, in the spirit of the Labor Covenant [of the International Labor Organization] in order that peace, freedom, and equality may rule the earth.'[58]

These promises of struggle were anchored in a long and quite specific list of concrete demands which included virtually every plank in the platform of the new ILO:

1. [recognition of] the principle that labor is not an article of commerce;
2. freedom of trade unionism;
3. abolition of child labor;
4. establishment of a minimum wage;
5. equal pay for equal work of male and female workers;
6. Sunday holiday each week;
7. eight-hour day and forty-eight-hour work week;
8. prohibition of night work;
9. appointment of women inspectors of labor;
10. institution of workers' insurance;
11. promulgation of a labor arbitration law;
12. prevention of unemployment;
13. equal treatment for national and foreign workers [in Japan];
14. public management and improvement of workers' housing;
15. establishment of a workers' compensation system;
16. improvement of home work;
17. abolition of indentured labor;
18. institution of general suffrage;
19. amendment of the Peace Police Law;
20. democratization of the educational system.[59]

In addition, the convention resolved to reorganize all existing labor unions arranged on the basis of mixed trades into genuine trade unions, to increase their federation into municipal and regional alliances, and actively recruit female workers. All of these measures were seen as essential to the strengthening of the Yūaikai for political struggle. To realize these objectives, the administrative specialization of the Yūaikai bureaucracy in national headquarters was increased with the establishment of separate bureaus responsible for different areas of policy and action; these included, among others, a Political Bureau, a Recruitment Bureau, a Women's Bureau, a Research and Publication Bureau, and a Finance Bureau.

Finally, to underscore the 1919 convention as a major point in the political development of the labor movement, the name of the Friendly Society was changed to Dai Nihon Rōdō Sōdōmei-Yūaikai. Although cumbersome, the title symbolized the new aggressive character of the former Friendly Society and its new political identity.

As if to demonstrate this identity at once, the Sōdōmei became politically active on a number of fronts after the 1919 convention: it sponsored national rallies against the Peace Police Law, supported universal suffrage and the legalization of unions, and demanded the right of the workers to select their own representatives in the Japanese delegation to the International Labor Organization free of manipulative government interference.[60]

The Sōdōmei was particularly anxious to undertake these initiatives in cooperation with other labor organizations in 1919 and 1920. It was realized of course that this cooperation might be difficult given the wide range of political philosophies which cut across the labor movement. The polarization between the anarchist Shin'yūkai and Seishinkai and the vaguely socialist Sōdōmei had already become a matter of great concern in the General Federation. Still, it was widely recognized throughout the movement that labor unity was worth striving for in view of the fact that the movement was still extremely small and weak, with only 100,000 – out of a total of 1,777,171 – workers organized into unions in 1919.

For this reason, the Sōdōmei cooperated with the anarchist Shin'yūkai and Seishinkai and six smaller groups to form the first labor front in Japan, the Rōdō Kumiai Dōmeikai (Alliance of Labor Unions), in 1920.[61] The Alliance received some notice in the Japanese press in 1920 by staging demonstrations against unemployment and for the abolition of the Peace Police Law and the enactment of a minimum wage law for labor, on May Day – the first May Day observed in Japan. Most of these demonstrations took place in Hibiya Park in Tokyo but similar meetings were held in Osaka and Kobe where they were attended chiefly by Sōdōmei members.[62]

The emotional matrix of this alliance of politically dissimilar labor organizations was a strong militancy that pervaded the entire labor movement, including the Sōdōmei, immediately after World War I. The reasons for this militancy were political and economic in character.

When Hara Kei – the 'Great Commoner', as he was known – took office as Prime Minister in 1918, the labor movement felt that his liberal party cabinet would be more responsive to popular demands for democratic change in Japan than the wartime cabinets. But as Watanabe Tōru and other writers have shown, Hara's cabinet was politically conservative; its refusal to meet the demands of the labor movement alienated labor from the so-called 'bourgeois' parties and made the Alliance of Labor Unions militant in its attitude toward the existing order.[63]

The militancy of the workers in these years also flowed from the impact of the postwar recession on Japan. This caused a precipitous decline in production and a corresponding unemployment crisis. By 1921, when the recession was in full swing, there were 189,363 workers unemployed.[64]

The immediate reaction of many workers to this crisis was to engage in industrial action as a protest against unemployment, as the record number of labor strikes (497) in 1919 indicates. The anarchists, writing in such organs as *Shakaishugi Kenkyū* [Studies in Socialism], *Rōdō Undō* and *Nihon Rōdō Shimbun* [Japan Labor Newspaper] attempted to convert these strikes into political conflict with capitalism, and a number of new, radical organizations came into being in 1920 for this purpose: the Nihon Shakaishugi Dōmei (Japan Socialist League); the anarchist L–L Kai (Land and Labor Society), organized by Arahata Kanson; and new anarchist unions such as the Tokyo Rōdō Undō Dōmeikai (Tokyo Labor Movement League) organized by Kondō Kenji, a disciple of Ōsugi Sakae.[65] These, and other 'black' unions, such as the Shin'yūkai and the Seishinkai, regularly published their own smaller newspapers in order to propagate the anarchist message of direct-action confrontation among the workers. Although it did not go so far in advocating class warfare leading to revolution, the official organ of the Sōdōmei, *Rōdō*, likewise expressed powerful protests against the ravages of unemployment caused by a system which they claimed was based on the systematic exploitation of the poor.[66]

This labor militancy did not last long. As the recession deepened in the early 1920s, and as unemployment mounted (in 1922, for instance, there were 216,722 workers unemployed),[67] the rank and file factory workers began to retreat from large-scale industrial protest. Even as early as 1920, the number of labor strikes fell to 282, from 497 in 1919; it dropped further in 1921, to 246.[68] When forced to choose between engaging in protests which might cost them their jobs and remaining passive, most workers generally opted for the latter.

However, in the years immediately following World War I, when anarchism exerted its strongest appeal in Japanese labor history, it was not readily apparent that labor militancy would eventually subside. For those workers who identified with socialism, being socialist meant being militant. It was indicative of the times that the most cautious of the Sōdōmei's leaders, Suzuki Bunji, could declare in 1919 that 'The time is fast approaching for the reconstruction of the world [based on the] destruction of the tyranny of the minority, of bureaucratism, and of capitalism, and the establishment of democracy.'[69]

Nor did these militant sentiments disappear entirely even after the unequivocal rejection of anarchism by the Nihon Rōdō Sōdōmei later in the 1920s. When the Sōdōmei became embroiled in a massive labor strike at the Kawasaki–Mitsubishi Shipyards in Kobe in 1921, the workers marched for days outside the company gates protesting against unemployment and the dismissal of key union leaders, and sang songs such as 'Rise up, ye laborers, rise up, capture the strongholds of capitalism'.[70] At one point, before the strike ended in defeat for the workers, Nishio Suehiro went so far as to advocate the burning of company property to wring concessions from management.[71] Although this proposal was not carried out, it illustrates the mood of the period.

In sum, labor's image of the past in 1919 and 1920 nurtured great hopes for the future of labor politics. In the years right after World War I, many participants in the labor movement believed it had reached a take-off stage in its historical evolution. They took confidence from two valuable lessons of the uneven development of the unions in the Meiji and early Taishō periods. The first was that for the labor movement to have any meaning and future in Japan at all, it had to combine the pragmatic development of the unions with political action; without strong unions the movement would remain forever vulnerable to the resistance of employers. Unless organized labor went beyond business unionism, it would be impossible to break down the existing barriers to workers' rights and improved conditions. The Sōdōmei therefore linked the growth of its unions with goals such as universal suffrage and the legalization of unions in its bid to contribute to the broad, democratic reconstruction of Japan.

The second lesson from the past was that political action undertaken by the labor movement, and any proletarian party which might arise to assist the workers, would only succeed if protracted conflict over political objectives and programs could be avoided in the ranks of labor. It augured well for the labor movement that the politically diverse groups in the Alliance of Labor Unions were willing to achieve a united front and bury their differences.

However, it was one thing to acknowledge these lessons from the past and begin to act upon them and quite another to remain guided by them. As the labor movement entered the 1920s, many questions concerning priorities remained. Should the movement give immediate priority to political struggle or should it first emphasize the institutional development of unions to allow a greater chance of success in the long run? To what extent were the politicization of the workers and the pragmatic building up of the unions likely to reinforce or impede each other? What forms should political struggle take? Should they include revolutionary, or reformist, strategies and to what specific ends? Finally, who should lead the way in settling these problems – the leaders of the labor movement or the rank and file workers themselves?

The answers to these questions depended upon many variables: ideological perceptions of political purpose, calculations of the aspirations and capabilities of the working masses, notions of existing options made possible by the nature of labor's environment, and personal ambitions on the part of labor leaders and their followers. Unfortunately, when the labor movement crossed the line from optimistic anticipation to the business of actually resolving these questions, the potential for labor unity and effective political protest dissolved in heated disputes over the future course of Japanese labor politics. It is to these disputes and their divisive repercussions in the labor movement that this book now turns.

2

Anarchism, socialism, and communism in the labor movement, 1920–1923

The political controversies reverberating throughout the Japanese labor movement for most of the 1920s may be analyzed in terms of three phases. From 1920 to mid-1922, when the Japanese Communist Party was formed, the main axis of tension lay between the anarchists and socialists in the movement. The second phase, from mid-1922 to late 1923, centered on rivalry between the anarchists and a tenuous coalition of socialists and communists. The third phase, stretching from late 1923 to 1928, was dominated by a fierce struggle between socialist and communist alignments for hegemony in the labor movement. This chapter focuses on the first two phases of conflict.

However, it is important to remember that these conflicts were largely confined to a small number of protagonists who felt that they possessed the key to the problem of organizing and politicizing the workers. The political consciousness of the great majority of workers, including both those in and outside of unions, remained unawakened and generally unaffected by the ideological implications of these rivalries.

Very few of the thinkers who invoked anarchist, socialist, or communist ideas in formulating their concepts of political action for the labor movement possessed more than a superficial understanding of these ideologies as discrete systems of thought. The latter had entered Japan from the West too recently to be fully assimilated into the intellectual life of the country. One writer cautions, 'To attempt any rigorous demarcation of ideological positions would be very misleading.'[1]

Nevertheless, if anarchism, socialism, and communism may be thought of as being different points on the ideological compass of Japanese labor politics, it is possible to identify in the thought and action of the participants a tendency to gravitate toward one or another of these points over time; some passed through several stages before committing themselves to a specific ideology. Many anarchists, in particular, or men who interpreted socialism in sufficiently militant terms as to make their ideology almost indistinguishable from anarchism, experienced shifts of this type prior to embracing communism as their paramount ideology. Others, who began by believing in more moderate forms of socialism, ended up affirming these convictions by moving from a nebulous to a more concrete understanding of what their ideas implied in the realm of practical action.

The impact of anarchism on these disputes was catalytic, sweeping through the Japanese labor movement like an electric shock. After World War I, the mood of many workers was stamped by an inchoate militancy which was exploited by radical labor organizers in their efforts to promote proletarian revolution. For a moment, anarchism met the emotional need of those workers whose impulse, forged in rage, was to lash out blindly at an oppressive social and political system. Yet, despite its powerful jolt, the current of anarchism proved short-lived. Under the changing conditions of the postwar recession, particularly amid severe unemployment, the emotional rage of the workers receded, or at least turned inward, and they recoiled from militancy.

Nor could anarchism, unlike socialism and communism, appeal to labor activists who were searching for coherent theories to direct them in a political course for the unions. Preoccupied with achieving a spontaneous revolution of the proletariat through direct action, and highly distrustful of bureaucracies and centralized authority in proletarian organizations, anarchism represented a conscious revolt against the desires of most participants in the Japanese labor movement for rational and authoritative interpretations of the position of the labor movement and its political path. The romantic, irrational approach of anarchism to class struggle appealed only to a minority of radicals, who so personalized political purpose as to render its imperative incomprehensible to others, and, as a result, failed to win widespread acceptance in the labor movement.

This flaw, originating in the thought of the leading anarchist thinker of this period, Ōsugi Sakae,[2] prevented the anarchists from mobilizing a mass following and enabled socialism and communism to gain ascendancy in the labor movement. The need to articulate strong political alternatives to the anarchist prescriptions for labor politics forced the socialists and communists to clarify their own positions in order to maximize their influence among the unions. Thus socialism and communism in the labor movement arose in reaction to the catalyst of anarchism.

The structure of the Dai Nihon Rōdō Sōdōmei-Yūaikai and labor conflict

Although almost every labor organization in Japan was somehow involved in the labor conflicts of this period, the main arena of these rivalries was the new Sōdōmei. Beginning with only 30,000 members, the General Federation was a small organization by today's standards but quite large in comparison with other labor groups in Taishō Japan. The Sōdōmei was also the only labor organization in Japan at the time possessing a national network of unions that included workers from most trades. Accordingly, it was regarded as the central pivot of the interwar Japanese labor movement. The fact that the Sōdomei enjoyed a certain respectability in the eyes of some government officials and business leaders also lent it an element of gravitas in the fledgling labor movement in the early 1920s.

The men holding the balance of power in the Sōdōmei in 1919 and thereafter were especially predisposed to view the General Federation as the basis for the expansion of the labor movement. Espousing a vague but nonetheless strong commitment to socialism, they attempted to make the Sōdōmei the driving wedge for socialist politics in the labor movement. By the same token, men with a far more radical vision of future labor politics were drawn to the Sōdōmei with the ultimate aim of taking it over and utilizing its promising resources for their own political purposes in the movement. The anarchists and, later, the communists realized that so long as the Sōdōmei adhered to socialist politics, their own influence in the labor movement would be limited, and therefore tried to undermine the General Federation as a step toward seizing control of its infrastructure. Certain weaknesses existing in the structure of the Sōdōmei enabled them, with varying success, to implement this policy of infiltration.

One such weakness resided in the command structure of the General Federation. On paper, the Sōdōmei was a highly centralized organization. The bylaws and regulations adopted by the 1919 convention clearly defined the authority of the executive committee in national headquarters to recommend policy, control funds, and generally direct the affairs of the Sōdōmei. The only qualification was that the entire membership should have to ratify the policy of headquarters through its representatives attending the Sōdōmei's national conventions.

The national structure presided over by the headquarters of the Sōdōmei extended downward through two large regional federations in

Western and Eastern Japan. These were the Kansai Rōdō Dōmeikai, founded in 1919, and the Kantō Rōdō Dōmeikai, organized two years later. Both federations consisted of numerous urban federations, or *rengōkai*, and beneath these, at the local level, individual unions. In theory, policies were made in Tokyo and communicated downward in the Federation through these interlocking administrative tiers, while the unions and urban and regional federations were responsible to national headquarters for carrying out these policies. They were also obliged to send a portion of their dues to the national treasury of the General Federation, administered by headquarters.[3]

This formal, bureaucratic command structure was held together by personal cliques embracing labor *oyakata* in national headquarters and their respective *kokata* and which were dispersed throughout the different administrative levels of the labor bureaucracy in positions of power. These cliques were informal in character and did not exist on paper. Accordingly, it is extremely difficult to be precise about their size. But it is certain that they were sufficiently pervasive to increase considerably the centralization of power in the Sōdōmei.

The three most important of these cliques belonged to Matsuoka, Nishio, and Asō. Nominally, they were *kokata* of Suzuki Bunji, the grand *oyakata* of the Sōdōmei, but in reality his hold over these men was weak. Suzuki's personal clique, established during the early Yūaikai period, had long since dissolved due to resignations and deaths among his close associates.[4] The real center of power in the Sōdōmei in the early 1920s was the triumvirate of Matsuoka, Nishio, and Asō.

Matsuoka and Nishio commanded the oldest and most extensive of these cliques, consisting of workers who had bound themselves to the two men through personal ties of loyalty in the early Taishō period. When Matsuoka and Nishio joined the Yūaikai, their *kokata* also joined, and as they rose to power in the Friendly Society, Matsuoka and Nishio relied upon these *kokata* to develop personal bases in the labor movement. The key members of Matsuoka's clique were Miki Jirō, who had worked with Matsuoka at the Muroran Steel Works, Uchida Tōshichi, Hirazawa Keishichi, and Genji Mochizuki. The most important man in Nishio's clique was Kanemasa Yonekichi, called 'my Chūgoku Toyotomi' by Nishio,[5] and relied upon to look after Nishio's power base in the Kansai area. Nishio had developed his own labor organization here, the Shokkō Kumiai Kisei Dōshikai, before entering the Yūaikai.

Asō Hisashi's clique consisted mostly of intellectuals who had taken part with Asō in the Shinjinkai: Tanahashi Kotora, Yamana Yoshitsuru, Akamatsu Katsumaro, Katō Kanjū, Kamijō Aiichi and others. Compared to the other cliques of the Sōdōmei, this was fairly new and small in scope – its main sphere of influence lay in the miners' section where Asō had been given special authority by the central executive committee in 1919.[6]

Perhaps the metaphor of feudalism best describes these cliques. Their penetration of the labor movement at all levels was facilitated by the role of the leading *kokata* as *oyakata*-lords toward their own personal followers in the areas under their control. The network of personal cliques can therefore be likened to a system of subinfeudation. Even the choice of words in Nishio's description of Kanemasa as his 'Chūgoku Toyotomi' indicates that the feudal metaphor was not lost on these men. Presumably, Nishio thought of himself, doubtless with a twinkle in his eye, as a latter-day Oda Nobunaga.[7]

Over the years, these allegiances tended to harden. Moreover, as time passed, they ramified extensively and became aligned with similar cliques in the agrarian union and socialist party movements. In many respects, the history of social protest in Japan can be written in terms of the interplay of these factions. Yet, the command structure of the Sōdōmei, including its formal and informal dimensions, was not as strong as it may seem. In reality, the centralization of power in the Federation was checked to a significant extent by the uneven distribution of executive power in the Sōdōmei and by the divisive effects of rivalry between the ruling factions.

The authority of the national executive was most respected among the Kantō organizations of the Sōdōmei where the proximity of the major urban federations of Tokyo and Yokohama to headquarters enabled Sōdōmei leaders to exercise direct, personal influence. Nevertheless, the dominance of Sōdōmei leaders in this area did not always go uncontested. On several important occasions labor revolts took place right under the eaves, as it were, of headquarters. But in the main, the hold of headquarters over the Kantō labor movement was fairly secure.

By contrast, it diminished in more distant regions, less susceptible to the direct interference of the national leadership. Thus, the powerful labor organizations of the Kansai industrial belt of Western Japan were less under the control of Sōdōmei headquarters than their counterparts in Eastern Japan. In administrative rather than solely regional terms, it can be said that Sōdōmei headquarters exerted the greatest influence over the labor bureaucracies of the Kantō and Kansai Rōdō Dōmeikai, peopled with trustworthy *kokata* who rarely wavered in serving the will of their *oyakata* in the national executive. Further down, at the urban federation and union local levels, it is apparent that the authority of national headquarters was much weaker. In other words, the vertical cliques emanating from Tokyo did not extend uniformly or pervasively to the grass roots of the General Federation.

This problem of administrative control over the lower echelons of the Sōdōmei was due to the previous rapid expansion of the Yūaikai. In the first years of the Friendly Society, when it was a very small and rather intimate organization, Suzuki Bunji managed to maintain his personal authority at the union local level by installing hand-picked labor bosses in positions of power. However, with its rapid growth during World War I, the picture changed abruptly. No longer did Suzuki regularly and personally consult with the men who administered the unions nominally under his control. They knew who Suzuki was, but Suzuki did not always know who they were.

In 1919, Matsuoka, Nishio, and Asō wrested power from Suzuki. However, lacking Suzuki's long association with the Yūaikai and his prestige as its creator, they found themselves at a disadvantage in not possessing personal links with many union bosses in the new Sōdōmei. Where these links existed, they were limited to certain areas. Nishio, for instance, had come to Sōdōmei headquarters from Osaka. Therefore he could claim to know most of the labor bureaucrats of the Osaka area, but not local leaders in other regions. Similarly, Matsuoka had cultivated a personal power base in the Kantō area and was on good terms with its labor leaders, but he was not familiar with union officials elsewhere. The same applies to Asō.

The anarchists, and to a far greater extent the communists, exploited this shallow penetration of national authority by establishing leverage at the local level, where the influence of Sōdōmei headquarters was weakest. Their challenge to the leaders of the Sōdōmei thus came from below.

This challenge was supported by the discord among the leaders of the three main factions in headquarters, and among their respective followers. There was less friction between Matsuoka and Nishio who shared a common worker background than between these two men and Asō, an intellectual. Jealousy between Matsuoka and Nishio, arising from their parallel ascendancy in the late Yūaikai, paled in significance next to their mutual distrust toward Asō and his toward them.

They tended to regard Asō and the other university graduates of the Shinjinkai faction as interlopers in the labor movement.[8] Asō's florid rhetoric, his associations with known labor radicals, and his extremely confident demeanor as a self-proclaimed socialist caused Matsuoka in particular to fear that the Shinjinkai activists might take the Sōdōmei too far, too fast along the road of political activism. While he shared their conviction that labor must involve itself in politics, Matsuoka was by nature much more cautious politically.

Conversely, Asō regarded Matsuoka and Nishio as being too bureaucratic and conservative to lead the labor movement.[9] To a certain extent, he shared the anarchist aversion toward these *rōdō kizoku*. Although cooperation with them in launching the Sōdōmei had been a necessity, it was not something Asō relished. In probing for weaknesses in the Sōdōmei, the anarchists and the communists hit upon the obvious tension which prevailed between these *oyakata*. They calculated that, by exacerbating this tension, their efforts to subvert the Sōdōmei from below would be facilitated by weakening it from above.

These weaknesses in the Sōdōmei command structure were aggravated by regional rivalry between the Kansai and Kantō organizations of the Federation. This has been mentioned in connection with the problem of headquarters' control over the movement, but regional rivalry was in fact rather more complicated. Again, like other problems in the Sōdōmei, it dated from the Yūaikai period.

Early in the Yūaikai it had been Suzuki's policy to weld the unions of the Kansai and Kantō areas, and elsewhere, into strong urban federations as a means of developing local solidarity which would benefit the labor movement as a whole. As an indirect consequence of this policy, some of the urban *rengōkai* had taken to publishing their own organs, the prime example being *Shin Kōbe* [New Kobe].[10] Local solidarity had also been enhanced by the development of urban consumers' cooperatives and welfare programs, as in Tokyo, Yokohama, Osaka, Kobe, and Kyoto, which continued to function in the Sōdōmei. Similarly, participation in local strikes had encouraged organized workers to identify strongly with their respective *rengōkai* in the big cities of Japan.

Inevitably perhaps, these local allegiances gradually took precedence over identification with the national labor movement. Localism was further reinforced by the autonomous development of the Kansai and Kantō labor organizations which, to employ the metaphor of feudalism once again, can be likened to feudal domains that jealously coveted their independence both from Sōdōmei headquarters and from each other. Like Chōshū, and other *han* in the late Tokugawa period who aspired to play independent parts in the drama of the Meiji Restoration, the Kansai Rōdō Dōmeikai and its Eastern counterpart, the Kantō Rōdō Dōmeikai, vied with each other in influencing the national politics of the Sōdōmei.[11]

The communists were more perceptive than the anarchists in taking advantage of the limited capacity of Sōdōmei headquarters to subordinate regional rivalries to its own unifying influence. Pitting one region against the other was one way to weaken the national cohesiveness of the General Federation and the overall authority of headquarters. In the same way, it appeared to these subversives that by establishing a foothold in the two major regional labor networks, their insurgency from below would be assured of eventual success. Neither the anarchists nor the communists wanted to destroy the infrastructure of the Federation. But loosening it was regarded as the precondition for capturing control of the Sōdōmei.

Yet another problem which weakened the Sōdōmei and presented the anarchists and communists with an opportunity to subvert from within was the polyglot nature of the Sōdōmei unions. The Sōdōmei inherited two basic types of unions from the Yūaikai. One included unions of workers in the large, modern, mechanized industries such as steel, machine-tool, chemical, electrical, and shipbuilding. These were large unions, in some instances numbering as many as 1,000 members.[12] Most of them were first organized, according to trades, during World War I. They were fairly stable in terms of membership, and they provided the skilled worker–leaders so essential to the Yūaikai and, later, to the Sōdōmei. Taken together, they were the cornerstone of the Sōdōmei's urban and regional federations.

But this group formed a minority in comparison to the second type of unions inherited from the Yūaikai. These included workers from the more traditional trades such as smiths, matchmakers, tatami-makers, deliverymen, sewer-maintenance workers, printers, soy sauce workers, brewers, and some female textile workers. Since these workers were mainly employed in small and medium-scale enterprises, their unions shared the characteristics of these firms. That is, they were small in size and their membership fluctuated according to economic conditions; for example, in times of recession, the output of these firms was reduced and workers laid off as a consequence.

In addition, the unions of this second category, most originating in the early Yūaikai, were not, strictly speaking, trade unions at all. In contrast to the first category, they included workers of mixed trades, organized on an enterprise basis. This format encouraged the identification of the workers with their enterprises, to the detriment of their identification with a horizontal, class-oriented, national labor movement. When contemporary writers complained about the absence of class-consciousness among the work force, they usually had these workers in mind. Due to the preponderance of the second type of unions in the Sōdōmei, the General Federation had a rather amorphous mass base.[13]

Judging that the prospects were brighter for building a politically aware, class-oriented labor movement around the workers in the large, mechanized industries than around their counterparts in the small and medium enterprises, the anarchists and the communists concentrated no less than the socialists on mobilizing these workers into unions, even to the point of trying to organize the skilled labor aristocracy whom they denigrated so often and attacked as a privileged stratum. At the same time, the anarchists and the communists calculated that the great mass of workers in the small and medium enterprises whose wages and conditions were poor in comparison to those of workers in larger enterprises would be receptive to radicalism. So, radical labor organizers in both the anarchist and communist camps concentrated on recruiting the 'true proletariat' in these factories while simultaneously trying to drive a wedge between them and the leaders of the Sōdōmei whom they accused of callously neglecting the interests of the factory poor. This was another crucial aspect of their insurgency from below.

A final weakness which aided the subversion of the anarchists and communists existed in the recruitment procedures of the Federation. In the manner of all social protest movements anxious to build up a membership as fast as possible, the Sōdōmei, like the Yūaikai earlier on, welcomed into its fold practically anyone who wanted to join. Little attention was paid to screening out workers whose past history contained signs of radicalism. A prospective member simply had to secure the sponsorship of several existing members and, at an induction ceremony held before the Sōdōmei flag at the union local, pledge loyalty to the Sōdōmei and agree to pay union dues.[14] This rather porous admissions procedure meant that radical labor organizers had no difficulty in entering the Sōdōmei with the intention of disruption.

In sum, because of its ramified national network of unions and the potential they represented for developing the labor movement as a political entity, together with weaknesses which made it seem that infiltration might succeed, the Sōdōmei appeared to radical labor organizers to be a juicy plum on the tree of Japanese labor. What might have been a constructive debate over labor's political options therefore became, very quickly, a struggle for power between competing camps in the Sōdōmei, more concerned about surpassing each other in gaining control of the labor movement than about containing their rivalries for the good of the unions.

The first phase of labor conflict in the 1920s: anarchism and socialism in the Sōdōmei, 1920–1922

The first sparks of controversy between anarchist labor organizers and the leaders of the Sōdōmei flew in the General Federation's inaugural convention of 1919. Here, anarchist delegates, led by two workers from the Tokyo Ironworkers' Union, Takata Waitsu[15] and Yamamoto Kenzō,[16] voiced strong opposition to the following issues: the Sōdōmei's support for universal suffrage, the projected name of the organization (they disliked the characters for 'Dai', or 'Greater', and 'Yūaikai' because to insert them into the new title would imply the compatibility of the Federation with imperial values and capitalism), and Suzuki Bunji's leadership as Sōdōmei chairman, for they considered him to be too bourgeois for the position.[17] These anarchist objections were all overruled in 1919, however, and as the convention ended, it seemed that the problem of anarchist dissent had been contained.[18]

But instead, this problem loomed larger on the horizon of the Sōdōmei even while negotiations were under way for the creation of the Alliance of Labor Unions in late 1919 and early 1920. During this period Takata and Yamamoto, assisted by Akiyama Kiyoshi, Sekine Kōshin, Shimura Teruō, and other anarchist labor organizers, formed a loose coalition of black unions in the Kantō wing of the Sōdōmei.[19] The leverage of this coalition became strikingly apparent in the inaugural convention of the new Tokyo *rengōkai*, which consisted chiefly of iron workers, on August 31, 1920.[20]

Much to the distress of Sōdōmei headquarters, this convention was the scene of an anarchist offensive aimed at passing policy resolutions which were contrary to the plans of Sōdōmei leaders. The tireless efforts of Takata, Yamamoto, and other anarchist delegates to drum up support for these proposals paid off when the convention resolved to oppose the General Federation's support for universal suffrage and to endorse the principle of a general strike. This meant that the Tokyo *rengōkai* was committed to backing similar resolutions in the next annual convention of the Sōdōmei, scheduled to take place in Osaka from October 3 to October 5.[21] In addition, the anarchists mustered enough support at the Tokyo *rengōkai* convention to oust one of the *rengōkai's* prominent officers, Hirazawa Keishichi, a *kokata* of Matsuoka's, from the organization. Thus, the anarchists had virtually captured the *rengōkai* as a fortress for their cause.[22]

These startling events alerted the leaders of the Sōdōmei to the necessity of checking anarchist influence in the General Federation before it spread elsewhere. But by October 1920, when the Sōdōmei held its annual convention, it was obvious that this would be a difficult task. One had simply to stand on the platform of the Osaka rail station several days before the opening of the convention to appreciate this. When the train bearing the Kantō delegates arrived, some of them stepped onto the station platform carrying small black flags. Shortly afterwards, they broke out into a militant labor song calling for the violent destruction of capitalism. Kagawa Toyohiko, present to welcome the Kantō delegates on behalf of the Kansai Rōdō Dōmeikai, was appalled at this open display of anarchist sentiment. At once, he drew back and proceeded to lead his own comrades in a milder chorus.[23]

The war of songs at Osaka depot poured over into a war of debates during the formal proceedings of the convention and at the informal meetings of delegates which followed each day's deliberations. Emotions ran high as the participants engaged in angry disputes over the political programs of the Sōdōmei. What had begun as a local anarchist insurgency against the ruling factions of the General Federation and their political philosophy, had now taken on national dimensions. Since the policy debates of the 1920 convention defined the most serious points of disagreement between the anarchists and the socialists in the Sōdōmei, and since the conventions of 1921 and 1922 (there was no national convention in 1923 because of the great earthquake that ravaged much of the Tokyo and Yokohama areas in September of that year) were largely sequels to the 1920 convention, the latter should be considered as an illustration of the polarization of the Sōdōmei between anarchist and socialist camps.

Although a great many issues came up for discussion in the 1920 convention, the two most important problems confronting the delegates concerned, first, the debate over direct action (*chokusetsu kōdō*) versus parliamentarianism (*gikaishugi*) and second, the debate over decentralization (*jiyū rengō*) versus centralization (*gōdō rengō*) as opposing emphases in the labor movement.

The clash over political priorities in the Sōdōmei began when Takata Waitsu triggered an outburst of applause from members of the anarchist L–L Kai sitting in the convention gallery by proclaiming, 'We absolutely must decide between direct action and parliamentarianism.' No sooner had Suzuki Bunji, in the chair, restored order than another anarchist delegate, from Kyoto, shouted, 'We reject the Diet!', which elicited further applause from anarchists in the convention.[24] Thereafter, it was clear that the proponents of direct action wanted the Sōdōmei and the entire labor movement to precipitate a massive general strike, to paralyze the economy and to incite worker wrath against the existing order. This militant mood was summed up later by one anarchist writer who stated, 'We do not say unions are useless. But they are effective only in building, not in the work of destruction – destruction must come before building.'[25]

It was only with great difficulty that Sōdōmei leaders were able to persuade the convention to reject direct action for parliamentarianism and thus support universal suffrage and legal and moderate initiatives on behalf of the workers and of democracy in general. For instance, Nishio Suehiro asserted that given the low political consciousness of the workers and the small size of the labor movement, a general strike would be impossible even if it were desirable and he did not think it was. He also pointed out wryly, 'To reject parliamentarianism but to debate this problem is itself an undeniable contradiction', for the essence of parliamentarianism was freedom of debate, not mob rule.[26] Kagawa Toyohiko agreed, stating, 'There are many faults in parliamentary politics...but it is rash to reject the Diet because unless we have universal suffrage, the people will never develop experience in the Diet' and will never play their historic role in Japanese politics.[27]

The strength of these arguments carried the day for the parliamentarian side in the Sōdōmei in 1920, and in subsequent conventions. But the socialist victory was qualified by the failure of the convention of 1920 to endorse universal suffrage as a specific goal of the Federation, preferring instead to put this matter before a policy review committee until the government showed signs of greater sympathy with this cause. Not until 1924 did the Sōdōmei again make universal suffrage one of its foremost goals in pursuing parliamentarian politics.

When the convention turned its attention to the structure of authority in the Sōdōmei, the debate over decentralization, advocated by the anarchists, versus centralization, supported by the socialists, also resulted in a victory for the latter. Speaking for the anarchists, Takata Waitsu and Yamamoto Kenzō argued that each union should be free to decide when to strike or when to undertake whatever action it wished, without having to obtain the prior approval of Sōdōmei headquarters. This position was consistent with their advocacy of 'spontaneous revolution' among the proletariat as the means of challenging the existing order. In reply, Nishio, Matsuoka, and other Sōdōmei leaders defended the principle of centralized authority in the Federation on the grounds that only the national leadership had a sufficiently comprehensive understanding of when strikes would succeed or fail, to judge whether they should be undertaken. If decisions in this regard were not made in headquarters, there was little point in having a national labor movement in the first place, it was argued. As the Sōdōmei's support for the great Kobe strike of 1921 later indicated, the proponents of centralization did not oppose strikes per se but only wanted the timing and planning of them to be left to the national leadership of the Federation.[28]

The anarchists also opposed, but without success, the Sōdōmei's support for the International Labor Organization, which they felt was too distant to help Japanese workers and which they believed was intrinsically worthless because it was a reformist rather than a revolutionary organization; the support of the Sōdōmei for collective bargaining, stressed in particular by Matsuoka Komakichi as an economic adjunct of parliamentarian politics; and so on. However, the anarchists did manage to have 'Dai' deleted from the title of the Sōdōmei; 'Yūaikai' remained, but it too was deleted under anarchist pressure in 1921. On the question of whether to continue support for the Alliance of Labor Unions, the anarchists and socialists agreed in 1920 that this was important. However, when the Alliance became the venue for similar clashes between anarchist and socialist labor groups, the Sōdōmei withdrew from it in early 1921, thus contributing to the collapse of the Alliance within a year after its formation.[29]

In retrospect, the 1920 convention revealed the capacity of the anarchists to stir up controversy in the Sōdōmei even though many of their more important proposals had been rejected. But the real significance of this convention lay in its general affirmation of parliamentary politics and the principle of centralization in response to anarchist demands for radical direct action and decentralization. To be sure, these main contours of Sōdōmei policy had been discernible in the convention of 1919; they were part of the legacy inherited from the Yūaikai. But in 1920 they hardened significantly; subsequent anarchist attempts to erase them met with failure. After 1920, socialism in the Sōdōmei was henceforth firmly identified with gradual, legal, evolutionary reformism wedded to pragmatic politics to build up the infrastructure of the union movement.

However, the anarchists continued to play the spoiler's role in certain sections of the General Federation, especially in 1921. Their position in the Tokyo *rengōkai*, the principal seat of anarchist influence, was strengthened that year by the addition of the Kokushoku Kumiai, or Black Union, founded by Watanabe Masanosuke after the collapse of his Nagamine Celluloid Union in 1920.[30] Like the Nagamine Union, the Black Union was centered in the Kameido district of Tokyo, where Watanabe lived, and was composed of celluloid workers, watchmakers, and printers. When Watanabe affiliated the Black Union with the Tokyo *rengōkai*, he and his organization were deemed valuable allies by Takata and Yamamoto in their continuous struggle to undermine the labor bureaucracies running the Sōdōmei.

The anarchists did achieve several notable successes in this struggle. For example, in July 1921 they managed to drive Tanahashi Kotora, a prominent member of the Shinjinkai faction in the Sōdōmei leadership, from his post as director (*shuji*) of the Tokyo *rengōkai*. The anarchists singled out Tanahashi for attack primarily because of an article he wrote in the January 1921 issue of *Rōdō* entitled, 'Rōdō kumiai e kaere' [Return to Labor Unions]. Tanahashi's message was that spontaneous revolution through direct action would achieve nothing in Japan. If organized labor expected to make progress, it would have to concentrate on the pragmatic development of the unions as a basis for parliamentary politics in the future. He declared, in calling upon the workers to abandon anarchist fantasies, 'The capitalists and the potentates fear much more one hundred quiet men solidly organized than they do a single courageous worker scuffling with the police. Workers! Return to the unions! Your kingdom is here!'.[31]

The anarchists leapt on Tanahashi for these views in the Tokyo *rengōkai* convention of 1921, creating such disorder that he felt compelled to resign from the *rengōkai*. Demoralized, Tanahashi in fact also broke entirely with the labor movement for several years, but returned to figure prominently in labor and socialist party activities during the late 1920s.[32] The anarchists also succeeded in hounding Kagawa

Toyohiko out of the labor movement in early 1922. Henceforth, Kagawa devoted himself to developing the agrarian union movement and later the socialist party movement in Japan.[33]

Anarchist influence is also discernible in some of the major labor strikes waged at the local level of the Sōdōmei in the early 1920s, for example, in the massive strike that erupted in 1920 in plants of the Fuji Gas Spinning Company. Here the Yūaikai Spinners and Weavers Labor Union received support from the anarchist Shin'yūkai and Seishinkai when they struck against the Company for its refusal to extend formal recognition to the Sōdōmei union. Spurred on by anarchist militancy, some of the strikers resolved 'even to die' for their cause during this clash with the Company, but the police were called in, and the strike resulted in the arrest of members of the Sōdōmei local along with Shin'yūkai and Seishinkai agitators, and then collapsed.[34]

However, despite all their efforts, the anarchists failed to divert the Sōdōmei from reformist socialism. Their disregard for organization and coordination, in preference for spontaneity, prevented them from expanding their influence beyond the precincts of such organizations as the Tokyo *rengōkai*. They were thus condemned to a peripheral position in the labor movement which was eroded still further by the growing reluctance of workers to listen to anarchist calls for militant direct action during the recession. Even such solidly anarchist bastions outside the Sōdōmei as the Shin'yūkai and Seishinkai failed to enlarge their numbers. By mid-1922, the anarchist labor movement, in and beyond the Sōdōmei, was in decline.[35] Its final eclipse as a major force in the ranks of Japanese labor was hastened by the sudden appearance of a new challenge: opposition from the Japanese communists.

The second phase of labor conflict in the 1920s:
anarchism, socialism, and communism in the Sōdōmei,
1922–1923

The formation of the Comintern-backed Japanese Communist Party in July 1922 ushered in the second phase of labor conflict in the 1920s, described by contemporary and later writers as the period of *ana-boru* (anarchist–bolshevik) rivalry.[36] In the short run, the greatest beneficiaries of this conflict were the socialists of the Sōdōmei who succeeded in working out a cooperative relationship with the communists that assisted them in destroying anarchism within the General Federation.

The immediate impact of the Japanese Communist Party (JCP) on the anarchist movement was to divert many leading anarchists to the communist cause, including, for example, Arahata Kanson, Yamakawa Hitoshi, and Sakai Toshihiko, all of whom had been strongly identified with anarchism together with Ōsugi Sakae. Of these men George Beckmann writes, 'As they studied developments in Russia in order to grasp the "realities of socialism", they began to realize that Russian communism was something very different from anarcho-syndicalism. They came to believe that communism, as the foundation of the successful Russian Revolution, would provide more practical guidelines for achieving the socialist transformation of Japan.'[37] In particular, they were attracted to Marxist–Leninist theories about the inevitability of an historic transition from capitalism to socialism throughout the world and, as important, to the idea that revolution could occur in Japan under the leadership of a vanguard proletarian party which, in contrast to the diffuse militancy of anarchism, would provide the organizational means to make this revolution possible.[38]

Beckmann and others have elsewhere discussed the conversion of Arahata, Yamakawa, and Sakai to communism and the subsequent role they played in forming the JCP.[39] It is instructive to consider why so many workers, including former anarchists, joined the communist movement. The case of Watanabe Masanosuke is fairly typical.

As his wife, Tanno Setsu, recalls in her memoirs, Watanabe was originally drawn into the anarchist movement by the ideas of Ōsugi Sakae, which had seemed compelling in pointing to the revolutionary liberation of the Japanese proletariat after World War I.[40] However, Watanabe was persuaded to abandon the anarchist cause for communism after reading an article written by Yamakawa Hitoshi, 'Musan kaikyū no hōkō tenkan' [The Change of Direction of the Proletarian Class] which appeared in the July–August 1922 issue of *Zen'ei* [Vanguard], a communist organ. Yamakawa was the leading theorist of the new JCP at the time; this article stated the Party's early policy toward the labor movement.

Like Tanahashi Kotora in the preceding year, Yamakawa's goal in writing this article was to condemn anarchism. Anarchism, he asserted, could never lead to revolution because it failed to appreciate the importance of organizing a mass base for political struggle. Echoing Tanahashi in his criticism of the minority of anarchists who dreamed of revolution but who did little to prepare for it, Yamakawa declared,

> Ten or twenty enthusiasts get together, dream about the next day of revolution and make big talk...At best, they would satisfy their 'rebellious

spirit' by taking 'revolutionary action' against a policeman and spending a night under police detention. Although they reject the capitalist system, they actually do not lay even a finger upon it. As long as they adhere to such a passive attitude, they become more isolated from the proletarian masses.[41]

Yamakawa went on, 'In all battle fronts against the control and power of capitalism...we must turn from the attitude of pure negation to positive struggle. This indeed is the change of direction the proletarian movement must adopt everywhere.'[42] In short, 'positive struggle' signified going 'to the masses', a phrase Yamakawa often employed in his writings, and organizing them into a disciplined revolutionary movement. The JCP would lead the way in this practical endeavor but it was clearly understood that the Party would work through existing institutions, such as the Nihon Rōdō Sōdōmei, which had already begun to organize the proletarian workers in their efforts to reach out to the masses. That is, the Party would try to make use of the centralized bureaucracy of the Sōdōmei and its union network in carrying out this important 'change of direction'.[43]

Yamakawa's well-argued refutation of anarchism and his insistence on a disciplined mass base in preparing for the liberation of the *musan kaikyū* immediately explained to Watanabe the failure of his previous struggles to follow Ōsugi's thought. It also persuaded him that strategies and tactics for revolution, which had proved successful in Russia, also existed for Japan. Therefore, Watanabe joined the JCP where he was welcomed by Yamakawa, Arahata, Sakai, and Tokuda Kyūichi as he had already made a name for himself as a radical labor organizer, first in the Nagamine Celluloid Union and more recently in the Black Union. When he joined the JCP, Watanabe was preoccupied with building up a third union, his earlier organizations having been repressed by the police. This was the Nankatsu Rōdō Kumiai (Nankatsu Labor Union), founded in 1922.

Under Watanabe's energetic leadership, the Nankatsu Labor Union quickly formed a vigorous focal point for communism in the labor movement. Watanabe endeavored to raise the political consciousness of his followers by conducting rigorous study of such works as the *Communist Manifesto*, printing pro-communist newspapers such as the *Nankatsu Jihō* [Nankatsu Review] and *Rōdō Kumiai* [Labor Unions], and waging militant labor strikes. Soon the Nankatsu Union became associated with what was called the revolutionary 'spirit of Nankatsu' in the communist labor movement. This phrase signified uncompromising loyalty to the JCP and a willingness to struggle on its behalf, whatever the risks.[44]

Other workers such as Sugiura Keiichi, Nabeyama Sadachika, Tsuji Taminosuke, Taniguchi Zentarō, Ichikawa Yoshio, Nakamura Yoshiaki and Watanabe Mitsuzō experienced a similar conversion to communism. Yamamoto Kenzō, very active with Watanabe Masanosuke and Takata Waitsu in the anarchist labor movement, also joined the JCP for reasons akin to those that motivated Watanabe.[45] Without the participation of these men, the JCP, then dominated by intellectuals, would never have developed a base in the factories during the 1920s.

Socialist–communist cooperation against anarchism in the Japanese labor movement was centered on the points of agreement found in the articles written by Tanahashi of the Sōdōmei, and Yamakawa of the JCP, in 1921 and 1922 respectively. The Sōdōmei and the JCP both insisted on developing the unions into a mass movement, on centralizing power in the movement to this end, and on avoiding adventurist direct action. 'Into the masses' was their joint slogan. The decision of the communists and socialists to work together in combating anarchism developed further from a series of informal meetings sponsored by the labor bureau of the JCP in 1922 and 1923 for the purpose of facilitating open-ended discussion of political options available to the labor movement.[46] These meetings were attended by leading communists, including Tokuda, Arahata, Yamakawa, and Sakai, together with a number of prominent men in the Sōdōmei. Among the latter were Asō Hisashi, Yamana Yoshitsuru, and Akamatsu Katsumaro, all of the Shinjinkai faction in the General Federation, and Nishio Suehiro and his right-hand man, Kanemasa Yonekichi.[47]

Although some of the Sōdōmei participants attended these meetings out of an intellectual curiosity, in order to learn more about communism and communist tactics for the labor movement, none of them, save Akamatsu, joined the JCP.[48] Rather, their collaboration with the communists was bred of expedience. They knew that working with the JCP posed certain risks, not the least of which was the risk of being exposed to police harassment against the JCP and anyone associated with it, however tenuous the connection. Another obvious risk lay in allowing the communists to gain a foothold in the Federation, for it was plain that the JCP wanted to infiltrate the Sōdōmei and eventually take it over. But these risks were judged to be worth running, if this is what it took to subdue the anarchists. The calculation that communism could be contained in the Sōdōmei once this goal of defeating anarchism had been achieved, turned out to be a serious mistake later on. But in 1922, this calculation made sense. The communists, in turn, welcomed good relations with the Sōdōmei because they, too, wanted to defeat anarchism which posed a threat to their own brand of revolutionary politics, in the unions. They hoped to preserve the Sōdōmei against the anarchists so that they could use the Federation as a ready-made labor base for the JCP's activities in the factories, without having to build from the ground floor up a communist union infrastructure in Japan.[49]

Thus the anarchists, whose position had already declined in the labor movement, found themselves the victims of socialist–communist attempts to eliminate their presence in the factories. The socialist–communist 'alliance', if it may be called that, worked against the anarchists in several ways. For instance, the socialists and the communists coordinated their attempts to outflank the anarchists in such 'black' bastions as the Tokyo *rengōkai* and the newly formed Kantō Rōdō Dōmeikai, organized in November 1921.[50] The leaders of the Sōdōmei endeavored to tighten the lines of control over these organizations from above while the communists undermined the anarchist unions from below. Ironically, the anarchists were put onto the defensive by some of their former comrades: Watanabe Masanosuke and Yamamoto Kenzō. Watanabe used his Nankatsu Union, now affiliated to the Kantō Rōdō Dōmeikai, to weaken the leverage of Takata Waitsu, as did Yamamoto in unions where he held sway. By early 1923, anarchist influence in the Kantō wing of the Sōdōmei had been successfully neutralized.[51]

Furthermore, belated efforts by the anarchists to expand into Western Japan were cut short by communist labor organizers, notably Nabeyama Sadachika, who worked assiduously to establish communist unions, particularly in Osaka. Sōdōmei leaders tacitly encouraged this endeavor because they thought that these unions would strengthen the General Federation against anarchism in the Kansai area, and also because, at the time, Nabeyama showed no signs of wanting to upset their power there.[52]

Also, both the socialists and the communists made anarchism the target of constant criticism in their publications during 1922 and early 1923.[53] They cooperated in smothering anarchist proposals at the 1922 Sōdōmei national convention. In addition, this convention passed several resolutions favored by the JCP and supported by the Sōdōmei leaders. These included demands for the recognition of the Soviet

Union by Japan and for the immediate withdrawal of the Japanese troops still in Siberia, where they had been sent in the famous Siberian Intervention of 1918. The fact that Nishio Suehiro cooperated with Akamatsu Katsumaro and Nozaka Sanzō, both members of the JCP, in writing these resolutions, illustrates the closeness of socialist–communist collaboration.[54]

Seen in the perspective of these developments, the death of Ōsugi in September 1923 was the final coup de grâce for the anarchist labor movement. Ōsugi had been arrested during a general crackdown on radicals (which, it will be shown, included many communists as well), carried out on the pretext of maintaining public order during the massive confusion following the September earthquake in the Kantō area.[55] His murder, along with that of his wife, Itō Noe, and a young nephew, shocked many of his friends and foes alike in the labor movement and made him something of a martyr in the history of Japanese radicalism.[56] But with Ōsugi gone, anarchism lost its only national symbol, leaving the political terrain of the labor movement now dominated by the socialists and the communists.

However, the decline of anarchism, though it simplified to a certain extent the political choices facing organized labor, did not conclusively resolve the dilemma of political choice. It merely shifted this problem to the new ground of conflict between socialism and communism. It remained to be seen whether the rationality of socialism or the rationality of communism would prevail in the Japanese labor movement. The prerequisite for the success of both was, fundamentally, the same: ideology – which still awaited further refinement and precision – had to be effectively related to practical action and made relevant to the factory masses. This latter problem weighed heavily on the minds of both Sōdōmei and JCP labor strategists. For instance, in an article written for *Rōdō* in 1921, one Sōdōmei writer lamented the 'antipathy toward politics' that was widespread among the workers as a consequence of the negative labor policies of the Hara government. He regretted the disillusionment of the workers with political activism of any sort.[57] Similar sentiments were expressed in 1922 by Yamamoto Kenzō, when he commented, 'I doubt the working class is revolutionary in spirit at all; it certainly lacks the consciousness of the Russian Bolsheviks.'[58]

Clearly, going 'to the masses' had only just begun.

3

The communist offensive and
the 1925 labor split

With anarchist labor in disarray, the stage was set for a struggle for power in the Sōdōmei between the socialists and communists. During the period 1923 to 1928 centrifugal, rather than centripetal, forces prevailed and multiple schisms resulted: the split of the General Federation in 1925, known as the *dai-ichiji bunretsu* ('first great split'), the subsequent polarization of the remaining labor movement into socialist and communist centers, and the ensuing fragmentation of the proletarian party movement. This chapter deals with the first of these catastrophes, the 1925 labor split, while the following two chapters trace the development of socialist–communist struggles in the labor and proletarian party movements through to 1928.

It took very little to unravel the loosely entwined strands of socialism and communism in the Nihon Rōdō Sōdōmei; their disentanglement was accomplished through successive shocks administered by the government's 'whip' against the Japanese Communist Party and elements of the anarchist movement in 1923. Put briefly, the government's policy was to destroy the Party and its influence in Japanese social protest movements while simultaneously enticing the socialists, with the 'candy' of concessions, into lasting political compromises with the status quo.

The Russian Revolution of 1917 had added a new and alarming dimension to Japan's traditional rivalry with Russia; now, Russia was an ideological as well as a military rival to Japan in Asia. A determination to contain communism in Asia had already prompted Japan's participation in the abortive Siberian Intervention of 1918 and inevitably, fear of the enemy without – Soviet Russia – led to fear of the enemy from within – communist subversion in Japan. That it would be guided and financed by the Russian Comintern made the spectre of subversion all the more formidable in the eyes of the government. Accordingly, the Home Ministry was entrusted with the task of containing 'bolshevik' activity in Japan.

In particular, the old fear that labor unions were enclaves of political subversion and 'dangerous thoughts' was revived in this period, even though the movement was still very small. In 1923, there were only 432 unions with a total membership of just 125,551 workers. By 1924, their number had increased to 469, with 228,278 members, representing 5.3 per cent of the total industrial work force. Two years later, at the beginning of the Shōwa period in 1926, Japan had 488 unions claiming a membership of 284,739 workers. In 1929, on the eve of the Depression, the labor movement had increased in size to 630 unions and 330,985 workers, but this was still only a fraction of the total industrial work force (6.8 per cent).[1]

However, the size of the movement was irrelevant in a country where most of officialdom still believed that *any* unions were a threat to the national order, especially given the Comintern's desire to spread revolutionary class-consciousness among the workers. The concentration of more than half of these unions in the modern machine and transport industries,[2] and the federation of some of them into various regional or industrial associations, caused additional concern.[3] Strategically located in important sections of industry and possessing the beginnings of horizontal organization, the unions were seen to be potentially dangerous to the *kokutai* (national polity) if they were allowed to be manipulated by the 'bolsheviks'.

The Sōdōmei, despite its relatively favorable image in such august organizations as the semi-official Kyōchōkai, was not exempt from these suspicions. Even before the formation of the JCP, uniformed police attended Sōdōmei public meetings regularly in order to detect signs of radicalism. When Kagawa Toyohiko, in addressing a labor rally, once alluded to the option of destroying capitalism (ironically, to discredit this argument), an officer drew his sword and shouted, 'stop your speech!'.[4] On another occasion, aptly remembered as the 'deaf-mute incident', Kanemasa Yonekichi was similarly interrupted during a speech at an Osaka labor rally whereupon he gamely continued his remarks in pantomime, to the amusement of his audience.[5] Anarchist labor organizations were subjected to greater harassment. Many of their journals were censored by the Home Ministry, and in many instances closed down, their editors arrested and imprisoned for allegedly violating the Peace Police Law. But it was the communists who felt the 'whip' of anti-radical repression most often, and most severely.

The first crack of the government's whip against the communists was delivered in the summer of 1923 when fifty known communists and their sympathizers were suddenly rounded up. These mass arrests seriously depleted the membership of the JCP,[6] but it suffered a second, more cutting stroke during the period of martial law in Tokyo which followed the Kantō earthquake in the September of that year. A virtual reign of terror existed in the Kameido industrial area where many communists in the Nankatsu Labor Union were killed by the police;[7] Watanabe Masanosuke survived only by virtue of already being in prison, as a result of the earlier arrests. Elsewhere in Tokyo, Ōsugi Sakae was murdered, and mobs, driven by rumors about the threat of communism, roamed through the streets looking for 'subversive' Chinese and Koreans, several thousand of whom were slaughtered in an ugly wave of indiscriminate violence.[8] Although the government was not directly responsible for these outrages, it is true that the press had inflamed anti-communism during the post-quake chaos, possibly with government approbation.

In early 1924, crippled by the 'white terror' of September 1923, those communists who had escaped the police dragnets decided to disband the JCP, leaving the affairs of the defunct Party to a rump bureau which, it was understood, would continue the penetration of other proletarian organizations against the day when the JCP would revive and use them for its revolutionary purposes. When informed of the Party's dissolution, the Comintern branded the Japanese communists as defeatists and urged the immediate rebirth of the JCP, a policy that was not carried out until December 1926.[9]

Through several articles in *Rōdō*, the Sōdōmei hierarchy expressed some sympathy with the beleaguered communists, and posed the pertinent question: what were the limits of the government's apparent plan to crush proletarian dissent in Japan?[10] Privately, however, Sōdōmei leaders feared that their links with the communists, however tenuous they had been, might precipitate similar repression of the General Federation by the police unless the Sōdōmei moved quickly to dissociate itself publicly from the communist movement. Thus, plans were laid in late 1923 to carry out a major 'change of direction', *hōkō no tenkan*, for the Federation in the next annual convention, scheduled for February 1924. Meanwhile, members of the Sōdōmei central committee who had been active in the communist movement, notably Akamatsu Katsumaro, cut their ties with the communists.[11] In particular, Akamatsu's repudiation of the communists was significant, for his was to be the guiding hand behind the 'change of direction' in the Sōdōmei.

Before discussing the policies and assumptions that comprised the Sōdōmei's 'change of direction', it should be noted that, strictly speaking, this so-called 'change' was perhaps rather less dramatic than it was made to appear. A 'change' did occur in the sense of rejecting communism to embrace socialism. But in reality the 'new' position of the Sōdōmei was just a comprehensive reaffirmation of the thought and action conspicuous in the Sōdōmei's earlier resistance to anarchism.

Further, it would be erroneous to attribute the 'change of direction' solely to the expedience of Sōdōmei leaders who now believed that the survival of the Federation depended on the projection of a moderate, socialist, political image. In fact, these men regarded the new policies of February 1924 as being consonant with what they interpreted as the 'trends of the times'. It seemed to them that the government, while 'whipping' the communists, was ready to extend a friendly hand to the socialists in the labor movement as demonstrated by the offer of the 'candy' of important concessions in this period. These included labor laws designed to demonstrate to organized labor that if it did cooperate with the State, then its major goals for the workers would come to fruition.

For example, the Health Insurance Law, enacted in 1922 to become effective in 1927, provided every worker covered by the 1911 Factory Law with health, accident, and, in the case of women, maternity insurance. This scheme was to be administered by the government through a new network of Health Insurance Societies.[12] The thrust of this legislation was augmented by the Amendment to the Factory Law in 1923 (to come into effect in 1926) which increased by 11 per cent the number of factories covered by the Factory Law. Whereas the 1911 Law had applied only to factories of fifteen or more workers, it was now extended to factories of ten or more. Also, whereas the original Law had set the minimum age for factory workers at twelve years and the maximum work time for women and children at twelve hours per day, the Amendment raised the minimum age to fifteen and reduced the number of hours for women and children to eleven.[13]

These were scarcely dramatic improvements. But they did signify progress and raised hopes that the government might soon conform across the board to the standards advocated by the International Labor Organization concerning conditions of labor. The passage of other labor laws in the 1920s reinforced this impression. Among them were the Employment Exchange Law of 1921, the Matches Manufacture Prohibition Law of the same year, the Seamen's Employment Law of

1922, the Seamen's Minimum Wage Law of 1923, and the Labor Disputes Mediation Law, enacted in 1926 to come into effect in 1927.[14] These laws were not without serious defects, as other writers have noted.[15] But they encouraged the belief that sooner or later the government would legalize unions, recognize their right to strike and bargain collectively, and free them from unreasonable constraints.

The impression that the government would tolerate political moderation in the labor movement was enhanced when Prime Minister Yamamoto Gombei announced, after the Kantō earthquake, that his administration was in principle favorable toward universal suffrage.[16] Unfortunately, nothing came of this until the coalition liberal party cabinet of Prime Minister Kato Kōmei (president of the Kenseikai, or Constitutional Association) came into office in June 1924. But the immediate response of the Sōdōmei to this declaration was to initiate a study of the problems involved in forming a proletarian party under the authority of its political bureau, led by Akamatsu Katsumaro.[17] Akamatsu also represented the Sōdōmei in a new organization, the Seiji Mondai Kenkyūkai (Society for the Study of Political Problems) – later renamed simply Seiji Kenkyūkai – founded in December 1923 by a diverse group of intellectuals including Abe Isoo, Shimanaka Yūzō, Kagawa Toyohiko, Suzuki Mosaburō and Takahashi Kamekichi. Their intention was to establish a proletarian party that would represent the factory workers and tenant farmers in the Diet once universal suffrage became law.[18]

These political initiatives taken by the Sōdōmei were based on a decision of the central committee in October 1923 to revive the Federation's support for universal suffrage.[19] And indeed in 1924, this became a major plank in the Sōdōmei's 'change of direction' platform. The considerable grass roots support for universal suffrage within the Sōdōmei is apparent in the many articles written by rank and file unionists that appeared in *Rōdō* during 1923 and 1924, urging the Federation to take the lead in forming a workers' party. For instance, a member of the Kantō Iron Workers Union wrote that with universal suffrage the labor movement would be able to rely on a labor party to defeat the 'entrenched bourgeois parties'.[20] Similarly, unions such as the Takazaki local of the Sōdōmei Kantō Brewers Union published their resolutions in *Rōdō* calling on the Sōdōmei executive committee to draw up guidelines for a labor party.[21]

Another positive sign that the 'trends of the times' were beneficial to a politically moderate labor movement was the government's decision in 1924 to allow the labor movement complete autonomy in selecting delegates to the ILO. Previously, the government had reserved the right to decide who would represent Japanese labor at the ILO by choosing from a list of nominees presented by labor. This list invariably included politically 'safe' men upon whom the government could rely to make only moderate demands for labor reforms in the forum of the ILO. The new arrangement, dispensing with this procedure, conformed to the rules of selection of the ILO itself, and, because the government felt the General Federation would be unlikely to name someone for this role who would be politically radical, favored the Sōdōmei. Beginning in 1924 with Suzuki Bunji, the Sōdōmei supplied most of the Japanese labor representatives to the ILO until Japan withdrew from that body in 1938.[22] Not surprisingly, the Sōdōmei reaffirmed its support of the ILO in the 1924 convention, greatly heartened by the government's change of mind on the ILO selection issue which, as one writer notes, sprang from the government's desire to offset international criticism of its former policy in this matter.[23]

The implication that the government's concession on the ILO selection issue showed a willingness to encourage moderate, as opposed to radical, labor was given weight when the government called on the Sōdōmei to help cope with the chaos caused by the Kantō earthquake in 1923. When they saw that the Federation behaved responsibly in providing emergency housing for homeless workers and in taking other relief measures, officials in the Home Ministry began to think that 'not all elements in the social movement were "dangerous" but rather there existed "sober" leaders who could be helpful'.[24] Naturally, the Sōdōmei was glad to confirm this impression.

Moreover, new developments overseas supported the view in the Sōdōmei that the 'trends of the times' presaged new breakthroughs for social democracy around the world, including Japan, and that the Japanese labor movement could contribute to this trend by adhering to moderate socialism in labor politics. The record of political success registered by the German Social Democratic Party and, more significantly, the election of a British Labour government in 1924, captured the imagination of Sōdōmei leaders. For instance, in arguing that the rise to power of the British Labour Party should inspire the emulation of the British labor movement by Japanese labor, Akamatsu Katsumaro wrote, 'Because English history and social circumstances differ from those of our country, it is impossible for our labor movement to follow in the footsteps of England in every respect. But if the working class [of Japan] stresses the development of democratic social reform', as in England, 'and if ours is essentially a moral labor movement, labor movements like ours can teach much even to the British labor movement'.[25] As conditions in Japan resembled those of England more than those of pre-1917 Russia, it was clear to Akamatsu that England, and specifically the British labor movement, was the superior model for Japanese labor.

All in all, these 'candy' concessions by the government and the 'trends of the times' both at home and abroad may not appear in retrospect to have been substantial enough to justify optimism as the Federation approached its 'change of direction' in 1924. Nevertheless they appealed enormously to men who were desperately anxious to believe that the political climate around them was becoming increasingly favorable to their goals, especially given the obvious capacity of the State to crush radical labor. It is in this context that the Sōdōmei's 'change of direction' must be appreciated for what it was: an attempt to keep pace with events rather than be overwhelmed by them.

The 'change of direction' of 1924 and 'realist socialism' in the Sōdōmei

The 1924 national convention of the Sōdōmei, held in Tokyo from February 10 to February 12, accompanied its resolutions in support of universal suffrage, the formation of a legal proletarian party, parliamentary tactics in seeking labor's objectives, and the ILO, with an official declaration which read:

> We must plan for the development of labor unions in our country by the following means: after the implementation of universal suffrage, we must use our rights to vote effectively;...we must promote the political awakening of the proletariat; and we must find ways and means of promoting our goals through participation in international labor conferences [i.e., the ILO].[26]

Nishio Suehiro, who helped to draft this declaration, hailed it and the new policies of the Sōdōmei's 'change of direction' as a triumph of 'realism' (*genjitsushugi*) and pragmatism over radicalism in the labor movement.[27] Neither he nor anyone else at the convention referred to 'communism' as such, presumably because of fears that to do so would confuse the authorities who otherwise might not have understood that the whole purpose of the convention was to demonstrate the Sōdōmei's opposition to this system of 'dangerous thoughts'. But as Nishio implied, it was clear that the Sōdōmei now repudiated everything the communists stood for: violent class struggle, the overthrow of the State, and ties with the Comintern.

Those communists who remained in the Sōdōmei even though the JCP had been dissolved were, of course, less enthusiastic than Nishio about the Sōdōmei's 'change of direction'. Men like Nabeyama Sadachika, Nakamura Yoshiaki, and Taniguchi Zentarō still clung to the communist view, first articulated by Yamakawa Hitoshi in 1922, that to support universal suffrage and parliamentary politics was to compromise class struggle and play into the hands of the 'bourgeois' parties who controlled the lower house of the Diet.[28] They therefore tried to amend the convention declaration to include such statements as 'Frankly, we do not expect full liberation of the working class by a Diet dominated by the bourgeoisie,' or 'The militant labor unions... may take advantage of modified policies given by the ruling class but they will never be corrupted by such policies.'[29] Another amendment kept the door open to possibly resorting to extra-parliamentary action: 'The movement for the liberation of the proletariat must henceforth change its tactics from time to time in accordance with the conditions of the enemy and the power of friends.'[30]

Though these amendments did not deflect the Sōdōmei from its 'new' policies, they nonetheless won the approval of the delegates, many of whom wanted to make it clear that their 'change of direction' did not signify total accommodation with the status quo. Moreover, the amendments were so vaguely worded that they could be interpreted as one wished. For instance, allusions to the 'enemy' plainly referred to capitalism but 'the power of friends' could be construed in two ways: for the socialists, as the general power of the workers; for the communists, the power of their own movement and, presumably, the Comintern.

So, too, were some of the Principles endorsed by this convention amenable to various interpretations: 'We shall engage in an all-out war against the oppression of the capitalist class...We firmly believe that the working class and the capitalist class cannot exist side by side. Through the power of labor unions, we shall...build a new society in which the working class is completely liberated.'[31] 'All-out war' against the capitalists could mean either struggling against the bourgeois parties in the Diet, as the socialists anticipated, or violent revolution, as the communists desired.

Similarly, the liberation of the proletariat could be attained by either socialist reformism or communist revolution, depending upon one's point of view. In other words, it was possible for the majority socialists in the 1924 convention to believe they had ratified a major 'change of direction' toward socialist labor politics and it was equally possible for the minority communists to feel that the Sōdōmei was still capable of being pushed into a more militant, communist direction. Consequently, the 'change of direction' of February 1924 temporarily postponed the final collision of both camps although the Federation's clear rejection of revolution in favor of reformism that month made such a collision almost inevitable.

The extent to which the Sōdōmei had embraced socialism out of a reaction to communism is revealed through an analysis of the so-called 'new' ideology of the Sōdōmei in 1924 – 'realist socialism' (*genjitsuteki na shakaishugi*) – and its primary exponent, Akamatsu Katsumaro. His upbringing as the son of a priest in the Nishi Honganji sect of Buddhism led him to emphasize a humanitarian concern for the down-trodden, while the influence of Christianity took him in the same direction. As a university student and a member of the Shinjinkai, Akamatsu had waxed eloquent in his enthusiasm for Karl Marx and his ideas. Typical of his thinking at the time of his entry into the JCP in 1922 was this statement:

> The basic drive of our reform movement is an ardent humanitarian spirit which, on a foundation of matter, strives to build a shining kingdom of true goodness and beauty which will rise above matter. While we do not believe in the whole of Marx's material view of history, yet we are deeply moved by the example of his moral life, he who sacrificed everything and died a martyr for the great cause of human emancipation.[32]

However, Akamatsu's experience in the JCP soured his enthusiasm for both Marx and the communist movement which he accused of waging 'formalistic struggle' (*kōshikiteki tōsōshugi*). This phrase signi-fied many things: the subordination of the proletarian class to the dictates of a communist vanguard party and an emphasis on bureau-cratism within the party that pandered to the Comintern; the tendency of the communists to undermine and split socialist organizations, thereby weakening proletarian solidarity; communist opposition to the Emperor system which drew the fire of the State against communist organizations; and the notion that the present corrupt bourgeois regime would be replaced by the 'dictatorship of the proletariat', a concept regarded by Akamatsu as inimical to genuine democracy.[33] In short, Akamatsu came to believe that the humanitarian face of communism was a false mask.

Akamatsu also became disillusioned with the materialist 'laws' of historical change inherent in Marxism-Leninism. To Akamatsu, Marx was mistaken in insisting that according to the dialectic of historical process, all societies pass through inevitable stages culminating in socialism, or that all societies were affected by the laws of change in the same, uniform ways.[34] Rather, Akamatsu held that the character of socialism in a given country would be shaped by the unique cultural attributes that the country had inherited from the past. In the case of Japan, they included a distinctive race (*minzoku*), a distinctive set of national myths, and above all, the Imperial institution. For socialism to succeed in Japan, it would have to adapt itself to these cultural attributes.

Akamatsu's rejection of communism led him to formulate his concept of 'realist socialism' in 1923 and 1924, a concept which he applied to the Sōdōmei's 'change of direction' and which he elaborated upon in numerous books such as *Shakai undō ni okeru genjitsushugi* [Realism in Social Movements], published in 1928; *Kaihō undō no shidō riron* [The Guiding Theories of Liberation Movements], written the next year; and *Shakai minshūshugi no hata no shita ni* [Beneath the Flag of Social Democracy] which appeared in 1930.

The central theme of these books was the bankruptcy of communism as a guiding light for the democratization of Japan. Of the communists, Akamatsu wrote in 1926, 'They know the world but not Japan... They look at the universe, not the earth; they are astronomers.'[35] By contrast, advocates of 'realist socialism', Akamatsu's alternative to communism, had their feet firmly planted on the ground of reality. In seeing the world and conditions in Japan realistically, instead of through the distorted ideological prism of Marxism, they appreciated the 'true rationality' of socialism which Akamatsu often described in the Japanese context as 'scientific Japanism' (*kagakuteki na nippon-shugi*).[36] As he explained repeatedly, 'scientific Japanism' rested simply on the proposition that for socialism to flourish in Japan, it would have to be combined with Japanese nationalism.[37]

'Realist socialism' in the spirit of 'scientific Japanism' was simply a rhetorical concept that Akamatsu used to condemn communism; it also referred to a specific set of objectives. First, Akamatsu asserted that the economic and political liberation of the proletariat from poverty and powerlessness should be accompanied by the liberation of the individual. For instance in *Kaihō undō no shidō riron* Akamatsu stated that the means of socialism were materialist (*busshitsuteki*) but the ends were humanist, oriented to the realization of *jinkakushugi* (individuality) in the life of each person.[38] And, since the liberation of the individual extended to everyone, he stressed that Japanese social democracy was concerned with not just serving the proletariat but other classes as well, especially the petty bourgeoisie – small factory owners, shopkeepers, and the like – whose deprivations he found similar to those of the 'propertyless'.

Second, 'realist socialism' aimed to liberate the Japanese race from the negative effects of capitalist materialism which blurred the distinctive development of Japanese racial culture by subjecting it to the harsh calculus of private profit.[39] Third, this philosophy signified reliance on peaceful, legal, and evolutionary reforms to achieve liberation. In economic terms this meant the legal nationalization of 'monopoly capital' and large-scale capitalist enterprises so that the control of production and the distribution of goods would be concentrated in the hands of the State which in turn would be responsive to the social needs of the masses. However, Akamatsu exempted the petty bourgeoisie from this process on the grounds that this class was a potential ally of the proletariat.

In the political sphere, the goal of 'realist socialism' was to reduce the power of the *genrō*, the Peers, the conservative bureaucracy, and the military through legislative reforms that would accentuate as the main center of policy-making in Japan the lower house of the Diet, elected by the people. The pressure for these reforms would come from proletarian political parties supported primarily by the labor and agrarian union movements. However, Akamatsu never questioned the power of the Emperor as the symbol of the race.[40]

In many ways 'realist socialism' was simply a reformulation of Yoshino Sakuzō's liberalism, which is not surprising since Yoshino was one of Akamatsu's former teachers at Tokyo Imperial University (and incidentally his father-in-law). But the theme of proletarian class struggle received greater emphasis in Akamatsu's writings than in Yoshino's, as did certain specific socialist objectives such as the nationalization of heavy industry. Still, Akamatsu's attitude towards liberalism was undeniably sympathetic. In his view, Japan in the 1920s was moving strongly in the direction of liberal democracy. The task of the socialists was to assist this trend in anticipation of later pushing the country's liberal evolution onto the path of social democracy, again through legal and peaceful strategies and tactics.[41]

'Realist socialism' was not a profound system of thought and, as later chapters will suggest, contained flaws that were to haunt those labor and socialist party organizations that accepted it as an authoritative statement of political purpose. Nor can it be said that the leaders of the Sōdōmei, not to mention the rank and file workers, had arrived at the same synthesis of values as Akamatsu who, in comparison with people such as Suzuki Bunji or Nishio Suehiro, was a more sophisticated political thinker. Nevertheless, these men were ready to follow Akamatsu's ideas in carrying out the Federation's 'change of direction' and in adhering to them in the future. Unfortunately, however, 'realist socialism' in the Sōdōmei was soon to shrivel from being a rather progressive vision of change into little more than an almost pathological anti-communism, due to the disastrous labor split of 1925 and its enormous, negative consequences for the labor movement.

The 1925 labor split

After the JCP was replaced by a rump bureau in early 1924, the communists concentrated on Yamakawa's earlier policy of penetrating other proletarian organizations in an attempt to seize control of them from within. The Comintern had also recommended this approach. According to the Bukharin Theses, propounded at the fourth Congress of the Comintern in late 1922, internal subversion was essential for the preparation of the proletariat for the first – bourgeois–democratic – stage of an envisioned two-stage revolution in Japan in which the proletariat would ally themselves with the petty bourgeoisie to overthrow capitalism. In the second stage this alliance with the petty bourgeoisie would be terminated and a socialist society established.[42] Cooperation with the socialists of the Sōdōmei, whom the communists regarded as being a part of the petty bourgeoisie, was, thus, an important feature of the first revolutionary stage.

The communist strategy of subversion in the Nihon Rōdō Sōdōmei was largely carried out by a flying wedge of communist unions centered in the Kantō Rōdō Dōmeikai and led by Watanabe Masanosuke who, by this time, had become one of the most effective labor organizers in the communist movement. Of special importance as the central pivot of Watanabe's initiatives was the Tokyo Tōbu Gōdō Rōdō Kumiai (Eastern Tokyo Amalgamated Labor Union) which consisted of the remnants of the Nankatsu Labor Union plus other workers whom the indefatigable Watanabe had recruited to the communist cause. The majority were iron workers, and altogether the Tōbu Kumiai numbered about 2,600 members.[43] Five other smaller unions made up the rest of Watanabe's power base in the Kantō Rōdō Dōmeikai.[44] All of them, like the Tōbu Kumiai, were affiliated with the Sōdōmei's Kantō Iron Workers' Union in the Dōmeikai.[45] Together, they aimed at seizing control of this Union as a first step toward subverting the Dōmeikai as a whole.

An opportunity to implement this scheme first arose through the Kantō Iron Workers' Union annual convention of late April 1924. Using tactics similar to those of earlier anarchist attacks on labor bureaucrats in the Sōdōmei, Watanabe's communist caucus amassed enough votes among the delegates to pass motions of censure against the chairman of the Union, Uchida Tōshichi, and the director, Doi Naosaku, both of whom were important *kokata* of Matsuoka Koma-kichi in Sōdōmei headquarters. These men were accused of being puppets of Matsuoka who cared little about the ordinary workers in the Union. They were also condemned as proponents of 'realist social-ism' which, according to the communists, was a philosophy of surrender to the bourgeoisie. After Uchida and Doi were driven from office in the Union, the communists engineered the election as Union chairman of one of their own men, Kawada Kenji. The Kantō Iron Workers' Union thus fell into communist hands.[46]

This communist victory set the stage for one of the most chaotic conventions in the history of the Sōdōmei, the annual meeting of the Kantō Rōdō Dōmeikai itself on October 5, 1924. During its proceedings, the communists pursued vigorously the tactics of criti-cizing Dōmeikai officials, all of whom were other *kokata* in Matsuoka's train. The chairman of the Dōmeikai, Taguchi Kinzō, was so personally maligned by Watanabe's caucus that he fell ill in the midst of the pro-ceedings and was forced to resign his post on the grounds of poor health. But this time, the Sōdōmei leadership was able to plug the gap of his withdrawal by successfully ensuring the election of Uchida Tōshichi as his successor. This was some consolation for Uchida who had been ousted earlier as chairman of the Kantō Iron Workers' Union.[47]

At one point in this tumultuous convention, Watanabe Masanosuke led a protest walk-out of the communist delegates as a demonstration of his scorn for the Dōmeikai leaders. According to several of his followers, who later recalled the convention in a taped interview, this ploy had not been planned in advance and some of the communists present had been quite surprised when Watanabe rose spontaneously from his seat. In fact, not all of his comrades followed him from the convention hall, so great was their confusion over his gesture.[48] However, although the communists had managed to throw the convention into chaos, they failed to gain support for their various policy positions which included criticism of 'realist socialism', parliamentary politics, and the leadership of the Sōdōmei.

Even so, the events of the conventions of the Kantō Iron Workers' Union and the Dōmeikai caused great consternation in Sōdōmei headquarters. Matsuoka took to spending his evenings in the libraries of Tokyo poring over accounts of European labor movements in order to discover effective ways of stopping the communists in the Sōdōmei. So diligently did he undertake this study that he earned the nickname of 'iron locomotive'.[49] Meanwhile, Matsuoka and the other Sōdōmei leaders on the central committee came under intensive pressure from the officials of the Kantō Rōdō Dōmeikai to expel the communist unions from the Sōdōmei.[50] The anti-communist wrath of these *kokata*, already boiling after the Dōmeikai convention, grew hotter still after an incident in which members of the Tōbu Kumiai staged a 'revolutionary court' which 'tried' certain Dōmeikai leaders in absentia for 'crimes' against the workers. In particular, this 'court' found these men guilty of intervening to negotiate an end to a labor strike precipitated by Tōbu extremists at the Daiwa Rubber Plant.[51]

However, Sōdōmei headquarters procrastinated on this demand for expulsion, regarding it as too extreme a measure. Therefore, the officers of the Dōmeikai, led by Uchida Tōshichi, expelled independently six of the communist ringleaders from the Dōmeikai: Watanabe Masanosuke and Sōma Ichirō, both of the Tōbu Kumiai; Kasuga Shōjirō of the Kantō Insatsu Rōdō Kumiai (Kantō Printers' Labor Union); and three men from the Kantō Iron Workers' Union, Kawada Kenji, Sugiura Keiichi, and Tatamatsu Ichitarō.[52] The Dōmeikai also served notice to the Sōdōmei central committee that it expected the committee to ratify these expulsions by the total expulsion of the six men from the Sōdōmei. Meanwhile, the six communists in question responded to the Dōmeikai's hostile initiative by organizing the communist network of unions in Eastern Japan into the Nihon Rōdō Sōdōmei Kantō Chihō Hyōgikai (Kantō Area Council of the Japan General Federation of Labor) in December 1924. The Chihō Hyōgikai, with more than 3,000 workers in its fold, became an instant rival of the Kantō Rōdō Dōmeikai in the Eastern wing of the Federation.[53]

The unilateral expulsion of these communists from the Dōmeikai and the creation of the Chihō Hyōgikai temporarily immobilized the Sōdōmei central committee which was beginning to sense that events were rapidly moving beyond its control. The committee held many meetings in November and December to debate what should be done in this worsening situation. Matsuoka and Akamatsu argued repeatedly that the only option open to the committee was to expel all communists from the Sōdōmei as soon as possible. But Suzuki Bunji, backed by Asō Hisashi and Nishio Suehiro, maintained that expulsion was too extreme a step. Their view prevailed, for the time being, and a special crisis committee consisting of Nishio, Suzuki, and Katō Kanjū, was established to solve the communist problem in an orderly fashion.[54]

These three 'peacemakers' held countless meetings with the communists in December 1924 and early 1925, hoping to persuade them to temper their criticism of mainstream Sōdōmei policy. On one occasion, Nishio travelled to Osaka to confer with the communist labor organizer Nabeyama Sadachika, Watanabe's counterpart in the communist movement in Western Japan, on ways in which to preserve unity in the Federation. Nishio successfully persuaded Nabeyama to formulate a compromise settlement between the communists and the Sōdōmei leadership. Nabeyama undertook to persuade Watanabe, Sugiura, and other key communist labor leaders in Eastern Japan to disband the Chihō Hyōgikai and resign from the Sōdōmei – steps intended to placate the labor bosses of the Kantō Rōdō Dōmeikai – providing that the Dōmeikai agreed to permit the communist unions to remain in its fold.[55] Nabeyama visited Tokyo for this purpose, only to find Watanabe totally opposed to this plan, thus destroying Nishio's effort to avert a final crisis.[56]

Sōdōmei headquarters then decided to ratify the communist expulsions from the Dōmeikai, in order to appease the Dōmeikai leaders. But the six communists who had been excommunicated from the Dōmeikai were not expelled from the Sōdōmei as a national organization and no action was yet taken to destroy the Chihō Hyōgikai for fear that to do so would wreak havoc in the Eastern wing of the Federation. Instead, the Chihō Hyōgikai was allowed to affiliate directly with Sōdōmei headquarters.[57] This was a cosmetic maneuver intended to give the Chihō Hyōgikai a 'legitimate' place in the Sōdōmei and soften its antipathy toward headquarters. These policies naturally infuriated the officials of the Kantō Rōdō Dōmeikai who regarded them as half-hearted. Uchida Tōshichi and others in the Dōmeikai still insisted on the total expulsion of the communists and the Chihō Hyōgikai unions from the Sōdōmei. This was the first priority for the Dōmeikai, at that time locked in a vicious struggle with the Chihō Hyōgikai for influence over the workers in the Kantō area – in the face of this struggle, preservation of unity in the Sōdōmei was regarded by the Dōmeikai as pointless. Dōmeikai leaders constantly branded the Chihō Hyōgikai as a front for the Comintern, while the Chihō Hyōgikai accused the Dōmeikai of being a 'reactionary bastion' of the *rōdō kizoku*.

Inevitably, these rivalries in the Sōdōmei were greatly complicated by the progress in the Diet toward the enactment of universal manhood suffrage in 1925. Early that year the government of Prime Minister Katō served notice that a bill for universal manhood suffrage would be presented to the lower house in February. This news accelerated the plans of the Sōdōmei's central committee to play a major role in the anticipated formation of a labor party.

The Sōdōmei central committee had already decided to initiate such a party by first establishing regional parties, based primarily on Sōdōmei unions, as a means of developing the kind of grass roots organization and experience essential to the success of a national proletarian party. The elections for office in city, town, and village councils and assemblies to be held in early 1925 were considered to be useful tests for the application of this strategy. Accordingly, on February 22, 1925, the Sōdōmei founded its first regional party, the Ashio Rikken Kokumintō (Ashio Peoples' Constitutional Party) which was, in terms of leadership, finances, and organization, an extension of the Sōdōmei's Ashio *rengōkai*.[58] Other similar parties followed: the Kyūshū Minkentō (Kyūshū Peoples' Constitutional Party), centered on the Kyūshū *rengōkai* in Hachiman City, April 6, 1925; the Chiba Minseitō (Chiba Democratic Party), based mainly on the Chiba Noda *rengōkai* of the Sōdōmei, July 13, 1925; and the Kansai Minseitō (Kansai Democratic Party), founded on July 18, 1925.[59]

As it was hoped, these local parties, relying heavily on Sōdōmei union support, did rather well in the local elections of early 1925. The Ashio Kokumintō elected seven men to the Ashio Assembly, the Kyūshū Minkentō four to the Hachiman City Assembly, and the Chiba Minseitō another four.[60] However, these parties, and the strategy that begot them in the Sōdōmei, came under communist attack in the Sōdōmei annual convention of March 15 to 17 in Kobe that year. The communists, principally Nabeyama, Taniguchi Zentarō, and Yamamoto Kenzō, accused the Sōdōmei of engaging in what they called 'Sōdōmei *teikokushugi*' or 'Sōdōmei imperialism' by trying to control the budding proletarian party movement for its own purpose. They also attacked the notion that regional parties had to come before a national party. What was needed, they insisted, was a national party that would represent all proletarian elements, not just the whims of Sōdōmei 'labor bosses'.[61]

Nevertheless, this convention, which took place amidst the bitter rivalry between the Chihō Hyōgikai and the Kantō Rōdō Dōmeikai in Eastern Japan and similar confrontations in the Kansai area, endorsed the Sōdōmei's rapidly unfolding political party strategy. A resolution was passed which read in part, 'The regional political movement of the proletariat is a favorable one, arising from the development of the unions and because it is an excellent training for the political movement of the proletariat, we must strive to carry it further. However, the ways and means of this movement must be controlled by [Sōdōmei] headquarters and its political bureau.'[62] A related statement by a delegate from the Kyūshū *rengōkai* reflected the majority view on this matter: 'It is necessary to organize the proletariat regionally and then we must establish a [national] party on this basis. . . .'[63]

The acrimonious debates between the communists and the Sōdōmei leadership over the Federation's political strategies in this convention magnified further the rift developing between both sides. However, they were in agreement over the necessity to voice strong objection to the new Peace Preservation Law (Chian Iji Hō), submitted by the Katō government to the lower house in February and approved there on March 7. This law, which was eventually approved by the upper house of Peers on March 19, promulgated on April 22, and put into effect on May 11, superseded the 1900 Peace Police Law (and in particular Article Seventeen of the latter which the Katō government had repealed) in the constraints it placed on social protest. Article One of the new Law stated:

> Anyone who organizes a group for the purpose of changing the national polity or of denying the private property system, or anyone who knowingly participates in said group shall be sentenced to penal servitude or imprisonment not exceeding ten years. An offense not actually carried out shall also be subject to punishment.[64]

The 1925 convention closed ranks and adopted an aggressive motion, submitted by the Kobe Gōdō Rōdō Kumiai (Kobe Amalgamated Labor Union) delegates which stated, 'It is clear that the recent Peace Preservation Law is an attempt by the government to rationalize [the use of] force to repress movements of the proletariat. We resolve to struggle tenaciously to resist this violent practice.'[65] A strong consensus plainly existed at this convention that the government intended the Peace Preservation Law to give increased power to the police to contain the proletarian parties that would emerge after the passage of universal manhood suffrage.

However, the knowledge that the Katō government was determined to achieve universal manhood suffrage, combined with recent memories of the opposition of communists in the 1925 Sōdōmei convention to Sōdōmei strategies for a proletarian party, stirred the Sōdōmei central committee into taking a hard line toward the communists in late March by demanding that the Chihō Hyōgikai be disbanded immediately. Sōdōmei headquarters also made it known that if the Chihō Hyōgikai did not comply, it would be expelled from the Federation.[66] However, the Chihō Hyōgikai refused to disband, and it defiantly organized a 'reform (*kakushin*) rally' of continuous demonstrations by its member unions in protest against 'Sōdōmei teikokushugi' in the labor movement.[67]

When faced with the options of expelling the communists or backing down, the leaders of the Sōdōmei procrastinated once again. For several months, they wavered between Nishio's recommendation to hold off on expulsion – a view he had retained despite all the trauma of that spring – and Matsuoka's demand to clear the Sōdōmei decks of communism. In April, Nishio made a last-ditch attempt to persuade the Chihō Hyōgikai to call off the 'rally' and its criticism of the Sōdōmei leadership.[68] But this failed and finally he and other 'softliners' in Sōdōmei headquarters capitulated to Matsuoka in May; seeing that the Universal Manhood Suffrage Law gave all males twenty-five years of age and over who had resided in their electoral districts for at least one year the right to vote, and that the electorate would be expanded from 3,000,000 to 12,500,000, Sōdōmei headquarters decided to purge the Federation of the communists in order to get on with the urgent business of forming a moderate and legal proletarian party which would be responsive to 'realist socialist' ideals.[69]

Thus, on May 16, Sōdōmei headquarters announced the expulsion of all communist individuals and organizations, including the Chihō Hyōgikai, from the General Federation. They were accused of subverting the Sōdōmei on behalf of the Comintern, an enemy of the *kokutai*.[70] Within a matter of days, the expelled unions replied by forming a labor federation of their own, on May 25, 1925. This was the Nihon Rōdō Kumiai Hyōgikai (Council of Japanese Labor

Unions).[71] It was nearly as large as the Sōdōmei, encompassing 10,778 workers in thirty-two unions in comparison with the Sōdōmei's 19,460 members organized into thirty-five unions.[72] The *dai-ichiji bunretsu* of the Sōdōmei was now a matter of historical record.

An analysis of the 1925 labor split

Predictably, the communists and the socialists blamed each other for causing the split. For instance, Yamamoto Kenzō argued that the fundamental conflict underlying the split had been between the 'bourgeois' social reformist leaders of the Sōdōmei and the militant majority of rank and file workers who had tried valiantly to keep the Sōdōmei from walking down the path of 'realist socialism' into a fatal compromise with capitalism. The Sōdōmei leaders, he asserted, had defied the 'true voice of the proletariat' in the Chihō Hyōgikai by expelling this group from the Sōdōmei.[73] Yamakawa Hitoshi echoed these views, adding that no one in the Chihō Hyōgikai had wanted the split to occur; the split was entirely the responsibility of the 'Sōdōmei imperialists'.[74]

Sōdōmei spokesmen interpreted the split differently. Matsuoka, for one, claimed that a small minority of radicals in the Chihō Hyōgikai had brought about the crisis through their defiance of the authority of Sōdōmei headquarters, authority recognized all along by the vast majority of unionists in the Federation. In reply to communist assertions that the split was a manifestation of a global conflict between the Second International and the Third International (the Comintern), Matsuoka said this was absurd: the Sōdōmei had not associated itself with the former and did not intend to. But he did allow that the split had international implications in that the communists of the Chihō Hyōgikai had acted on behalf of the Comintern.[75]

In retrospect, this latter charge was erroneous. Though communist labor organizers had followed the Comintern blueprint for internal subversion, carrying this strategy through to the point of splitting the Sōdōmei was definitely not part of this blueprint. Indeed, the Comintern had summoned Watanabe Masanosuke to Shanghai to confer with its agent, L. Heller, in early May 1925, so that Heller could advise him to preserve the unity of the Japanese labor movement to the end that the 'left-wing and the right-wing unions could cooperate', as envisioned in the Bukharin Theses.[76] But by this time it was too late to avoid the anti-communist expulsions in the Sōdōmei. Later, the Comintern went

on record by saying, 'The policy of the Japanese communists in splitting up such organizations as the Sōdōmei was...radically wrong.
The existence of mass proletarian movements is a prerequisite for the
normal and healthy development of the communist party.'[77]

Thus, ironically, the Comintern blamed the communists for the split,
as did the Sōdōmei leaders. But this too was not entirely correct.
Admittedly, the communists had brought matters to a boil, particularly
in using the Chihō Hyōgikai to challenge the authority of Sōdōmei
headquarters. But it is not certain whether men like Watanabe ever
desired the split; certainly others in the communist cause, notably
Nabeyama Sadachika, did not. A good many of them wanted to
preserve the Sōdōmei in order to be able eventually to take it over,
rather than to have to build up a new pro-communist labor federation.[78]

At any rate, whatever responsibility the communists may have had
for the split was shared by the Sōdōmei as well, not so much by Sōdōmei
headquarters, although it carried out the final expulsion, but rather by
middle-level and local labor leaders who pressed headquarters to take
an increasingly strong line against the communists. In contrast to such
national leaders as Suzuki, Asō Hisashi, and Nishio, all of whom
delayed on the expulsions in order to try and salvage the unity of the
Federation, the Uchida Tōshichis, the *kokata* of these elites, were quite
prepared to see the Sōdōmei fractured if that was the price that had to
be paid for protecting their own positions in the Sōdōmei hierarchy
which were most directly under communist siege. Ultimately, the
Sōdōmei leaders in headquarters capitulated to this anti-communist
pressure from below after arriving, albeit reluctantly, at the same conclusion about the need to maintain their own authority in the Federation.

Aside from the question of how communist and Sōdōmei labor
leaders conducted themselves in the 1925 labor split, there remains the
problem of the role of the rank and file unionists in this turbulent affair.
Given the fact that labor leaders on both the communist and socialist
sides justified their actions in terms of political ideology, it would be
tempting to attribute a similar tendency to the rank and file. For some
of them, this would be valid. But whether most of the rank and file in,
for example, the Chihō Hyōgikai or the Kantō Rōdō Dōmeikai,
thought of themselves as communists or socialists and whether they
were politically conscious in this ideological sense is rather doubtful.

One might more safely conjecture that the majority of workers in both organizations were simply swept along by events without being aware of their political ramifications. It is probable that the majority of workers in the Chihō Hyōgikai revolted against the reigning factions of the Sōdōmei because they believed that the latter had grown unresponsive to the needs of the workers by clinging to power in the labor movement, power which they would not share. Communist propaganda to the effect that the Sōdōmei leadership symbolized 'Sōdōmei imperialism' fed this resentment. For their part, the majority of workers in the Dōmeikai, and in the Sōdōmei generally, remained loyal to Sōdōmei headquarters out of personal respect for men like Suzuki or Matsuoka who symbolized stability and authority in the labor movement as opposed to the unsettling, rebellious insurgents who openly flaunted these attributes. In either case, the conflict between communism and socialism was secondary from the perspective of the rank and file.

However, there is little question that the labor elites of the Sōdōmei who took it upon themselves to define political strategies and tactics for the General Federation regarded the 1925 labor split as being essentially political in origin and that they based their subsequent endeavors in the field of labor politics on this interpretation. In view of what was to follow, the *dai-ichiji bunretsu* of the Sōdōmei freighted the Sōdōmei's recent, socialist 'change of direction' with a heavy commitment to wage an all-out war against communism within the labor movement just at a time when, with universal manhood suffrage a reality, neither the labor movement nor the emergent proletarian party movement could afford such a campaign. The 1925 labor split occurred, then, at a most unpropitious time. It divided the labor movement into two rival camps which quickly became embroiled in internecine struggles, confounded attempts to organize a single united proletarian party, and made it easier for the government to divide and rule the unions.

As ominously, the split took place amidst significant developments in the factories which provided the immediate context for Sōdōmei–Hyōgikai rivalry. Because these developments were nearly as important as the government's 'whip and candy' policy in determining the future course of Japanese labor politics, they are discussed in some detail in the next chapter.

4

Industrial paternalism and Sōdōmei–Hyōgikai rivalry in the factories

During the 1920s, the structure of Japanese industry, the nature of industrial labor markets, and the system of labor relations in the factories underwent fundamental changes, which strongly affected the development of the unions and their political behavior in this decade and the next. The main trend in industry throughout the interwar period lay in the direction of industrial dualism as characterized by a widening gap between, on the one hand, a large number of small and medium-sized enterprises each employing relatively few workers and possessing relatively scarce capital resources and, on the other, a small number of very large enterprises, all employing many workers and possessing immense capital resources.

To illustrate this pattern of dualism in terms of numbers of employed workers: small enterprises of from 5 to 9 workers accounted for 45.8 per cent of all private industry in 1919, and those with 10 to 99 workers, 49.1 per cent. Factories of from 100 to 499 workers accounted for 4.3 per cent while factories employing 500 or more workers, for only 0.8 per cent.[1] In 1934 the situation was similar: factories in the first category comprised 56.5 per cent; the second, 39.7 per cent; the third, 3.1 per cent; and the last, of 500 or more workers, only 0.7 per cent.[2]

The many smaller enterprises that coexisted, like pygmies, alongside of the *zaibatsu* (financial combine) giants on the horizon of Japan's industrial structure contributed significantly to Japan's industrialization. William Lockwood observes, referring to data for 1934, 'If all establishments of less than 100 operatives are considered together, we find that plants of this size contributed 45 to 50% of the gross output of Japanese manufacturing in 1934.'[3] However, in terms of productive output their achievement was counter-balanced by the productive capacity of the *zaibatsu* in many critically important areas. Kozo Yamamura states in this regard:

> By 1929, the firms owned or controlled by the Mitsui, Mitsubishi, and Yasuda zaibatsu along with the giant, nationally-owned Yawata, produced

93.6 per cent of the total output of pig iron, 83.1 per cent of the steel and 83.5 per cent of processed steel products. In the ammonium sulphate industry, the Mitsui and Mitsubishi firms by 1930 virtually divided the total output between them...Oji Paper and Fuji Paper, both directly controlled by Mitsui, produced 65.4 per cent of the total output of paper in 1929.[4]

If one examines the question of industrial dualism in terms of capital concentration, the gap between the *zaibatsu* and the small and medium enterprises is equally impressive.

During the Taishō period, as the economy underwent the First World War boom and then a long recession, the dual structure emerged to stay. By 1929...the small firms (those capitalized at 100,000 yen or less) constituted 71.1 per cent of all firms, but they collectively accounted for only 3.2 per cent of the total capital of all firms. This is a decline of 8.6 per cent from the relative magnitude observed in 1909. On the other hand, the largest firms capitalized at more than 5 million yen increased from 38 to 733, and they increased their relative share of capital from 36.2 per cent to 65.1 per cent during the twenty years.[5]

The complex question of why the Japanese economy in the interwar period evolved along the lines of industrial dualism lies outside the scope of this book, which is concerned rather with assessing the influence of industrial dualism on the labor movement. A discussion of dualism in relation to accompanying trends in the labor markets and in labor relations during the 1920s and 1930s is therefore necessary.

As explained in Chapter 1, a pattern of fluid labor markets characterized by a high degree of mobility, particularly in the careers of skilled workers, predominated in Japan until after World War I. Moreover, during the postwar recession, when industrial recovery became imperative, employers undertook, with increasing success, to bring labor markets under their control as part of their policy of *sangyō gōrika*, or industrial rationalization. This included such innovations as the introduction of automatic machines, assembly-line production, the standardization of products, and so forth which were intended to cut labor costs, raise labor productivity, strengthen competitive power, and increase production for an internal market where purchasing power rose later in the decade.[6]

In order to be successful, the technological innovations of industrial rationalization necessitated innovations in labor relations to ensure the availability of a new kind of worker who could be brought fully under employer control while performing the 'one-skill, repetitive, small operations'[7] of the assembly line. The procedures that were accordingly implemented for the recruitment, training, and supervision of the work force, and for binding the workers firmly to the enterprise, have been described as 'industrial' or 'corporate paternalism'.[8]

Under these evolving arrangements in labor relations, employers recruited young male workers directly from the schools into the factory, trained them in company-run training programs, and bound them to the factory through a number of incentives designed to curtail their mobility. Prospective workers were screened by company recruiters and were required to meet certain educational and health standards set by the company. This task, and the business of training and supervising the workers, was entrusted to an expanded *rōmu* (labor management) section in factories which practised industrial paternalism.

In theory, of course, and to some extent in practice, decision-making which would affect the workers was to be carried out at the upper echelons of management under the supervision of the company president and his board of directors. In fact, the day-to-day responsibility for managing the work force fell to the *rōmu* section, in cooperation with the highest grades of blue-collar workers on the shop floor.[9] The position of the latter in the factory hierarchy may be ascertained from contemporary trends in the systematic ranking of factory personnel. Although the precise terms and gradations that became prevalent in the ranking system under *sangyō gōrika* differed from company to company, the system generally included the following classifications.

White-collar workers, who performed managerial functions in the enterprise, were known collectively as *shain* (company officials) and *shokuin* (staff employees). The former occupied the upper echelons of the management hierarchy and the latter the lower ranks. The *shain* were classified as *jōkyū shokuin* (top-grade employees) and *kakyū shokuin* (low-grade employees), depending upon their position. In general, the *jōkyū shokuin* held degrees from Japanese universities or higher technical schools (*semmon gakkō*). The *kakyū shokuin* possessed degrees from middle schools and technical schools at the middle school level of the Japanese educational system.[10]

For their part, the blue-collar workers were generally classified as *kōin* (factory workers). Typically, they were divided into the following grades: *shokuchō* (foremen), *kōchō* (workshop foremen), *kumichō* (workbench foremen), *kōin* (workers) and *minarikō* (apprentice workers). Another important distinction was made between *jōyō-kō* (regular workers) and *rinji-kō* (temporary workers). The basic educational requirement for the blue-collar workers was the possession of a primary school certificate.[11]   .

The systematic ranking of factory personnel in this manner entailed the precise definition of the responsibilities and duties of each grade of worker, including white- and blue-collar employees. In general, the foremen of various grades cooperated with white-collar management in directing the affairs of the work force at the production level. The important point for this study is that the entire system was designed to bypass the previously significant role of the *oyakata* skilled 'all-round' worker who in the past had been prominent as a labor recruiter and training supervisor.

Employers considered that the *oyakata* skilled craftsman – the 'man of moods', the 'wanderer' – was anachronistic in the new system of labor relations. The institution of new company recruitment procedures under the control of the *rōmu* section rendered him dispensable in the recruitment of labor. The assembly-line techniques of production and in-company training programs further obviated the need for his services on the shop floor in the training of the work force. *Sangyō gōrika*, in other words, made him expendable. He did not, of course, disappear overnight in factories where *sangyō gōrika* was attempted. Often, he was retained until the new recruitment and training programs were fully implemented. And, as Ikeda Makoto points out, the *oyakata* skilled worker was frequently bought out by the new system through being grafted into the lower echelons of management as a *shokuchō*, where he would serve the company until he retired and passed from the factory scene.[12] Some *oyakata* turned to the labor movement to resist this erosion of their power in the factories. But most of them blended into the new system because it offered them concrete incentives to do so. The same incentives had the effect of binding the rest of the work force very closely to the company.

Most histories of Japanese labor relations discuss these incentives in connection with *nenkō seido*, or 'length of service system', which was an important feature of industrial paternalism.[13] Perhaps the most important incentive for the worker to remain with the firm was provided by the *nenkō jōretsu chingin* wage system under which wages and promotions were calculated on the basis of seniority, length of service in the firm, and the occupational status of the worker in the rank system of the factory. Skill per se was not a formal element in these calculations but, as many studies point out, there did exist a general correlation between skill, seniority, and rank.[14] The longer the worker stayed with the firm, the more he could expect to receive in terms of regular pay increases and promotions up through the *kōin* ranks. Beginning wages were pegged low, at levels sufficient to support only the individual worker.[15] This contrasted with the World War I period when skilled workers commanded wages high enough to support both themselves and their families.[16] With promotion based on seniority, the worker could look forward to annual increments in basic wages as he underwent apprentice training and rose up the factory ladder. In addition, wages were supplemented by various bonuses, such as that received at the end of each year, and allowances that were paid on such occasions as layoffs, dismissals, and most significantly, upon retirement. The retirement allowance was usually generous and came in a lump sum, while the bonuses and allowances helped to compensate for what was a rather low wage scale.[17]

It was clearly to the worker's advantage to remain in the firm of his original employment in order to benefit from the *nenkō* wage system and periodic promotion. If he moved elsewhere, he risked having to start all over again in accumulating the seniority essential to these benefits. Accordingly, the *nenkō jōretsu chingin* wage system contributed greatly to the verticalization of the labor market and the reduction of its fluidity. Compartmentalization of the wage system from one company to another was a related result of these practices.[18]

A second important incentive in this system binding the worker to the firm was the implicit assumption that he would be retained by the company for the duration of his career. Guaranteed lifetime employment (*shūshin koyō*) was seldom written into the labor contracts of the 1920s and 1930s but it was generally recognized as an integral part of the *nenkō* system.[19] The prospect of employment security meant a great deal to the worker affected by the system; more often than not, he was eager to serve the company out of gratitude for this security. As might be expected, *shūshin koyō* also eroded the fluidity of the labor market.

A third incentive fostering loyalty to the firm was its provision of various welfare facilities and services which reflected the old paternalistic notion of noblesse oblige on the part of management toward the workers in the field of non-wage benefits. These included company-run health clinics, educational programs, dining halls, nurseries, baths, barber-shops, and recreational facilities.[20] These benefits were provided either free to the workers or at low cost. Taken together, they balanced the effects of low wages and created an atmosphere of *jigyō ikka* (enterprise family) thus fulfilling their intended function.[21]

These features of *nenkō seido* provided the cornerstone of industrial paternalism in the interwar period. As Hazama Hiroshi and Ronald Dore show in their respective studies of the history of Japanese industrial relations, the models for the *nenkō* system had originated earlier in strategies adopted by the management of such government-run enterprises as the Yokosuka Shipyard to rationalize production and labor relations in the Meiji period.[22] By 1900, the essential ingredients of *nenkō seido* had become firmly established in a growing number of public, and private, enterprises.[23] In the 1920s, they emerged with even greater pervasiveness. One study comments, 'By the middle of the 1920s, management had made considerable progress in instituting the new hiring and reward systems. Labor turnover declined, the length of continuous service increased, and industrial relations generally became more stabilized. . .in contrast to the preceding periods of high labor mobility.'[24]

However, three important qualifications must be made concerning the spread of the *nenkō* system in interwar Japan. First, the system was never intended to apply to the entire work force; it was implemented for the white-collar workers and the *jōyō-kō* of the *kōin* stratum alone, and the various benefits discussed above did not extend to the *rinji-kō*. They were added to that part of the work force on temporary contracts when management needed their services in times of industrial growth. Conversely, they were dismissed when production contracted. Unlike the *jōyō-kō*, they had no prospects for employment security. Their function was to provide a valuable cushion of labor which could be expanded or reduced as requirements dictated, thus enabling the company to continue the provisions of the *nenkō* system for the permanent workers. Without the *rinji-kō*, the practices of the *nenkō* system would have been impossible.[25]

Second, the development of the *nenkō* system was confined to the factories who could best afford these innovations, that is, the large enterprises of Japan. Its scope did not extend to the great mass of medium-sized and small enterprises which were characterized by a constant shortage of capital; frequent bankruptcy, especially in the postwar recession and during the financial crises of the late 1920s and the Depression; low wages; and a generally horizontal labor market in which the workers, many of whom were *rinji-kō* dismissed from the large firms, continued to move from one factory to another as in the Meiji and early Taishō periods. Mikio Sumiya observes: 'In the very small businesses, where working and business conditions are poor, the authoritative family pattern (e.g., master–servant relations) prevailed and neither paternalistic industrial relations nor the lifetime employment nor length of service systems existed.'[26]

The third qualification is that not all large enterprises which dominated industry put industrial paternalism into practice and those that did rarely combined all of the institutional features of the *nenkō* system in the precise balance suggested by the preceding discussion of the industrial paternalism model. But the *nenkō* system represented the wave of the future in Japanese industrial relations during the 1920s. After Japan's defeat in World War II, industrial paternalism became synonymous with labor relations in Japan.[27]

Enough has been said about industrial paternalism to permit an analysis of the effect of changes in labor relations on the politics of the labor movement. Specific case studies relating to this problem are presented later in this discussion of Sōdōmei–Hyōgikai struggles in the factories. In more general terms, industrial paternalism influenced the labor movement as follows. First, and most obviously, the institutions of industrial paternalism threatened the labor movement ideologically. The ideal of *onjōshugi* had not changed. What was new was its institutional consolidation in the *nenkō* system. One of the major purposes of the system was to create harmony and stability in the factories in keeping with the principles of paternalism and *shūjū kankei* (hierarchical relations) between labor and management. The idea of workers forming associations based on separate interest or class was still regarded as anathema by employers. If anything, the old value of paternalism was reinforced all the more in the context of the *nenkō* system.[28]

Second, industrial paternalism spawned the application of many techniques employed by management to check the growth of labor unions. Sometimes employers simply outlawed unions by fiat. But usually they preferred a more oblique approach to the neutralization of the unions in their factories. It was especially significant that where unions had already penetrated factories, employers tried to bend them into an enterprise union (*kigyōbetsu kumiai*) mold.[29] This was not particularly difficult since most of the unions in such federations as the Nihon Rōdō Sōdōmei were already unions of this type. Sumiya estimates that well over half of Japanese unions in the interwar period were 'vertical', or *kigyōbetsu kumiai*.[30]

The verticalization of unions in interwar Japan was reflected in the low rate of union federation. In 1926, for instance, of the 488 unions in existence, only 210 – with a combined membership of 165,845 (out of a total of 284,739 unionized workers) – were federated in one way or another.[31] By 1931, the number of unions had risen to 818, embracing 368,975 workers out of a total industrial work force of 4,729,436 workers (7.9 per cent of the total work force).[32] This represented an all-time high for labor union membership in interwar Japan. But of these unions, 386, with a total membership of 182,827, were not federated.[33] Thus, while the rate of unionization increased, that of federation did not, even though the number of labor federations in Japan had risen from fifty-two in 1926 to sixty-one in 1931.[34]

The management's encouragement of the *kigyōbetsu* model for unionism was manifested in a number of policies. One was the tactic of negotiating closed shop agreements with enterprise unions in order to buttress their position in the factories and eliminate the intrusion of workers who identified with horizontal unions or organizations, like the Hyōgikai, objectionable for their political radicalism. At the same time, it must be noted that collective bargaining to any other ends was steadfastly resisted by employers. No law compelled them to engage in collective bargaining with labor and most of them were loath to do anything which would be interpreted as even a tacit recognition of the unions. Those unions which pursued collective bargaining in the 1920s (and later) to enhance their status in the factories were nearly always disappointed. As George Totten observes, 'Only in two or three instances did a company agree to collective bargaining, but merely to the extent of being willing to listen when the unions wanted to raise a question. The causes for defeat arose from management's extreme distaste for dealing with any labor organization and from the workers' inexperience in negotiation with management.'[35]

Another tactic in management's strategy of neutralizing the labor movement was to set up *kōjō iinkai* (works councils). These were deliberative committees including representatives of management and labor which were supposed to discuss and iron out problems at the plant level. To the extent that the councils included men from the enterprise union local, they implied a tacit recognition of that local as the voice of the workers. But in terms of actual function, their purpose was to tie the local, and the workers generally, to the company. In most cases, the *kōjō iinkai* were little more than sounding boards where management exhorted the workers to serve the company rather than agencies for the solution of factory problems.[36]

Still another tactic to reinforce the trend toward enterprise unionism was the establishment of a company union (*goyō kumiai*) which would be under the thumb of management. It was not uncommon for employers to form such a union in order to reach closed shop agreements as a means of keeping other unions out of the factory. And, where other unions existed, company unions were used to offset their influence.[37]

Finally, management often required the workers to sign oaths of loyalty to the firm. This tactic had the effect of developing enterprise consciousness with or without *kigyōbetsu kumiai*. One such pledge ran as follows:

> As I recognize the spirit of paternalism which is the basis on which the Kanegafuchi Spinning Company is operated, and trust that the Company will guarantee the stability of our livelihood, I will refrain from joining in any agitation and go quietly about my work. I give my solemn oath and sign this statement for future reference.[38]

Another typical pledge stated, 'I shall obey shop rules as to hours of work and wages...You may discharge me at any time at your convenience, or in case of improper conduct on my part.'[39] Such oaths were powerful constraints on the workers. If broken they could lead to dismissal. Members of unions who were obliged to sign these oaths knew that if they stepped out of bounds they would endanger the survival of the union and risk losing their own jobs.

It is clear, then, that employers used the *kigyōbetsu kumiai* model to undercut the influence of horizontal, federated labor unions while at the same time fostering the paternalistic ideal of *jigyō ikka*. However, they were unalterably opposed to the legalization of unions. They fought such a measure through various business pressure organizations which had been formed to influence the government in the area of economic strategy.

The first of these organizations dated from 1878 when the Tokyo Metropolitan Chamber of Commerce (Tokyo Shōhō Kaigisho) was established. After the passage of the Chambers of Commerce Act in 1890, the National Federation of Chambers of Commerce became an important center of business opinion. A more recent business lobbying organization was the Nihon Kōgyō Kurabu (Japan Industrial Club), a powerful group of leading industrialists and financiers, formed in 1917. In 1922, the Nihon Kōgyō Kurabu combined with other business groups to establish an umbrella business lobby, the Nihon Keizai Renmei (Japan Economic League) which became the principal political spokesman for the National Federation of Chambers of Commerce. Yet another powerful business association which was more directly involved in helping to elect pro-business candidates to the Diet was the

Jitsugyō Dōshikai (Businessmen's Voluntary Association), founded by the famous industrialist, Mutō Sanji, in 1923.[40]

These business organizations were particularly effective in blocking government attempts to legalize trade unions in the hope of stabilizing labor relations in the 1920s and 1930s. The seriousness of the government's purpose in this connection is attested by the creation in 1922 of the Shakai Kyoku (Social Affairs Bureau) in the Home Ministry, which for all intents and purposes functioned like a Labor Ministry in collecting labor statistics, supervising programs relating to worker welfare, administering employment agencies and the health insurance program, enforcing the Factory Law, and designing government policy toward the International Labor Organization.[41]

It has been said of the Shakai Kyoku that its activities, which also included the drafting of bills to legalize unions, were 'an indication that among the bureaucrats of the Ministry of Home Affairs, which dealt mainly with police administration, there were top officials who were adaptable to world trends after World War I' in the field of labor relations.[42] However, where the legalization of unions was concerned, the Shakai Kyoku's bills, when presented to the Diet, were repeatedly defeated, mainly due to organized business lobbying.[43]

A third, related, consequence of industrial paternalism in large factories was the crowding of the unions into the domain of the small and medium-sized enterprises which lacked the resources to emulate the strategies of industrial paternalism in larger firms. Within these smaller enterprises, the unions were able to capitalize on worker discontent with the prevailing poor wages and working conditions. In most instances, the key figure in mobilizing this dissent was the skilled *oyakata* worker who, like the majority of workers, had not found a place of security in the big enterprises which implemented industrial paternalism.

As the labor movement became increasingly concentrated in these enterprises, the problems facing the unions inevitably reflected those of the enterprises themselves. For example, size was one such problem. Like the firms in which they were located, these unions tended to be small in scale. Of the 432 unions in Japan in 1923, 117 had 49 or fewer members, 100 had 99 or fewer, 160 had 499 or fewer members; 26 unions claimed from 500 to 999 workers, 23 had from 1,000 to 4,999 members, and 6 had 5,000 or more workers on their rolls.[44]

Most of the unions in the Sōdōmei and the Hyōgikai were small in size. In 1928, for instance, the Sōdōmei's largest union comprised about

6,000 muslin workers in the Tokyo *rengōkai*; except for a handful of other unions whose membership stood at around 3,000 workers each, the great majority of the Federation's unions were well under 1,000 members strong and in some cases included only several hundred or fewer members.[45] The Hyōgikai's biggest union that year, the Metal Workers' Union in the Kantō Chihō Hyōgikai, numbered 3,900 workers; the remainder were much smaller.[46] Both the Sōdōmei and the Hyōgikai remained clusters of many small unions except for several which, despite their relative size, were still small by modern standards. The capacity of these unions to exert influence in the labor movement stood in proportion to their small dimensions, particularly when it is remembered that a union rarely included all workers in a factory.

However, the labor movement was hindered by more than size in these small and medium-scale enterprises; acute union instability mirroring the instability of the enterprises presented a severe impediment. A striking feature of the interwar union movement was the high rate of organizational attrition and collapse. Many reasons for these adverse trends can be cited. Some unions folded for lack of effective leadership. Others fell apart when the firms in which they were organized collapsed in bankruptcy. Still others were nudged into oblivion by company unions like those which appeared in many large firms. Finally, many unions died out in the wake of massive layoffs following particularly severe labor strikes. This last fate was often encountered by those unions in the Hyōgikai.

To illustrate the problem of union attrition, Koji Taira estimates that two-thirds of the unions in existence in 1923 had vanished from the scene by 1929, the average rate of attrition in this period being 11 per cent. Unions founded between these years survived at the following rates: 36 per cent from 1924, 56 per cent from 1925, 66 per cent from 1926, 69 per cent from 1927, and 91 per cent from 1928.[47] Figures on union attrition are unavailable for the 1930s but the problem can be said to have remained acute throughout the interwar era. Taira remarks, 'In this state of organizational instability, long-term union strategies with lasting effects on the labor market process were hardly possible.'[48]

In sum, the indirect effects of industrial paternalism on the unions in small and medium-scale enterprises were as important as the direct effects in the large firms. Before proceeding to a more specific discussion of the influence of industrial paternalism on Sōdōmei–Hyōgikai rivalry, the question arises, why did industrial paternalism succeed in becoming so pervasive in Japan? Certainly the raw power of capital in the large firms was one reason. Industrial management successfully seized the initiative in determining the course of labor relations simply because nothing stood in its way. Another factor was the support given by the government to the goals of *sangyō gōrika*, in recovering from the post-World War I recession, and from the Depression of 1929–1931.

However, industrial paternalism also succeeded because many workers wanted it to. Given the attractions of the *nenkō* system, and particularly the security it offered to workers, it is hardly surprising that the workers were co-opted into this system to the detriment of their interest in labor unionism. Robert Cole sums up this point by saying that the system provided 'a map whose contours and gradations were easily grasped by the participants', including the workers, 'and whose contents proved highly attractive'.[49] Although the system reduced their sense of independence, 'From the worker point of view...the benefits apparently outweighed the costs.'[50] Worker enthusiasm for the *nenkō* system was by no means passive. Another source states, 'Giving up mobility based on skills, workers began to *demand* permanent employment in their work places. This was consistent with the emerging ideal of lifetime employment, especially in large firms' (my italic).[51]

Demands of this sort came principally from the young male worker who wanted the security of employment offered by the *nenkō* system. The prospect of being recruited, trained, and rewarded by the company made him enthusiastic about becoming a loyal member of the factory family. But the demand also arose from the *oyakata* skilled worker, once he realized that if he adjusted to the wave of the future, he could preserve at least a portion of the status that he had enjoyed in the past. For many of these men, the problem was not so much how to resist industrial paternalism but rather how to avoid being squeezed out of the system. While young workers aspired to becoming *shokuchō* (foremen) someday, the *oyakata* skilled workers wanted to retain this status.

The position of *shokuchō* was indeed worth coveting. The foreman was like a lord in the plant, although he could not expect to rise further in the rank system. His duties included the checking of the production line, coaching workers in their jobs, and maintaining order at the work place. He was respected by his peers, his subordinates, and his superiors, while he enjoyed other benefits accompanying his job. On occasion, special dinners were given by the company in his honor, especially upon his retirement. Becoming a *shokuchō* was, thus, the life-long ambition of many workers under industrial paternalism.[52]

The attractions of the *nenkō* system hindered the recruitment of new blood from the skilled worker stratum in the interwar period into institutions such as the Sōdōmei. Thus, throughout its history, the General Federation remained dominated by men who had joined the labor movement during the days of a fluid labor market before industrial paternalism became the norm in the 1920s. They represented an earlier generation of skilled workers who had committed themselves to full-time careers as labour movement leaders as part of the rebellion of the *oyakata* against capitalism in the first years of Taishō. For men like Matsuoka and Nishio, status as respected leaders in the labor movement compensated somewhat for their trials and tribulations in the movement. But for others who entered the work force in the 1920s and 1930s, membership of the factory family was far more attractive than that of an embattled labor movement.

In sum, industrial paternalism, within the context of dualism and changes in the labor markets of the factories, imposed rigid limitations throughout the interwar period on the development of the labor movement, comparable in effect to the political limitations under which the movement operated. Seen in this light, the battle for hegemony between the Sōdōmei and the Hyōgikai over the labor movement was a drama whose script, the destruction of the Hyōgikai and the gradual absorption of the Sōdōmei into the existing order, was largely foreordained by the shared environment of these two rivals.

Sōdōmei–Hyōgikai rivalry

The Hyōgikai was a formidable challenger to the Nihon Rōdō Sōdōmei. It was administered from a national central headquarters, with a bureaucracy as ramified and effective as that of the Sōdōmei. Its concentration of union strength in the Kantō and Kansai industrial districts enabled it to challenge the Sōdōmei in the areas where the General Federation had developed its largest following. In addition, the Hyōgikai benefited from strong labor support in Hokkaidō, the Tōhoku area of Northern Japan, and Shikoku, regions where the Sōdōmei achieved only superficial penetration.[53] The Council of Japanese Labor Unions also became a potent rival on the rough terrain of socialist party politics, to the consternation of the General Federation.

The militant character of the Hyōgikai, in sharp contrast to the moderation of 'realist socialism' as practised in the Sōdōmei, sprang from the Council's links with the Japanese communist movement and, after December 1926, with the Japanese Communist Party. The Hyōgikai never called itself a communist front but in effect, this was what it was. Almost all of the Hyōgikai's leaders belonged to the JCP: Noda Ritsuta (chairman),[54] Nabeyama Sadachika (head of the propaganda and publications bureau which put out the Council's organ, *Rōdō Shimbun*), Mitamura Shirō (head of the political bureau), Aogaki Zen'ichirō (head of the Hyōgikai's finance bureau which received most of its funds from membership dues and from the Comintern via the JCP), and Taniguchi Zentarō (head of the research bureau) are examples.[55]

Other prominent communist leaders in the labor movement such as Watanabe Masanosuke and Sugiura Keiichi, also held great power in the Hyōgikai although they did not occupy positions on the Hyōgikai central committee. Watanabe's Tōbu Kumiai was one of the strongest in the Council's network of unions. Moreover, as head of the JCP's labor bureau, Watanabe played an important role in maintaining liaison between the Party and the Hyōgikai elites. He is credited with having designed the administrative structure of the Council and its formal platform and major policy statements.[56] Although the rank and file members of the Hyōgikai did not for the most part belong to the JCP, the interconnection between the Council's leadership and the Party enabled the latter to work through the Hyōgikai in building up communist influence among the factory workers. Ultimately, however, the Hyōgikai's function as a communist front organization caused its repression along with other communist front groups, and the JCP itself, in 1928.

The militancy of the Hyōgikai manifested itself in the first national convention of the Council in late 1925 which pledged 'to resist the capitalists' exploitation by means of organization and struggle, to maintain and improve working conditions... [and] to emancipate the working class'.[57] The convention resolved to prepare the workers for struggle by developing their class consciousness: 'It is the responsibility of labor unions to educate the working masses to free themselves from the capitalist frame of mind and to promote organized activities of workers based on the principles of class consciousness.'[58] Specifically, the workers of the Hyōgikai were to be educated into class consciousness and to develop a commitment to proletarian democracy through special study and action 'cells' established within the unions for the purposes of learning basic Marxist theory under the guidance of Hyōgikai 'cadres' and of implementing Hyōgikai policy.

The structure of the Hyōgikai and the procedures for the definition of policy adopted in the Council were intended to reinforce worker class consciousness and uncompromising dedication to the goal of proletarian democracy in Japan. Nationally, the Hyōgikai consisted of district councils, including the Kantō District Council (Kantō Chihō Hyōgikai), the Fukushima District Council (Fukushima Chihō Hyōgikai), the Osaka District Council (Osaka Chihō Hyōgikai) and so forth.[59] Although power was concentrated in national headquarters in Tokyo, the various councils were permitted considerable autonomy in running their affairs. This arrangement was intended to contrast with that of the Sōdōmei, whose national headquarters nominally reigned supreme.

Within the Hyōgikai unions and the councils, and indeed in national headquarters, the spirit of democracy was, in theory, enhanced by the procedures of democratic centralism.[60] For example, all Hyōgikai workers were free to participate in debates over policy, with their respective cells as the centers for their involvement. But once policy was decided upon, they were expected to conform to it without dissent. In theory, if not always in practice, the 'tyranny of bureaucracy' was to be avoided at all levels of the Council. The will of the majority would prevail in this, a labor federation which belonged to the working masses, not to a privileged coterie of *rōdō kizoku*, as in the Sōdōmei. By emphasizing the democratic participation of the workers in decision-making, it was hoped, as the 1925 Hyōgikai convention declared, to 'achieve maximum fighting power [that] would enable the concentration of the will and action of the . . . working people'.[61]

The 'fighting power' of the Hyōgikai was most clearly demonstrated in the militant labor strikes waged by the Council. The strike was a primary weapon in the Council's arsenal of tactics because Hyōgikai leaders believed, as had Watanabe Masanosuke in the Nankatsu Union, that the political education of the workers would take place in the course of strikes, where revolutionary theory would be linked to practical action, as well as in Hyōgikai study cells. The Council thus became conspicuous in the wave of strikes that continued to sweep the country in the mid-1920s (293 in 1925, 495 in 1926, 383 in 1927, and 393 in 1928).[62] According to one source, 'In 1926 alone, over 5,000 Hyōgikai members were detained by the police and 196 imprisoned because of strikes.'[63] Most of these strikes were over low pay and poor working conditions but Hyōgikai leaders regarded them as integral parts of a broader strategy to weaken the foundations of capitalism by upsetting production. Therefore, the strikes conducted by the Council were frequently pressed to the limit by their participants without thought of the consequence for the unions involved; this usually meant destruction by the company, in cooperation with the police who monitored every Hyōgikai activity in this period.[64]

In comparison with the Hyōgikai's emphasis on the primacy of strikes, the Sōdōmei's position on strikes was more restrained. Although by no means inactive on the strike front,[65] the Sōdōmei regarded strikes as a last resort, after negotiation with management over worker grievances had failed. In an emergency national convention held in October 1925 to assess the damage of the 1925 labor split, the Sōdōmei resolved 'to continue active resistance to capitalism and the rising tide of reaction' by stressing collective bargaining campaigns to raise worker wages, improve their work conditions, and end unemployment.[66] Nothing was said about waging 'an all-out war' against capitalism, as had been promised in the 1924 convention. Capitalism would be opposed by the Sōdōmei mainly in the Diet and through the quiet, pragmatic development of strong labor union institutions – not primarily on the picket lines. This conformed to the spirit of 'realist socialism', whose conciliatory aspects had clearly become more pronounced in the General Federation after the 1925 labor split, and distinguished the Sōdōmei from its militant rival in the labor movement.

Sōdōmei leaders claimed, with some justification, that they were doing a better job than the Hyōgikai in creating stable and effective unions and that the Council wasted its resources on dramatic, but futile, strikes. The example of the Numazu local of the Sōdōmei Kantō Bōshoku Kumiai (General Federation Kantō Spinning Workers' Union), organized in 1927, bears this out. This local was well known in the Sōdōmei for its comprehensive range of mutual aid activities, including a strong consumers' cooperative linked to that of the Kantō Rōdō Dōmeikai, with which it was affiliated, and the generous provision of funds for the victims of industrial accidents, layoffs, bereaved families that had lost their loved ones in death, women who needed money to buy clothes for their children, weddings, and so on. The local also won respect for its vigorous efforts to organize youth and women and integrate them into the affairs of the Union. It established a special youth bureau, which sponsored a youth league, and a journal beamed at young workers in Numazu; representatives of the youth league attended the executive meetings of the local leadership. Akamatsu Tsuneko, the sister of Katsumaro, frequently travelled to Numazu from Tokyo in order to assist the women's bureau in the provision of classes for the female workers of Numazu. They were taught how to sew, cook, and plan the family budget, and were introduced to the arts of flower arrangement and tea ceremony for relaxation. The women's bureau lobbied in the factory for improved living quarters and better child-care facilities. It became a model for other Sōdōmei organizations where women were prominent among the membership.[67]

The Numazu local's annual conventions were lively affairs at which resolutions were passed on matters of policy with every intention of presenting them at the annual conventions of the Kantō Rōdō Dōmeikai and the Sōdōmei. The workers at Numazu proved responsive to policies handed down from Sōdōmei headquarters and contributed to the Sōdōmei's political support of the socialist party movement and other Sōdōmei unions, such as the one at Noda in 1927 and 1928, when they were engaged in large-scale labor disputes with management.[68] In short, while the Numazu local's institutions and programs were neither spectacular nor militant, they symbolized the kind of pragmatism that typified the Sōdōmei's approach to the labor movement.

Perhaps the contrast between the character of the Sōdōmei and that of the Hyōgikai and their differences in strategy and tactics can best be conveyed by examining their concepts of political education for the workers. Like the Hyōgikai, the Sōdōmei professed to be concerned with raising the class consciousness of the workers. However, the General Federation's approach to this problem differed considerably from the Hyōgikai's and produced different results. While the Hyōgikai relied upon study–action cells as the principal vehicle for building class consciousness, the Sōdōmei educated its workers in various labor schools (*rōdō gakkō*). In the former, Marxist theory was related to militant action, while the curriculum of the latter inculcated the value of democracy in the workers through the cultivation of their personal skills and general knowledge in a broad program of liberal education.

The General Federation had begun to form labor schools throughout Japan in the early 1920s. Typical were the Tokyo Rōdō Kōjōkō (Tokyo Labor Factory School) and the Rōdōsha Kyōiku Kyōkai (Workers' Education Society).[69] Their general mandate was to bring to the workers the benefits of culture' as promised in the Sōdōmei's 1919 convention. Accordingly, their classes, usually held in the evening, included lectures by such distinguished educators as Yoshino Sakuzō and Horie Kiichi and various Sōdōmei officials on social ethics, the basic principles of trade unionism, economics, law, politics, and history. Classes were also conducted on the operation of modern machinery and, for female pupils, in the techniques of flower arrangement and tea ceremony, as at Numazu. Kamijō Aiichi, who was a cardinal figure in the development of the Sōdōmei's *rōdō gakkō*, estimates that as many as 3,600 workers regularly attended the classes of the Rōdōsha Kyōiku Kyōkai.[70] This indicates that some of the labor schools were large-scale operations.

In broad terms, the purposes of the labor schools were twofold: to make the ordinary worker a morally responsible citizen, and to foster his identification with a labor movement that spoke for his interests and required his dedication and commitment. In some respects these two objectives were contradictory. The first, which reinforced the general thrust of formal education in the State school system, was avowedly nationalistic. It reflected the widely held belief that the individual should subordinate his own interest to that of the community as a whole and that the universal claims made on his loyalty by the State were to be fully honored. The second objective, on the other hand, assumed that the particularistic pursuit of self interest on the part of the individual and groups was legitimate and that all citizens possessed basic human rights that justified social protest if they were not recognized by the State.

This contradictory emphasis in the labor schools flowed from the tension between the universal aspects of nationalism and the particularistic dimensions of socialism and labor unionism in the thought of Akamatsu Katsumaro. But Akamatsu believed he had resolved this tension. It will be recalled that he stressed the unique attributes of Japanese culture as something to be valued in a socialist movement. It followed naturally that training in social ethics, with special attention to the moral obligation of the workers to honor and serve the Emperor, would occupy a high place in the curriculum of the *rōdō gakkō*. The importance of moral virtue was not new in the Sōdōmei. In the early Yūaikai, Suzuki Bunji had emphasized the moral uplift of the workers through the inculcation of Christian virtue.[71] Akamatsu had merely elaborated upon Suzuki's approach by accentuating its nationalistic implications.

But identification with the national community of Japan and its values did not mean, for Akamatsu, the acceptance of unjust practices which denied the individual rights of the workers. Loyalty to the State did not automatically signify worker loyalty to factory management when the latter insisted upon a concept of paternalistic collectivism in the factories that failed to acknowledge the equality of the workers with management as human beings possessing the same rights. In brief, Akamatsu believed it was entirely justifiable to oppose capitalism while supporting the Emperor out of a spirit of patriotic duty. The whole point of holding lectures on unionism, politics, economics and law in the *rōdō gakkō* was to educate the workers into an awareness of how society functioned and how they, as individuals with basic human rights, could serve both their self interest in realizing those rights and the interests of the State. Thus, nationalism and individualism were but two sides to the same coin of Akamatsu's 'realist socialism'.

In sum, the educational philosophy of the Sōdōmei, which bore significant implications for the political behavior of the General Federation, contrasted sharply with that of Hyōgikai. The Hyōgikai tried to create a revolutionary subculture rooted in Marxist values for the embattled community of workers in the Council by denying the legitimacy of the central values of imperial culture in order to free the workers from the 'capitalist frame of mind'.[72] In contrast, the Sōdōmei planted itself firmly within the imperial culture of Japan, admitted the legitimacy of the central values of the latter, and encouraged their application in the life of the labor movement. The Hyōgikai placed exclusive emphasis on the collectivism of proletarian class consciousness; the Sōdōmei did not ignore this priority but its concept of collectivism was oriented more to nation than to class so that it increasingly interpreted class in a diffuse, nonspecific sense to mean a broader category than just the workers and farmers of the *musan kaikyū*. This explains why the General Federation was ultimately absorbed into a nationalistic New Order which brooked no tolerance for particularism. Even the emphasis on individualism in the Sōdōmei served to check the Federation's concern for class consciousness by putting a high premium on the individual rather than on the proletarian class in bringing about the civic integration of the workers into the national community.

As they endeavored to recruit workers into their respective organizations while simultaneously discrediting each other, the Sōdōmei and the Hyōgikai projected images of themselves which accorded with their dissimilar approaches to labor politics. The Sōdōmei advertised itself, in countless leaflets passed out at the factory gates to workers who came and went, as a 'Japanese' labor organization which supported the *kokutai* while advancing the interests of the workers. The Sōdōmei's propaganda typically portrayed the Hyōgikai as a communist front manipulated by the Comintern – as a non-Japanese, 'foreign' entity that had no place in the country. The workers were told that if they wanted to improve their situation in the factories, they should join the General Federation, a stable and pragmatic organization with a long history going back to the Yūaikai.[73]

Conversely, Hyōgikai propaganda asserted that it was the only truly 'progressive' labor organization in Japan because it alone was based on the principle of militant class consciousness and struggle against capitalism. Proof of this, it was attested, lay in the readiness of the Council to commit its resources to labor strikes on behalf of the workers, which the Sōdōmei was less anxious to do. Propaganda rivalry of this kind was most virulent: quite often, Sōdōmei and Hyōgikai leafleteers stood uneasily together outside the factory gates like competing hawkers at a circus, promoting their respective sideshows. Meanwhile, *Rōdō* and *Rōdō Shimbun* traded blistering critiques of their opponents in the labor movement in an escalating war of rhetoric, the intensity of which surpassed even the earlier exchanges between the anarchists and their rivals.[74]

The average factory worker must have been rather puzzled by this rivalry, lacking as he did any notion of what unions were, let alone a knowledge of where the Sōdōmei and the Hyōgikai stood in the spectrum of labor politics. The picture became all the more blurred when a third labor federation appeared on the scene in 1926, offering itself as a 'centrist' (*chūritsuteki*) alternative to the two combatants on the left and the right and as a bridge for their eventual reunification. This was the Nihon Rōdō Kumiai Dōmei (Federation of Japanese Labor Unions). The political orientation and the reasons for the formation of the Dōmei are reserved for discussion in the next chapter. It suffices to say here that the Dōmei tried to steer a middle course between its rivals by combining their respective terrains in a program that blended the Hyōgikai's militance with the Sōdōmei's quiet pragmatism.

For instance, in its first annual convention, in 1927, the Dōmei served notice that it intended to raise worker class consciousness in order to 'oppose economic exploitation and the political oppression of the capitalists from the standpoint of class struggle'.[75] But this rhetoric, which resembled the Hyōgikai's, was accompanied by pledges to emphasize the concrete realization of nearly every goal espoused by the

Sōdōmei, including such objectives as an eight-hour work day, forty-eight-hour work week, further improvements of the Factory Law, and so forth. The Dōmei also pledged to wage strikes vigorously – like the Hyōgikai – but only when there seemed to be a good chance of winning tangible benefits for the workers – a proviso shared by the Sōdōmei. The Dōmei was likewise active in supporting a 'centrist' socialist party in opposition to the left-wing party backed by the Hyōgikai and the right-wing socialist party supported by the Sōdōmei in the 1920s. However, the principal conflict in the factories remained that of the Sōdōmei and the Hyōgikai since the Dōmei suffered from having a blurred identity in the labor movement for reasons that will be made clear later.

Each of the three rival labor organizations attempted to outflank their rivals by forming blocs with other labor organizations. The Sōdōmei's bloc was the largest. By 1928, it included the Nihon Kaiin Kumiai (Japanese Seamen's Union) of 81,534 workers, the Kaigun Rōdō Renmei (Naval Labor League) with 42,896, the Kangyō Rōdō Sōdōmei (General Federation of Labor in Government Enterprises) which had 14,042 members, and the Nihon Kaiin Kyōkai (Japan Maritime Officers' Association), an organization comprising about 11,124 workers.[76] The Nihon Kaiin Kumiai, founded by Hamada Kunitarō in 1921 as an outgrowth of the Yūaikai Kaiinbu (Friendly Society Seamen's Department), was the largest single labor union in Japan, its members taken from seamen in the merchant marine. Due to its loose affiliation with the Sōdōmei, based upon Hamada's close association with Suzuki Bunji, the Nihon Kaiin Kumiai constituted a formidable bulwark of the Federation in Japanese labor politics. Personal connections between Kawamura Yasutarō, head of the Kangyō Rōdō Sōdōmei, and Suzuki also accounted for the close relationship between the Kangyō Union and the General Federation. Kawamura's organization embraced arsenal workers, mainly from army arsenals, and workers in government-run steel plants, the tobacco monopoly bureau, and other government enterprises. It was a small union but its strategically-placed workers were a valuable asset to the Sōdōmei in penetrating large, government-administered industries.[77]

This was also true of the Kaigun Rōdō Renmei whose members were chiefly workers in naval arsenals. The Kaiin Kyōkai, an outrigger of Hamada's union, included ships' officers in the Japanese merchant marine. Altogether, the Sōdōmei bloc, which was supplemented by several other, smaller organizations, encompassed 184,315 workers in

1928, including roughly 40,000 from the General Federation itself.[78]

The Dōmei's bloc, on the other hand, encompassed the Nihon Rōdō Kumiai Sōrengō (General Alliance of Japanese Labor Unions), 14,155 workers strong, the Shichū Dōmei (Stewards' Federation) of 5,600 workers, and the Nihon Kōfu Kumiai (Japan Miners' Union) of 910 members. The Sōrengō had developed out of the earlier anarchist labor movement under the leadership of Sakamoto Kōsaburō who had broken with Nishio Suehiro, his one-time friend in the Osaka labor movement, during the early Taishō period. The Shichū Dōmei was composed of ships' stewards, with its base of operations in Osaka. The Kōfu Kumiai, formed originally by Asō Hisashi, was strongest in Kyūshū. The collective strength of the Dōmei's bloc in 1928 was about 45,000 members, more than half of whom came from the Dōmei.[79] The Hyōgikai, with a membership of about 36,000 in 1928, commanded a less sizeable bloc of militant unions, most of which were dominated by the metal and machine trades in the Kantō region.

With the consolidation of these three blocs, centered on the Sōdōmei, the Hyōgikai, and the Dōmei respectively, the confrontation between the three federations was amplified beyond their own individual strength. Yet, despite the rivalry of their rhetoric, all three federations, and their allies, were subject to the same conditions dictated by industrial paternalism. Heavily concentrated as they were in the small and medium-sized enterprises of Japan, they experienced great difficulty in expanding their independent leverage in the larger plants where industrial paternalism predominated. Several illustrations of this problem, based on the work of Professor Komatsu Ryūji of Keiō University, may be cited.[80]

I. Organized labor at the Shibaura Manufacturing Company. Beginning in 1905, the Shibaura Manufacturing Company had made steady progress in instituting an in-company technical training program for its workers, a program of general education, and numerous welfare benefits, including special payments to injured and dismissed employees. By 1920, it held out the prospect of permanent employment for its *jōyō-kō* employees who received wages and promotions on a graded basis according to seniority. In other words, this company was well on the way toward developing industrial paternalism when the Sōdōmei and several smaller organizations formed the first union at Shibaura, the Shibaura Rōdō Kumiai (Shibaura Labor Union) in December 1921. Even though the Sōdōmei had gone on record in favor of the principle of organizing workers by trades in its inaugural convention of 1919, the Shibaura Union functioned in the manner of an enterprise union. Its locals, as at the Company's plants at Ikegai and Ishikawajima, were closely tied to management in a cooperative relationship that rendered their association with the Union at large, or indeed with the Sōdōmei itself, almost superfluous.[81]

Not everyone in the Shibaura Rōdō Kumiai supported this emphasis. The Union was soon rocked by disputes between an anarchist caucus, mobilized by the energetic Takata Waitsu, and the mainstream Sōdōmei group, over whether to accept the Company's insistence on the enterprise model. The anarchists opposed it, arguing that the 'free' (*jiyū*) association of unions based on trade was essential. In time, their caucus withdrew from the Union and joined the newly formed, and anarchist-dominated, Kikaikō Kumiai Rengōkai (Association of Machinists' Unions) which had arisen in March 1921.[82]

This rupture notwithstanding, the Shibaura Rōdō Kumiai enjoyed a fairly tranquil existence until the 1925 labor split. At the time of the formation of the Hyōgikai, some of the Union locals split off and formed new locals affiliated with the Kantō Kinzoku Rōdō Kumiai (Kantō Metal Workers' Union). This was established as a Hyōgikai bastion in August 1926, and brought the Sōdōmei and the Hyōgikai into direct confrontation at Shibaura. The Kinzoku's locals heaped criticism on the Sōdōmei's for accepting the enterprise model and refused to write into their rules anything which would support this model. At the same time, plans were laid to alter the Kinzoku locals, which like those of the Sōdōmei at Shibaura were mixed, into locals based on trade. This effort, however, failed, when the Company refused to allow any such change. Komatsu concludes that the Hyōgikai's rhetoric in emphasizing trade unionism as the basic principle of organization melted away in the reality of the de facto enterprise unionism characterizing both the Hyōgikai and the Sōdōmei organizations at Shibaura.[83] Significantly, when the Sōdōmei union helped to organize a works council with the cooperation of the Company, the Hyōgikai locals linked to the Kinzoku union supported this endeavor. In the end, both federations supported the tactic of collective bargaining with the works council as the medium, despite the Hyōgikai's theoretical aversion to both councils and bargaining. In short, the Company remained in control of the union movement at Shibaura from start to finish.[84]

II. Organized labor at the Tokyo Steel Company. The history of the labor movement at the Tokyo Steel Company reflects the same trends toward enterprise unionism. In this case, the story concerns the Sōdōmei alone. The Federation first penetrated Tokyo Steel in 1926 when Miki Jirō, of the Matsuoka faction, a foreman at the steel works, founded the Seikō Rōdō Kumiai (Steel Workers' Union). It seems that the Company welcomed this Union as a way of keeping the radical Hyōgikai out of the plants. Soon after it was formed, the Company signed a closed shop agreement with the Union, stipulating that all organized workers at Tokyo Steel had to belong to this Union. The Sōdōmei welcomed the agreement because it too wanted to prevent the Council from establishing a base at Tokyo Steel.[85]

As at Shibaura, the management of Tokyo Steel had by this time developed many of the institutions of industrial paternalism in keeping with *sangyō gōrika* after World War I. Company-sponsored worker welfare facilities and mutual relief programs were particularly strong. Elements of the *nenkō* wage system were also discernible. Significantly, the Company encouraged the Union to expand its welfare programs, and, in particular, to establish consumers' cooperatives for the workers. The Union was also encouraged to develop a workers' education program. All of these endeavors were financed by the Union's dues (fifty *sen* per annum for men, thirty for women) but it is noteworthy that the Company also provided financial support to the Union. For instance, the Company paid regular instalments into the Union's Relief Fund.

Eventually, the formal agreement with the Union was refined and amplified. It stated that the Company could exercise the right to keep out 'leftists', implying that objectionable members of the Union could be dismissed, if the Company saw fit, with the Union's acquiescence. It also stated that the Company was under no obligation to give in to Union demands over wages and other issues if the Company regarded them as intolerable. According to Komatsu, the skilled workers who monopolized the leadership of the Union – men such as Miki Jirō – were willing collaborators with the Company in creating a situation in which the Union was easily manipulated by management. They saw nothing wrong in cooperating with the Company in conforming to the *kigyōbetsu kumiai* model if this benefited the workers at Tokyo Steel. It mattered little to them that such a course contradicted the Sōdōmei's formal advocacy of unions based on trades to preserve the horizontal, class character of the labor movement.[86]

III. Organized labor at the Ishikawajima Shipyards Company. The picture at the Ishikawajima Shipyards Company in Tokyo was more complicated but it also illustrates the drift toward enterprise unionism in the labor movement during the 1920s. This Company, like many others, had begun to innovate in labor relations after the Russo-Japanese War. By 1920, its recruitment procedures were much the same as those described under industrial paternalism. It had by then also established in-factory training programs and a workers' education program to raise the quality of the work force. Other features of the *nenkō* system were implemented by the management later in the decade.

The Yūaikai had established a union in this Company in 1912. It comprised several locals, all mixed – none was organized by trade. The union was known as the Yūaikai Kikai Gikō Rōdō Kumiai (Friendly Society Machinist–Artisans' Union). In 1919, however, another union was organized at Ishikawajima, the Zōki Senkō Rōdō Kumiai (Ships' Engineers' Labor Union). This was strongly anarchist in orientation and opposed the enterprise model of its rival. Komatsu states that its appearance prompted Company management to encourage the more moderate Sōdōmei union and its enterprise formula in order to isolate and weaken the Zōki group. Thus, while the Sōdōmei made some headway in organizing the *jōyō-kō* workers at Ishikawajima, who were by this time being absorbed into the *nenkō* system, its rival was confined mainly to the *rinji-kō*.[87]

The Zōki Senkō Rōdō Kumiai tried for a time to incite strikes at Ishikawajima and supported the battle against the Sōdōmei waged by the anarchist labor organizations in the ill-fated labor front, the Rōdō Kumiai Dōmeikai. But, while it professed to speak for the rank and file unskilled temporary workers, its leaders were, like those of its rival, skilled workers. Realizing as they did that their Union would only become popular if it offered concrete ways to help the workers, they adopted a program of pragmatic action which was very similar to that of the Sōdōmei union; it included cooperatives, relief programs for the sick and injured, and so on.[88]

This sort of pragmatism was already becoming discernible when in the heat of *ana-boru* conflict, many of the Zōki leaders went over to 'bolshevism'. As the events of 1925 raced toward the final split of the Sōdōmei that year, the Union threw its support behind the Kantō Chihō Hyōgikai and, after the split occurred, the Hyōgikai itself. Like its counterpart at Shibaura, its locals became affiliated with the Hyōgikai's powerful Kinzoku Rōdō Kumiai. As at Shibaura, then,

Ishikawajima became the battleground of rival Sōdōmei and Hyōgikai organizations.[89]

However, both of them were soon faced with an ingenious initiative undertaken by the Ishikawajima management in order to blunt their progress. Although the Company had hoped to use the Sōdōmei Union to offset radical labor in its factories, it concluded that, to ensure the defeat of the Hyōgikai, it would be necessary to form a third union, a company union (*goyō kumiai*). This was known as the Nogi Kōsha (Nogi Workers Society) and its title hints at the Company's motivation. General Nogi was a hero of the Russo-Japanese War who committed suicide in 1912 upon the death of Emperor Meiji in order to follow his Sovereign in death, emulating the old feudal tradition where samurai gave up their lives for this purpose. Nogi's act had won great public acclaim because it demonstrated his spirit of patriotism. Evidently, the Ishikawajima management believed that this spirit could be fostered among the workers so that they would work patriotically for both the Company and Japan.[90]

For reasons that are unclear, the Nogi Kōsha was renamed the Jikyō Rōdō Kumiai (Strenuous Efforts Labor Union) in later 1926. This at least clarified its identity as a bona fide union but the conservative emphasis on worker diligence was retained by the new title. The goals of this company union were to inspire the workers to work for the strengthening of the national polity and to raise their 'industrial spirit'. Above all, the Jikyō Rōdō Kumiai stood for absolute harmony between capital and labor. The head of this Union was Kaeno Shin'ichi, a foreman at Ishikawajima.[91]

By 1928, when the Hyōgikai fell and its Union at Ishikawajima was destroyed along with it, the Jikyō Rōdō Kumiai had become the dominant labor organization at the Shipyards. The Sōdōmei Union, which had survived the repressions of 1928, remained on the scene as a weak competitor. In terms of practical activities, however, its programs and those of the Jikyō were nearly identical. Their cooperatives, educational programs, and the like functioned fairly smoothly side by side, and representatives of both organizations sat on the works council, set up by the Company several years previously to enhance industrial peace. Both were enterprise unions which fit nicely into the industrial paternalism that typified Ishikawajima.[92]

These three brief case studies show that whether the union was affiliated to the Sōdōmei or to the Hyōgikai, it generally ended up in the *kigyōbetsu kumiai* mold with strong attachments to management.

Sōdōmei leaders rationalized their acquiescence to this trend by saying that tactical compromises with management were necessary to establish a foothold in the factories. They reasoned that the goal of reforming capitalism from within could not otherwise be achieved. They believed that the best response to industrial paternalism was to turn enterprise unionism to their own advantage, as for instance in using enterprise unions to bargain collectively with management. This pliant posture was consistent with their ideology, 'realist socialism', which emphasized pragmatic flexibility and adaptation to changing circumstances. They did not abandon their fidelity to trade unionism in their rhetoric. But they were prepared to compromise this ideal when the choice came down to enterprise unionism or no unionism at all.

The challenge of industrial paternalism to the labor movement caused greater agony in the Hyōgikai and the Dōmei, also buffeted by the same pressures exerted on the unions by the *kigyōbetsu kumiai* model. With every surrender of a Hyōgikai union to the enterprise model, the prospect for creating a mass base of class-conscious workers dedicated to the overthrow of capitalism receded. Thus, the Hyōgikai was also obliged to adjust to industrial paternalism in order to keep its unions above water in the large enterprises. The tactic of waging militant strikes had, by 1927, resulted in the closure of so many Hyōgikai unions that any other response was out of the question. Rather than rise to the Hyōgikai cause in the midst of these strikes, the repeated failure of the latter had flattened the resolve of the workers to struggle. Faced with this erosion of support, and a seemingly intractable situation in the large enterprises where management was so powerful, the Hyōgikai reassessed its tactics in 1927, announcing in its annual convention of May that year that henceforth it would walk the path of 'realism' (*genjitsushugi*) by stressing the evolutionary development of unions and initiatives, including collective bargaining with management, to secure higher wages and improved work conditions for the workers. Costly strikes were to be avoided, for the time being, to give the Council time to shore up its flagging strength. The Hyōgikai platform was revised to include many objectives long sought for by the Sōdōmei: a higher minimum wage, unemployment relief at public expense, greater protection for women and children, and above all, the legal right of unions to exist and bargain collectively.[93]

Some contemporary critics of the Hyōgikai such as Nishio Suehiro greeted the Council's moderation in 1927 as a positive sign that the Hyōgikai would abandon its previous militancy in favor of pragmatic union-building policies similar to those of the Sōdōmei. As Nishio saw it, the Hyōgikai had rejected the ideas of Fukumoto Kazuo in 1927. After displacing Yamakawa Hitoshi as the main theoretician in the Japanese communist movement following the Comintern's censure of Yamakawa for his part in dissolving the JCP earlier in the 1920s, Fukumoto had stressed revolutionary doctrinal purity and militant political struggle at the expense of unionism.[94] It seemed to Nishio that the Council's 'new' course reflected a return to Yamakawa's insistence on developing the unions by endorsing programs and goals that would appeal to the rank and file workers. Since the Sōdōmei had been pursuing this policy all along, Nishio felt that the Hyōgikai's new 'change of direction' vindicated the wisdom of the Sōdōmei's own 'realism'.[95]

Whether the Hyōgikai would have adhered to its moderate policies for very long or whether the 1927 convention constituted only a temporary tactical adjustment to the recent costliness of militant strikes and to the weakness of the Council's unions in large enterprises where industrial paternalism prevailed will never be known, for within a year the Hyōgikai was faced with extinction. Its ranks were seriously depleted by the government's mass arrests of known and suspected communists in March 1928 during another police crackdown against the JCP.[96] Then, in April 1928, the Home Ministry prohibited the Hyōgikai and several other organizations thought to be under the influence of the JCP, including the 'legal left' party supported by the JCP, the Zen Nihon Musan Seinen Dōmei (All-Japan Proletarian Youth League), and the Shinjinkai.[97] Another serious blow to the communist movement was the death of Watanabe Masanosuke, one of its most able labor organizers, who was killed later in 1928 in a struggle with Japanese police in Taiwan after escaping from the police in Japan.[98]

The government's anti-communist campaign of 1928 ended the struggle between the Sōdōmei and the Hyōgikai for influence among the workers, which had raged with bitter intensity after the 1925 labor split. The Sōdōmei and its allies remained vigilant in opposing communist influence in the labor movement after a successor to the Hyōgikai arose later in 1928. But, since neither this organization nor the JCP, which continued its embattled existence, proved as strong as the communist movement had been in the past, the Sōdōmei's ongoing war against communism would be fought with rather less urgency than in the mid-1920s, and largely as a function of the Federation's attempt to preserve itself from other new threats in the Depression period.

However, the Sōdōmei's rivalry with the Hyōgikai had left a deep and enduring impression on the Federation. Its desperate efforts to distinguish itself from the radical Hyōgikai in the public eye had pushed the Sōdōmei even further into a cooperative relationship with its wider political and economic environment, a tendency reinforced by the warping influence of industrial paternalism on the horizontal linkages of the union movement in the large enterprises. Moreover, the Federation's anti-communism had strengthened the Sōdōmei's resistance to cooperation with other labor organizations in the rest of the non-communist labor movement unless they accepted the Federation's moderate brand of political socialism coupled with a practical emphasis on labor unionism as the basis for labor unity in the future. This was also the Sōdōmei's uncompromising criterion for achieving unity in the proletarian party movement which had been fragmented by many of the same tensions that had polarized the labor movement in the course of Sōdōmei–Hyōgikai conflict from 1925 to 1928.

5

Labor and the socialist party movement, 1925–1928

From 1919 to 1925, the Nihon Rōdō Sōdōmei had been forced by its own avowed commitment to political action and by the absence of a legal proletarian party to combine its functions as the mainstay of the labor union movement with those of a surrogate socialist party. This dual role had placed a considerable burden on the Sōdōmei's shoulders. The Federation had suffered bitter internecine conflict because both its leaders and their opponents had assumed that the outcome of their struggle for power in the labor movement would be decisive in determining the future political course of other social movements. Their disputes over the role that organized labor should play in Japan had become increasingly uncontrollable, as the 1925 labor split revealed.

The assumption that political conflict in the unions was significant for the entire range of proletarian organizations that comprised, however loosely, the 'Taishō democracy movement' remained intact even though the enactment of the Universal Manhood Suffrage Law in 1925 promised to transform the role of the Sōdōmei and the Hyōgikai from operating in effect as surrogate parties to that of providing a bona fide, independent socialist party with the support it would inevitably require from the urban workers. Both federations felt a duty to prevent the other from controlling the ideology, strategy, and tactics of the new party lest their own concepts of political priorities and action, which they now defended with fanatical zeal in the labor movement, would cease to have any impact on the cause of Taishō democracy in general.

With the consequent diffusion of labor conflicts into the nascent socialist party movement, the latter was soon destined to experience the same pattern of schism that had thrown the labor movement into disunity: the direct, and indirect, consequence of Sōdōmei–Hyōgikai struggles was the emergence of not one, but three, socialist parties in 1925 and 1926, each of which possessed its own labor base. The ensuing competition between these socialist alignments, which also included elements of the agrarian union movement, among others, virtually nullified the collective impact that the socialists might have registered on Japanese politics in the years ahead, and condemned their efforts to futility almost as soon as the socialists entered the new arena of parliamentary politics in the Diet.

The involvement of the Sōdōmei and the Hyōgikai in the socialist party movement began one month after the labor split when the two federations accepted invitations from the Nihon Nōmin Kumiai (Japan Farmers' Union) to send representatives to a deliberative conference of various proletarian organizations. Its purpose was to plan and establish a united socialist party that would represent the interests of the *musan kaikyū* in the Diet. Since its inception in 1922, the Nōmin Kumiai had made good progress in mobilizing the tenant farmers of Japan into unions. By 1925, it claimed 70,000 members, most of whom had been transformed from small landlords into tenant farmers during the post-war recession when their agricultural income had been sharply reduced by the downward plunge of prices of raw silk, rice, and other farm products, a trend that was to continue throughout the interwar period.[1]

Embracing a socialist program which centered on legislation to relieve the distress of the rural poor by reducing rents and introducing other reforms, the Nōmin Kumiai leaders – Sugiyama Motojirō and Kagawa Toyohiko – calculated that this program would succeed only if the organizational potential of the agrarian unions could be linked to that of the labor movement, so that the anticipated socialist party would be provided with a solid base in the villages and factories.[2] Worried that the labor movement was in danger of drifting aimlessly under the shock of the recent split, they took it upon themselves to seize the initiative in forming a socialist party as soon as possible in preparation for the next prefectural and national elections.

Sugiyama and Kagawa knew that they were placing the enterprise of organizing a cohesive socialist party in grave risk by inviting the two hostile labor federations to take part in its formation. But they judged that any party that did not include the Sōdōmei and the Hyōgikai would lack the kind of labor base necessary to be effective in the Diet. Moreover, they hoped it would be possible to contain the rivalry between the Federation and the Council by subsuming them into a broad proletarian front that would also include, besides the Nōmin Kumiai itself, the Seiji Kenkyūkai, the Suiheisha (Levelling Society, founded in 1922 to liberate the *burakumin*, or *eta*),[3] the Musan Seinen Dōmei (Proletarian Youth League, also formed in 1922),[4] and several other labor groups such as the Kangyō Rōdō Sōdōmei, thought to be strategic because of their inroads into government enterprises.[5] However, this strategy, which seemed sensible at the time, backfired on the Nōmin Kumiai: once the conference was convened and a joint committee of its participants was established, the Sōdōmei and the Hyōgikai clashed immediately over the prickly issue of which organizations had the right to be involved in launching the new party.

Nishio Suehiro and Asō Hisashi, speaking for the General Federation at the conference, made it plain that the Sōdōmei opposed the participation of the Hyōgikai, the Kenkyūkai, the Suiheisha, and the Musan Seinen Dōmei in the proceedings on the grounds that all of them were communist-front organizations. They also charged that the Seiji Kenkyūkai had no business taking part because it was merely a loose coalition of intellectuals with no established constituency among the workers and farmers.[6] This bitterness toward the Kenkyūkai stemmed from the Sōdōmei's withdrawal of support from that organization following the Kenkyūkai's shift to the left politically earlier in 1925.[7] The Sōdōmei insisted that the only groups that should be involved in the establishment of a socialist party were the Nōmin Kumiai, representing the farmers, the Sōdōmei, standing in for the workers, and organizations like the Kangyō Rōdō Sōdōmei who shared the Sōdōmei point of view on the need for a politically 'responsible' socialist party.

This hard line taken by the General Federation clearly manifested its increasing anti-communism after the 1925 labor split. Reactions in the conference to the Sōdōmei position were just as uncompromising. Watanabe Masanosuke, selected by the Hyōgikai to represent its views at the conference, passionately condemned the Federation for obstructing the important business of forming a socialist political front by engaging in unnecessary bickering over the credentials of the participants in an attempt to take control over the proceedings. Watanabe became so emotional in the course of his exchanges across the conference table with Nishio and Asō that the Hyōgikai decided to replace him with a cooler man, Nakamura Yoshiaki, on the joint committee.[8]

Ultimately, the very strained proceedings of the committee reached a crisis point in October 1925 when a Sōdōmei motion stipulating that the Seiji Kenkyūkai, at least, should withdraw from the committee was defeated in a general vote of the participants. Remarking that the vote proved conclusively that the Hyōgikai and the Kenkyūkai were in collusion on behalf of communism, Nishio announced the withdrawal of the General Federation from the committee.[9] This move was duti-fully followed by the exodus of the Kangyō Rōdō Sōdōmei which was anxious to take its cue from the General Federation.[10] Eventually, the Hyōgikai also withdrew, calculating that because of these disruptions, the conference was bound to fail. However, the Nōmin Kumiai leaders pressed on with their plans for a socialist party and, in cooperation with the remaining organizations on the committee, established the Nōmin Rōdōtō (Farmer Labor Party) on December 1, 1925. But, to the dismay of its adherents, within hours of the Party's formation it was ordered to close down by the Home Ministry. The Ministry alleged that the Nōmin Rōdōtō was 'too radical', presumably because of the participa-tion of the Seiji Kenkyūkai.[11]

At this point, it looked very much as if the task of organizing a united socialist party was beyond the capacities of the socialist move-ment. However, the Nōmin Kumiai leaders decided to make a second attempt. This time, they hoped to build the party around their own unions and moderate labor organizations such as the Sōdōmei and the Kangyō Rōdō Sōdōmei, with a view to expanding the party's mass base to include other, more leftist groups in the future. Accordingly, the Sōdōmei and the Kangyō Rōdō Sōdōmei were invited to participate in planning the party, but the Hyōgikai, the Kenkyūkai, Seinen Dōmei, and Suiheisha were not. Kagawa and Sugiyama also counted on the moderating influence of Abe Isoo, Takano Iwasaburō,[12] Horie Kiichi, and Yoshino Sakuzō to make the new negotiations a success. These men, as recognized 'elders' of the Taishō democracy movement, helped smoothe the way, and after further consultations, the groups concerned established the Rōdō Nōmintō (Labor–Farmer Party) on March 5, 1926.[13] Sugiyama was elected chairman; Miwa Jusō, a young lawyer closely associated with Asō Hisashi through their common Shinjinkai connections, was made General Secretary. Abe, Takano, Kagawa, and Suzuki Bunji, Matsuoka Komakichi, Nishio, Asō, and others from the Sōdōmei all sat on the Party's central committee.[14] Because of the moderate complexion of the committee, the government made no move to prohibit the Rōdō Nōmintō.

However, the new Party soon fell into disarray. Not long after its formation, Kagawa and Sugiyama argued that it should open its doors to all proletarian organizations to give the Rōdō Nōmintō a truly mass base.[15] They included the Hyōgikai in this proposal, along with the Seiji Kenkyūkai and other groups. To mollify the Sōdōmei, they pro-posed that members of the Hyōgikai be allowed to join the Party as individuals, not as official representatives of the Council. The same admissions procedure would apply to the Kenkyūkai, the Suiheisha, and the Seinen Dōmei.

As might have been expected, the Sōdōmei objected strenuously to this proposal, arguing that it would radicalize the Rōdō Nōmintō. When the proposal came up for a vote on the Party central committee in April, it passed, nine votes to eight. But, due to the closeness of the vote, the open-door admissions policy was not implemented immediately. During the summer and early autumn of 1926, the General Federation tried to reverse this policy in countless, heated discussions on the Party central committee. Meanwhile, the Hyōgikai sent petitions to Sugiyama, asking that its members be permitted to enter the Rōdō Nōmintō. Sugiyama and Kagawa continued to express sympathy with this request, the Sōdōmei accusing them of having fallen under communist influence. On October 24, the General Federation abruptly announced its withdrawal of support from the Rōdō Nōmintō and all of the Sōdōmei officials on the Party central committee resigned their posts. Once again, pro-Sōdōmei labor organizations that had been involved in the affairs of the Party followed the exodus of the General Federation.[16]

After this split in the Rōdō Nōmintō, the Hyōgikai and the Seiji Kenkyūkai stepped into the vacuum left by the Sōdōmei's departure. Soon, the Rōdō Nōmintō fell under the indirect control of these two organizations. Even the Nōmin Kumiai, which had worked hard to establish the Party, suffered an erosion of its influence in Party affairs when Sugiyama was displaced as chairman, in a central committee election, by Ōyama Ikuo, an intellectual who had become the dominant voice in the Seiji Kenkyūkai and who was basically sympathetic to the Hyōgikai in the labor movement.[17] Henceforth, the Rōdō Nōmintō comprised the 'legal left' of the socialist party movement, as distinguished from the illegal Japanese Communist Party, with which Ōyama and other Rōdō Nōmintō leaders wanted to cooperate.

In the Sōdōmei, sentiment was bitter toward what some Sōdōmei leaders, such as Nishio, regarded as the treachery of the Nōmin Kumiai's Kagawa and Sugiyama in complying with communist desires on the Party's admissions policy.[18] In retaliation, the Sōdōmei central committee decided to press ahead in its plans to establish a party which would be true to the principles of 'realist socialism' in order to counterbalance the influence of the Rōdō Nōmintō. Accordingly, when in November 1926 Yoshino, Abe, and Horie, all of whom had also left the Rōdō Nōmintō out of sympathy with the Sōdōmei's position, invited the Sōdōmei to participate in talks for a moderate socialist party, the invitation was eagerly accepted.[19] After rather hurried deliberations, these talks resulted in the formation of a second proletarian party, the Shakai Minshūtō (Social Democratic Party) in Tokyo, on December 5, 1926.[20]

The Shakai Minshūtō was intended by its founders, as its chairman, Abe Isoo, explained in the inaugural convention, to be the Japanese equivalent of the British Labour Party.[21] Indeed, Suzuki Bunji had suggested that the Party be called the 'Nihon Rōdōtō' (Japan Labor Party) for this reason. However, Akamatsu Katsumaro argued that the name should be Shakai Minshūtō to emphasize the aim of the Party to represent the *musan kaikyū* in general, not just the workers.[22] Observing the Party's founding convention, Yamakawa Hitoshi quipped that really, the Party ought to have been named the 'Nihon Sōdōmeitō' (Japan General Federation of Labor Party) since, aside from Abe, and the Party's General Secretary, Katayama Tetsu, most of the men on the Shakai Minshūtō central committee were officials from the Sōdōmei, including, among others, Suzuki, Matsuoka, Nishio, Asō, and Akamatsu.[23] Yamakawa's caustic sarcasm also arose from the fact that this Party pledged at its opening ceremonies to begin building branches around Sōdōmei unions as a step toward developing a national infrastructure.[24]

The Shakai Minshūtō was, thus, a coalition of moderate labor groups led by the Sōdōmei and well-known intellectuals, who comprised the so-called right wing of the socialist movement. The predominance of the Sōdōmei in this Party and the presence of men like Abe and Yoshino on the central committee lent the Party a certain gravitas in the socialist movement because it seemed to center on groups and individuals who had long been active in 'Taishō democracy'. Yoshino's participation in the Party was thought to be particularly significant for it marked a break from his former liberalism and his espousal of 'realist socialism'.[25] Since Abe was chairman, the Party could reasonably claim to represent continuity with the Meiji socialist movement as well.

With the rise of the Shakai Minshūtō, the socialist party movement was polarized into right and left wings, largely a direct consequence of the socialist–communist conflict which had originated earlier in the Sōdōmei. However, the General Federation was also the epicenter for yet a third eruption which complicated the party movement even further by producing a 'centrist' socialist party later in 1926. Once again, the clash between 'realist socialism' and communism figured prominently, although less directly than before, in this new development.

To elaborate, during the events which had precipitated the 1925 labor split, Asō Hisashi and his faction in the Sōdōmei had vigorously supported the Sōdōmei from the dissidence of unions that were to coalesce in the Hyōgikai. Asō had also endorsed the Sōdōmei's withdrawal from the Nōmin Rōdōtō and the Rōdō Nōmintō. However, privately, Asō had begun to entertain deep misgivings toward the 'spoiler's' role that the Sōdōmei had played in these gyrations. It seemed to him that the other leaders of the General Federation had become too entrenched in their anti-communist crusade to see the importance of cooperation with other groups in the creation of a united socialist party, a move which Asō believed to be absolutely necessary if the socialist movement was to have any leverage in the Diet at all.

Therefore, Asō undertook secret conversations with others in his faction, including Miwa Jusō, Katō Kanjū, Kamijō Aiichi, Asanuma Inejirō, and two powerful workers, Iwauchi Zensaku and Fujioka Bunroku, to plan the formation of a third proletarian party which would mediate between the Rōdō Nōmintō on the left and the Shakai Minshūtō on the right.[26] Early in these discussions, which occurred in late 1926, none of these men thought that this initiative would necessarily lead to their splitting from the Sōdōmei itself. They believed it possible for the Sōdōmei to support two proletarian parties in the interim before their eventual reunification, along with the Rōdō Nōmintō, into a united political front.[27]

Asō's plan did not come to the attention of the other Sōdōmei factions until November 24, 1926, when the *Asahi Shimbun* newspaper published a statement by him in which he disclosed his desire for a 'centrist' proletarian party.[28] Until then, Matsuoka, Suzuki Bunji, and Nishio had believed Asō to be with them in planning for the Shakai Minshūtō. Indeed, Asō had given this impression by conducting negotiations toward the Shakai Minshūtō with Yoshino Sakuzō, his *sempai* (senior) from his Tokyo Imperial University days, and with Abe Isoo and Horie Kiichi, on behalf of the Sōdōmei's central committee.[29]

The *Asahi Shimbun* article precipitated demands for Asō's expulsion from the Sōdōmei on the part of the Kantō Rōdō Dōmeikai and other organizations in the General Federation.[30] Greatly perturbed by Asō's apparent betrayal of Sōdōmei policy, Matsuoka, Nishio and Suzuki supported this demand in a special session of the Sōdōmei central committee, whereupon Asō and eleven others in his faction were summarily expelled from the General Federation on the eve of the Shakai Minshūtō's formation.[31] The expulsions triggered the exodus of about 6,000 workers in the Sōdōmei loyal to Asō.[32] Principal among them were the coal miners whom Asō and Katō Kanjū had organized earlier on. These workers immediately established their own labor federation, the Nihon Rōdō Kumiai Dōmei, mentioned in the last chapter, and on December 9, just four days after the formation of the Shakai Minshūtō, Asō and his followers founded a centrist socialist party, the Nihon Rōnōtō (Japan Labor–Farmer Party) in Tokyo. Asō was its chairman; Miwa Jusō, its General Secretary.[33] The new party looked to the Rōdō Kumiai Dōmei for its main labor support.

The expulsion of Asō and his faction from the Sōdōmei was clearly carried out for a mixture of personal and ideological motives. Neither Nishio nor Matsuoka had ever trusted Asō as an intellectual. His surprise revolt against them seemed to confirm their suspicions of his maverick qualities. More importantly, Asō had committed the error of calling for a reunification of the labor and party movements on the basis of cooperation with the pro-communist Hyōgikai and the Rōdō Nōmintō to which the Sōdōmei leaders were now vigorously opposed. The idea that the Asō faction could somehow remain in the Sōdōmei while supporting a centrist party and not the Shakai Minshūtō seemed to these men totally naive and quite unacceptable. Hence his expulsion.

A similar mixture of personal and ideological considerations had prompted Asō's revolt against the Sōdōmei and its political inclinations. To him, the worker-leaders of the Sōdōmei had subordinated proletarian unity to their obsessive desire to preserve personal power in the labor movement. Moreover, their increasing political conservatism had made them more 'bourgeois' than proletarian in mentality. They had interpreted 'realist socialism' as a rationalization for cooperating with capitalism rather than opposing it.[34] That they were even prepared to work hand in hand with conservatives in the political establishment was apparent, in Asō's view, from the so-called '*Minshū Shimbun*' incident. Soon after the formation of the Shakai Minshūtō, it was rumored that Suzuki Bunji and other Sōdōmei leaders had accepted money from a prominent member of the House of Peers to finance the *Minshū Shimbun*, the newspaper of the Shakai Minshūtō. Although this was never proven, Asō believed the rumor and concluded that the Sōdōmei and its allied party were willing to be maneuvered by the government for the sake of blunting the edge of other proletarian labor and party organizations.[35]

There is no doubt that those who followed Asō out of the Sōdōmei into the centrist movement were motivated by their ideological opposition to 'realist socialism'. Like Asō himself, these men hoped the centrist organizations could somehow pull the others together before the cleavages of 1925 and 1926 hardened beyond redemption. But personal factors also figured in their decision to participate in a new wing of the socialist movement. For instance, Kamijō Aiichi confided to Nishio Suehiro in 1926 that he did not know whether Asō, Miwa, and Tanahashi Kotora were right or wrong in splitting from the Sōdōmei and the Shakai Minshūtō. But he felt he had no choice but to go along with them because he respected them as individuals.[36] Okada Sōji, another member of the Asō faction, expressed the same sense of personal loyalty to Asō in an interview with the author.[37] Kikukawa Tadao, another of Asō's *kokata* who had been with Asō in the Shinjinkai, is also quoted as having said that he did not have anything personally against the Sōdōmei or the Shakai Minshūtō but that he had felt compelled to follow Asō's lead because Asō was his *sempai* in the Shinjinkai.[38]

For the workers who joined the Kumiai Dōmei, it would seem that the opportunity to play leading roles in a new labor movement after they had been denied influence in the Sōdōmei was at least as important as any personal fidelity to Asō or political calculations based on ideology. Iwauchi Zensaku, for example, told the author that the Kumiai Dōmei had appealed to him as an alternative to the 'realist socialism' of the Sōdōmei and to the communism of the Hyōgikai. He wanted to be more politically progressive than the Sōdōmei but he could not bring himself to embrace communism. Centrist socialism represented a middle ground. But Iwauchi also remembers feeling resentful against the bureaucratic elites who ran the Sōdōmei; he joined the Kumiai Dōmei to escape from their authority and in order to have a say in building up a new labor federation.[39] To some extent, his expectations were fulfilled. On the other hand, the Dōmei was, from the start, ruled not by workers but by intellectuals in Asō's faction. Its chairman was Tanahashi Kotora. Kono Mitsu, another intellectual loyal to Asō, was second in command in the Dōmei.[40]

As in the case of the 1925 labor split, the historian who seeks to determine the saboteur of the dream of proletarian unity in the socialist party movement must sift through much polemic for the answer.

This time, the evidence suggests that the policies of the Sōdōmei leadership were chiefly to blame for the fragmentation of the socialist parties and for the second major split (*dai-niji bunretsu*) of the Federation itself when the expulsion of Asō and his clique caused the breakaway of 'centrist' labor unions from the Sōdōmei in 1926.

To be sure, this was not the view of the Sōdōmei. Akamatsu Katsumaro, for instance, accused the Hyōgikai of sabotaging the cause of proletarian unity in the Nōmin Rōdōtō and the Rōdō Nōmintō by trying to isolate and discredit the Sōdōmei and other moderate organizations. In the rhetoric that became typical of Sōdōmei leaders in this period, he asserted that the Hyōgikai was a communist front and a 'Russian-style' organization subservient to the JCP and the Comintern. Any party supported by the Hyōgikai was guilty of the same sins. By contrast, the Sōdōmei and the Shakai Minshūtō represented 'Japanese' socialism in their respect for the Emperor.[41]

Akamatsu was likewise bitter toward the 'centrists'. He accused Asō and his faction of 'opportunism' in opposing the Sōdōmei and its political ally, the Shakai Minshūtō.[42] Akamatsu and other Sōdōmei writers stated that while the Sōdōmei regarded the idea of a single proletarian party as 'beautiful' in the abstract, such a party was an impossibility given the divisions of the labor movement.[43] Cooperation with either the legal left or the centrists would amount to cooperation with communism, a policy which was contrary to the ideology of 'realist socialism' and one that would surely bring down the government's wrath on the right-wing socialists as well as everyone else in the socialist movement.

Yet, despite the logic of some of these points (in particular, the last one seemed partly vindicated by the government's repressions of 1928), the fact remains that it was the Nihon Rōdō Sōdōmei which aborted the cause of proletarian political unity in 1925 and 1926. By abandoning the Nōmin Rōdōtō and the Rōdō Nōmintō, the General Federation deprived them of the considerable strength under its command in the labor movement. Without the Sōdōmei, the Rōdō Nōmintō was especially vulnerable to repression for being a radical organization dominated by the communist-leaning Kenkyūkai and the Hyōgikai. Had the Sōdōmei remained in this Party, it is at least possible that the government might not have been so quick to close it down in 1928, preferring instead to rely on the Sōdōmei and other moderate groups to make the Rōdō Nōmintō more 'responsible' politically.

Furthermore, the Sōdōmei's involvement in the formation of the

Shakai Minshūtō added to the institutional fragmentation of the proletarian party movement by creating another, right-wing, party which
competed with the Rōdō Nōmintō and whose creation precipitated the
dai-niji bunretsu of the Sōdōmei itself and the rise of a third socialist
party, the Rōnōtō. Although Asō Hisashi might be held responsible for
complicating the socialist party picture by forming the Rōnōtō, the fact
that he saw it as a possible bridge to unity between the Rōdō Nōmintō
on the left and the Shakai Minshūtō on the right indicates the degree of
his enthusiasm for proletarian political unity which the Sōdōmei did not
share.

In short, while other organizations, including even the Hyōgikai, had
been willing to risk cooperation with one another to create a socialist
party front, the General Federation had refused to take this risk. It had
permitted its antagonism toward the Hyōgikai to intrude into the
politics of the socialist party movement. Opposing the Hyōgikai was
more important to Sōdōmei leaders than reaching compromises with
their arch-rival for the sake of proletarian party unity. Thus, a valuable
opportunity was lost in 1925 and 1926 to represent the *musan kaikyū*
in the Diet with one voice. Because, as Yamakawa Hitoshi perceptively
pointed out, the Sōdōmei would not countenance a party which it was
unable to dominate, the socialist party movement as a whole suffered
the effects of internal division which it could scarcely afford in its
formative stages during the mid-1920s and thereafter.[44]

Socialist labor–party alignments, 1926–1928

Contemporary Japanese observers described the three labor–party
alignments of these years in terms of a left–center–right division. The
Rōdō Nōmintō was said to represent the left wing or *sayoku*, of the
socialist political movement; the Rōnōtō the centrist, or *chūritsu*,
element; and the Shakai Minshūtō, the right wing, or *uyoku*. The
same terminology was also applied to the labor bases of the parties,
the Hyōgikai, Kumiai Dōmei, and Sōdōmei, respectively.[45]

Recently, however, scholars have found it more useful to portray
these alignments in terms of *kei* or cliques. This approach, which is used
here, was first systematized in English-language research on Japan by
George Totten. Totten observed that the cliques which emerged in the
1920s in the Japanese socialist movement remained intact through
the interwar period and indeed that they extend into the present as
well.[46]

The principal cliques included the Shaminkei or 'Socio-Democratic' clique, composed of persons associated with the Shakai Minshūtō; the Nichirōkei or 'Japan Labor' clique, linked with the centrist Rōnōtō; and the Rōnōha or 'Labor–Farmer Faction' which generally supported the Rōdō Nōmintō on the legal left. It should be noted that although these categories take their names for the most part from party titles, the cliques extended into the mass base organizations which supported these parties. Thus the Sōdōmei is grouped along with, and is seen as part of, the Shaminkei; the Rōdō Kumiai Dōmei organization is part of the Nichirōkei; and so forth.[47]

The important attributes of the Shaminkei were very similar to those of its main labor base, the Nihon Rōdō Sōdōmei. They included 'realist socialism' as the political ideology of the Shaminkei and a corresponding emphasis on rationalism, gradualism, legalism, parliamentarism, progressive social reformism, and a strident anti-communism. In terms of class orientation, the Shaminkei professed to speak for the *kinrō kaikyū* (literally, the 'devotedly laboring class').[48] The *kinrō kaikyū* embraced nearly anyone who depended upon his own labor for income: factory workers, farmers, salaried employees, professionals, shopkeepers, and so on. The distinguishing characteristic of this concept of class was that it included people who 'own a certain amount of property but not enough to live on without working. What the whole class had in common, then, is not necessarily lack of property, but lack of security.'[49]

The liberation of the *kinrō kaikyū* as a class, and of its members as individuals whose self-fulfillment was regarded as an important aim of the socialist movement, typified the Shaminkei approach to class struggle against capitalism. But this struggle was to be conducted within the boundaries of respect for the fundamental principles and symbols of Japanese nationalism. The nationalism of the Shaminkei is illustrated by an incident involving Nishio Suehiro after he had been elected to the Imperial Diet on the Shakai Minshūtō ticket. Once, Nishio had attended a reception for Emperor Hirohito, dressed in an ordinary business suit rather than the formal attire customary on such occasions. Because of this indiscretion, he was called in for questioning by the police, who accused Nishio of deliberately defying ceremonial custom in order to show disrespect for His Majesty. Nishio was astounded at this allegation. In all sincerity he told his interrogators that he had simply forgotten to wear formal attire because of his great excitement at meeting the Emperor who, he declared, was 'sacred' and so grand that he stood 'above the clouds' in relation to his people.[50] It never occurred to Nishio, or anyone else in the Shaminkei, to oppose the Emperor system of Japan.

In Takagi Ikurō's critical opinion, based on a study of the Shaminkei, the nationalism that typified the Shaminkei rested on the false assumption that capitalism could be opposed without simultaneously opposing Japanese nationalism and the Emperor system. He perceptively suggests that the Shaminkei was so preoccupied with the philosophy of individualism and a nationalistic concept of socialist political purpose that it never formulated a theory of State which recognized the mutual interdependence of Japanese capitalism and nationalism under the Emperor. This lacuna was particularly notable in Akamatsu's 'realist socialism'. Akamatsu's myopia, according to Takagi, led to the co-optation of the Shaminkei by nationalism and the long-term collapse of the Shaminkei's struggle against capitalism. But, Akamatsu was not alone in his conceptual failure to perceive the link between capitalism and the Emperor system. Abe Isoo, Yoshino Sakuzō, and other Shaminkei thinkers were guilty of the same error.[51]

The Rōnōha, which had the indirect support of the communists, and the centrist Nichirōkei, possessed an altogether different political character. They sought to champion the interests of those elements in society who lacked any property – the *musan kaikyū*. They consciously used this term to distinguish themselves from the Shaminkei and its broader *kinrō kaikyū* concept. For the Rōnōha and the Nichirōkei, the *musan kaikyū* included the workers and the farmers, but not the petty class. They also used the term '*puroretariāto*' (proletariat), but with narrower reference to the most progressive stratum of the *musan kaikyū*, which was, in their view, the factory workers.[52]

The Rōnōha and the Nichirōkei socialists also differed from the Shaminkei in their concept of liberation. In general, they emphasized the liberation of the *musan kaikyū* as a collective force from the fetters of capitalism. They did not lay much stress on the liberation of the individual, which they felt to be a 'liberal', petty bourgeois priority. They also believed that the liberation of the *musan kaikyū* would eventually require a political revolution in Japan. Everything they did was in preparation for this anticipated event. But until conditions were ripe for revolution, they were prepared to strike a legal, parliamentarian posture in order to build up proletarian strength in the Diet, although they retained the option to review the appropriateness of such tactics and to shift to a more revolutionary emphasis as circumstances dictated.

The Rōnōha and the Nichirōkei relied upon their own instincts to know when such a shift should take place. The communists who backed the legal left, on the other hand, were willing to trust to the wisdom of the Comintern in deciding strategy and tactics.[53]

Commitment to revolution, of course, implied the desire to achieve the overthrow of both capitalism and the Emperor system. The strongest statement of this militant objective was made by the communists. The Rōnōha and the Nichirōkei were more equivocal about the Emperor. One gets the impression from their writings in the interwar period that their opposition to the Emperor system was more rhetorical than real, in comparison with the position of the communists. Even so, as Takagi suggests, the legal left and the centrists were more perceptive than the Shaminkei in seeing that the capitalist order and the Emperor system were mutually interdependent, which explains why they dismissed 'realist socialism' as a petty bourgeois, middle-class ideology and combined their attack on capitalism with denunciations of nationalism and imperialism in general, unlike the Shaminkei.[54]

The historical rise of the Nichirōkei has already been mentioned in connection with schisms in the labor movement. The Rōnōha, which emerged independently of the labor movement as a leftist alternative to communism during the course of disputes between men like Yamakawa Hitoshi and the Comintern after Yamakawa's break from the Japanese communist movement, need not be analyzed at length in this study.[55] It suffices to say that while both the centrist Nichirōkei and the Rōnōha advocated cooperation with the communists in waging class struggle, the Nichirōkei placed the greater emphasis on creating a massive socialist front that would include organizations led by the Shaminkei. The Rōnōha was not entirely opposed to such a front, but doubted the effectiveness of the front if it included the right-wing socialists because of their tendency to compromise with capitalism, nationalism, and imperialism. So the Rōnōha interpreted the Shaminkei.

Thus, the Rōnōtō concentrated on weaving an alliance with the centrist socialists (hoping to radicalize the latter) while the Nichirōkei endeavored to keep open the lines of communication to both the Shaminkei on its right and the Rōnōha and the communists on its left. For its part, the Shaminkei refused to have anything to do with the Rōnōha and the communists, although it was prepared to undertake ad hoc cooperation with the centrists in hopes of eventually weaning them away from the legal left.

Despite these cleavages in the socialist party movement, it is noteworthy that the political platforms of the Rōdō Nōmintō, the Rōnōtō, and the Shakai Minshūtō were very similar. Only minor differences of nuance can be found in reading them together. For instance, the Principles (*kōryō*) of the Rōdō Nōmintō stated:

1. We, taking into consideration the special national characteristics of this country, aim at the complete emancipation, political, economic, and social, of the proletarian class.
2. We aim at reforming by legislative means the present unfair conditions regarding land, production, and distribution of wealth.
3. We aim at the overthrow of the established political parties which represent only the interests of the privileged classes and at the thorough reform of the Imperial Diet.[56]

By comparison, the Principles of the Shakai Minshūtō went as follows:

1. We aim at the establishment of a political and economic regime with the working class as its foundation on which we believe the sound development of national life depends.
2. We aim at reforming by every rational means the capitalist system of production and distribution, the present condition of which is, we believe, injurious to the people's interests.
3. We oppose the established political parties which only represent the privileged classes and also the radical parties which ignore the processes of social evolution.[57]

The official policy statements of the centrist Rōnōtō, which need not be reiterated here, ran along the same lines. Except for point three in the Shakai Minshūtō Principles, the Shakai Minshūtō and the Rōdō Nōmintō were, in fact, practically indistinguishable in their *kōryō* even though they stood at the opposite ends of the socialist political spectrum. It is little wonder that some contemporary observers found it hard to tell these parties apart judging from their formal statements of policy.[58]

The three socialist parties were also quite similar in their specific programs of action. On matters pertaining to labor, for instance, all three called for the legalization of unions, legislation to arbitrate labor disputes, reduction of work hours, various measures to improve working conditions, and a higher minimum wage. Relatively greater emphasis on labor questions was asserted by the Shakai Minshūtō than the others, because of the insistence of the Sōdōmei upon this priority. But in general, the parties covered the same terrain in the area of labor objectives. Similarly, all three parties expressed demands on behalf of the tenant farmers such as legalization of their unions, legislation to arbitrate their disputes with landlords, rent reduction, and so forth. Party platform planks concerning the farmers were most developed by the Rōdō Nōmintō, which had the greatest support of the farmers thanks to the Nōmin Kumiai, and by the Rōnōtō. The Shakai Minshūtō, by comparison, devoted relatively little attention to the farmers but did not ignore them completely.[59]

The Shakai Minshūtō, Rōnōtō, and Rōdō Nōmintō were likewise unanimous in demanding reform of the educational system, public relief for small and medium factories, nationalization of utilities, social security, tax reform, and cuts in military spending. Moreover, they placed equal emphasis on opposing the conservative influence of the *genrō, hanbatsu* (ruling cliques), and the established 'bourgeois' parties. The Shakai Minshūtō was clearest in supporting the Emperor system but the Rōnōto and the Rōdō Nōmintō also professed loyalty to the Emperor, albeit in perfunctory terms.[60]

Furthermore, they agreed on certain specific objectives in the area of foreign affairs. They all called for 'people's diplomacy' which meant the end of secret agreements between governments; racial equality; freedom of migration; and the principle of noninterference in the internal affairs of other nations.[61] Similarly, the parties opposed all manifestations of Japanese imperialism. For instance, on the China question, they criticized the military expeditions sent to China by the administration of Prime Minister Tanaka Giichi (president of the Seiyūkai) in 1927 and 1928. The landing of Japanese troops at Tsinan in 1928 was said to be the first step in Tanaka's plan to make the Shantung area a special preserve for Japanese capitalists at the expense of the Chinese. In general, the Shakai Minshūtō, Rōdō Nōmintō, and Rōnōtō declared their support for the 'Chinese people' against Japanese militarism and imperialism. However, only the Shakai Minshūtō voiced strong support for the government of Chiang Kai-shek in Nanking. After Chiang split from the Chinese communists in 1927, the Rōdō Nōmintō and the Rōnōtō tended to side with the latter in their attitude toward Chinese political developments.[62]

The socialist alignments in Japan did differ, however, on the issue of international linkages. The Shaminkei backed the International Labor Organization, which was opposed by the other two cliques. Thus, when the Secretary General of the ILO visited Japan in December 1928, he was hosted only by the Sōdōmei and the other organizations in its labor bloc which sent representatives to meet him at the pier in Yokohama.

Unlike their European counterparts, none of the Japanese socialists associated themselves with the Second International. But the Shaminkei professed some sympathy for it while the legal left opposed it in preference to the Third International, the Comintern. Correspondingly, the Shaminkei opposed the Third International. The Nichirōkei waxed ambiguous on this question but implied tacit support for the Third International.[63]

In connection with this, the Shaminkei was enthusiastic about forging links with other moderate Asian labor movements. As early as 1925 Suzuki Bunji had broached the matter of a possible congress of Asian labor unions in discussions with an Indian labor representative at the ILO.[64] Similar proposals along the same lines were made by the Sōdōmei later in the 1920s, although nothing came of them until the 1930s. By contrast, the Hyōgikai was interested solely in establishing links with the Pan-Pacific Trade Union Secretariat, a Comintern-influenced organization located in Shanghai.[65]

A difference of policy toward the Soviet Union also existed. The Rōdō Nōmintō emphasized the defense of Russia as the 'land of workers and farmers'. The Shakai Minshūtō, in line with its anti-communism, extended no such support. The Rōnōtō carved out an intermediate position on the Soviet issue by expressing general admiration for the Soviet Union without, however, doing so in strong terms.[66]

Since the socialist parties were generally mirror-images of one another in terms of their respective programs, it is unlikely that these programs were decisive in perpetuating the rivalry that existed between the Rōdō Nōmintō, Shakai Minshūtō, and Rōnōtō. Rather, personal antagonisms and ideological differences supplied most of the vitriol for their continuing, corrosive conflict. Yet, because their programs were fundamentally the same, they had trouble distinguishing themselves from each other in the eyes of the voters. This was particularly true of the centrist Rōnōtō which sought to occupy a middle ground between its socialist competitors, just as the Nihon Rōdō Kumiai Dōmei tried to clarify its identity while being sandwiched in between the Sōdōmei and the Hyōgikai in the labor movement. But neither the centrist party nor its labor base overcame the problem of blurred image, and both remained weak in comparison with the right and left wings of the socialist movement.

To reiterate, the socialist party movement in the 1926–1928 period consisted of a confused array of alignments, each possessing its own ideology, definition of class interest, and approaches to problems of strategy and tactics, but all overlapping to some extent in their various platforms and programs of political action. However, despite their disunity, the socialist parties in the late 1920s together offered the most vigorous advocacy of progressive alternatives to the existing order that Japan had yet witnessed. Moreover, during their early years the socialist parties displayed certain signs of potential effectiveness as bearers of 'Taishō democracy' in the future by virtue of a promising pattern of articulation with the grass roots social movements, including organized labor, which supplied the parties with their main popular support. This may be illustrated in the case of the Shakai Minshūtō and the Nihon Rōdō Sōdōmei on the right wing of the socialist movement, first with regard to their interaction in the 'Great Noda Strike' of 1927–1928 and second, in the coordination of their activities during the elections of 1927 and 1928.

Learning the ropes of socialist opposition: labor–party articulation in the Great Noda Strike

The labor strike at the Noda Soy Sauce Company in the town of Noda (Chiba Prefecture) from September 1927 to April 1928 was the longest in duration of any industrial action in Japan until then. It began when the Company rejected the demands of the Noda local of the Sōdōmei's Kantō Brewery Labor Union for higher pay, improved working conditions, and recognition by management of the local as the spokesman for the workers in collective bargaining. From the start, the Sōdōmei central committee wanted to make the strike a showcase for its support of worker grievances to demonstrate that the Hyōgikai's accusations of softness were ill-founded and that the General Federation was not above waging militant strikes when negotiations for the attainment of worker rights failed.

In his detailed study of the Noda strike, Totten observes that the Noda local had become very active politically since its establishment in 1921.[67] In 1925, the local had inaugurated the Noda Labor School, the program of which gave greater weight to political activism than was usually the case in the Sōdōmei's labor schools.[68] After the enactment of universal manhood suffrage, the local had been instrumental in founding the Chiba Minseitō which later became a strong pillar of the Shakai Minshūtō.[69] Totten writes, 'political action had, by the time of the strike, become a normative aspect of local union activities' at Noda.[70] Since the owner and management of the Soy Sauce Company supported the Seiyūkai, the Noda strike rapidly assumed the character of a political confrontation.

The strike was as large in scale as it was long in duration. Out of a total of 2,092 workers at Noda, 1,358 took part. Refusing to make any concessions, the Company began firing strikers in December 1927 and hired temporary workers to take their place so that production of its soy sauce products, which came onto the market bearing the familiar label of Kikkōman, could continue. The Company also hired strike-breakers who attacked the workers demonstrating peacefully on their picket lines. By early 1928, emotions ran high at Noda. Already, the Sōdōmei central committee had poured money into the local's strike fund and Sōdōmei leaders went to Noda regularly to give advice on how to keep the strike alive. The general responsibility for supervising the strike was given to Matsuoka Komakichi. It was hoped his long experience in the labor movement would assist the beleaguered local.[71]

Significantly, the Shakai Minshūtō also decided to throw its weight behind the workers, a step that was taken after the Party's first annual convention of December 1927.[72] Party officials were sent to Noda to observe the strike and to lend assistance. At the same time, the Party organized a national boycott of the Company's products (the first time this was done in connection with a strike) in order to arouse public awareness of, and support for, the strike.[73] In their campaigns during the elections of February 1928, Shakai Minshūtō candidates constantly defended the strikers against the Company and Shakai Minshūtō men who won seats in the Diet frequently took to the Diet floor to criticize the Company and the 'reactionary' Tanaka cabinet which had backed the Company in the strike.[74] In short, the Party made the strike into a cause of its own and did much to publicize nationally the crisis at Noda.

Unfortunately for the strikers, the Noda strike ended in failure. Before it reached a final stage, Matsuoka tried in desperation to persuade the famous entrepreneur, Shibusawa Eiichi, a former friend of Suzuki Bunji and vice president of the Kyōchōkai, to mediate in the dispute. However, Shibusawa declined. Finally, only 300 of the strikers were permitted by the Company to return to their jobs. The rest were dismissed and blacklisted; the strike 'in effect destroyed the union'.[75]

However, in assessing the wider significance of the Noda upheaval, Totten states that because the strike prompted the Company to later upgrade working conditions and establish a wage system based on the seniority of permanent workers at Noda in order to assuage past grievances, 'The improvement of the conditions of the workers clearly came through the threat or exercise of collective action by the workers.'[76] The view that labor strikes such as the one at Noda generally served to pressure management into making concessions to the workers in this period is also shared by Koji Taira who writes, 'The prevalence of industrial disputes...indicates that workers, with or without the unions' help, had some notion of minimum tolerable standards...and were able to enforce these basic demands on employers when the latter grossly transgressed workers' customary expectations...By this kind of veto power, workers and unions were telling employers of the minimum price that had to be paid for employing labor services.'[77] Taira concludes that the role of the unions in waging strikes 'seems to suggest that unions sharpened the issues and intensified confrontation to such an extent that workers and employers were forced to take clearer stands than they would otherwise have taken',[78] and that although the labor movement was small in scale, 'the power of unions displayed through industrial disputes frightened the government and employers' into granting concessions to labor.[79]

It is perhaps debatable whether the unions did in fact have this much 'veto power' in dealing with management or whether strikes 'frightened the government and employers' as much as Taira suggests.[80] On the other hand, given the tendency of employers and the government to fear industrial disruption, the strikes of this period and the involvement of unions in them may well have induced the establishment to respond flexibly to worker demands in many instances, particularly when it became apparent, as at Noda, that the union concerned had not operated in a political vacuum but rather that it had enjoyed the full support of a new and assertive socialist political party. For their part, the Sōdōmei and the Shakai Minshūtō had demonstrated at Noda the potential achievements for the goals of social democracy by cooperating on an issue that concerned them both: the Sōdōmei dispute had given the Party an opportunity to gain considerable public visibility by taking a strong stand in the Diet on behalf of the Noda strikers while the Federation had been able to use the Party to draw attention to its cause.

Labor, socialist politics, and the elections of 1927 and 1928

The potential benefits of labor–party articulation in the political sphere for the growth of the Japanese socialist movement in the future were also evident in the close cooperation of the Sōdōmei and the Shakai

Minshūtō in their mutual endeavor to develop the Party as rapidly as possible and to elect Party candidates to seats in the prefectural assemblies and the Diet in 1927 and 1928, respectively.

From the beginning of their relationship, the Sōdōmei and the Shakai Minshūtō were distinct, autonomous organizations. Indeed, the political bureau of the Sōdōmei had insisted on labor's autonomy vis-à-vis a national proletarian party as early as 1925 in its report to the Sōdōmei convention of that year. This emphasized that the Federation should follow the examples of the British and German socialist labor movements in maintaining a separate identity in relation to its socialist party ally.[81] Accordingly, the Sōdōmei adopted the formula of encouraging its workers to join the Shakai Minshūtō as individuals rather than have the unions automatically affiliate with the Party as groups.[82] Labor's autonomy from the Party was emphasized for a further reason: if the Party was too closely identified with the labor movement, its appeal to other proletarian groups such as the agrarian unions, and to the petty bourgeoisie, would be lessened.[83]

Nevertheless, it was clear that the Sōdōmei and the Shakai Minshūtō would work closely together, and that in the political sphere they would act in unison. As promised in the Party's inaugural convention, most of the thirty-seven branches that were founded across the country, and a regional party federation established in Tokyo during the first year of the Party's existence had Sōdōmei organizations as their nuclei.[84] For instance, the Kanagawa branch of the Shakai Minshūtō, established on December 11, 1926, relied almost exclusively on the Sōdōmei's Kanagawa Federation which supplied the branch with most of its members (except for Katayama Tetsu, the branch chairman) and even its offices, which were located in the same building that housed those of this *rengōkai* in Kawasaki. Indeed, the inaugural ceremonies marking the founding of the branch resembled those usually conducted on the occasion of the opening of a new Sōdōmei union. All of the speakers were Sōdōmei officials including Suzuki, Nishio, Matsuoka, and Akamatsu who exhorted the assembled throng, composed mostly of Sōdōmei workers, to support the branch of the Party as if it were a Sōdōmei union. Above them the Sōdōmei flag flew next to that of the Shakai Minshūtō, symbolizing the close links between the two organizations.[85]

The tight interdependence of the Sōdōmei and the Shakai Minshūtō was also apparent in the national leadership of the Party, for in most instances the same men who served on the Sōdōmei central committee also served in this capacity on the Party's executive. Moreover, the Sōdōmei central committee was the principal source of election campaign funds for the Shakai Minshūtō, and, when Sōdōmei unionists joined the local Party branch, they paid fifty *sen* per annum to the branch, ten *sen* of which went to the Shakai Minshūtō national treasury.[86]

But the most significant illustration of the articulation between the Sōdōmei and the Shakai Minshūtō was the role played by the Sōdōmei's political bureau in advising the Party central committee on electioneering strategies and techniques, beginning with the prefectural elections of 1927 and in 1928 the first national elections since the passage of Universal Manhood Suffrage. Virtually every aspect of the Party's campaigns in these elections originated in the political bureau of the General Federation.[87]

The campaign preparations for these elections were very thorough. For example, at a special conference called by the Shakai Minshūtō and the Sōdōmei in July 1927 to plan for the prefectural elections, arrangements were made to determine a list of candidates for the Party ticket, produce campaign posters and leaflets, coordinate national electioneering tours by prominent Party officials who were to speak on behalf of the candidates, distribute campaign funds to the candidates, and so forth.[88] Special committees were also established to study the election laws in order to avoid infractions and to study local conditions in the interest of identifying slogans which might appeal to the electorate.[89] The Party also appointed its own inspectors to watch the polls for signs of election interference by the authorities or the opposing parties.[90] Similar plans were laid in anticipation of the 1928 general elections.[91]

The electioneering techniques that resulted, which were typical of those implemented by the other proletarian parties, may be illustrated by several examples taken from the 1928 elections. Since election regulations prohibited the use of the radio, the telephoning or interviewing of voters in house-to-house canvassing, parades, or the wooing of votes through entertainments involving the offering of food or drinks, a premium was necessarily placed on winning votes through the medium of public campaign oratory and the drawing of attention to candidates through the use of posters and bills (the sizes of which were also regulated).[92] Accordingly, in his campaign for the Diet from the Osaka fourth district, Suzuki Bunji, supported mainly by the Sōdōmei's Osaka *rengōkai*, spent most of his time giving speeches in the district and supervising the pasting up of posters bearing pictures of himself and describing him as the 'father of the labor movement' or as 'the distinguished Japanese labor delegate to the International Labor Organization'.[93]

A typical scene in Suzuki's campaign was an address he delivered to an assembled crowd from the balcony of the Ukita Inn opposite the Osaka train station. Appealing for votes, Suzuki said 'I have been active for twenty years in the proletarian movement...The majority of the laboring classes (*kinrō kaikyū*) of this country are now in a state of unrest. It is the duty of the government today to pacify this unrest by meeting the needs of the livelihood of the people...' After this speech, Suzuki's assistants distributed campaign bills among the crowd.[94]

Katayama Tetsu, running in 1928 for election from the Kanagawa second district, also gave campaign speeches in which he elaborated on the Shakai Minshūtō's election slogans, 'Heavy taxes on the wealthy, reduced taxes on the poor!', 'Lower interest rates, rent, and prices!'.[95] Katayama recalls, too, how he personally went around the district pasting up campaign posters and helping his assistants prepare campaign signs which were displayed during his speeches.[96] Asō Hisashi, running from the Tochigi first district on the Nihon Rōnōtō ticket, campaigned in similar fashion as he tried to muster votes among the copper mining workers in the Ashio region.[97]

All of the proletarian candidates in 1928 received much support from their respective organized labor bases. For instance, Sōdōmei unionists were conspicuous in doing the various jobs, such as making and distributing posters and bills, associated with the Shakai Minshūtō campaigns and in some instances acted as campaign managers for the candidates in their regions (as with Kanemasa for Nishio in the Osaka third district), a strategy that was intended to arouse voter enthusiasm among the unions for Shakai Minshūtō candidates. Meanwhile, *Rōdō* regularly covered the campaigns in its pages, emphasizing the particular merits of each candidate and his contributions to the labor movement, past and present. Extensive biographical sketches of the candidates were also published in *Minshū Shimbun*, the Party organ. Suzuki Bunji and Abe Isoo received the greatest attention in this respect as the Party sought to capitalize on their considerable public visibility – Suzuki's as 'father of the labor movement' and Abe's as a long-time participant in the socialist movement and as head of the Party.[98]

Yet, despite all these vigorous efforts, the Shakai Minshūtō and the other proletarian parties did not fare well in the elections of 1927 and 1928. In 1927, between them, they managed to elect only twenty-eight of 204 candidates to the prefectural assemblies; thirteen from the Rōdō Nōmintō, four from the Nihon Nōmintō (Japan Farmers' Party) organized by Hirano Rikizō in 1926, three each from the Shakai Minshūtō and the Nihon Rōnōtō, and five others from assorted local proletarian parties.[99] In the 1928 general elections, the leftist parties entered eighty-eight candidates but elected only eight to the Diet. Suzuki, and Abe, who ran from the Tokyo second district, Nishio and Kamei Kan'ichirō (from the Osaka third and Fukuoka second districts respectively) were the successful candidates from the Shakai Minshūtō while other prominent candidates in that Party, including Katayama and Akamatsu Katsumaro, ran and lost.[100]

Ōyama Ikuo, head of the Rōdō Nōmintō and Asō Hisashi, head of the Rōnōtō, also ran and lost. The only victorious candidate from Asō's party was Kawakami Jōtarō who later became one of the most important men in the centrist socialist camp.[101] Aside from the proletarian parties, the Seiyūkai, which had been in power before the elections, emerged with the balance of power still in its hands in the lower house, but only by a one-vote margin over the Rikken Minseitō (Constitutional Democratic Party, formed in 1927 as a successor to the Kenseikai), so that, along with several other small splinter groups in the Diet, the proletarian parties possessed a 'casting vote'.[102]

The poor showing of the proletarian parties, particularly in the 1928 elections, arose from a multiplicity of factors. First, very few of their candidates, with the exception of Suzuki or Abe, had much public visibility among the electorate, and suffered at the polls accordingly. Second, it is likely that many voters were suspicious of any and all parties associated with 'socialism' and hence failed to give these parties their vote. Third, lack of funds prohibited the proletarian parties from committing the vast financial resources commanded by the major established parties to their campaigns. Abe, for instance, spent only 5,610 yen in his campaign,[103] and Katayama less than 2,000 yen.[104] This contrasted with the 50,000 yen spent per candidate by the Seiyūkai and Minseitō, each committing approximately five million in the elections of the interwar period.[105] As one writer observed in 1929, 'The lavish use of decorated posters is expensive; the hiring of halls and telephones is an added burden; the election law requires a deposit of two thousand yen to be forfeited in case the candidate fails to win a certain percentage of votes and finally there exists in some constituencies an active competitive bribery.'[106] Clearly, the limited funds of the proletarian parties were no match for these expenses.

Fourth, the proletarian parties often experienced disruption of their campaigns at the hands of the police or other opponents. Their 'election workers were arrested and political meetings suppressed on flimsy excuses', in what has been described as an attempt at 'systematic oppression' of proletarian candidates.[107] To cite the example of Asō Hisashi's 1928 Ashio campaign, 'The Ashio Copper Mining Company...brought severe pressure upon the miners, threatening dismissal and actually suspending ten employees for political views while the aid of the police was secured to close public halls and break up evening meetings.'[108] So great was the Company's determination to block Asō that it contributed money to both the Seiyūkai and Minseitō candidates in this election.[109]

Fifth, by failing to coordinate in placing candidates, the proletarian parties fell prey to the exigencies of Japan's multi-member single vote system of proportional representation in which each district sent from three to five men to the Diet. All too often the proletarian parties undercut each other by running more candidates than they could reasonably expect to see elected in a given district. 'An analysis of the electoral returns [in 1928] indicates that if the labor parties had effected agreements in nine districts where their candidates opposed each other, the proletariat would have had a good chance to send seventeen members to the Diet instead of eight.'[110] But because coordination did not generally take place and because the proletarian candidates spent as much time attacking their left-wing party rivals as they did the established parties, they succumbed to what Maurice Duverger has called the fate of 'permanent minority parties' in this type of electoral system.[111]

All of these problems continued to bedevil the proletarian parties in the 1930s although their electioneering tactics, generally much the same as in 1927 and 1928, later included various attempts at coordination in the placement of candidates from the different parties to avoid the sort of mutual splitting of proletarian votes which ate into their performance in 1928. Indeed, the imperative of greater coordination was seen immediately after the 1928 elections when the Shakai Minshūto took the lead in forming a joint-consultative committee of proletarian members of the Diet with the other parties so that at least in the Diet the otherwise divided socialist movement could speak with one voice.[112]

Political strategists in the Sōdōmei and the Shakai Minshūto, disappointed that the Party had done so poorly in 1927 and 1928, tried to determine what action to take in the future to strengthen the Shakai Minshūtō at the polls. One early step in this direction was the formation of the Nihon Nōmin Kumiai Sōdōmei (Japan General Federation of Farmers' Unions) in 1927, intended to lend the Party more support from the countryside where the Nihon Nōmin Kumiai displayed an impressive capacity to deliver votes to the Rōdō Nōmintō.[113] The Nichirōkei followed suit by forming a similar rural political organization, the Zenkoku Nōmin Kumiai (National Farmers' Union), to support the Rōnōtō.[114] In addition, the Shaminkei laid plans to attract more votes from the salaried workers, who were regarded as part of the *kinrō kaikyū*, the Party's natural constituency.[115] But it remained axiomatic in the Shaminkei that organized labor, centering on the Nihon Rōdō Sōdōmei and its labor bloc, was still the main core of popular support for the Shakai Minshūtō.[116]

This latter emphasis on the indispensable ties between the Shakai Minshūtō and the Sōdōmei reflected the fact that without the support of the Federation and its labor bloc, the Party would scarcely have been a viable alternative to the Rōdō Nōmintō and the Rōnōtō in proletarian party politics and that without the support of the Shakai Minshūtō in the Diet, the Sōdōmei could not expect to make much headway in achieving labor reforms through a progressive alliance with an ideologically 'responsible' socialist party in the cause of 'realist socialism'.

However, the same emphasis on the ultimate priority of Sōdōmei–Shakai Minshūtō cooperation within a divided socialist movement also reflected a far more negative reality pertaining to the socialist movement in general: the lasting cleavages of the socialist parties which diminished their capacity to assist the social movements now reliant upon them in the quest for democratic reforms. Without the resolution of the problem of labor disunity, such a disastrous contribution to proletarian party disunity in the 1920s, these splits would continue. Kenneth Colegrove, writing in 1929, expressed this problem as follows:

> The fundamental problem confronting the new parties appears to involve the difference between labor unions and labor parties. The former movement aims to organize the workingmen for the purpose of the collective bargain. The latter aims to secure an adequate voice for the proletariat in the legislative halls of the nation. Both movements are phases of the class struggle, but distinctive phases. The present trend in the labor movement has been not toward an all-Japan federation but rather in the direction of federations of the right and left. Hence, until a greater degree of political

unity appears in the economic organization of labor, political cohesion cannot be assured.[117]

In the late 1920s, it was not inconceivable that if the labor movement could be united in the interests of fostering unity between the proletarian parties, Japan might yet gradually evolve in the direction of social democracy. As a more recent student of the period has remarked in characterizing the situation which confronted the labor movement on the threshold of the Depression,

> In politics, there was a glimpse of leverage even in the Imperial Diet when the social democrats...got a 'casting vote'. Even sections of the bureaucracy were more favorably disposed than was business to the enactment of a labor law that would give legal sanction to unions and collective bargaining agreements. The military was comparatively quiescent at the time, suffering from internal factional quarrels. In this environment, it was not a foregone conclusion that 'sound' union–management relations could not develop.[118]

Unfortunately, however, when new and adverse conditions in the economic and political environment of labor developed during the Depression period of 1929–1932, prodding elements of the labor and socialist party movements to close ranks for the sake of survival, the dynamics of cooperation at the labor and political party levels of 'Taishō democracy' were dissimilar: whereas the socialist parties sought unity mainly to defend socialism, the labor movement, influenced by the Sōdōmei and its increasing conservatism, sought unity primarily to defend unionism. In this endeavor it retreated from its previous commitment to socialist politics into a depoliticized zone of action that all but neutralized organized labor as a factor in the struggle for democracy.

6

Labor's retreat from socialist politics, 1929–1932

From the time of its 'eruption' late in the First World War, the labor movement had made the achievement of democracy in Japan through political action its central mission. Although the precise definition of democracy and the specific means to achieve it had been variously interpreted in different sections of the movement, in general, democracy had signified the liberation of the workers from political and economic deprivation and the attainment of their basic human rights. This movement was part of a larger impulse to rebuild Japan in a new image of freedom and equality, either through reform or revolution.

In this context, the liberal–capitalist order, epitomised by the *kisei seitō* (established parties) and the *zaibatsu*, had out of expedience granted to the moderate mainstream of the labor movement, comprising the Nihon Rōdō Sōdōmei, the Nihon Rōdō Kumiai Dōmei, and their respective blocs, a certain maneuvering space for the pursuit of reformist socialism on condition that these organizations would act as a buffer between liberalism and capitalism on the one hand and anarchist and communist labor in the factories on the other. Organizations such as the Sōdōmei had sought to exploit this situation by adhering to the 'realist socialist' assumption that the encouragement of the progressive aspects of liberalism in the short run would eventually result in the elimination of the exploitation of the workers under capitalism. After the enactment of Universal Manhood Suffrage in 1925, it had been axiomatic in the General Federation, and throughout the moderate labor movement, that organized labor would support a socialist party movement working to this end by representing the workers and seeking legislation on their behalf in the Diet in the broader cause of social democracy.

Since the socialist labor movement operated at the sufferance of liberalism and capitalism, the success of these strategies depended on the good health of liberalism and, ironically perhaps, on the continued good health of capitalism, the fate of which was inextricably linked to the fate of liberalism. But, despite the fact that the so-called 'liberal' 1920s marked the zenith of the *kisei seitō* and the *zaibatsu*, the truth is that neither Japanese liberalism nor Japanese capitalism was very strong.

In the 1920s, liberal party politicians often spoke of the lower house of the Diet as being the 'center' of politics (*gikaichūshinshugi*),[1] and of liberal party government as being the 'normal path of constitutional government' (*kensei no jōdō*).[2] But the powers of the lower house continued to be curtailed by the Meiji Constitution and it is doubtful whether liberalism represented the 'normal' trends of the times as its proponents, and indeed some socialists, believed. Historians have shown that because of their insecurity in relation to the Peers, the bureaucracy, and the military, the liberal parties compromised with these elites in attaining and maintaining political power in this decade, at the expense of any progressive potential inherent in Japanese liberal political philosophy.[3]

Moreover, although Japanese capitalism, particularly the burgeoning strength of the *zaibatsu*, seemed unassailable, Japan's uneven economic growth in the complex 'economic muddle of the 1920s'[4] revealed that its accomplishments in this period were offset considerably by serious problems. These included the chronic weakness of banking institutions, the vulnerability of small and medium enterprises to extinction in times of reduced economic growth, and the continued sluggishness of the agricultural sector after World War I.[5]

Nor did Japanese capitalism prove to be a strong ally of political liberalism. As Robert Scalapino remarks, 'In the absence of a theory which would recognize the legitimacy of private interests, there was a compulsion on the part of the business class to protect and advance its interests', working through the liberal parties which shared the same objective, 'with minimal resort to open political action or democratic procedures'.[6] He adds, 'In Japan, capitalism created great social and economic problems...without building any solid liberal foundations in its society. It could produce neither spectacular improvements in living standards nor a dynamic new political philosophy. Consequently, it operated', along with liberalism in general, 'under the threat of revolutionary attack, with few of the circumstances present which would encourage democratic tactics or moderation'.[7]

As long as this revolutionary attack had come from anarchism and communism on the left, the liberal–capitalist order was in little danger, for it could mobilize national support for the defense of the *kokutai* from the menace of leftist radicalism in the 1920s. The consequent fit between liberalism, capitalism, and nationalism had compelled the socialist movement, particularly its right wing, to attach itself to the established order in an attempt to make socialism compatible with all three. But when, in the Depression and thereafter, the revolutionary attack came from the right, feeding on a groundswell of sentiments loosely described by historians as 'ultranationalism',[8] the liberal parties and the *zaibatsu* were thrown onto the defensive.

Inevitably, their insecurity and decline, beginning in 1929, produced a parallel crisis in the socialist movement which also felt threatened by the same forces that had placed liberalism and capitalism under siege. This was, again, especially true of the Shaminkei socialists in the labor and proletarian party movements who had identified most closely with the status quo under liberalism and capitalism. One by one, elements of the socialist movement therefore abandoned socialism to survive in the new circumstances of the Depression period. Significantly, this retreat from socialist politics began not at the level of the proletarian parties in the socialist movement but rather, at the lower level of the movement's labor base, specifically in the Nihon Rōdō Sōdōmei and its labor bloc.

Labor's environment in the Depression, 1929–1932

Before examining the withdrawal of labor from socialist politics and assessing its significance, it is necessary to recapitulate briefly the well-known economic and political factors prompting this retraction in the 1929–1932 period. To begin with, there is no doubt that the economic impact of the Depression, beginning in 1929, greatly heightened the insecurity of the Japanese labor movement and contributed significantly to the weakening of labor's commitment to socialism.

In the early stages of the Depression, the government of Japan was administered by the cabinet of Prime Minister Hamaguchi Yūkō of the Minseitō. He had come to power in July 1929 after his predecessor, Tanaka Giichi, had resigned, taking responsibility for the murder by the Japanese Kwantung Army in Manchuria of the puppet warlord, Chang Tso-lin.[9] Believing that the collapse of the New York stock market was only temporary, the government returned to the gold standard (effective January 1930) with the result that the economy was strained beyond control. As Hugh Patrick points out, this measure was taken 'when the world economy had just begun to toboggan down into the most serious and extended crisis it has ever had to suffer'.[10]

As world prices plunged, prices in Japan followed suit because 'accelerated deflation in Japan could not keep pace'.[11] Wholesale prices in Japan, which had already plummeted at a rate of 20 per cent in the 1925–1929 period, dropped by another 20 per cent in 1930.[12] This trend was especially calamitous in the price of raw silk which fell 50 per cent after the bottom dropped out of the American silk market which had absorbed much of Japan's silk exports in the 1920s.[13] Thus, Japanese silk exports correspondingly fell in value during 1930 to only 53 per cent of their value at the 1929 rates.[14] This trend persisted in 1931. The price of rice in Japan also fell in 1930, due in part to an almost ironical abundance of the rice harvest.[15]

The result was chaos in Japanese villages and the effects continued for most of the 1930s as the rural economy remained crippled by the Depression.[16] But the effect of the Depression on industry was similarly catastrophic, albeit less sustained than on the rural economy. The collapse of Japan's international markets caused a sudden drop in production and the liquidation of hundreds of firms (823 in 1930 alone, according to one source),[17] most of which were in the small and medium categories of industry. The hardest hit by the Depression were those in the textile industry which increasingly lost its dominant position in the industrial economy in favor of heavy industry; this trend was encouraged by the subsequent reflation policies of Finance Minister Takahashi Korekiyo which, by investing intensively in heavy industry, encouraged a relative shift from textiles to heavy industry during the 1930s.[18]

In general, the government's strategy for dealing with the impact of the Depression on industry was to promote *sangyō gōrika* (industrial rationalization) in order to improve the efficiency of, and lower the production costs in, depression-ridden enterprises. A Bureau of Industrial Rationalization was established in the Ministry of Commerce and Industry in 1930 to this end.[19] Under the Bureau's recommendation, and that of the Finance Ministry, the government also invested massive infusions of capital from the Bank of Japan into heavy industry which enabled the *zaibatsu* to emerge from the Depression in complete domination of the industrial economy whereas small and medium-scale firms, which did not receive such support, withered in relative importance.[20] As a result the tendency toward industrial dualism, already prevalent in the 1920s, was accelerated still further.

The increasingly dualistic structure of industry benefited the large firms, moreover, in the sense that they were able to absorb the skilled workers, whom they needed to expand production during the recovery period, from weaker, smaller firms that were forced to shut down or retrench in this period. Koji Taira states, 'On the strength of superior conditions of employment' and higher wages, 'large firms during the 1930s were able to hire as many workers as they wanted at the standards of quality and skill they prescribed without necessarily [or constantly] raising wages relative to other firms and industries'.[21] Large firms were also able to retain, and add to, their skilled workers by dismissing the cushion of *rinji-kō* as a means of cutting costs in the 1930s.

The implementation of *sangyō gōrika* on a greater scale than ever before during the Depression meant that all of the features of the *nenkō* system and techniques of assembly-line production, discussed earlier in relation to industrial paternalism, multiplied in heavy industry during the 1930s.[22] These trends worked against the labor movement in the same ways that they had in the 1920s. Unions in large firms were pressed increasingly into the *kigyōbetsu kumiai* mold, leaving the horizontal thrust of the labor movement even more confined to the precarious domain of the small and medium enterprises, with all of the attendant problems for unions noted earlier.

The immediate repercussions of the Depression for the factory workers were unprecedented in severity, if rather uneven in nature. In the aggregate, skilled workers did not fare too badly. Those skilled workers in the large, modern plants suffered only a slight reduction of their money wages – their real wages actually rose between 1929 and 1933.[23] Indeed, for them, real wages reached an unprecedented high in 1931.[24] But the situation was quite different for the mass of unskilled labor. The sharp fall in prices eroded the money wages of unskilled workers and their real wages fell by 20 per cent in the Depression before they stabilized again in the mid-1930s.[25] The effect of these trends was most noticeable in small and medium-scale firms.

Another problem caused by the Depression for the workers was massive unemployment, as a result of cut-backs in production. Between 1928 and 1931, factory employment dropped by 13 per cent.[26] Not until 1933 did it reach the 1928 levels again.[27] Contemporary figures vary widely on rates of unemployment. In the national census of October 1930, the figure stood at 322,527 unemployed. But, according to statistics published by the Social Affairs Bureau of the Home Ministry, there were 340,000 unemployed workers in January that year. The Bureau put unemployment in December 1930 at 362,000.[28]

By contrast, two private, independent surveys registered the number of unemployed by the end of 1930 between 2,370,000 and 3,150,000 workers.[29] Similarly high estimates were also recorded by different elements of the labor movement.[30] As Ōkōchi Kazuo suggests, virtually every survey conducted by the government, labor, or private sources rested on questionable sampling techniques, which makes it difficult to ascertain precisely how many workers were unemployed during the Depression.[31] Still, even the more modest figures suggest the awesome scale of the unemployment problem in this period, particularly in small and medium enterprises.

Confronted with massive insecurity, the workers of Japan struck hard and often in the Depression. For example, in 1931 alone, there were 2,415 labor disputes, involving 152,161 workers – an all-time high for industrial action in interwar Japan.[32] Most of these disputes concerned the traditional issues which had troubled the workers in the past and which had become even more serious in the Depression: unemployment, wage cuts, and the absence of any effective unemployment relief. Whereas in 1928 14.6 per cent of the disputes had involved protest over wages, in 1930 this issue gave rise to 32.1 per cent. Similarly, while 17.7 per cent of disputes in 1928 were over dismissals of workers, this problem was central in 28.1 per cent of disputes in 1930.[33] In many instances, these grievances, and others, such as poor work conditions, were combined in strikes.

In general, the entire atmosphere of the Depression period can be summed up in the phrase 'restless movement'. In Tokyo, and in other cities, it was as common as in the West to see crowds of unemployed workers in their *mompei* (baggy trousers) milling about in parks and on street corners, or waiting in soup lines maintained by the Salvation Army. Huge labor rallies were constantly staged in city parks; the demonstrations of May Day in 1930 and 1931 were among the strongest ever seen at Hibiya Park in Tokyo.[34] When strikes erupted, they were often frenzied. During the continuous strikes at Tokyo Muslin, for instance, streaming crowds of angry workers marched, with arms locked, on the Company gates, to the beat of a large drum placed at the head of their surging ranks. But they were repeatedly driven back by hired strike-breakers using water hoses. When the Company retaliated by dismissing the strike leaders, the protest grew all the more ferocious.[35]

Although most of the strikes in the Depression were by workers who had not been organized into unions, unions were often spontaneously

involved. For example, the Osaka *rengōkai* of the Sōdōmei reported
that it had engaged in fifty labor disputes from late 1930 to November
1931. Altogether, 3,592 of its members had taken part.[36] Sōdōmei
unions were also active in the great Tokyo Municipal Tramway strike
of 1929, the rash of disputes that occurred in many Japanese spinning
mills in 1930 and 1931, and a major series of struggles at the Tokyo
Muslin Company, also in 1930 and 1931, to name but a few.[37] Perhaps
because of this involvement, the General Federation attracted new
members in the Depression. By late 1931, it had 44,209 workers
organized into sixty-eight unions and eight sizeable regional labor
federations.[38] Other labor organizations also swelled. As mentioned
earlier in this study, the rate of unionization in interwar Japan peaked
in 1931 with 368,975 workers, or 7.9 per cent of the work force,
organized into 818 unions.

Some socialists were persuaded by the deleterious economic conditions of the Depression and the attendant new wave of labor unrest
that capitalism was about to collapse in Japan, and indeed throughout
the West, and that therefore the time was ripe for moving ahead quickly
toward the long-awaited socialist reconstruction (*kaizō*) of the country.
According to Uchida Sakurō and Okada Sōji, who told the author in
separate interviews that this represented their feelings in the Depression,
this bold reading of events was especially prevalent in the centrist
socialist ranks, in which both men had been active.[39] It was also the
predominant attitude in the remnants of the Japanese communist
movement, to be discussed shortly.

However, when one looks at the labor and party organizations of the
Shaminkei socialists, one finds quite a different interpretation of events.
Admittedly, the pages of *Rōdō* and *Nihon Minshū Shimbun* rever-
berated with extended criticism of the government for the way in which
it handled the Depression, pointing out that the policies of industrial
rationalization had done little for the beleaguered small and medium-
sized enterprises, for the masses of unemployed workers, or for the
depressed citizenry of rural Japan.[40] And Shaminkei representatives in
the Diet aggressively attacked the government in the same vein in that
forum, as for instance when Nishio Suehiro accused the government of
pursuing *sangyō gōrika* 'at the expense of the workers', particularly
where unemployment was concerned.[41]

But at no time did any member of the Shaminkei in either the Nihon
Rōdō Sōdōmei or the Shakai Minshūtō ever express the view that
Japanese capitalism was on the brink of collapse or that the time was

ripe to escalate the struggle for socialism. On the contrary, it was a foregone conclusion, particularly in the Sōdōmei, that a situation of great danger now prevailed for the labor movement in the Depression. Fears were expressed that the government, then under public criticism for its Depression policies, might seek to deflect this criticism by stirring up public fears of socialist and communist revolution from the labor and proletarian party movements. If this occurred, it would not matter that the Shaminkei in the past had opposed communism by adhering to moderate 'realist socialism': all socialist movements would become a target for repression along with the communists if they made the mistake of thinking that the Depression had created an opportunity to pursue socialist politics in an aggressive manner.[42]

Rather, the Shaminkei argued that the politics of class conflict as advocated by the Nichirōkei and the far left should be unequivocally ruled out in favor of the politics of compromise with capitalism and liberalism to help solve the momentous problems of the Depression. This meant that labor should support the Shakai Minshūtō in the passing of emergency legislation to assist *sangyō gōrika* and alleviate the sufferings of the *kinrō kaikyū* which the economic crisis, and some of the solutions inherent in the government's approach to industrial rationalization, had posed for this stratum.[43] The corollary of this policy in the Sōdōmei was the peaceful and orderly negotiation of collective bargaining agreements with employers as a means of reducing unemployment and raising wages, issues which, the Sōdōmei argued, were uppermost in the minds of the majority of workers who, being gripped in the vice of the Depression, did not care much about socialist rhetoric.

Thus, while the Shakai Minshūtō pressed for laws to legalize unions, sanction collective bargaining, and provide greater relief to the unemployed and the distressed small and medium-scale enterprises, Sōdōmei leaders rushed into the breach when their unions became involved on their own volition in labor strikes, and negotiated settlements with management before these strikes could result in the destruction of the unions concerned. To cite but one example, when the Sōdōmei's Tokyo Spinners and Weavers' Union became embroiled in a massive strike against the Greater Japan Spinning Company in 1929, demanding reinstatement of workers recently dismissed by the company due to retrenchment, recognition of the Union, reduction of night labor, and so forth, Matsuoka Komakichi, as chairman of the Sōdōmei's Kantō Rōdō Dōmeikai to which this Union was affiliated, successfully interceded to negotiate an agreement with management whereby many of these demands were met, including Company recognition of the Union.[44]

Critics of the Sōdōmei denounced this type of action and the Federation's generally cautious response to the Depression crisis as a betrayal of class struggle in pursuing the politics of compromise. But the Sōdōmei defended its priority of protecting the unions as a 'rational' and 'realistic' policy necessitated by the fact that the institutions of the labor movement had been placed in grave jeopardy by the Depression. This obsession with the insecurity of the unions was an important element in the Federation's deliberate abdication of socialist politics inasmuch as it was felt in the Sōdōmei that to engage in political struggle on behalf of socialism was a luxury that the labor movement could no longer afford, given that the first task was now to save the unions from extinction.

The Sōdōmei's disengagement from socialist politics during the Depression period must also be seen against the background of political developments in Japan and internationally, for they, in combination with the economic impact of the Depression, seemed to portend that the new, prevailing 'trends of the times' had become distinctly inauspicious for socialist labor politics.

First, apprehension on this score in the labor movement sprang from the dramatic cycle of right-wing terrorist attacks on prominent liberal party politicians and business leaders in the early 1930s. The shooting of Prime Minister Hamaguchi (who later died from his wounds) in November 1930, the murder of the former Finance Minister Inoue Junnosuke in February 1932, the assassination of Baron Dan Takuma, head of Mitsui, in April that year, and the assassination of the then-Prime Minister Inukai Tsuyoshi in May 1932, along with other terrorist plots and intrigues involving elements of the military and self-styled civilian patriots, disclosed that Depression Japan was being swept by a resurgent nationalism that threatened to extinguish any individuals and movements that did not ride this tide.[45] The appeal to some Japanese of the agrarian utopianism of men like Tachibana Kōsaburō and Gondō Seikyō,[46] and the national socialism of Kita Ikki and Ōkawa Shūmei,[47] all of whom were involved in some of the terrorism of this period, and whose ideas clearly represented a revolt against the values and institutions of liberalism and capitalism in Japan, likewise reinforced the impression that Japan had entered a new stage of historical development unfavorable to social democracy.

There were, of course, many dimensions to this revolt, but those most visible – the passionate desire for a new 'Shōwa Restoration',[48] to save Japan from the weakness of liberalism, and a general antipathy toward things Western in preference for things Japanese – reflected a less apparent but nonetheless severe alienation of many Japanese from symbols of authority and ways of life that had been more or less taken for granted in the past. Professor Maruyama has described this alienation and breakdown of values as leading to what he calls an 'atomized' type of personality in Japan during this period who

> bitterly suffers from the actual or imagined state of uprootedness and the loss of norms of conduct (anomie). The feeling of loneliness, anxiety, fear, and frustration brought about by the precipitous change of his environment characterizes his psychology. Just because he is concerned with escaping from loneliness and insecurity, he is inclined to identify himself totally with authoritarian leadership or to submerge himself into the mystical 'whole' expressed in such ideas as national community, eternal racial culture, and so on.[49]

The history of Japan in the Depression and thereafter could well be written in terms of the rebellion of this 'atomized man' against a sense of meaninglessness that had attended the process of modernization in Japan under liberalism and capitalism in the recent past. The vocabulary of ultranationalism which stressed the restoration of sacred traditions and the elimination of profane Western cultural influences became his vocabulary and dictated his response to contemporary events. 'Overcome the modern', signifying the taking of control of modernization as it had evolved under liberalism and capitalism and investing it with a new meaning in accord with a new sense of national identity and purpose, became his slogan.[50] Given this type of mass psychology, which pervaded the ranks of labor as well as society in general, it may be said that labor's drift away from socialism after 1929 into an accommodation with nationalism developed essentially from the 'politics of despair'.[51]

A second political factor behind labor's abandonment of socialist politics was the unfolding consequences of Japan's aggressive foreign policy in the early 1930s. Japan's clash with the Western powers over the issue of naval arms limitations at the 1930 London Naval Conference,[52] her conquest of Manchuria in the Manchurian Incident of 1931 culminating in the creation of the puppet regime of Manchukuo in 1932,[53] and Japan's subsequent break from the League of Nations in 1933 after the League had censured Japan's activities in Manchuria, seriously estranged Japan from the West politically, just as the Depression had loosened the ties between Japan and the West economically.

These developments nurtured an embattled, isolationist mentality in Japan and the conviction that the Japanese Empire must be protected in a climate of growing conflict with the liberal West, whose decline in the Depression was seen to parallel the decline of liberalism within Japan. Moreover, the rise of the national socialist movement under Hitler in Germany in 1933 and the apparent strength of the Fascist countries of Europe in comparison to the liberal democracies made it seem as if the trends of the times internationally were no longer conducive to liberalism, or to socialism which in England, for example, had flourished within a liberal political environment. From this perspective, labor's retreat from socialist politics in the 1929–1932 period and thereafter was justified in the Sōdōmei and other labor organizations in its bloc on the grounds of being a 'rational' response to new international conditions, just as their earlier embrace of 'realist socialism' had been a 'rational' response to the now-superseded world conditions of the mid-1920s.

A third critical political factor that pushed socialist labor toward its quiescent political position was the rapid rise of an ultranationalist labor movement on the right and a persistent, albeit weakened, communist movement on the left. An illustration of the former was the growing strength of the Jikyō Rōdō Kumiai, centered in the Ishikawajima Shipyards Company, alluded to in Chapter 4. In the late 1920s, the Company had increasingly employed the resources of this Union to help break labor strikes. By 1930, other labor groups at Ishikawajima had been all but nullified, leaving the Jikyō Rōdō Kumiai as the dominant organization. In 1929, the Jikyō Union had joined a patriotic labor front which included similarly conservative unions in other Kantō-area factories. This body, known as the Busō Rōdō Renmei (Chivalrous Labor League) numbered 4,000 workers at its inception.[54] In 1930 it was renamed simply Nihon Zōsen Rōdō Renmei (Japan Shipbuilding Labor League), and was then 7,000 members strong.[55]

The central objective of the Renmei was to create a 'Great Right-Wing' (Dai Uyoku) labor front for the defense of Japan against leftist radicalism.[56] Accordingly, the Renmei became the core of an umbrella organization known as the Kokubō Kenkin Rōdō Kyōgikai (Labor Council for Donations to National Defense) in December 1932, mainly at the initiative of the Jikyō Union, the single most important organization in this front.[57] The next year, the front was to expand to include a total of ten labor organizations, combined into the Nihon Sangyō Rōdō Kurabu (Japan Industrial Labor Club) whose ideology was *nipponshugi*, or 'Japanism'. [58]

To anticipate further developments in the history of this front, in 1936 it spawned a number of auxiliary bodies, typical of which was the Aikoku Rōdō Kumiai Zenkoku Kondankai (All-Japan Roundtable of Patriotic Labor Unions). The Kondankai served as a forum for the discussion of national problems and the participation of patriotic labor in the defense of the country.[59] The leading figure in the Nihon Sangyō Rōdō Kurabu and also in the Kondankai was Kaeno Shin'ichi, the powerful leader of the Jikyō Rōdō Kumiai at Ishikawajima. By the mid-1930s, the front had developed a membership of over 134,000 workers.[60]

Other rightist labor organizations, some of which will be discussed in due course, also emerged in the early 1930s. Their appearance on the scene startled the Sōdōmei and a good many other labor organizations in the Sōdōmei's train into fears that unless they set aside their previously affirmed socialism, they would run the risk of being overtaken by their new challengers on the right in the race to organize the factory workers into unions. Furthermore, while in the 1920s the Sōdōmei had flown the banners of 'realist socialism' to distinguish itself from and discredit communism, the presence of a stridently anticommunist right-wing labor movement in the 1930s which was also strongly opposed to socialism, deprived the Sōdōmei of even this prerogative.

The 'communist problem' in the labor movement had not entirely vanished after the fall of the Hyōgikai in the spring of 1928, for elements of the Hyōgikai had regrouped to form the Nihon Rōdō Kumiai Zenkoku Kyōgikai (National Conference of Japanese Labor Unions) in the December of that year. Zenkyō, as it was known, was very clear about its links with the struggling Japanese Communist Party, which had also regrouped in late 1928. For instance, Zenkyō proclaimed in 1929, 'In order to liberate the working class from the pits of oppression, to destroy capitalism, and to achieve communism, our Council must be under the political leadership of the Japanese Communist Party...and must preserve the class character of left-wing unionism.'[61]

As it turned out, Zenkyō never amounted to much. With a core of only 5,600 workers, concentrated in the Kantō area, Zenkyō was constantly hounded by the police and in later 1929 it went completely underground where it eventually petered out.[62] As for the JCP, it remained on the scene well into the 1930s but by 1933 was a spent force. Most of its leaders were in jail that year and some of them, notably Nabeyama Sadachika and Sano Manabu, disheartened their comrades who remained at large by announcing dramatically from their cells their conversion from communism to nationalistic support of the Emperor.[63]

Nevertheless, as long as any communist labor movement remained in existence, communism was still a bête noire for the Sōdōmei and its allies in the labor movement, as can be seen in the so-called *dai-sanji bunretsu* of the General Federation in 1929. Unlike the labor splits of 1925 and 1926, which originated in Tokyo, this one occurred in Osaka where a small group of iron workers' unions in the Sōdōmei's Osaka *rengōkai* led by Yamanouchi Kanetomi, Ōya Shōzō, and Suzuki Etsujirō – who were part of what was known as the 'Yamanouchi faction' – rebelled against the Sōdōmei's anti-communism on the grounds that the leaders of the Federation were guilty of 'bureaucratic chauvinism' in refusing to form an alliance with other leftist labor organizations against capitalism. In particular, the Yamanouchi faction called upon the Sōdōmei to ally with the centrists and the communists and build a proletarian labor front. This faction also opposed Sōdōmei support for the ILO.[64]

The Sōdōmei leadership initially responded to this revolt, which had surfaced in the spring of 1929, by attempting to persuade the Yamanouchi faction of unions to desist from attacking Sōdōmei policies. Since Osaka was Nishio's labor base, he was especially active in this endeavor. However when the Yamanouchi faction remained implacable, Sōdōmei headquarters expelled the unions under the control of this faction – about 5,000 workers in all – from the Federation in August 1929. The official reason given for the expulsion was familiar: the groups in question were pro-communist and therefore could not be tolerated in the Sōdōmei. Later, the Yamanouchi faction members were expelled from the Shakai Minshūtō for the same reason.[65]

In retrospect, the Yamanouchi faction was not pro-communist as the Sōdōmei and the Shakai Minshūtō had alleged. Rather, Yamanouchi, Ōya, and Suzuki Etsujirō had merely associated themselves with the cause of labor unity in a manner reminiscent of Asō Hisashi in 1926. Although the Yamanouchi faction formed a new labor federation immediately after the 1929 labor split in Osaka (the Rōdō Kumiai

Zenkoku Dōmei or National Federation of Labor Unions), in June 1930 this was merged with the centrist Nihon Rōdō Kumiai Dōmei which thus became Zenkoku Rōdō Kumiai Dōmei (National Labor Union Federation).[66]

The more general point to be emphasized from this latest tear in the Sōdōmei's fabric is that the Federation, already fixed in its determination to fight communist influence in the labor movement, was obliged to continue this struggle in the 1930s, less because communism was a serious threat than because the prevailing nationalistic climate of the times required a powerful anti-communist position. But whereas in the 1920s the Sōdōmei had advocated socialist labor politics as an alternative to communism in the labor movement, in the 1930s the perceived risk of adhering even to moderate, 'realist socialism' amidst the onslaught of ultranationalism, reduced the Federation to presenting nonpolitical labor unionism pure and simple as the safest alternative to communism. Soon, the Sōdōmei would discover that anti-communism without socialism and based solely on patriotism would, as a formula, make it very difficult to distinguish the Federation from the right-wing nationalist labor movement in the eyes of the workers and that therefore the latter would prove to be more eager to join the swelling ranks of such organizations as the Jikyō Rōdō Kumiai than they were to join the Sōdōmei.

The retreat from socialism to labor unionism, pure and simple, 1930–1932

The process whereby the Nihon Rōdō Sōdōmei and its labor bloc turned inward politically, away from socialism to an overwhelming preoccupation with labor unionism in the Depression period was a gradual one, discernible in a number of contexts. In analyzing it, one must distinguish between the form and the content of Sōdōmei policies, for in most instances, the superficial form of the Federation's commitment to socialist politics and to the specific support of the Shakai Minshūtō was retained, but without sustaining the content of socialist political purpose. The first example was the Sōdōmei's performance in the general elections of February 1930.

The socialist party movement entered the 1930 elections with the same basic right-wing, centrist, and left-wing alignments as in 1928, although in some instances party names had changed to reflect recent permutations in the proletarian ranks. Besides the Shakai Minshūtō, the movement consisted of the Nihon Taishūtō (Japan Masses' Party) – originally the Rōnōtō – and a smaller party, the Zenkoku Minshūtō (National Democratic Party) in the centrist camp, and the Shin Rōdō Nōmintō (New Labor–Farmer Party) – more commonly known, and referred to here, as the Shin Rōnōtō – on the left. In general, developments in the socialist party movement from 1928 to 1930 may be summarized as follows.

The first attempt to revive the legal left with a successor to the ill-fated Rōdō Nōmintō, banned by the Home Ministry in the spring of 1928, occurred in the July of that year when remnants of the Rōdō Nōmintō, excluding Ōyama Ikuo, founded the Musan Taishūtō (Proletarian Masses' Party). This was composed of men who felt that Ōyama, who was then contemplating the formation of a 'new' Rōdō Nōmintō, was less keen to restore unity to the socialist movement by cooperating with the centrists, for whom they themselves had much sympathy. Before long, in December 1928, the Musan Taishūtō did merge with the Rōnōtō, becoming the Nihon Taishūtō.[67]

A second leftist party arose soon after, in January 1929, when other elements of the defunct Rōdō Nōmintō, again excluding Ōyama, established the Rōnō Taishūtō (Labor–Farmer Masses' Party). This was based in, and largely confined to, Kyoto. Led by Mizutani Chōzaburō, a former associate of Ōyama's, this Party criticized Ōyama for being too sympathetic toward a possible merger between a legal left party and the centrists. This was precisely the opposite assessment of Ōyama to that made by the founders of the Musan Taishūtō. But Mizutani's local party did not last long on the left wing of the socialist movement. Mizutani would experience a change of heart after the 1930 elections and combine his organization with the centrist Nihon Taishūtō which, accordingly, changed its name once again to the Zenkoku Taishūtō (National Masses' Party) on July 20, 1930.[68]

Still anxious to organize a national, legal left party, Ōyama next founded the Shin Rōnōtō in November 1929.[69] It consisted of elements in the original Rōdō Nōmintō who had remained loyal to him. But because Ōyama wanted to avoid the impression that the Shin Rōdō Nōmintō was as radical as the police had believed its predecessor to have been, he purged this Party of men like Professor Kawakami Hajime who had been in the past, and continued to be, in favor of working covertly with the communists.[70] Hence, the Shin Rōdō Nōmintō was less militant than the Rōdō Nōmintō; ideologically, it was akin to the Nihon Taishūtō. But in the Depression its rhetoric stressed militant class struggle and uncompromising resistance to capitalism to a greater degree than the Nihon Taishūtō's.

The Zenkoku Minshūtō had been organized on the eve of the elections by Ōya Shōzō, one of the protagonists in the 1929 labor split of the Sōdōmei.[71] It was mainly limited to Osaka where Ōya, who had not followed Yamanouchi and Suzuki Etsujirō into the centrist party led by Asō Hisashi, provided the Zenkoku Minshūtō with a small labor base of unions under his own personal control. However, after the 1930 elections, Ōya would merge his party with Asō's party which changed its name yet once more on July 5, 1931, from Zenkoku Taishūtō to Zenkoku Rōnō Taishūtō (National Labor–Farmer Masses' Party), with Asō still at the helm.[72] This additional permutation in the centrist political camp had a further significance because it involved the merger between the latter and Ōyama's Shin Rōnōtō.

In the labor movement, the principal elements entering the 1930 elections were those coalesced around the Sōdōmei and the Nihon Rōdō Kumiai Dōmei. The restoration of a legal left labor organization to continue the work of the Hyōgikai in supporting the Rōdō Nōmintō did not occur until April 1931 when Ōyama and his followers, seeing that they could hardly rely on the illegal and underground Zenkyō, organized the Nihon Rōdō Kumiai Sōhyōgikai (General Council of Japanese Labor Unions). Like its predecessor, the Hyōgikai, Sōhyō, as it was informally called, was based on regional councils. However, there were only three of them and Sōhyō's support was chiefly confined to metal workers. Ōyama hoped to increase the size of Sōhyō, which never exceeded the 11,400 membership it reached in 1932, by linking it to those moderate elements whom he endeavored to lure away from the Zenkyō. This failed, however, since Zenkyō persistently accused Sōhyō, and virtually all other labor organizations, of being 'yellow' politically, a term that referred to their compromises of class struggle and accommodation to capitalism. The weakness of Sōhyō proved to be a decisive factor in Ōyama's later decision to merge the Shin Rōnōtō with the centrist socialist party.[73]

As in 1928, the Sōdōmei's political bureau prepared assiduously for the 1930 elections and worked closely with the Shakai Minshūtō executive to determine a slate of candidates, raise funds, schedule electioneering tours by labor and party officials, and, above all, to settle on a list of slogans designed to appeal to the electorate.[74] The slogans, and the Party's election platform in general, were dominated by themes that were considered to be of great importance to the labor movement, including demands for the legalization of unions, unemployment relief, and opposition to the government's program of industrial rationalization, particularly its failure to care for smaller enterprises where many workers had been made redundant.[75]

Moreover, special emphasis was given in the Sōdōmei to the election of men from its ranks such as Nishio and Suzuki Bunji, running from the Osaka third and fourth districts respectively, for it was expected that they would be under stiff competition from candidates associated with the Yamanouchi faction in the Zenkoku Minshūtō.[76] Priority was likewise placed on Matsuoka Komakichi's campaign in the Tokyo fifth district, his first entry into the electioneering lists.[77]

In these respects, the Sōdōmei's preparations for the 1930 elections resembled those of 1928; the form of the Federation's cooperation with the Shakai Minshūtō seemed unchanged. But in the campaign itself, candidates from the Sōdōmei on the Shakai Minshūtō ticket concentrated exclusively on issues pertaining to the security of unions, making little or no reference to socialism, and in this they demonstrated that the content of their commitment to socialism had become virtually negligible.

A study of Matsuoka's campaign speeches for instance reveals that he barely mentioned socialism at all.[78] This was not true, however, of those Shakai Minshūtō candidates such as Katayama, who had not arisen from the ranks of labor. But even Katayama, whose ideological fidelity to socialism cannot be questioned, found it risky to allude to *shakaishugi*. On one occasion, when he stated, 'We are socialists, not communists', the police interrupted his speech to warn him against mentioning either socialism or communism.[79]

Indeed, police surveillance was tighter than ever in this campaign. Whenever proletarian candidates mounted the podium to give campaign speeches, as many as two or three policemen were often found sitting behind desks on the same platform, pencils poised to jot down 'subversive' utterances.[80] And, occasionally, proletarian campaign workers scuffled with the police. In one incident, when Katayama's assistants were approached in the street by police for questioning, they threw watermelons and potatoes from a nearby truck at the officials before running off, so great was their hatred of police harassment.[81]

But when the election results were in, it was clear that the Sōdōmei's strategy of concentrating on essentially nonpolitical issues pertaining to unionism had not paid off. Although Nishio won election to the Diet, Suzuki, who had encountered the predicted competition from the

Zenkoku Minshūtō in his district, lost this election, as did Matsuoka. The only other Shakai Minshūtō candidate to reach the Diet was Katayama, who credited his victory to the fact that he had neutralized the former opposition he had received from a (non-Sōdōmei) worker candidate in 1928 by persuading this man to act as his campaign manager in 1930.[82] The other proletarian parties did as poorly. Only Ōyama was elected in the Shin Rōnōtō. Most of the leaders of the centrist Nihon Taishūtō, including Asō, Kawakami Jōtarō, Kono Mitsu, Tanahashi Kotora, and Katō Kanjū, were unsuccessful. Only Asahara Kenzō and Matsutani Yojirō reached the Diet from this party.[83] All in all, the proletarian parties had captured five Diet seats, a loss of three from 1928. As for the liberal parties, the 1930 elections resulted in a Minseitō government.[84]

It is significant that in its post-mortem of this election, the Shakai Minshūtō singled out the growing 'weakness of the labor movement' as a major reason for the Party's dismal performance, although other factors, including police interference, lack of campaign funds, and the like were also noted.[85] The implication was that Sōdōmei and its labor bloc had, in addition to being thwarted in places like Osaka by new rivals as a consequence of the 1929 labor split, let the Party down in adopting a low profile on the question of the Party's socialist image.

A second example of how the Sōdōmei had pulled back from socialism in the defense of the nonpolitical goals of labor unionism was the way in which the Federation mounted its determined campaign for the legalization of labor unions in 1930 and 1931. The fact that the Federation worked with the Shakai Minshūtō in the Diet in seeking this objective suggests superficially that the Sōdōmei still identified itself with the Party's socialist ideology. But this is to see the situation only in terms of form. Once again, it must be reiterated that the Sōdōmei was using the Party to maneuver politically for a goal that had long been sought in the labor movement and which, in the Depression, seemed more crucial for labor than ever. However, whereas in the late 1920s the Sōdōmei had struggled for the legalization of unions as part of a general socialist view of national reform benefiting the proletariat, and although for the Party this remained the case in the Depression, from the Sōdōmei's point of view, the campaign to legalize unions was now to be fought without reliance upon socialism as a justifying vision for the attainment of labor's rights. On the contrary, it was judged in the Federation that the only way to succeed in the campaign was to quietly dissociate unionism from socialism.

The decision to escalate attempts to legalize unions was made immediately after the Minseitō government declared in December 1929 that it would support a labor union law. This announcement was made by Yoshida Shigeru, head of the Home Ministry's Social Affairs Bureau whose staff was already preparing a government draft of a labor union bill. Yoshida explained the purpose of the legislation as follows:

> *The purpose of a Labor Union Law is to eliminate social obstacles facing the labor movement and to make it more moderate and orderly. Labor unions are the natural product of the present economic system and no one can prevent their birth and growth.* But because they have no status in law, there have been unnecessary disputes between labor and management...The government always intends to promote the sound development of industries through cooperation between labor and management and genuine cooperation can be achieved with giving the labor unions a legal position and working with them...*It is inconceivable that the promulgation of this Law will foster class struggle or hinder the development of industry.* [My italics.][86]

The Sōdōmei greeted this announcement as an enlightened statement of governmental policy toward labor unionism which entirely conformed to its leaders' vision of the function of labor unions: they served to stabilize relations between labor and management for the benefit of national recovery from the Depression.[87] Other elements in the labor movement were less sanguine about the government's labor policy. They feared that Yoshida's emphasis on making the labor unions 'more moderate and orderly' implied a coercive attitude, especially since it was clear that the Minseitō administration wanted to prevent class struggle during the crisis of the Depression. Even so, they were prepared to cooperate with the Sōdōmei and the Shakai Minshūtō and help to pass a progressive labor union law, which now seemed possible due to the backing of the majority party in the lower house of the Diet. Accordingly, at the behest of the Shakai Minshūtō and acting under the prodding of the Sōdōmei, a joint committee of all socialist members of parliament was established in early 1930, after the elections, to coordinate their activities for this purpose.[88]

The committee immediately began to draft a socialist labor union bill for presentation to the 1930 Diet. Much of this work was done by Katayama Tetsu, the Shakai Minshūtō's lawyer who held a Diet seat, and Miwa Jusō, whose legal expertise had long been recognized by the Nichirōkei. Unfortunately, the 1930 Diet session soon became bogged down in dissension between the Minseitō and the Seiyūkai on other issues relating to Depression-period policy and ended without the socialists having an opportunity to present their bill for debate. This gave the opposition to a labor union law, centered in the business community, time to mobilize its forces before the matter of legalizing unions came up for debate in the 1931 Diet.

Initially, the main opposition to the legalization of unions came from the Nihon Kōgyō Kurabu. As soon as Yoshida had made public the government's interest in a labor union law, Club officials, such as Baron Dan Takuma, sent letters to the government asking that it reconsider this policy.[89] Indeed, Dan, accompanied by Baron Gō Seinosuke and Kimura Kusuyata, other leading lights in the Club, made frequent visits in 1930 to the offices of Home Minister Adachi Kenzō to lobby against the labor union bill.[90] And, in early 1931, before the Diet reconvened, Club officials took the lead in organizing a powerful business lobby against the bill, the Zenkoku Sangyō Dantai Rengōkai (National Association of Industrial Organizations), or Zensanren.[91] Its chairman was Fujihara Ginjirō, president of the Oji Paper Company. He presided over a blue-ribbon board of thirty-seven men who, as directors of Zensanren, included most of Japan's leading industrialists and financiers; some were from the Nihon Kōgyō Kurabu.[92]

Zensanren opposed the legalization of unions on the familiar grounds that to sanction their existence would be to open the floodgates to 'dangerous thoughts' in the body politic. Zensanren officials were also sensitive to the fact that in late 1930 the Sōdōmei and its labor bloc had formed a national committee, which included some centrist labor unions, to orchestrate a running series of demonstrations all across the country on behalf of a labor union law. These demonstrations were usually held outside the offices of the Chambers of Commerce in Japan's prefectural capitals and in Tokyo. Zensanren was a prominent target of the rallies after its formation in 1931.[93] Naturally, organized business interpreted these demonstrations as evidence that unless the unruly masses were constrained, to prevent the collapse of public order, Japan would fall prey to proletarian revolution. Concessions to the proletariat, such as a labor law, were out of the question.

Weighed down by other more pressing items on its agenda, the government was anxious to avoid protracted conflict in the 1931 Diet concerning the labor union law. But Home Minister Adachi organized a series of roundtable discussions, to be held at the Home Ministry, to which representatives of labor and business would be invited to air their views on this issue, with the aim of reaching an agreement acceptable to all parties involved. The first of the discussions was scheduled for late December 1930. The socialists were eager to take part. Matsuoka, Nishio, and Miwa Jusō went to the Home Ministry on the appointed day with great expectations, as the spokesmen for labor. They thought that, with Adachi's support, they could overcome the objections of business leaders to the bill. However, upon arrival, they were informed that the latter had not come. The business officials invited by Adachi had sent a note explaining they would not sit down with labor men because such an act would imply approval of unions.[94]

Undaunted, Adachi tried again. Later that month, he succeeded in persuading business leaders to sit down with representatives of the labor movement at the conference table. As soon as Adachi opened the meeting, Fujihara, who was spokesman for the business side, demanded to speak first. He stated flatly that the labor men present did not really represent the mass of factory workers but only a tiny minority of unions. He also said that unions were either communist or pro-communist and were therefore a serious threat to the *kokutai*. He referred everyone present to a booklet he had written on the danger of unionism in Japan. When Adachi argued for a more flexible view of the labor movement, Fujihara remained impassive and intractable.[95]

Similarly futile roundtable talks were held in early 1931 before the beginning of the Diet session.[96] Finally, when the Diet reconvened, both the Home Ministry and the socialists' joint committee presented drafts of a labor union bill. Space does not permit a discussion of the differences between the two drafts. In any case, the socialists soon withdrew their draft in order to support the government's. This decision was mainly due to Nishio Suehiro who argued that the labor movement would have a better chance of attaining a union law if it closed ranks behind the government to overcome resistance from the Seiyūkai. When Miwa Jusō objected that this amounted to capitulation to the government's more conservative bill, which did not include the right of unions to bargain collectively or provision for the protection of workers from arbitrary dismissal by employers, Nishio retorted pointedly that the government's bill would be better than no bill at all. After Nishio's view was finally accepted, the joint committee authorized him to work out a plan with Home Minister Adachi to ensure the passage of the government bill.[97]

After lively debate in the Diet, this bill cleared the lower house. However, when it reached the Peers, it was sent back to committee where representatives of Zensanren testified against it at the invitation of certain Peers. Fujihara stated Zensanren's position. He charged that most of the labor disputes in the Depression had been instigated by unions. A law to destroy, not sanction, unions was necessary, he said. Unions were also dangerous to the national polity because they harbored 'dangerous thoughts'. They were harbingers of armed revolution. To make a maximum impression on the Peers, the courtly Fujihara also declared that the socialist parties were out to destroy the upper house altogether. The issue was thus portrayed as a test of power between the Peers and the socialists. The force of these arguments induced the Peers to stall the bill in committee where it languished as the session closed.[98] This was the end of the battle over the legalization of unions; although labor continued to press for this legislation in future years, it never again had the support of the government, which was soon immobilized by the political crisis beginning later in 1931.

It should not be implied that the chances for success on this issue would have been stronger had labor stressed the connection between a labor union law and any grand socialist design for the reconstruction of the country. It is probable that the labor union law battle was doomed to failure because of the strength of organized business in lobbying against it, whatever arguments were put forward on behalf of this legislation. Still, the fact remains that in deliberately avoiding any possible connection between the labor union bill and socialism, the Sōdōmei in particular had taken another step in its retreat from socialism.

Yet a third step in this direction was the Sōdōmei's evolving concept of a united labor front and its attempt to construct it in 1931. From first to last in this endeavor, the Sōdōmei, obsessed with the conviction that labor unity was indispensable given the threats to unionism in the Depression, wanted this front to serve as a viable force for the protection of labor unionism; the possibility that the front would have any other, political, priorities was never seriously countenanced.

Sōdōmei headquarters first decided to explore the possibility of greater labor unity in the spring of 1931 when, at the instigation of the General Federation, talks were begun with the centrist Zenkoku Rōdō Kumiai Dōmei and another labor group, the Nihon Rōdō Kumiai Sōrengō (General Alliance of Japanese Labor Unions).[99] These talks were brittle. Neither the representatives of the Sōdōmei, Matsuoka and Nishio, nor the spokesmen for the Dōmei, including Kamijō Aiichi, Yamanouchi Kanetomi, and Ōya Shōzō (who had by this time rejoined the Yamanouchi clique in the centrist labor movement) were able to entirely thrust aside memories of recent conflict between the two organizations. Indeed, because Sōdōmei leaders had foreseen that the talks would be strained, they had asked Hamada Kunitarō of the Nihon Kaiin Kumiai to act as chairman of the deliberations in order to provide the discussions with a relatively impartial leadership. Although Hamada had been a staunch member of the Shaminkei labor movement, he was considered by all to be objective and his large union was judged by everyone present to be indispensable to any cooperation that might ensue.

Whether the Sōdōmei had initially envisioned the objective of the negotiations as a full-scale merger is not entirely clear. In any case, very early in the talks, it became clear that such a merger was out of the question. Matsuoka opened the deliberations by stating that if a merger was accomplished, the Sōdōmei and its bloc, comprising the largest phalanx in the labor movement, should have the right to fill the majority of executive posts that would be created in the merger's central committee. This was firmly rejected by Kamijō Aiichi who did not want to see the Sōdōmei dominate the future coordination of policy and action. Kamijō argued that any committee that might arise to undertake liaison between the participating organizations should consist of representatives from all the groups involved, in equal numbers.[100]

Seeing that the talks were in danger of becoming bogged down in disputes over questions of representation and the distribution of power at the expense of discussing larger issues of economic and political policy, Hamada Kunitarō broke this potential impasse by suggesting that the groups involved consider forming a loose coalition in a kind of 'club' rather than waste time talking about a full-scale merger which, it was obvious, none of them was ready to undertake. The merit of this formula was that the federations would retain their own separate identities while benefiting at the same time from greater joint consultation in facing common problems.[101] This proposal was finally agreed upon and on June 25, 1931, the talks resulted in the formation of the Nihon Rōdō Kurabu (Japan Labor Club). It was understood that if, after a trial period, their cooperation in the Kurabu proved successful, they might take up the option of fully merging together at some point in the future. Altogether, the Kurabu consisted of fourteen labor organizations, including those in the Shaminkei and Nichirōkei labor blocs, with a combined membership of 224,000 workers. Its chairman was Hamada, by mutual consent of the member organizations, to preserve the notion of impartial leadership.[102]

From its inception, the Nihon Rōdō Kurabu was an omnibus organization in which the only liaison ever achieved came about through the meetings of its unwieldy executive committee; this was made up from representatives of the Sōdōmei, the Dōmei, and other labor groups in roughly equal numbers, as the centrists had insisted should be the case.[103]

On the surface, the Kurabu projected something of a progressive political image. It stood for 'anti-communism', 'anti-anarchism', and 'anti-fascism', which were later amended to include 'anti-communism', 'anti-capitalism', and 'anti-fascism'.[104] On a more positive note, the Kurabu endorsed 'social democracy', signifying the primacy of legal, gradual, and 'rational' tactics in pursuit of democratic reform.[105] Formally, the Kurabu did not commit itself to any particular socialist party.

However, as the relatively greater emphasis in the Kurabu on economic policies made clear, 'social democracy', 'anti-communism', 'anti-capitalism', and 'anti-fascism' were more like perfunctory nods to a dwindling enthusiasm for socialist politics than they were evocative, inspiring statements of dynamic political purpose in the Nihon Rōdō Kurabu. The real concern of the Kurabu, like the Sōdōmei itself, was with '*kenjitsuteki na kumiaishugi*' (sound unionism), a slogan which had become prevalent in the Sōdōmei during the Depression.[106] As in the General Federation, 'sound unionism' was understood to mean the practical development of union institutions and programs to assist the livelihood of the workers, and the advocacy of labor legislation to legalize unions, sanction collective bargaining, and provide impartial arbitration of labor disputes. Sound unionism also signified the Kurabu's strong support for the principles and goals of the International Labor Organization. In brief, sound unionism connoted all of the laborist emphases engendered in the Sōdōmei and its bloc.

The Shin Rōnōtō, the Nihon Rōdō Kumiai Sōhyōgikai, Zenkyō, and the Japanese Communist Party opposed the Kurabu because they felt that it had gone too far in adopting nonpolitical, labor-oriented priorities. The communists were especially critical of the Kurabu for its opposition to their movement. But significantly, some elements of the Nichirōkei were also against the Kurabu. Katō Kanjū was convinced that the Kurabu's sound unionism implied that the organization was a 'social-fascist manifestation of the new fascist trend' in Japan.[107] He branded the Kurabu's 'anti-capitalism' and 'anti-fascism' as insincere because it was obvious, Katō thought, that these policies would be meaningless so long as they were acted upon in accordance with the conciliatory prescriptions of 'sound unionism' rather than militant class struggle. In Katō's opinion, only proletarian class struggle could beat down the threat of fascism in Japan.

Accordingly, Katō rallied a number of unions under his influence in the Nichirōkei labor movement, consisting mostly of coal miners' unions, to form an organization to oppose the Nihon Rōdō Kurabu. This was the Zenrō Kurabu Haigeki Tōsō Dōmei (National Labor Struggle Combination to Boycott the [Japan Labor] Club) founded in November 1931.[108] The elites of the Zenkoku Rōdō Kumiai Dōmei, led by Kono Mitsu, tried in vain to dissuade Katō from carrying on with his protests. When he remained adamant, they decided that they had no alternative but to expel him from the Zenkoku Rōdō Kumiai Dōmei, in 1932. This was followed by Katō's resignation from the Zenkoku Rōnō Taishūtō and his break from its leader, Asō Hisashi.[109] Later, in 1937, Katō organized a party of his own, the Nihon Musantō (Japan Proletarian Party) to carry out a final struggle with 'fascism'.

Despite such opposition, the Kurabu continued to expand, numbering 280,000 members by the autumn of 1932. Thus, at the initiative of the Sōdōmei, it was decided to symbolize the Kurabu's gathering momentum by adopting a new name on September 25, 1932, when the Kurabu became the Nihon Rōdō Kumiai Kaigi (Congress of Japanese Labor Unions).[110] Hamada remained as chairman but the real power behind the Kaigi was wielded by Matsuoka Komakichi, in his role as vice chairman. Aside from the new name, however, the Kaigi was indistinguishable from the Nihon Rōdō Kurabu. It continued to adhere to sound unionism as its first priority which, as before, superseded the largely ornamental three antis of 'anti-communism', 'anti-capitalism' and 'anti-fascism'. *Sangyō kyōryoku* (industrial cooperation) was now just as prominent in Kaigi affairs as it had become in the Sōdōmei.[111]

The Nihon Rōdō Kumiai Kaigi is rarely discussed in Japanese accounts of the 1930s, if indeed it is mentioned at all. One exception is the work of Shirai Taishirō. In his opinion, the Kaigi represented a significant achievement for the labor movement by creating solidarity among the unions. The very existence of the Kaigi less than ten years after the first splits in the labor movement is regarded as noteworthy. Observing that the growing cohesiveness of the labor movement in the 1930s was a positive trend in reaction to the increasing strength of organized business lobby groups such as Zensanren, Shirai states that if the Kaigi is evaluated in terms of its sound unionism emphases, it represented great potential in the historic quest of Japanese unions for security and gains on behalf of the workers. Because they have over-looked the importance of this fact, other scholars of the labor movement have unwisely ignored the significance of the Kaigi.[112]

All this may be true. Doubtless the Kaigi deserves some 'rehabilitation' in Japanese labor history. Yet the point remains that the Kaigi, like the Kurabu before it, was still a loose coalition of divergent labor organizations whose sole common denominator was an agreement on a rather narrow range of goals, based on nonpolitical sound unionism, for the labor movement. Any gains that might have been registered by the Congress in the pursuit of these goals were largely precluded by the political timidity and conservatism of the Kaigi in the face of the 'prevailing national circumstances' that seemed unpropitious for social ism. Thus, to the extent that the Sōdōmei had been the driving force behind the evolution of the Kaigi, the Sōdōmei's own withdrawal from socialist politics had served to depoliticize a major cross-section of the Japanese labor movement in the early 1930s, the outward form of the Kaigi's nominally political 'three antis' notwithstanding.

A fourth aspect of the Sōdōmei's retreat from socialism, in which not even the form of socialist labor politics was retained, is apparent in the Federation's response to the Manchurian Incident. At first, the Sōdōmei observed a cautious silence on the subject. For instance, the Sōdōmei's annual convention of November 15 to November 17 1931 did not address itself at all to the fighting that had raged in Manchuria since the inception of the Incident in September.[113] In fact, neither the Sōdōmei nor the Nihon Rōdō Kurabu (nor the Kurabu's successor, the Kaigi) ever took an official stand on the Incident.

When individuals in the Sōdōmei expressed their views, however, these were generally equivocal or sympathetic to Japan's actions in Manchuria. For example, an unsigned article assessing the Incident in the February 1932 issue of *Rōdō* began on a somewhat critical note as the writer stated it was hard to see how the Japanese Kwantung Army could claim to be an 'army of liberation' in freeing the peoples of Manchuria from the yoke of China, as alleged in Japanese propaganda, when it was obvious that the Kwantung Army intended to annex Manchuria into the Japanese Empire. But then the writer pointed out that Japan had to protect her interests abroad in view of the monopoly of the world's resources by the United States, Britain and France through colonial rule. The article ended with the observation that there was nothing intrinsically unhealthy about Japanese nationalism in this regard; it was a legitimate reaction to Western imperialism in Asia. The inference was that the Manchurian Incident was justifiable.[114]

It is possible that this article was written by Nishio Suehiro. At least, Nishio voiced much the same sentiments when as a part of the Japanese labor delegation to the ILO in 1932 he addressed the ILO assembly at Geneva with these remarks:

> The majority of delegates attending this conference are of the white race, representing the various countries of Europe. The white race, which once had only one-fourteenth of the land of the world, now has taken over more than three-fifths of the entire globe and has subjected more than one-third of the world's population to its domination. It has concluded antiwar pacts which have guaranteed territorial possessions and permanent peace under conditions extremely unfavorable to the colored races. Are the International Labor Organization and the League of Nations going to set up policies of appeasement recognizing this illogical state of affairs, this unfair present situation?[115]

Nishio also criticized the findings of the League's Lytton Commission which had censured Japan in Manchuria.

The Sōdōmei's tacit support for the Manchurian Incident became clearer in January 1932 when the General Federation, with great public fanfare, mounted a 'home front' campaign designed to raise money for the relief of families suffering from the loss of loved ones at the front. Sōdōmei unions were exhorted to pay condolence money to worker families in this category. Matsuoka chaired this campaign and viewed it as a good method of demonstrating concrete patriotic support for the nation. A similar campaign was sponsored by the Japan Labor Club, in which Matsuoka was also instrumental.[116]

In contrast to the Sōdōmei's reaction to the Manchurian Incident, the proletarian parties, including the Shakai Minshūtō, opposed the Incident, to varying degrees. One month after the beginning of the Incident, the Shakai Minshūtō published a statement on the war in *Nihon Minshū Shimbun* condemning the Japanese *gunbatsu* (military cliques) for attempting to seize Manchuria. The statement also claimed that the military was only a pawn of the *zaibatsu* who wished to exploit Manchuria for their own purposes.[117] Thus, although the Party, in this and subsequent statements, did not entirely oppose the Manchurian Incident, it remained more critical of it in general than the Sōdōmei. The other proletarian parties were even more consistent in attacking the Incident. The Sōdōmei's retreat from socialism on this critical issue, where one might have expected a socialist labor movement to take a harder stand in opposing Japanese imperialism abroad, had not extended into the proletarian party movement, at least not yet.

The last and perhaps the most important context wherein the Sōdōmei's deliberate withdrawal from socialist politics manifested itself was in the general relationship of the Federation to the socialist party movement in 1932. Entering the general elections of February that year, the socialist parties included the Shakai Minshūtō and the centrist party, which had changed its name once again when in July 1931 Ōyama Ikuo had closed down the legal Shin Rōnōtō to merge his forces with Asō Hisashi's organization. The latter then became the Zenkoku Rōnō Taishūtō, referred to earlier. Another party, which was politically to the right of both of these organizations, had also emerged by the time of the elections: the Kokumin Shakaitō Soshiki Jumbikai (Preparatory Committee for the National Socialist Party). Its origins will be discussed shortly.

As before, the Sōdōmei went through the motions of supporting the Shakai Minshūtō in the 1932 elections, emphasizing again the same labor union issues that had figured so prominently in 1930, to the exclusion of any broader socialist vision of the Party's purpose. To be sure, the Shakai Minshūtō joined the other proletarian parties in ridiculing the Seiyūkai as the 'Seiyū Mitsui' and the Minseitō as the 'Minsei Mitsubishi' because of the connection of the liberal parties with powerful *zaibatsu* interests.[118] And, with differing degrees of emphasis, the proletarian parties attacked the Manchurian Incident as an intolerable instance of aggression.[119]

However, in the case of the Shakai Minshūtō, these rather assertive policies were defined not in cooperation with the Sōdōmei's political bureau, which, for its part, emphasized labor union issues with a single mindedness reminiscent of 1930, but rather by party elders such as Abe Isoo who were still determined to maintain a socialist critique of contemporary trends. The Sōdōmei did give some support to such candidates as Nishio Suehiro and Matsuoka but their campaigns were waged without reference to socialism; both men tried to focus on the legitimacy of labor unions and laws on behalf of the workers as their chief emphasis. Even then, however, the 1932 elections were a dismaying disappointment for labor candidates and indeed for the socialist parties in general. Suzuki Bunji, Nishio, Matsuoka, and other key Shakai Minshūtō candidates were defeated, with only Abe, Kamei Kan'ichirō, and Koike Shirō entering the Diet. The Zenkoku Rōnō Taishūtō also suffered defeat at the polls, electing only Matsutani Yoshirō and

Sugiyama Motojirō. Again, the proletarian parties had won only five Diet seats, a paltry showing compared with the liberal parties, of which the Seiyūkai emerged the victor.[120]

The one bright consequence of the 1932 elections was that after years of undercutting each other, the Shaminkei and Nichirōkei parties decided to merge together in order to create a socialist united front at the polls. The Sōdōmei had reason to be sympathetic to this development, for one of its most important leaders, Nishio Suehiro, owed his election defeat in 1932 to a failure to work out an agreement with the Zenkoku Rōnō Taishūtō whereby it and the Shakai Minshūtō would avoid placing candidates in districts where only one had a chance of winning. In this case, Nishio had been opposed by Ōya Shōzō in Osaka, with the consequence that both men lost.[121]

The merger of the Shakai Minshūtō and the Zenkoku Rōnō Taishūtō into the Shakai Taishūtō (Social Masses' Party) on July 24, 1932 in Tokyo did not come about easily; both parties experienced internal dissension and splits over this issue. In the Shakai Minshūtō great confusion arose in the spring of 1932 when, to the surprise of nearly everyone, Akamatsu Katsumaro declared that instead of merging with the centrists, whom he said were still 'pro-communist', the Party ought to help in forming a national socialist political front to support Japan in a time of peril. Akamatsu explained that he had been convinced by the Manchurian Incident, of which he strongly approved, that this was the 'patriotic duty' of the socialist movement.[122]

Unknown to the Shakai Minshūtō, Akamatsu had in fact already begun to work for a national socialist party through private consultation with Shimonaka Yasaburō, a move which had resulted in the formation of the aforementioned Kokumin Shakaitō Soshiki Jumbikai in January 1932. Shimonaka was the leader of this group which also had the support of Sakamoto Kōsaburō who in the end had not taken his General Alliance of Labor Unions into the Nihon Rōdō Kurabu but instead committed this organization to the new national socialist movement. Suzuki Etsujirō, of the Yamanouchi clique in the Nichirōkei, also participated in the Jumbikai.[123] Working behind the scenes, Akamatsu had persuaded these men to delay the conversion of the Jumbikai into a bona fide party until he could persuade the Shakai Minshūtō to join with it, hence the tentative name of the Jumbikai.[124]

The complex reasons for Akamatsu's activities in 1932 need not be elaborated here save to say that, as his writings of this period reveal, Akamatsu had concluded that socialism had to be made compatible with nationalism so that the socialists could continue their efforts on behalf of the 'people' (he now referred to them as the *kokumin*) while also serving the nation.[125] His earlier concept of 'scientific Japanism' remained intact. Only now the tension that had resided in it between the 'rationality' of socialism and his notion of *kokuminteki na unmei* or 'racial destiny' had slipped in favor of the latter category in his thought. However, the other leaders of the Shakai Minshūtō were not persuaded by Akamatsu's proposals, which they regarded as a sell-out to the State. Thus Akamatsu was expelled from the Party in April 1932 along with Koike Shirō and about forty other men who had become sympathetic to his ideas. Once this happened, the way was cleared for joining the Zenkoku Rōnō Taishūtō.[126]

Similarly, in the Zenkoku Rōnō Taishūtō, the role played by Akamatsu in the Shakai Minshūtō was played by Oya Shōzō who opposed amalgamation with the latter and argued for aligning the Party with the projected national socialist party. After failing in this endeavor, Ōya joined Akamatsu and Shimonaka in planning the national socialist party.[127] However, ultimately, two parties emerged from these maneuverings because of disagreements over who should be chairman. Akamatsu established the Nihon Kokka Shakaitō (Japan State Socialist Party) while Shimonaka formed the Shin Nihon Kokumin Dōmei (New Japan Nationalist Federation). Their platforms were nearly identical although the Kokka Shakaitō stressed 'State socialism' whereas its rival emphasized 'Japanism'. Both looked to Kaeno Shin'ichi's labor front for support in the factories.[128]

When it finally took place, the merging of the right-wing and centrist socialist parties into the Shakai Taishūtō held much promise for the socialist party movement. An equitable division of power between both sides was agreed upon with Abe serving as President, Asō as General Secretary, and Miwa Jusō as Treasurer. The membership of the central executive committee was carefully balanced between both factions in equal numbers. This was likewise the case with a larger central committee consisting of no less than 100 men. Virtually every person who had been prominently associated with the Shaminkei and Nichirōkei sat on the latter; Yoshino Sakuzō, Takano Iwasaburō, Imai Yoshiyuki, Baba Tsunego, Suzuki Bunji, Nishio Suehiro, Hamada Kunitarō, and many others were included.[129]

In addition, the Shakai Taishūtō served notice that socialism was still very much alive when it proclaimed in its official Platform: '1. Our party will fight for the sake of protecting the livelihood of the workers, farmers, and the masses of the working people in general. 2. Our party aims at the overthrow of capitalism and the liberation of the pro- letariat.'[130] 'Anti-communism', 'anti-capitalism', and 'anti-fascism' were invoked as slogans as the Party listed virtually every reform that had been championed by the socialist party movement in the past: abolition of repressive laws such as the Peace Preservation Law; aboli- tion of the Peers; reform of the tax system; the passage of a labor union law and other laws benefiting the workers; the right of women to vote; and, in the area of foreign policy, the end to protectionist trade barriers around the world and the peaceful resolution of international problems through such steps as a Russo-Japanese Non-Aggression Pact and, more vaguely, recognition of the 'true independence' of Manchuria.[131] On the matter of its class orientation, the Shakai Taishūtō professed to speak for the *kinrō taishū* (masses of working people); the language of this concept reflected a compromise between the Shaminkei's *kinrō kaikyū* and the Nichirōkei's *musan kaikyū*.[132]

But if it seemed that the Shakai Taishūtō was girding its loins for the defense of socialism, this was not the case with the Nihon Rōdō Sōdōmei. Of course, the Federation was prepared to back the Party in a formal sense. However, its support was to be conditional on the Party's capacity to serve unionism, not socialism. Any doubts on this matter were clarified within several months of the Party's formation, particularly when Matsuoka Komakichi replaced Suzuki Bunji as chairman of the Sōdōmei in the Sōdōmei's annual convention of November 3–5, 1932.

In fact, for all intents and purposes, Matsuoka had taken over the reins of the Sōdōmei in November 1931, when at the Federation's con- vention in that year Suzuki Bunji had submitted his resignation as chairman, explaining it was time to step aside to allow a worker to assume this post. Suzuki had also stated that he wanted to devote all of his energy to the socialist party movement, hence his decision to give up office in the Sōdōmei.[133] Matsuoka, as Director of the Federation, had therefore become de facto chairman of the Sōdōmei. He was formally elected to this position in the 1932 convention.

At once, Matsuoka declared that henceforth he would as Sōdōmei chairman, spend all of his time serving the cause of 'sound unionism' in the labor movement. He gave notice that he would therefore not run again for election to the Diet and that his role in the new Shakai Taishūtō would be minimal. Politics, Matsuoka affirmed in so many words, could be left to the socialist party movement.[134]

This was quite a different set of priorities for Matsuoka as an individual and for the Sōdōmei as an organization than Suzuki had come to believe in. The contrast is significant: it symbolized the retreat of the Sōdōmei, which was followed by that of the Nihon Rōdō Kumiai Kaigi, from involvement in socialist politics and a turning inward toward priorities such as sound unionism that were seen to be essentially nonpolitical. A certain irony can be detected in this rearrangement of goals. Suzuki, who had founded the Yūaikai as a nonpolitical organization, had decided that socialist politics now took precedence over labor unionism, pure and simple. Matsuoka, who had taken part in the transformation of the Yūaikai into the Sōdōmei because of his belief that unions should engage in political action, now believed that sound unionism, which resembled the goals of the early Yūaikai, took precedence over political action. In giving Matsuoka control of the Sōdōmei, Suzuki had in effect returned the Sōdōmei to the past.

Matsuoka's concept of priorities was shared widely throughout the Sōdōmei, as the 1932 convention indicated. To begin with, the convention adopted a new platform that was strikingly similar to the original Yūaikai's. It read,

1. In accordance with our mutual ideals, we aim to improve and perfect the individual worker through the development of his consciousness, technical skills, and moral character.
2. We will endeavor to promote the reform and prosperity of working conditions by means of autonomous organizations and discipline of the workers.
3. We aim at the construction of a sound, new social order through a basic reform of capitalism on the basis of prevailing national circumstances.[135]

The reference to 'moral character', reliance on 'discipline' and the building of a 'sound' social order were all reminiscent of the early Friendly Society. In addition, the statement that the reform of capitalism would be conditioned by 'prevailing national circumstances' made it clear that the Federation would not actively resist these 'circumstances' in reforming capitalism.

Then, as if to back up the new, conservative 'change of direction' taken by the Sōdōmei in 1932, the convention voted to delete the former ruling that had been in effect prior to the establishment of the Shakai Taishūtō, namely, that 'Male members of the Sōdōmei twenty years or older shall in principle join the Shakai Minshūtō.'[136] Instead, the convention endorsed Matsuoka's view that 'Relations between the Sōdōmei and the Shakai Taishūtō will be different from the relations

between the Sōdōmei and the Shakai Minshūtō...it is no longer
necessary to apply Article Ten [the aforementioned section of the
Federation's Constitution governing labor–party relations] to the
Shakai Taishūtō.'[137]

These steps, taken to widen the distance between the Sōdōmei and
the Shakai Taishūtō and stemming from the belief that the goals of
sound unionism would be imperiled if the Sōdōmei were to identify
itself too closely with a party that seemed determined to defend socialism, were accompanied by a lengthy resolution drafted by the Sōdōmei
central committee which explained that originally the Yūaikai had
made labor unionism its central priority. However, over the years, due
to the absence of proletarian parties and the influence of anarchist and
communist ideas in the 1920s, the labor movement had been deflected
from this goal into political struggle. The platforms of the Sōdōmei had
been altered from time to time in accordance with these changing
emphases. Now in the present 'period of emergency' (*hijō jidai*) – an
explicit allusion to the manifold economic impact of the Depression in
Japan, 'the worsening of international relations in the aftermath of the
Manchurian Incident', and to the threats of communism and 'fascism'
– the time had come for the labor movement to return to its first
principles, to an emphasis on labor unionism as an end in and for
itself.[138]

With that, the convention proceeded to make *sangyō kyōryoku*,
which Suzuki Bunji had popularized in the early Yūaikai, a paramount
emphasis, thus clearly indicating that the Sōdōmei would strive above
all to assist the government and business in the implementation of the
policies of industrial rationalization within the context of harmonious
relations between labor and management.[139] Although unstated, the
implication of this general policy was that the Sōdōmei was prepared
to give up even symbolic resistance to the trend toward 'enterprise
unionism' which industrial rationalization continued to reinforce.
Needless to say, as *sangyō kyōryoku* ascended in importance, any
vestiges of commitment to class struggle, even on the basis of moderate
'realist socialism', decreased in relative significance. As the convention
came to an end, there was little doubt that the Sōdōmei's retreat from
socialism, begun early in the Depression period, would continue into
the foreseeable future, even as the new Shakai Taishūtō, which would
necessarily have to rely on labor organizations like the Sōdōmei, was
making its bid to preserve socialism as a political force in Japan.

Organized labor and socialist politics, 1929–1932: in retrospect

Referring to the institutions of the Japanese labor movement, Koji Taira suggests that in 1932 the movement had entered its 'dying stage'.[140] This characterization, which he applies to the capacity of the movement to achieve tangible goals on behalf of the workers, would perhaps be acceptable were it not for the formation of the Nihon Rōdō Kurabu and the Nihon Rōdō Kumiai Kaigi. Although structurally porous, they nonetheless represented labor alliances of a type and on a scale unknown in Japan prior to 1932. Their general advocacy of sound unionism and their continued support for the progressive goals of the ILO manifested a new vigor of sorts in labor's defense of the workers' livelihood.

Perhaps the metaphor of death is more valid if one applies it to labor's commitment to socialist politics, which had indeed begun to 'die' in the 1929–1932 period. Or, an alternative metaphor in this regard is suggested by Mayer Zald and Roberta Ash who use the term 'becalmed' to describe social movements that have lost much of their original vision but which, remaining ambivalent about the future, somehow manage to keep going by treading water for a time before they finally sink beneath the waves, the victims of their own atrophy of mission and a repressive environment.[141] The process of becalming set in when the Nihon Rōdō Sōdōmei, the Nihon Rōdō Kurabu and the Nihon Rōdō Kumiai Kaigi undertook to gradually divorce themselves from socialist politics in the early 1930s.

As Zald and Ash point out, the literature on social movements is replete with examples of social movements suffering this fate of 'becalming'. In many instances, writers on social movements have explained the process of becalming as a function of tendencies in the leadership toward bureaucratization, oligarchization, and the 'routinization of charisma'.[142] In this type of analysis, it is suggested that when administrative elites take power from the original charismatic founder of a movement, the 'mobilization' function performed by the latter in rallying the movement to a compelling vision of purpose gives way to the function of 'articulation' in which emphasis is placed on fitting the movement into its immediate environment and the function of 'integration' emphasizing the development of solidarity and cohesion within the movement.[143] As James Scoville puts it in referring to labor organizations that Zald and Ash would describe as 'becalmed', they become overwhelmingly oriented to the 'survival imperative of institutions' which eclipses in significance any other, broader goals they may have once embraced.[144]

This, in a word, was what had occurred in the Sōdōmei. By the time Suzuki Bunji passed the leadership to workers like Matsuoka and Nishio for whom the 'survival imperative' of their labor institutions was the overriding priority in the Depression period, the General Federation had become locked into its retreat from socialist politics in order to save the unions from what was believed to be the possibility of imminent destruction. Thus, the Sōdōmei in the early 1930s can be described in much the same way that Joel Seidman characterizes most labor movements:

> The union traditionally has been an insecure agency operating in an in-secure world, dependent upon its fighting strength for survival; its leaders, at the local as well as the national level, have overwhelmingly thought in terms of current issues, of solutions for problems that immediately confront them. Their long-run goals, needless to say, influence their decisions, but primarily they are men pragmatic in their philosophy and flexible in their methods, determining their objectives in the light of shifting considera-tions: the economic conditions of industry, the policies of the government, the state of public opinion, the existence of rival unionism, the fighting power of the employer, and the loyalty and discipline of the union membership.[145]

A similar becalming of political purpose did not occur in the newly-formed Shakai Taishūtō in this period. This was due to the compara-tively stronger charisma of such political leaders as Abe and Asō in the Party and to the fact that most of the Party's leaders were intellectuals, more strongly motivated by an ideological fidelity to socialism than the worker elites of the labor movement. Socialism remained for them an important, inspiring, overall objective. But soon the political conser-vatism of the labor movement would undermine the Shakai Taishūtō as it defined strategies for political struggle in the future. Men in the Party who clung to socialism would become disillusioned with the political becalming of the mass-based social movements to which they looked for support. They would give up any notion of carrying out a democratic reconstruction of Japan from below and dream instead of achieving a socialist 'renovation' (*kakushin*) of Japan from above by assisting the New Order which arose later in the 1930s and whose nature they did not comprehend.

7

Labor becalmed, 1932–1936

The Nihon Rōdō Sōdōmei and other organizations in its labor bloc such as the Nihon Kaiin Kumiai and the Nihon Rōdō Kangyō Sōdōmei continued their retreat from socialist politics well into the middle of the 1930s, fully determined to carry through their pledge to realize the goals of nonpolitical sound unionism for the workers. They made little attempt to reassess the appropriateness of this emphasis in the context of crisis politics in Japan during this period. The only systematic endeavor in the early 1930s to transcend the immediate situation facing the labor movement and develop a comprehensive theory of the labor movement that would relate unionism to political purpose came from a member of Asō Hisashi's faction in the labor movement, Kikukawa Tadao. Of special interest is a book written by Kikukawa in 1931, entitled *Rōdō kumiai soshiki ron* [On the Organization of Labor Unions].

In brief, Kikukawa claimed that the Japanese labor movement had an historic mission that transcended its battle against 'the repression of the unions by the ruling classes',[1] namely, to play its part alongside labor movements in the West in the prevention of a second world war. He argued that such an event was a distinct likelihood now that imperialist rivalries for raw materials and foreign markets throughout the world were about to escalate because capitalism both in the West and in Japan had reached the monopoly stage of its development. The problem in the Japanese case, he admitted, was how to repoliticize the labor movement which was being gradually turned away from socialist policies, including opposition to imperialism and war, by such organizations as the Sōdōmei that had been seduced by the 'fallacious' ideas of 'British Fabian reformism',[2] to the point where they could not see the imperative of political struggle.

Kikukawa's solution to this problem was multi-faceted: first, the labor movement must be made to recover its commitment to class struggle in order to overthrow the *zaibatsu* and the governments which served them before these agencies of Japanese capitalism dragged Japan into war. Second, organized labor must resist the trend toward enterprise unionism which threatened to extinguish the class consciousness of the proletariat. Third, the unions must be made to give greater support to, and receive the political guidance of, the socialist parties, which were still determined to oppose capitalism, imperialism, and war. Because Kikukawa had the greatest faith in the centrist labor movement based in the Zenkoku Rōdō Kumiai Dōmei, he called upon it to rejuvenate the dormant socialism of the Sōdōmei and other labor organizations in the Shaminkei fold.[3]

Kikukawa retained these views for quite some time following the publication of his book. The outbreak of the Manchurian Incident, which seemed to confirm his prediction of a new aggressive phase in Japanese imperialism, reinforced his thinking all the more in the 1932–1936 period. Others in the Zenkoku Rōdō Kumiai Dōmei rallied to Kikukawa's ideas in these years with the result that new strains were introduced into the evolving labor front, the Nihon Rōdō Kumiai Kaigi, where the Zenkoku Rōdō Kumiai Dōmei and its bloc coexisted rather uneasily with the Sōdōmei and its allies. From 1932 to 1936, the former increasingly emphasized militant class struggle in the labor movement while the latter, as in the earlier 1930s, clung rigidly to the politics of compromise.

Kikukawa's ideas are cited here because they indicate that some men, at least, in the labor movement had not been intimidated by the political and economic circumstances of the Depression period into taking an extremely cautious approach to labor's priorities. Whether or not the Japanese labor movement would have been able to realize the historical mission defined for it by Kikukawa in 1931 and thereafter, had labor paid heed to his call to arms, is a matter greatly debated in Nichirōkei and Shaminkei recollections of the 1930s. This dispute may strike one as academic in view of the fact that, in 1936 and after, the labor movement was obviously too small and weak to even survive, let alone take the offensive for socialism in preventing war or achieving a socialist reconstruction of Japan.

But where it pertains to the 1932–1936 period, this dispute cannot be lightly dismissed as academic. Research on the history of Japan in the 1930s has not demonstrated conclusively that the nation's drift toward political authoritarianism and war late in the decade was the inevitable consequence of earlier events and trends. While it is unlikely that the Shakai Taishūtō and a politically committed labor movement

would have been able to stop this drift, and though it must be acknow-
ledged that the very remote prospects for carrying out a socialist reconstruction of Japan that may have existed in the relatively more favorable political atmosphere of the 1920s had grown even more remote in
the 1930s, it is suggested here that the instability and fluidity of
Japanese politics from 1932 to 1936 at least held open the possibility
of a different evolution from that which led later to the New Order
and Japan's subsequent plunge into World War II. In appreciating
the indeterminate nature of labor's political context prior to 1936, men
like Kikukawa saw that the darkness of the 'dark valley' (*kurai tanima*)
in the early 1930s was due more to the grey of political ambiguity than
to the black of direct political oppression, unlike their fear-laden
counterparts in the Sōdōmei.

Labor's environment, 1932–1936

After the assassination of Prime Minister Inukai in 1932, Japan entered
a protracted period of bureaucratic, non-party rule that lasted until
World War II. Inukai's immediate successors were Admiral Saitō
Makoto, whose cabinet was in office from 1932 to 1934, and Admiral
Okada Keisuke, Prime Minister from 1934 to 1936. During these
administrations, the screws tightened on the labor movement politically
and economically. But not so completely that the labor movement was
entirely deprived of room for political action.

It has been shown elsewhere that the overwhelming preoccupation of
the Saitō and Okada governments was with industrial recovery, military
self-strengthening, and problems of national defense.[4] Diplomatic
problems also weighed heavily on the government in this period, such
as the League's censure of Japan in Manchuria, to which the Saitō
administration reacted by withdrawing Japan from the League. Expectations of war, rampant at the time, were expressed in a remark by
General Ishiwara Kanji in 1933 that 'The coming war with the Anglo-
American nations will be mankind's last war, to be fought for the
unification of world civilization...'[5]

Given this febrile atmosphere of ultranationalism and war-mobilization, it is tempting to conclude that the labor movement was faced with
overwhelming threats to its very existence in the early 1930s, just as
Sōdōmei leaders had concluded. This was certainly true for radical
labor. The policy of anti-communism adopted by previous liberal party
cabinets was continued by their successors.

However, the non-communist labor movement was not repressed

until 1936 and even after that one cannot speak of it succumbing to the whip of a police state. There is no evidence that the Japanese government wanted to break the back of non-communist labor in the 1932–1936 period. None of the organizations in the Nihon Rōdō Kumiai Kaigi experienced the kind of police arrests that were suffered by Zenkyō, for instance. On the contrary, the bureaucratic administrations of Saitō and Okada resembled earlier liberal party governments in their pursuit of a policy of 'whip and candy' toward the labor movement. Indeed, in 1934 the Okada administration declared that it would support the principle of legalizing unions in order to stabilize labor relations, a continuation of the Minseitō government's stated position of 1929.[6] The Okada government did not sponsor any action in line with this declaration, unlike the Minseitō administration, but clearly it was not determined to destroy the labor movement either.

Although the demise of liberal party government was inauspicious for organized labor, care must be taken not to exaggerate either the power or the authoritarian character of the Saitō and Okada governments. The truth is that they were constantly buffeted by conflicting demands concerning national defense readiness from different sections of the Japanese military. Lacking any basis of popular support and immobilized by fears of continuing rightist terrorism, these were weak and short-lived governments that came and went because they could not provide Japan with decisive leadership in domestic and foreign affairs.

The fact that the Saitō and Okada administrations were hostages to rivalries in the Japanese military relates to an equally important point: the military in this period was too internally divided and too preoccupied with its own problems to pose a serious threat to the labor movement between 1932 and 1936. Despite the military's increasing influence over national politics the armed forces were not monolithic. Rather, they were driven by ideological and personal factionalism, as for instance in the well-known Imperial Way (*Kōdō-ha*) and Control (*Tōsei-ha*) struggle, by conflicting concepts of military priorities and by differing predictions of the enemies of Japan, and the measures Japan should take to wage war against them.[7] On occasion, these rivalries boiled over into violence – the murder of General Nagata Tetsuzan of the Control faction by a member of the Imperial Way faction being a case in point.[8] And, as earlier in this turbulent decade, the military continued to be the source of terrorist plots designed to spark a 'Shōwa Restoration'.[9]

The military, then, was too consumed by its internal conflicts to take much notice of the labor movement in this period, much less contemplate the movement's destruction. Similarly, although ultranationalist sentiments were scarcely congenial to the labor movement, it would appear that ultranationalists in and outside the government and the military were more concerned with liberal dissent against their ideas than they were about the labor movement or the Shakai Taishūtō. An illustration is the fate in 1935 of Professor Minobe Tatsukichi of Tokyo Imperial University who was publicly condemned by conservatives in the Imperial Diet for ideas that he had long held but which were regarded as treasonous in the 1930s. In particular, Minobe was pilloried for advocating that the Emperor was no more than an 'organ of State' rather than an embodiment of the State, as his attackers, who included liberal politicians in the Seiyūkai and Minseitō, held. Ultimately, Minobe resigned his position in Law at the University as a consequence of these attacks.[10] This was a much-publicized blow to liberalism but it did not affect the labor movement directly.

To reiterate, labor's political environment had not deteriorated to the point where the Sōdōmei's self-imposed retreat from socialist political purpose was, strictly speaking, necessary in an objective sense. In fact, it was probably premature, albeit perhaps understandable from the particular perspective of men like Matsuoka Komakichi and Nishio Suehiro. In this connection, the mentality of Kikukawa and the other Nichirōkei labor leaders who subscribed to the ideas of his book in 1931 and thereafter contrasted markedly with the mentality of the Sōdōmei leadership and, indeed, with that of the government and the military in this period. Kikukawa may have over-estimated the capacity of the labor movement and the Shakai Taishūtō to influence events. But at least he had based his concepts of what might be done on the basis of realistically perceiving the fundamental ambiguity and inconclusiveness that characterized labor's political environment.

By contrast, although they did so in different ways for different ends, both the Shaminkei labor leaders and the civil–military establishment defined policy in accordance with distorted perceptions of reality and apprehensions of what might happen, not what was actually happening around them. This, in turn, led them to inadvertently transform fear into reality. At the government level of decision making, once the government and the military succumbed to the view that war was inevitable, they set about to prepare for war rather than to undertake policies designed to prevent war, with the result that over the years

Japan became increasingly estranged from a hostile West and vulnerable to war.[11] Similarly, once elements of the labor movement, such as the Sōdōmei, had decided that the narrow cause of unionism had to take precedence over political struggle on behalf of socialism, and once they had embarked on the politics of compromise and the compromise of politics, they ordained, by their own hand, that their subsequent co-optation by the government at the end of the decade would be quick and ignominious.

Turning to labor's economic context in the 1932–1936 period, pressures mounted against the unions in the factories, but here again circumstances in these years were not so conclusively negative as to cut off all possibilities for the survival of a politically committed union movement. Riding on the strength of heavy industry, Japan recovered rather quickly from the Depression. After 1932, Japan experienced a 'second industrial revolution' (the first one being that which stretched from mid-Meiji to 1929).[12] Capitalism had been politically discredited but the same strategies of industrial paternalism which had gathered momentum in the 1920s were continued and expanded in the context of *sangyō gōrika* so that the earlier *zaibatsu*, and 'new' *zaibatsu*, increased their domination of the national economy.[13] But this trend did not fundamentally alter the position of the labor movement in relation to industry, although this position remained weak in the period under review.

As Japanese industrial production began to climb again in late 1931, the country enjoyed a new export boom. From 1930 to 1936, exports rose from 1,435 million yen to 2,641 million yen.[14] The bulk of these were cheap textile goods but increasingly they included heavy industrial products. The export boom saw a change in the general regional distribution of Japanese exports. Though, for the first time, Japan exported more to the United States in this period than she imported from that country, Japan also sent goods to other countries in Asia, Oceania, South America, Africa and Europe with increasing consistency.[15] This trend produced fears in the West that Japan was 'dumping' cheap products on the world economy to the detriment of indigenous industry. Such fears led to protective tariffs and quotas against Japanese goods which only served to drive Japan even further away from the West.[16]

As before, production boomed through a government policy of heavy loans on favorable terms to industry, which stimulated industry to the point where manufacturing output rose 63 per cent from 1930 to 1936 and mining 34 per cent.[17] It was mentioned earlier in this study that growth trends were especially discernible in the heavy industrial sector. In addition, statistics show that while consumer goods production rose by only 33 per cent in this period, producer goods rose by 83 per cent.[18]

As might be expected, Japan's 'industrial revolution' of the 1930s militated in many ways against labor unionism. Large factories, where the institutions of industrial paternalism proliferated, were increasingly difficult for the labor movement to penetrate. Using figures for 1933, for instance, Taira estimates that of 560,532 workers in private enterprises employing 500 or more workers, only 32,049 belonged to unions. This was a very low figure considering that there were 125,170 workers in private firms of this category of 500 or more workers where unions were permitted to exist. The picture in public enterprises with 500 or more workers was also bleak. In this category, of a total of 196,534 workers, only 46,100 workers belonged to unions in 1933.[19]

In those instances of unions in large factories, the tendency was for their workers to identify increasingly with the interests of their firms rather than with the goals of the labor movement because of the continuing attractiveness of benefits offered by the institutions of the *nenkō* system, such as job security, automatic pay increases, and ancillary welfare benefits, all of which made the unions, as vehicles to achieve the same goals, irrelevant and redundant. This is why Kikukawa had emphasized the incompatibility of enterprise unionism and political struggle.

Unions, then, were largely confined to small and medium-scale factories where, without the presence of industrial paternalism, it was relatively easier for the labor movement to organize those workers who remained discontented with low wages and poor conditions. Also, the unions in these firms did not have to contend so much with the phenomenon of *goyō kumiai* (company unions) and *kōjō iinkai* (works councils), which employers in large firms used more regularly to blunt the progress of unions in their midst. Thus, most of the growth experienced by the labor movement in this period was confined to these firms. By 1936, the movement included 420,589 workers out of a total work force of 6,090,116 workers, in 973 unions – which represented a unionization rate of 6.9 per cent, in contrast to the figures cited earlier for 1931: 368,975 workers in 818 unions out of a total of 4,729,436 industrial workers, or a unionization rate of 7.9 per cent, the differential in the rates of unionization being explained by the increase in the total work force between 1931 and 1936.[20]

In other words, the trend of continuing weakness in large firms and of continuing confinement to small and medium firms in the 1930s did not differ basically from that of the 1920s. Certainly this trend was not in itself justification for breaking the link, which had been forged under similar conditions in the 1920s, between unionism and socialist politics.

Perhaps one can sympathize with the discouragement of Japanese labor leaders later in the decade when the numerical strength of the labor movement declined, first in gradual patterns of ebb and flow, and then, at a cascading rate (the number of unionists fell to 359,290 in 1937, rose slightly to 375,191 in 1938, dropped again to 365,804 in 1939, and finally to a paltry 9,455 in 1940 on the eve of the movement's extinction; the number of unions in this period declined to 731 in 1938, 517 in 1939, and 49 in 1940).[21] But in the 1932–1936 period, it was impossible to foresee that the movement would sink to these depths. In that period, when labor organizations like the Sōdōmei became becalmed politically, the trend was toward moderate growth in terms of the number of unions and unionists, if not in the rate of unionization. Like the distribution of the unions, the actual size of the movement ought not to have been a factor in pushing the Sōdōmei and its bloc in the direction of political meekness.

Concerning the level of industrial protest in the 1932–1936 period, statistics reveal that it declined. The comparative quiescence of worker protest is illustrated by the fact that whereas in 1931 there were 2,456 labor disputes including 993 strikes and other instances of work stoppage in which 64,536 workers had participated, in 1936, there were 1,975 disputes including 547 strikes involving a total of only 30,900 workers.[22] But this pattern of industrial action, while perhaps confirming the view of Sōdōmei leaders that most workers were not ready for militant political struggle, was essentially peripheral to the decision to back away from political involvement since that decision had been made in the Depression period when the level of industrial unrest had been much higher. Nor was it possible, from 1932 to 1936, for Sōdōmei leaders to justify their political becalming on the grounds that the dwindling number of strikes was due to police repression of the workers who took part. Instances of repression were too few for this view to prevail. Rather, the decline in worker protest in this period was due to the general improvement of employment opportunities and wage levels during Japan's recovery from the Depression.

It was not until the late 1930s that industrial protest slackened dramatically or that its decline was caused by the direct intimidation of the workers by the police, including workers in the few unions that remained on the scene and which engaged in industrial protest from time to time (in 1940, there were 718 labor disputes, involving 32,160 workers – 226 of these disputes actually resulted in strikes).[23] Even as late as 1937, the year in which Japan became enmeshed in a massive war on the continent, Japan experienced 2,126 labor disputes, 628 of which were strikes, involving 123,730 workers.[24] However, as in 1931, the impact of these disputes on the Sōdōmei was to reduce the militancy of the Sōdōmei – in 1937, to the point of renouncing the right of labor to strike altogether, in order to support the nation at war.

In sum, with respect to the prevailing economic conditions which affected the labor movement in the 1932–1936 period, the actual situation of the unions in the factories remained no better and not much worse than what they faced earlier on. If anything, the improvement in the employment picture in this period partially reduced the pressure on the unions which had suffered attrition during layoffs in the Depression period. However, this favorable change was regarded by the Sōdōmei elites as a green light for pursuing nonpolitical sound unionism, to strengthen union institutions in and for themselves, not as a positive development that might have strengthened the unions for political struggle.

In pursuit of sound unionism, 1932–1936

The difference between Kikukawa's perception of necessary action and the viewpoint of Shaminkei labor concerning the immediate priorities of the labor movement is strikingly revealed in an article that appeared in the May 1933 issue of the Sōdōmei organ, *Rōdō*. The (unidentified) writer asserted flatly that labor unions were neither 'political organizations' nor 'struggle organizations'. Rather, they were 'economic organizations' whose mandate was simply to improve the livelihood of the workers through the policies of sound unionism. The article referred to 'certain intellectuals' who wanted to deflect labor from this goal into futile political causes.[25] Whether the latter reference was an allusion to Kikukawa's book is unknown. But a clearer repudiation of his ideas is unimaginable.

Given this narrow concept of the role of unionism, it is scarcely surprising that in the 1932–1936 period the Shakai Taishūtō's 'anti-communism', 'anti-capitalism', and 'anti-fascism' were, in the Sōdōmei, merely weak adjuncts to sound unionism. For example, with regard to 'anti-communism', when the communists Nabeyama Sadachika and

Sano Manabu announced their conversion to nationalism in 1933, Matsuoka took that opportunity to declare once again that the General Federation, for its part, had always fought communism and would continue to do so in the future as it endeavored to realize the goals of sound unionism out of patriotic conviction that unionism could serve the interests of the State. At the same time, Matsuoka remarked that he wished Nabeyama and Sano had not been quite so strident in professing their new-found nationalism because their dramatic 180-degree about-face from communism to nationalism made it harder for organizations like the Sōdōmei, which had always supported the *kokutai*, to register as dramatic an impact on public opinion in demonstrating their support of the nation.[26]

As for 'anti-fascism' the Sōdōmei leaders were more apprehensive about a budding national socialist labor movement than they were about the role of fascism in national politics in the 1932–1936 period. When they spoke of 'fascism', it was in connection with national socialist (and Japanist) labor organizations that crystallized in the 1930s, not in reference to rightist terrorism, Shōwa Restoration fanaticism, or the growing power of the military in government. Nor, for that matter, can one find political commentaries in *Rōdō* and other sources which might have suggested any links between 'fascism' in Japan and fascism in Italy and Germany.

In addition to the patriotic labor front that gained momentum under the auspices of organizations like Kaeno Shin'ichi's Jikyō Rōdō Kumiai, mentioned in the last chapter, the new national socialist parties originating in 1932 organized 'fascist' labor organizations of their own. For instance, the day after Akamatsu formed the Nihon Kokka Shakaitō in May, he and Ōya Shōzō organized the Nihon Kokka Shakai Rōdō Dōmei (Japan State Socialist Labor Federation), consisting of unions that had bolted from the Zenkoku Rōdō Kumiai Dōmei with Ōya on his withdrawal from the Zenkoku Rōnō Taishūtō in order to assist Akamatsu in the national socialist movement. The Nihon Kokka Shakai Rōdō Dōmei also relied upon the support of an organization founded by Akamatsu earlier on, which had accompanied him out of the Shaminkei labor and party movements – the 3,000-member Postmen's Brotherhood. By 1933, the Nihon Kokka Shakai Rōdō Dōmei numbered roughly 20,000 members and was a major base among the workers for the Nihon Kokka Shakaitō.[27]

To some extent, the threat posed by this right-wing labor movement was mitigated by subsequent cleavages in the national socialist movement during the early 1930s. It has been related how Akamatsu and Shimonaka ended up by forming separate parties in 1932. The complexity of the national socialist movement deepened the following year when Akamatsu, after disagreements with his followers, bolted from the Nihon Kokka Shakaitō, to organize a Japanist party known as the Kokumin Kyōkai (Nationalist Society).[28] Meanwhile, Koike Shirō, who had accompanied Akamatsu out of the Shakai Minshūtō, had split from Akamatsu to form yet another national socialist party, the Aikoku Seiji Dōmei (Patriotic Political Federation) in 1932. The national socialist labor movement also twisted its way through similar vicissitudes. For instance, Ōya's Nihon Kokka Shakai Rōdō Dōmei lost a substantial number of unions in 1933; their secession was due to personal rivalries and resulted in the formation of a Japanist labor federation, the Nihon Sangyō Gun (Japan Industrial Army).[29]

The distinction between national socialist and Japanist labor and political organizations was not insignificant in undermining the cohesiveness of these groups on the right. Although both types professed loyalty to the State, the national socialist organizations combined this with programs to benefit the proletariat, a term which they defined in various and often diffuse ways, such as the '*kokumin*' (people). That is, they tended to base themselves on some notion of class interest. By contrast, Japanist organizations regarded the 'people' as comprising the racial collectivity of the entire social order, not any particular class; they also tended to be more obscure than the national socialists in suggesting concrete solutions to contemporary social problems that would involve the State's playing a greater role in mediating between the capitalist class and the disadvantaged.

These divisions aside, the combined forces of national socialist and Japanist movements on the right were regarded in the Sōdōmei as a dangerous menace to sound unionism. First, in general terms, they seemed to be sympathetic to the basic ideals of a Shōwa Restoration and hence were linked in the minds of Sōdōmei leaders with political terrorism and intolerance toward all organizations that were, or had been, socialist in orientation. This would include the Sōdōmei. Second, the similarity between many of their ideas and those of the Shaminkei labor movement made it very difficult for the latter to distinguish itself from the former.

For instance, while the Sōdōmei professed to speak for the *kinrō kaikyū*, this concept of class did not differ fundamentally from the national socialists' concept of the *kokumin* as the beneficiary of its endeavors. Both concepts referred to the workers, farmers, and the petty bourgeoisie. Then, too, the Sōdōmei and similar labor organizations had trouble in distinguishing themselves from the national socialists and the Japanists in taking positions on sensitive questions of foreign policy. The enthusiastic support of the nationalists and self-proclaimed Japanists for Japan's imperial mission in Asia compelled the Sōdōmei to come out more strongly in supporting Japanese policies abroad in order to avoid the impression of being less patriotic.

So, in the spring of 1933, *Rōdō* declared that the new regime in Manchukuo deserved Japan's full diplomatic, economic, and military support because Manchukuo, like Japan, was based on the principle of *ōdō seiji* (righteous government). In this, the Emperor of Manchukuo, Pu Yi, was seen to be as much as a manifestation of the Kingly Way as the Japanese Emperor, Hirohito. The Sōdōmei also criticized the League of Nations, and the West generally, for failing to grant diplomatic recognition to Manchukuo as a sovereign country. Similarly, the Federation dropped all past support for the Nanking regime of Chiang Kai-shek which it described as a reactionary collection of 'selfish' military cliques who had no support from the Chinese people.[30]

Furthermore, the Sōdōmei had difficulty in dissociating itself from the national socialists with regard to 'anti-capitalism', a goal which they, too, shared. The Sōdōmei's commitment to 'anti-capitalism' had already been compromised by such policies as *sangyō kyōryoku*. Matters were worsened when it became obvious that the national socialists (who also spoke in terms of 'industrial cooperation') took the same line as the Sōdōmei in appealing to the government to intervene more pervasively in the economy in hopes that the government would, by so doing, assist the proletariat in escaping from the chains of capitalist exploitation. Many of the ideas held by Akamatsu in the Sōdōmei on this point, residual traces of which remained in the Federation, now found expression in the national socialist movement where Akamatsu had become a leading figure.

In general, therefore, much of the wind was taken out of the Sōdōmei's sails by the national socialists and Japanists in their pursuit of objectives strongly resembling those of the Sōdōmei. Even the Sōdōmei's concept of sound unionism, with all its emphasis on concrete pragmatic gains for the workers, was replicated in national socialist and Japanist labor organizations who also claimed to champion the interests of the workers in the amelioration of their lot. In this connection, the Nihon Rōdō Sōdōmei operated under two disadvantages, one of which was also shared by its new rivals on the right wing of the labor movement.

The first was that the Sōdōmei, having recently turned its back on the nexus between unionism and socialism, offered no political alternatives to the political content of the national socialist and Japanist labor and party movements. The political substance of the Sōdōmei's former 'realist socialism' had been removed, leaving only sound unionism, which was not a positive political ideology at all. Thus, the Sōdōmei, which had virtually denied politics, found itself faced with rivals on the right who still linked unionism to political action. Because of this, the national socialists and Japanists were able, far more than the politically inert Sōdōmei, to offer political, as well as economic solutions to contemporary problems, which must have appealed to those workers who joined their organizations. This was, after all, a period in which the inconclusiveness of Japanese politics made many men anxious for effective political answers to the enigma of preserving national power, social cohesion, and national purpose abroad.

Secondly, the Sōdōmei, and the national socialist labor movement in particular, were in danger of being trapped by the logical implications of their own nationalism of the 1930s. Ironically, they could not afford to be too nationalistic because there were limits as to how far organizations that based themselves on some notion of class interests (however vaporous and diffuse this notion actually was) could go in expressing patriotism without succumbing to demands from the ultra right that all sectarian interest groups of this nature should demonstrate their unity of spirit and purpose with the greater collectivity of the race and nation by dissolving themselves in a time of national peril.

To some extent, the national socialists could avoid this trap as long as they retained their belief that social movements from below could work in tandem with a progressive State in bringing about national socialism from above. If this succeeded, then theoretically it would not matter whether the grass roots organizations of national socialism ended up by dissolving themselves into a new national order, characterized by national socialist ideas and institutions, to serve the proletariat and the nation.

By contrast, it was axiomatic in the Shaminkei labor movement that the indispensable prerequisite for the achievement of sound unionism in Japan was the maintenance of a permanent labor union movement which could represent the interests of the workers in dealing with management and government to solve concrete problems affecting labor. The Sōdōmei was willing to have the assistance of a reform-minded government in this endeavor but at no time did its leaders believe that advances for labor required the total destruction of interest-group pluralism for the sake of all-embracing social unity in conformity with the needs of the State. However, lacking the ideas and vocabulary to translate this fidelity to the principle of labor-pluralism into political terms, the Sōdōmei exposed itself, to a far greater degree than the national socialists, to co-optation by the existing order without having any trace of satisfaction that the dissolution of the labor movement would at least facilitate the realization of certain progressive political goals, goals which in fact the Sōdōmei had ceased to entertain anyway.

Thus, accused by the left (Katō Kanjū, Kikukawa Tadao, the communists) of being too rightist, and condemned by the right (Akamatsu Katsumaro, the national socialists and Japanists) of not being rightist enough, the Sōdōmei plodded along in pursuit of sound unionism in the hope that by keeping a low political profile it could somehow serve the workers and avoid the perils of politics. Because the Federation's energies – and those of the labor bloc allied to the Sōdōmei – were exclusively concentrated on the focal point of sound unionism from 1932 to 1936, Shaminkei labor managed to kick up a great deal of dust in a frenzied flurry of activity, creating the impression of forward progress. But when the dust settled, it was clear that the Sōdōmei had merely been thrashing about in one place and that very little had been achieved on behalf of *kenjitsuteki na kumiaishugi*.

The quest for sound unionism took the form of many different initiatives that were seen to be interrelated in serving the goals of sound unionism. As stated earlier, these goals were the legitimation of unions as the representatives of labor, the recognition of labor's right to strike and bargain collectively, the passage of labor laws to fulfill the concrete goals for labor in the Sōdōmei's charter (and that of the International Labor Organization), and the freeing of labor from such legislation as the 1925 Peace Preservation Law, generally regarded as a vehicle for intimidating social movements although in fact it was not used directly against the Sōdōmei itself.

The Sōdōmei central committee and its chairman, Matsuoka Komakichi, placed greatest emphasis on collective bargaining in achieving the goals of sound unionism. This emphasis was not new in the Federation; for many years the Sōdōmei had waged a more or less continuous campaign to strike collective bargaining accords with employers. Over the years, these endeavors had met with little success.

But this did not daunt Matsuoka. When he launched a new and intensive collective bargaining campaign in the Sōdōmei national convention of 1932, he made it clear that the Federation would commit all its resources to the campaign to make it a success. He stated that if the Sōdōmei could accumulate an impressive number of de facto collective bargaining agreements with employers, then it would be easier for the labor movement to outflank the anti-labor policies of organizations like Zensanren. Matsuoka scrupulously avoided the implication that there was any connection between the campaign and socialism. Collective bargaining, he said simply, was the sine qua non of sound unionism and nothing more.[31]

From the beginning, Matsuoka took personal charge of the campaign. Practically every speech he gave or article he wrote in the 1932–1936 period related in one way or another to the campaign. It was his personal obsession. He continually exhorted all officials in the Sōdōmei, from the members of the central committee down to the union local chiefs, to press vigorously for collective bargaining agreements with employers. He tried to stimulate interest in the campaign by promising to publish its results, naming successful unions, in the pages of *Rōdō* as an incentive toward greater efforts. Rallies were held with collective bargaining as the object of worker demonstrations. Collective bargaining for the sake of sound unionism became a cause célèbre for the Sōdōmei in these years.[32]

However, the campaign proved to be a dismal failure. Taira estimates that in all of Japan there were only 121 bargaining agreements in existence by 1936, most of them having been produced in the 1932–1935 period. In all, they covered a total of 136,000 workers, 114,000 of whom were seamen in organizations such as the Kaiin Kumiai, where management viewed the agreements as a good way of blunting worker militancy.[33]

It would be fair to say that, as in the 1920s, these agreements were not worth the paper they were written on – if they were written down at all, for many were merely oral contracts. Without a law compelling employers to recognize the unions as agents in collective bargaining, it was possible for employers to simply refuse to engage in negotiation. When they did sit down and talk with the workers, they often preferred to do so in connection with the *kōjō iinkai*, over which they held much influence. And, when agreements were struck, they were often aborted by employers who unilaterally abrogated them or refused to abide by them. Taira remarks, 'One could hardly imagine that...collective bargaining of this kind could have affected the working of the labor market to any great extent.'[34] Since most of the agreements concluded only applied to small and medium enterprises (just sixteen were struck in firms employing 500 or more workers), their impact was confined to these firms.[35]

In desperation, Matsuoka and his colleagues in Sōdōmei head-quarters escalated their exhortations to the rank and file to support the campaign. In April 1933, for instance, Matsuoka declared that the campaign was the zenith of labor's 'struggle' against capitalism.[36] But these attempts to whip up enthusiasm in the campaign could not compensate for the obvious disappointment of its results. In June 1933, an unsigned article in *Rōdō*, possibly written by Matsuoka himself, admitted that the campaign was not proceeding satisfactorily because union bosses were not pushing hard enough in dealing with manage-ment. The article vainly tried to breathe new life into the campaign by arguing that in Italy, France, and Britain collective bargaining was becoming increasingly common and represented a 'modern' develop-ment that Japan should emulate.[37]

Hoping to discover why the campaign was not turning out well, Matsuoka held a series of roundtable discussions or *zadankai*, to which he invited union bosses to analyze the campaign. A number of problems were identified. One union boss remarked that the workers in his union were reluctant to back the campaign in his factory because they were suspicious that the campaign manifested a 'sell-out' to management. To this Matsuoka replied that it was the duty of the union leaders to educate the workers into an appreciation of the value of the agree-ments.[38] On another occasion, unionists at these discussions revealed that the campaign was being upset in their unions by pro-communist workers who had infiltrated the unions in order to agitate against the campaign. One union boss admitted that he had not known there were communists in his union until the company called in the police to arrest them. He offered to resign to take responsibility for this 'oversight'. Matsuoka refused the offer but angrily berated the man for carelessness. Matsuoka said it was a poor union boss who did not know what was going on in his union.[39]

Another union leader raised a rather different problem in the course of one *zadankai*. He said that former communist workers who had joined his local had converted to national socialism and were plotting to displace him. The boss of a different union then chimed in with the remark that, in his company, management actively supported a national socialist union which was used to weaken the Sōdōmei local. Management was trying to seduce Sōdōmei workers to join the more conservative unions by promising them bottles of *sake*, money, and, in some cases, the enticements of women hired by the company. During this particular discussion, it was agreed that this type of threat from national socialist organizations was by far the most serious challenge the Sōdōmei had faced to date, and that this threat had distracted many Sōdōmei locals from supporting the collective bargaining campaign. A further serious problem cited in this *zadankai* was the development of management-backed works councils (in 1936, there were 274 of them in Japanese factories) used by companies to outflank and neutralize the demands of union locals.[40]

These *zadankai*, which offer a good insight into the internal problems of the Sōdōmei from the perspective of union bosses, were published verbatim in *Rōdō* to assist the readership in coping with the obstacles faced by the campaign. Similarly, articles appeared which referred to the few cases in which the campaign had resulted in fairly promising collective accords. In several, the agreements raised wages and in one case management even agreed to pay money to support a union-run labor school.[41] Much publicity was also given to Matsuoka's repeated visits to certain major companies in 1934 when he tried to persuade prominent industrial leaders that the spirit of the collective bargaining was that of *sangyō kyōryoku*.[42]

But the campaign dragged on ineffectually. Even the nominal support given to it by the Kumiai Kaigi, at Matsuoka's behest, was of little help. The Zenkoku Rōdō Kumiai Dōmei and its bloc in the Kaigi did not participate significantly in the campaign and writers like Kikukawa constantly criticized it as a useless diversion from the militant struggle against capitalism.[43] More disquieting still for the Sōdōmei leadership was the fact that several of Matsuoka's *kokata* began to express reservations about the campaign. For instance, Miki Jirō told Matsuoka that he was worried that the campaign might result in agreements which would convert Sōdōmei unions into little more than company unions, or *goyō kumiai*. Miki also wondered what the difference was between unions covered by these agreements and those which had been neutralized by works councils, despised by him as management's instruments to co-opt the unions.[44] Such second thoughts, and the passivity of many Sōdōmei union bosses toward the campaign, indicated that Matsuoka's crusade for sound unionism was wearing thin in the Federation.

Matsuoka was reluctant to abandon the campaign, but by 1936 he allowed it to peter out. Although the Sōdōmei continued to pay lip service to collective bargaining late into the decade, for all intents and purposes the Federation abandoned this initiative for sound unionism. Perhaps the significance of the campaign, other than the fact that its failure proved the futility of sound unionism in the 1930s, was that its disappointing results prodded the Sōdōmei leadership to become more aggressive in seeking the assistance of the government in whittling down the opposition of management to unionism. With increasing regularity, Sōdōmei leaders expressed their desire to make the labor movement a strong bastion of support for the government's policies toward such problems as trade protectionism in the West in exchange for the government's sympathy toward unions.[45]

The most important manifestation of this attitude occurred in 1934 when the Sōdōmei persuaded the Nihon Rōdō Kumiai Kaigi to hold public discussions on how the labor movement could assist economic growth as desired by the government. This idea originated in a special committee established by the Kumiai Kaigi to study ways in which the government could be encouraged to 'guide the economy' for the benefit of the workers and of the nation. The committee considered that the best way to accomplish this was to invite officials from the Prime Minister's office, the Home Ministry, the War Ministry, the Navy Ministry and the Kyōchōkai, to confer with Kumiai Kaigi leaders in open-ended talks on prevailing economic problems. When the talks were convened in 1934, the guest list had been expanded to include representatives of the Shakai Taishūtō, journalists from all of the important daily newspapers and certain business organs such as the *Tōkyō Keizai Shimbun* (Tokyo Economic News) to publicize the discussions. Zensanren was represented by Fujihara Ginjirō.[46]

Nothing came from these discussions in 1934. Yet, the labor movement had carried off something of a publicity stunt in coordinating the talks, which demonstrated the patriotic concern of the unions to play a responsible role in economic growth. Although several years passed before the government increased its powers in the economy, the Sōdōmei continued to lobby for this objective in the hope that somehow government intervention in industrial relations would yield positive results for the workers and for unionism. Nichirōkei labor waxed hot and cold over this endeavor in the early 1930s but later leapfrogged past the Shaminkei in demanding vigorously that the government take charge not only of the economy but of the labor movement as well.

A second initiative on behalf of sound unionism consisted of various demonstrations of support by Shaminkei labor for the policy of *sangyō gōrika* and economic recovery from the Depression in the 1932–1936 period. This initiative fed into the collective bargaining campaign. Early in the campaign, it was hoped that labor's support of *sangyō gōrika* would impress management with labor's responsible attitude toward economic growth so that employers would look more favorably on the unions and the practice of collective bargaining. When it became obvious that employers remained hostile to unions and the principle of collective bargaining, Sōdōmei leaders calculated that perhaps their support of *sangyō gōrika* would induce the government to side with labor in forcing employers to the collective bargaining table since the government desired stability in labor relations as one of the prerequisites of economic recovery.[47] However, like the collective bargaining offensive, this initiative only served to make the Shaminkei labor movement more submissive in relation to both management and government; nothing concrete was gained for sound unionism.

For instance, in addition to displaying symbolic support for *sangyō gōrika* during the discussions with government and business leaders sponsored in 1934, the Sōdōmei went out of its way to discourage its unions from taking part in the strikes of the 1932–1936 period. The Sōdōmei did not yet renounce the right of labor to strike, nor did it abstain entirely from engaging in certain strikes during these years. But in the main, the official stance of the Federation was to avoid strikes because they would hinder the principles of *sangyō kyōryoku* and *sangyō heiwa* (industrial peace), which were paramount.[48]

More significantly, the Sōdōmei dropped even its token resistance to enterprise unionism, one of the important byproducts of *sangyō gōrika* in the continuing spread of institutions and practices associated with industrial paternalism in the large factories. By doing so, the Sōdōmei hoped to preserve what little leverage it retained in such firms. However, this conciliatory policy toward enterprise unionism undermined the thrust of sound unionism: in truth, most of the concrete goals sought by the Sōdōmei as part of its advocacy of sound unionism – such as job security, higher wages, and improved working conditions – were being met with greater effectiveness by employers who implemented the institutions of the *nenkō* system in their factories than the labor movement could possibly hope to accomplish.[49]

At least among the skilled workers of these firms, it proved almost impossible for the labor movement to attract them into unions because their bread was being buttered, so to speak, by the employers. They did not, in short, need the unions to achieve job security and higher wages, because the *nenkō* system promised them, in theory if not always in practice, permanent employment, and gave them automatic wage increases based on seniority. They seemed to have reasoned, in not flocking to the Sōdōmei, why bother with unions? This of course was also the thinking of employers. Because the Sōdōmei had no convincing answer to this question, and because by forsaking socialist idealism it had no political reason for compelling the workers to join unions, it made little headway in expanding its position in the large factories.

A third type of initiative undertaken to realize sound unionism in this period involved the strengthening of the unions themselves. Since most of the unions were in small and medium enterprises, this move was intended to increase the recruitment of new workers into the Shaminkei labor movement by persuading them that strong unionism was the key to acquiring concrete benefits through their dealings with management in these factories. Indeed, a vital aspect of the union-strengthening program was the launching of annual '*toppa*' (break-through) recruitment campaigns, in which the Sōdōmei set targets of growth at 10,000 new members per year.[50] The idea of scoring an impressive breakthrough in the size of the Sōdōmei and similar labor organizations in the Shaminkei labor camp dovetailed with the collective bargaining offensive waged in this period: it was thought that the greater the number of workers in the labor movement, the more likely employers would be to take the movement seriously and work in harmony with it.

Unfortunately, despite the tremendous effort at recruitment, the growth of the Sōdōmei remained painfully slow. By January 1936, the membership stood at 55,000 workers organized into eighty-three unions, including ten regional federations besides the Kantō and Kansai Rōdō Dōmeikai. Other labor organizations also failed to increase their dimensions dramatically. The Zenkoku Rōdō Kumiai Dōmei claimed a membership of 45,000 in 1936, including forty-five unions.[51]

The union-strengthening program centered on the following: the 'rationalization' of union bureaucracies through administrative training classes, conducted in Sōdōmei labor schools, so that union leaders could improve their techniques of budget-management, program planning, and recruitment;[52] the expansion of the labor schools to attract new workers by offering the 'benefits of culture' and learning (in some instances, as in the case of the Sōdōmei's Japan Labor School in Tokyo, the Sōdōmei received funds from the Imperial Household Agency, the Home Ministry, and the Tokyo Metropolitan Government to support its educational emphasis);[53] the expansion of welfare programs such as Sōdōmei-sponsored medical clinics and consumer cooperatives which sold daily necessities at prices lower than the regular market rates;[54] the construction of labor halls around the country to house union offices and give the visual impression of solidarity to the labor movement (the largest was the Rōdō Kaikan, or Labor Hall, in Tokyo where the Sōdōmei headquarters was located – it included many meeting rooms, kitchen facilities to feed large crowds, all contained within a large concrete edifice of several floors);[55] and the proliferation of regional labor newspapers such as the Kanagawa Federation's *Kanagawa Rōdōsha Shimbun* (Kanagawa Workers' News) and the *Rōdōsha Shimbun* (Workers News) published by the Osaka Federation.[56]

Without entering into much detail, it seems that some of these programs for union-strengthening struck a responsive chord at the local level of the Sōdōmei. For example, efforts to improve the management of union budgets proliferated with the consequence that this sphere of union affairs improved markedly. An illustration is the Kawasaki local of the Sōdōmei's Steel Manufacturing Labor Union in 1933 where, after it was discovered that the treasurer had embezzled funds, the control of union finance was overhauled and a better system of accounting and reporting instituted.[57]

The Sōdōmei's labor schools also expanded in this period. For instance, the Osaka Labor School reported 'In the *rengōkai*, in the unions, and in the locals, a passion has developed' for the lectures and courses provided by the School.[58] Enrollments in the Tokyo-based Japan Labor School likewise grew, with classes in labor–management relations and other courses numbering over 200 students each.[59] In 1933, the Japan Labor School reported that 4,302 people had attended thirteen lectures given at the School's central campus and that a further 9,879 people had attended twenty-three lectures, sponsored by the school, in outlying districts.[60]

Consumer cooperatives flourished as well. New ones came into being, for example, in the Fuji Steel Local of the Sōdōmei's Kanagawa Iron Workers' Union, the Kawasaki local of the Asano Cement Factory, the Awaki local of the Osaka Metal Workers' Union, and so forth.[61] Certain locals, such as the Sōdōmei's Steel Workers' Hyōgo Local, were singled out in *Rōdō* for special praise due to their achievements in building up cooperatives, not to mention various programs of mutual aid in the area of health, unemployment relief, and other benefits.[62] Labor halls also dotted the local scene with increasing frequency. For instance, the Sōdōmei's Steel Workers' Kokura Local in Fukuoka Prefecture proudly reported that, through rigorous savings, it had managed to construct a new labor hall in addition to forming a new consumers' cooperative for its workers.[63] Similarly, a new labor hall was constructed by the Hachiman Local, consisting of workers in the Japan Pipe Company, Chiba Prefecture, with the help of the Company which contributed 200 yen to the endeavor.[64]

A fourth quite different initiative to advance the cause of sound unionism was the establishment, largely under the auspices of the Sōdōmei working in conjunction with the Nihon Rōdō Kumiai Kaigi, of the Ajiya Rōdō Kumiai Kaigi (Asian Labor Union Congress) in 1934. It will be recalled that the idea of such a congress had originated with Suzuki Bunji in the late 1920s. In the early 1930s Matsuoka and Nishio were keen to revive this concept as a means of broadcasting the goals of sound unionism beyond Japan into Asia, while demonstrating that Japanese labor could be of service to the State by supporting some of Japan's general objectives in Asia. They intended the Congress to be an Asian forum for the criticism of Western imperialism in the region by Asian labor. Since Suzuki remained enthusiastic about this project, he assisted the Sōdōmei leaders in making the Congress a reality. It was formally established at its inaugural session at Colombo in Ceylon (now Sri Lanka) in May 1934.[65]

Unfortunately for its architects, the Congress had the support of only a few countries, which made its name rather pretentious to say the least. At Colombo, the only labor movements represented were those of Japan, India, and Ceylon. After the 1934 meetings, it was hoped to expand the organization to include other Asian nations. But at the next convention of the Congress, held in the Sōdōmei's main Labor Hall in Tokyo in May 1937, the only nations represented were Japan and India.

The principal sponsors of the Congress, the Sōdōmei and its labor bloc in the Nihon Rōdō Kumiai Kaigi, tried their best to portray the 1937 convention as an important milestone in Asian labor history, and they endeavored to accentuate the leadership of Japanese labor in the Congress. Suzuki, who was elected to chair the 1937 proceedings, was hailed by Matsuoka as the 'father of the Asian labor movement' as well as the 'father of the Japanese labor movement'. But clearly, the Congress was a moribund organization. The third meeting, scheduled for 1939, never took place, and in 1940 the Congress was formally disbanded.[66]

In looking back at the Sōdōmei's concentrated campaigns for sound unionism in the 1932–1936 period, it is evident that, in the aggregate, they were unsuccessful in accomplishing any major gains for the unions. Collective bargaining had failed because employers simply did not want it and were not compelled by law to engage in it; since *sangyō kyōryoku* was not accompanied by aggressive political action for legislation that would have sanctioned the existence of unions and their right to bargain collectively, cooperation with *sangyō gōrika* and industrial paternalism only emasculated further the independence of the unions in large industries by reinforcing management's hand in dealing with the labor movement; the *toppa* recruitment campaigns had not attracted significant numbers of workers into the unions; programs to strengthen the unions had some impact but were not by themselves comprehensive enough to raise the tone of the entire Sōdōmei union network; and the Asian Labor Union Congress had been only an interesting, but quite irrelevant, sideshow in the offensive for sound unionism.

Perhaps the goals of sound unionism were progressive, as far as they went. But they were not advanced far enough. Because they were not linked with an overarching concept of political action, or with the strong support of socialism in the Shakai Taishūtō – the sole political institution in a position to assist sound unionism in the Diet – the campaign for *kenjitsuteki na kumiaishugi* was no more than a rear-guard action on the part of labor organizations who had lost sight of the fact that labor reforms could not be attained in a country where management and government remained indifferent, and in many respects hostile, toward labor unionism as a permanent and viable element in Japanese labor relations. In the end, all that had been achieved in pursuing sound unionism as a goal in itself was to make the labor movement more politically docile than ever.

The establishment of the Zen Nihon Rōdō Sōdōmei, January 1936

Undoubtedly, the most important consequence of the unfolding failure of sound unionism from 1932 to 1936 was the decision of the Sōdōmei to merge with the Zenkoku Rōdō Kumiai Dōmei to produce a single labor organization in 1936. The decision to approach the Nichirōkei labor movement for this purpose was based on the calculation by Sōdōmei leaders that the only way to make any progress with sound unionism, which they continued to regard as their paramount objective, was to add the resources of the Dōmei to the Sōdōmei's, a step which was also expected to strengthen cohesion within the Nihon Rōdō Kumiai Kaigi so that the latter would be more effective in working on behalf of sound unionism. Matsuoka and Nishio, as Sōdōmei chairman and director, respectively, were aware that the Dōmei had been rather critical of sound unionism. But they also knew that the leaders of the Dōmei had seen the imperative of joining the Sōdōmei in a new labor merger to complement, in the labor movement, the recent political unification of both factions in the Shakai Taishūtō.[67]

Thus, merger negotiations were undertaken, with the Sōdōmei participants hoping that the new step toward labor unity would result in a stronger campaign for sound unionism while Dōmei leaders saw it as a way to strengthen the political links between the labor movement and the Shakai Taishūtō for the benefit of socialism.

The conflicting concepts behind the merger made the negotiations toward the reunification of the Sōdōmei and the Dōmei, begun in the autumn of 1935, very tense. When Matsuoka and Kono sat down to discuss linking their two federations, it was as if they were two enemies compelled to strike a truce for the benefit of their respective causes rather than as two allies reaching out to one another to consolidate their organizations for a common purpose. With great difficulty, they agreed on a power-sharing plan modelled on that of the Shakai Taishūtō in which Matsuoka would be chairman of the merger, with Kono and Nishio serving jointly as vice-chairmen. The rest of the merger's executive committee would be balanced in equal numbers by men from both federations. It was also agreed to build the platform of the organization, to be called the Zen Nihon Rōdō Sōdōmei (All-Japan General Federation of Labor), around the twin objectives of the Shaminkei's nonpolitical sound unionism and the Nichirōkei's commitment to political struggle.[68] But this compromise did not signify consensus concerning the merger's ultimate priorities. Rather, the Shaminkei and Nichirōkei labor groups were to pursue their own, conflicting aims in future years, which meant that the Zen Nihon Rōdō Sōdōmei often moved in two opposite directions at the same time during its brief existence.

The Zen Nihon Rōdō Sōdōmei was inaugurated at a general convention of the two federations in Osaka on January 15, 1936. The choice of Osaka was intentional, for it was there that the most recent major labor split had occurred in the Sōdōmei, in 1929. Speeches given by Matsuoka and Kono at this convention pointed out that such labor schisms were things of the past; henceforward, the labor movement would proceed on the basis of unity. Soon after the convention, the headquarters of the Zen Nihon Rōdō Sōdōmei was installed at the Rōdō Kaikan in Tokyo, built recently by the old Sōdōmei. At the time of its establishment, the new Federation claimed about 90,000 members.[69]

However, despite these professions of optimism and good will at the convention, it had already become obvious that not everyone was happy with the merger. On the eve of the convention, the creation of the Zen Nihon Rōdō Sōdōmei was roundly attacked by elements of the Nichirōkei labor movement in Osaka, an attack which showed that the wounds of the 1929 split had not entirely healed. It will be recalled that one of the leading figures in the 1929 labor split had been Suzuki Etsujirō of the Yamanouchi clique. In 1932, Suzuki had taken part in preliminary discussions with Shimonaka Yasaburō and Akamatsu Katsumaro on the subject of a national socialist party. But Suzuki had not given his support to this project ultimately, apparently having entertained second thoughts about national socialism. In 1936, he ridiculed Kono and Kikukawa for linking the Zenkoku Rōdō Kumiai Dōmei with the conservative Sōdōmei, claiming that this would destroy the struggle against capitalism.[70]

Kono and Kikukawa won him over to acceptance of the merger by arguing that, on the contrary, the merger would help overcome the political conservatism of the Sōdōmei, to the advantage of political struggle against capitalism. Suzuki then dropped his criticism but he remained uneasy about the merger after it took place. Suzuki is mentioned here because his dissent indicates that, from the start, the Zen Nihon Rōdō Sōdōmei was subject to the possibility of schism. More importantly, Suzuki Etsujirō was instrumental, along with Kono and Kikukawa, in later destroying the merger by advocating the dissolution of the labor movement to support the New Order which all of these men subsequently regarded as the vehicle for the realization of socialism in Japan.

Had not the Sōdōmei and the Dōmei entered the merger with conflicting ideas as to its purpose, the rise of the Zen Nihon Rōdō Sōdōmei in 1936 would have indeed been a major accomplishment in ending divisions in the labor movement dating back to the mid-1920s. As it was, however, the rivalry between the right wing and center of the movement merely continued under the one roof of the Zen Nihon Rōdō Sōdōmei, for this organization was built on ideological and organizational contradictions that made it doubtful whether it could effectively serve any of the objectives defined for it in future years.

The ideological contradictions were apparent in the ambivalent character of the merger's platform. On the one hand, the Zen Nihon Rōdō Sōdōmei stood for sound unionism and support for the ILO. It also espoused 'realism', a concept interpreted to mean practical economic programs for the benefit of the workers. These emphases reflected the nonpolitical priorities of the Shaminkei side of the merger. On the other hand, the Zen Nihon Rōdō Sōdōmei proclaimed its adherence to 'anti-communism', 'anti-capitalism', 'anti-fascism', together with strong support for the Shakai Taishūtō, stances regarded by the Nichirōkei side as being of great importance.[71] Outwardly, a link had been restored between labor unionism and socialist politics in the Zen Nihon Rōdō Sōdōmei. But in reality, they remained as separate polarities that claimed the allegiance of the two sides of the merger without being integrated into a basic, comprehensive consensus as to where the labor movement was going in the 1930s.

In terms of organization, the Zen Nihon Rōdō Sōdōmei was less a full merger than a partial coming together of two distinct labor movements who retained their full identities within the merger. The Matsuoka and Nishio factions of the Shaminkei, and Asō's Nichirōkei faction, which extended downward into the merger from the Shakai Taishūtō's centrist flank, remained completely intact. Indeed, their lines hardened all the more as the Shaminkei and Nichirōkei labor factions endeavored to consolidate their relative positions in the merger.

In addition, the regional federations of the old Sōdōmei and Dōmei were brought into the Zen Nihon Rōdō Sōdōmei without modification.[72] The only integration between them occurred at the national level of the merger where Sōdōmei and Dōmei labor bureaucrats served together on the new Federation's central committee. The funds controlled by the committee were derived from union dues collected separately by these federations from both the Shaminkei and Nichirōkei camps. *Rōdō*, the organ of the old Sōdōmei, continued as the mouthpiece for the Zen Nihon Rōdō Sōdōmei but all the other local publications that had evolved over the years in the Sōdōmei and the Dōmei continued their separate existence, unaffected by the union of the two labor movements. In sum, although they nominally now functioned as one organization, the Sōdōmei and the Dōmei were, in reality, still two discrete organizations tied to each other in a fashion that can only be described as tenuous at best.

Given these ideological and institutional cleavages in the Zen Nihon Rōdō Sōdōmei, it was inevitable that the Shaminkei and Nichirōkei sections of the merger would articulate differently with the corresponding factions of the Shakai Taishūtō. Here, it is necessary to make it plain that the intra-factional relationships encompassing the socialist party and labor movements were quite different. As intellectuals with strong personal ties to Aso Hisashi, the head of the Nichirōkei in the Shakai Taishūtō, Kono and Kikukawa, as his *kokata*, were willing and eager to apply Aso's political ideas which he had propounded in the 1920s to the Zen Nihon Rōdō Sōdōmei. The vertical ties between Aso in the Party and these men in the labor movement were, thus, very strong.

By contrast, although the worker-leaders of the Shaminkei section of the Zen Nihon Rōdō Sōdōmei, Matsuoka and Nishio, deeply respected Abe Isoo, head of the Shaminkei faction in the Party, they regarded themselves as Abe's *kokata* only in the loosest sense, if indeed at all.[73] They were their own men more than they were Abe's men. Consequently, any political leadership Abe might have provided the labor movement was quite superficial. Abe was unable to impress upon Matsuoka and Nishio the importance of political action in the labor movement, unlike Aso in dealing with his *kokata*. These factors produced a situation in which one half of the Zen Nihon Rōdō Sōdōmei – the Nichirōkei half – was responsive to the goals of the Shakai Taishūtō while the other half – the Shaminkei side – was not. This must be borne in mind when considering the complex permutations that later took place in the labor and socialist party movement.

However, the resonance between Aso's political ideas and those of his *kokata* in the labor movement before the labor merger of 1936 ought not to be overemphasized. In the long run, later in this decade, Kono and Kikukawa followed Aso without equivocation, with disastrous consequences for the labor movement. But in the early 1930s, some of Aso's ideas, springing from his desire to experiment with new alternatives for the socialist movement, did not appeal to them. Because Aso did not take these ideas very far in this period, and because his *kokata* opposed them, they were not to become significant in determining the political behavior of the Nichirōkei until later in the 1930s, by which time Aso and his *kokata* acted in complete agreement.

Preserving socialism in the Shakai Taishūtō, 1932–1936

While different sections of the labor movement continued to disagree in this period over the role of organized labor in Japan, the Shaminkei and Nichirōkei intellectuals in the Shakai Taishūtō generally concurred in their belief that a class-oriented, mass-based socialist movement, depending on the combined strength of grass roots labor and agrarian organizations and the Shakai Taishūtō, should continue to pose socialist alternatives to capitalism, fascism, and imperialism insofar as circumstances permitted. But during the Depression, Asō Hisashi had drifted apart from the other leaders in the Party in his political analysis of contemporary events and possible strategies that the Party should adopt in response to these events.

Asō had always believed, because of his neo-Marxian views, that the fall of Japanese capitalism would be inevitable. When the Depression hit Japan, he jubilantly predicted that this climactic event was about to take place.[74] In contemplating what the socialist movement could do to facilitate the collapse of capitalism and build a new socialist order in its wake, Asō came to the conclusion that extraordinary steps were justified to make a socialist reconstruction of Japan possible. Specifically, he envisioned a cooperative alliance between the socialist political movement and the Japanese army.

The idea of working with the army to achieve socialism apparently gained stature in Asō's thinking as a result of personal contacts with such army men as General Nagata Tetsuzan of the Control faction whom he met in the early 1930s (just when is not clear), and with Ōkawa Shūmei, to whom he was introduced by their mutual friend, Kamei Kan'ichirō, in 1931.[75] It seems that Ōkawa in particular aroused Asō's interest in cooperating with the army to bring about what Ōkawa, the leading national socialist thinker in Japan at the time, termed a basic 'renovation' or *kakushin* of Japan. Ōkawa interpreted this to mean a 'Shōwa Restoration' that would emphasize the power of the military in politics in the interests of greater planning and coordination for economic growth geared to war-mobilization. Asō interpreted '*kakushin*' as being roughly the equivalent of his earlier notion of a 'rational' socialist reconstruction (*kaizō*). As time passed, it was to become manifest that in fact the two terms were quite dissimilar in meaning but this was not apparent to Asō in 1931.

Asō was likewise inclined to view the army as an ally of socialism because he discerned 'proletarian' elements in the army. By this he meant men from village backgrounds who, consequently, would be sympathetic to socialism as a solution to the innumerable problems of rural Japan which had worsened in the Depression.[76] Thus, convinced that the military represented a progressive force against capitalism, Asō recommended to the central committee of the Shakai Taishūtō in 1934 that the Party should establish links with the military. He stated, 'The situation in Japan makes necessary a rational alignment of the proletarian classes with the army if a social reformation is to be achieved by the overthrow of capitalism.'[77]

Yet, Asō's proposal that the Shakai Taishūtō join hands with the army in 1934 was completely rejected by the Shaminkei and Nichirōkei socialists in the Party. Abe Isoo, Katayama Tetsu, and Suzuki Bunji of the Shaminkei thought that Asō had been seduced by the army into thinking that *kakushin* as advocated in the military was the same as *kaizō*, or socialist reconstruction, just as Akamatsu had fallen prey earlier to the delusion that social democracy and national socialism were one and the same.[78] They asked Asō, had not the army been involved in fanatical terrorism? Had it not plunged Japan into the Manchurian Incident? That the army might help to create a socialist new order in Japan was unthinkable to them. They were supported in their arguments by Miwa Jusō, Kawakami Jōtarō, and Kono Mitsu of Asō's own faction. Miwa, for instance, said it was 'absurd fantasy' to think that the army was a democratic organization because it contained 'proletarian elements'. In his opinion, the army was associated with fascism.[79]

These exchanges with Asō were, of course, carried on behind the scenes in the Shakai Taishūtō and can only be reconstructed through the recollections of the men involved. It seems that the Shaminkei socialists in the Party were convinced that Asō was walking down the path taken in 1932 by Akamatsu. They thought of themselves as good nationalists, but not as fascists. Asō's plan struck them as playing into the hands of fascism. Asō's *kokata* likewise believed Asō had gone too far in proposing an alliance with the army. Ultimately Asō agreed to withdraw his proposal in 1934.[80] But the proposal foreshadowed a similar plan developed by him later in the decade, when he envisioned an alliance between the socialist party movement and the New Order government of Prince Konoe Fumimaro after he decided that Konoe was sympathetic to socialism.

Conceivably, Asō might have toyed with the idea of working with the army in the early 1930s whether or not most of the labor movement had grown politically quiescent. In any case, it is very likely that one of the factors behind his advocacy of this alliance was his disappointment with the political becalming of much of the labor movement in 1931 and 1932. Certainly the conservative trend in the movement in those years could hardly have inspired Asō's confidence in his long-held dream of achieving 'socialism from below'. One may surmise that he began to think of achieving 'socialism from above' in league with the army because of this. Later in 1936 and 1937, Asō recovered his vision of 'socialism from below' due to unforeseen events that shook his confidence in the army as a progressive, democratic force in Japan. But only momentarily: other options for the socialist movement, prefiguring 'socialism from above', subsequently governed his thought and action as soon as Japan went to war against China in mid-1937.

Apart from these inconclusive controversies revolving around Asō in the inner recesses of the Shakai Taishūtō, the Party maintained a generally consistent set of socialist positions on major domestic and foreign affairs problems in the 1932–1936 period. It criticized the 'bourgeois parties', the growing influence of the military in politics, the power of the Peers and conservative civilian bureaucracy, '*keisatsu seiji*' (police politics) as manifested in the 1925 Peace Preservation Law, and the fascist national socialist party and labor movements. Several new wrinkles were added to the Party's domestic programs: the advocacy of 'people's banks' and credit institutions and the idea of a 'people's inflation' which was understood to mean the channelling of massive government funds into welfare projects to benefit the poor. The Party also opposed very strenuously the heavy appropriations by the Diet for military development, on the grounds that this policy fanned the flames of an international arms race which could lead to war.[81]

In the area of foreign affairs, the Shakai Taishūtō continued to advocate genuine independence for Manchukuo from Japan and it advocated the 'socialization' of the Manchukuo economy to protect the inhabitants of the region from the threat of Japanese capitalist interests, interests which had imbedded themselves increasingly in Manchuria. And, when Japan withdrew from the League of Nations, the Shakai Taishūtō condemned this policy as catastrophic for Japan's relations with the West.[82] Thus, the Party coupled 'anti-communism', 'anti-capitalism', and 'anti-fascism' in domestic affairs with what was essentially a policy of anti-imperialism in foreign affairs. Democracy, not authoritarianism; internationalism, not isolation; peace, not war – these were its main planks from 1932 to 1936.

Since, taken together, the Shakai Taishūtō's domestic and foreign policy positions constituted an alternative to those of the other parties, it managed to carve out an identity of sorts, in the eyes of some Japanese voters, as a Party which sought progressive change. This helped the Party in amassing votes in the prefectural elections of 1935 and the national elections in 1936, not because voters wanted to endorse social- ism but because they were increasingly disillusioned with the liberal parties and with the inadequate leadership provided by weak govern- ment in this period. In the 1935 elections, the Shakai Taishūtō and various local socialist parties increased their seats in prefectural assemblies from seventeen (as of 1931) to thirty-eight.[83] This was not a spectacular gain, but it was promising. Possibly if the Party had not been challenged by the national socialist political movement, which garnered twelve prefectural assembly seats in 1935, it would have gained even more leverage in local assemblies that year.[84]

Encouraged by the results of the 1935 elections, the Shakai Taishūtō entered the elections of February 1936 in high anticipation of improving its position in the Diet. These 1936 elections followed the dissolution of the Diet by Okada, who called for new elections, the first in four years, to stave off a threatened no-confidence motion from the Seiyūkai. Working closely together, Abe Isoo and Asō decided to adopt strong election slogans for the Shakai Taishūtō campaign. These in- cluded, in their translated versions, 'The Established Parties or the Masses' Party?', 'One Solid Vote for the Masses' Party!', 'Carry Out the Renovation of the Country!', and in a more nationalistic vein, 'Enrich the People, Defend the Nation!'.[85]

In addition, the Shakai Taishūtō fought the 1936 elections on the basis of its so-called 'three pillars', which were broad policy planks under the respective headings of the 'Reform of the Structure of the Nation' (*Kokunai Kikō Kaikaku*), 'Industrial Policy' (*Sangyō Seisaku*), and 'Financial Policy' (*Zaisei Seisaku*). The first pillar incorporated demands for the abolition of the House of Councillors and the Peerage system, reform of the electoral districts, the amalgamation of the War and Navy Ministries into one Defense Ministry, and the establishment of a Social Ministry.[86] The hallmark of the Party's 'Industrial Policy' was the demand for the nationalization of heavy industry.[87] In the area of 'Financial Policy' the Party focused on tax reforms benefiting the poor at the expense of the rich and a number of related social policies including legalization of labor unions, a tenant farmers' law, and other measures which 'we advocate as social policies for the purpose of building a socialist society'.[88]

Benefiting from the fact that for the first time in a general election Shaminkei and Nichirōkei candidates had campaigned on a united ticket without undercutting each other at the polls, the Shakai Taishūtō emerged from the 1936 elections with eighteen seats in the Diet. Although the Party was still very weak in comparison with the victorious Minseitō which had elected 205 candidates and with the runner-up Seiyūkai which had captured 174 seats, it seemed at last that the socialist party movement in Japan was on the move.[89] Those of the Shakai Taishūtō candidates who reached the Diet that year included Abe Isoo, Katayama Tetsu, Kamei Kan'ichirō, Suzuki Bunji, Kawamura Yasutarō (the only prominent worker to win a Diet seat), Asō Hisashi, Miwa Jusō, Kono Mitsu, Asanuma Inejirō, Kawakami Jōtarō, Sugiyama Motojirō, and seven others.[90]

However, the fact that this list includes only one worker and that the entire slate of Shakai Taishūtō candidates, including those who lost as well as those who were successful in 1936, consisted overwhelmingly of intellectuals who were prominent in Party affairs, indicates the extent to which the Party's advocacy of socialist objectives depended heavily on the enthusiasm of its intellectual elements. Still very cool to politics, Matsuoka Komakichi, the chairman of the new Zen Nihon Rōdō Sōdōmei, did not campaign in 1936. Nor did Nishio Suehiro, who had participated in every previous campaign. Whereas the Nichirōkei side of the Zen Nihon Rōdō Sōdōmei had worked energetically to elect Shakai Taishūtō candidates from Asō's faction in the Party, the Shaminkei side of the labor merger had done so only with a half-hearted, perfunctory, enthusiasm.

The contrast between the two factions in the Zen Nihon Rōdō Sōdōmei in assisting, or failing to assist, the Shakai Taishūtō also applies to the labor organizations in their respective blocs outside of the Federation which remained intact and loyal to either the Nichirōkei or Shaminkei labor leaders in the Federation. Those groups in the Nichirōkei bloc were active in supporting the Party; those in the Shaminkei bloc, with the exception of Kawamura Yasutarō's Nihon Kangyō Rōdō Sōdōmei, which eagerly backed its leader in the elections, were relatively passive about mobilizing votes, even for such Shaminkei luminaries as Abe and Suzuki Bunji. Thus, neither the Zen Nihon Rōdō Sōdōmei nor the Nihon Rōdō Kumiai Kaigi, to which the

Federation and these two blocs belonged, constituted a solid wall of labor support for the Shakai Taishūtō in 1936. On the contrary, a good half of this labor movement, still obsessed with the priority of non-political sound unionism and still becalmed in its attitude toward socialism, remained inert when it came to supporting the Shakai Taishūtō's effort to preserve socialism as an alternative possibility in Japanese politics.

Thus, it would be erroneous to think that the successes of the Shakai Taishūtō in 1936 were due significantly or even in modest measure to the support it received from organized labor. The Party did relatively well in 1936 because, as the Party of 'renovation', it appealed to many voters disillusioned with the Okada government and who wanted to register a protest against it. It is also likely that many voters supported the Shakai Taishūtō to combat the rising influence of the military. This was less due to a basic aversion toward the military than to fears of more violence stemming from factional rivalries within the armed forces. In these years, the army had a public image as a volatile, unpredictable force that could not be fully trusted even though it could not be opposed because of its necessary role in defending the nation from foreign perils.

Just how volatile the army was became strikingly clear six days after the 1936 elections when, on February 26, elements of the Japanese army staged a major insurrection in Tokyo. The immediate impact of this crisis was a sudden change of government involving the resignation of the Okada cabinet, which had not been dislodged by the election results, and the rise of a new government that undertook policies, with the help of the Control faction in the army, which for the first time placed the non-communist labor movement in Japan in direct jeopardy. Like men rudely awakened from deep sleep, the Shaminkei labor leaders in the Zen Nihon Rōdō Sōdōmei were jarred by the insurrection and its aftermath of repression into the realization that because the new threats to the labor movement were essentially political, a political response was required to stave off these threats and save the unions. As they rushed to the Shakai Taishūtō for assistance in their panic, the Party itself closed ranks for a final defense of socialism. However, this revitalization of a labor–party alliance was soon brought to an abrupt end with the outbreak of the China Incident (Shina Jihen) in July 1937.

8

Toward dissolution, 1936–1940

Though the labor and socialist party movements had not been involved in the February 26th Incident, they suffered from the circumstances surrounding its repression. One of the first measures taken by Prime Minister Hirota Kōki, who had succeeded Okada on March 10 after the suppression of the Incident, was to use the martial law directive, which had been imposed during the insurgency, to justify the prohibition of May Day demonstrations as part of the government's endeavor to ensure public order in the wake of the Incident.

Organized labor protested vigorously against this policy. For example, Matsuoka Komakichi, Nishio Suehiro, Kono Mitsu, and Kikukawa Tadao visited the Home Ministry on behalf of the Zen Nihon Rōdō Sōdōmei and the Nihon Rōdō Kumiai Kaigi to tell Home Ministry officials that the ban on May Day constituted an arbitrary and indiscriminate repression of labor. Matsuoka asserted, 'The prohibition of May Day is clearly unjust. It will only encourage the highhandedness of the capitalists. Instead, you should take steps to promote harmony between capital and labor. Your lack of perception concerning the labor movement is outrageous.'[1]

The Shakai Taishūtō engaged in similar protests. Typical was Asō Hisashi's statement in the Diet, during his interrogation of Hirota over the imposition of the ban, that the prohibition of May Day jeopardized the freedom of speech guaranteed in the Constitution. Asō further declared that the ban would surely draw the scorn of other advanced countries; Western opinion would be incensed at this manifestation of blatant authoritarianism in Japan.[2] But Hirota was unruffled, replying simply, 'On this matter of May Day, your alleged world opinion of the West is of no concern to me.'[3] When Asō took this opportunity to argue that the government ought to legalize unions because unions were accepted in Western countries, Hirota rebuked him by saying that what was good for the West was not necessarily good for Japan.[4] Not surprisingly, the Shakai Taishūtō's continued efforts on behalf of a labor union law failed completely under this and subsequent administrations.

Another blow to the labor movement, delivered by the Hirota cabinet after the February 26th Incident, was even more ominous in its ramifications. In September 1936, Hirota suddenly ordered the Home Ministry to dissolve the Nihon Kangyō Rōdō Sōdōmei, most of whose unions were located in army and navy arsenals. The order itself had originated in the War Ministry, an office now opposed to labor unions like those in the Kangyō Rōdō Sōdōmei, which were seen as obstacles to the rationalization of industrial production for military purposes.[5]

The Nihon Kangyō Rōdō Sōdōmei, under Kawamura Yasutarō, had always been a major element in the Shaminkei bloc of labor organizations. It was also an enthusiastic member of the Nihon Rōdō Kumiai Kaigi. Hence, its dissolution aroused great consternation in the labor movement. Again, Matsuoka made frequent visits to governmental offices to protest against this step. On several occasions, he talked with the War Minister, General Terauchi Hisaichi. When he asked Terauchi point blank whether the army intended to eventually close down all labor union organizations, Terauchi denied this possibility. But it was, he said, the army's view that labor unions had no place in military arsenals.[6] Matsuoka was still worried. Ultimately, however, he could do nothing to prevent the immediate closure of the 15,000-man Kangyō Rōdō Sōdōmei, on September 23, 1936. This federation was the first moderate labor organization in Japan to suffer direct repression.

Hirota's imposition of martial law, his prohibition of May Day demonstrations, and his interdiction of the Kangyō Rōdō Sōdōmei were regarded by the labor movement as the first steps toward the creation of a fascist police State, a process which would eventually consume the unions. So, whereas in the recent past the movement had been largely uncritical of governmental policies, now anti-government protestations poured forth with sudden force, like rushing water spilling over the top of a dam. In the autumn of 1936, practically every issue of *Rōdō* carried articles attacking the Hirota government, and labor leaders in the Zen Nihon Rōdō Sōdōmei and the Kumiai Kaigi openly accused Hirota of aiding and abetting fascism in Japan.[7] The labor movement also pressed the Shakai Taishūtō to mount a strong attack on Hirota in the Diet, which it did very energetically.[8] An opportunity to widen this attack was unexpectedly granted the labor and socialist party movements in the national elections of April 1937.

The national election of 1937: new optimism in the Shakai Taishūtō

The tenure of the Hirota administration was cut short by army–party rivalries. Even Hirota was surprised when his War Minister, Terauchi, told the Diet on several occasions that Japan needed to develop a 'controlled unified State' which, in the process of 'renovation', would be rid of all the political parties.[9] These statements drew the fire of the liberal parties as well as that of the Shakai Taishūtō. Politicians from the Seiyūkai, for example, publicly condemned the military for wanting to impose a military dictatorship on Japan after the February 26th uprising.[10] Out of contempt for the parties and for Hirota himself, Terauchi resigned his portfolio, bringing down the Hirota cabinet in February 1937. When the next administration under Prime Minister Hayashi Senjūrō, a general, further alienated the parties by refusing to include anyone from the Seiyūkai or the Minseitō in his cabinet, their mounting protests prompted him to call a new general election, scheduled for April 1937.

Although it was clear that the results of this election would not affect the continuation of bureaucratic, non-party government, the liberal parties and the Shakai Taishūtō resolved to wage a strong campaign of protest against the authoritarianism of the cabinet in early 1937. Within the Shakai Taishūtō, the Shaminkei, led by Abe Isoo, and the Nichirōkei, with Asō Hisashi at the helm, cooperated in launching the boldest campaign ever attempted by either socialist faction in the inter-war period.

Significantly, the February 26th Incident destroyed Asō's hopes for forging an alliance with the army to bring about a socialist renovation of Japan. The Incident itself convinced him that the army was too unstable and unpredictable to be relied upon as a progressive force in Japanese politics. Then, the statements of General Terauchi to the effect that political parties were inimical to a new order worried Asō, who interpreted them to mean that the ascendant Control faction was hostile toward the parties and would someday engineer their destruction.[11] More generally, Asō Hisashi, and other socialists in the Shakai Taishūtō, feared that the Japanese political system had reached the brink of a systemic collapse. The army, bureaucracy, *zaibatsu*, and liberal parties had reached a position of stalemate in their competition for power and influence while the Emperor was powerless to provide a unifying influence; the Meiji Constitution itself was in jeopardy. Asō feared that unless socialism could offer an effective solution to fascism as an alternative to a military dictatorship imposed by the army, there would be no stopping the country's disastrous plunge into fascism. Thus, in his own campaign for election to the Diet, Asō Hisashi stressed the menace of the military as the vehicle of fascism in Japan.[12]

Other Shakai Taishūtō candidates did likewise. For example, Miwa Jusō condemned the army and the *zaibatsu* for trying to gain political control of the country. He charged that their alliance would draw Japan into imperialist war abroad. Like Asō, Miwa declared many times in his campaign that Hayashi was a 'fascist' front-man for the military. At the same time, Asō, Miwa, and most other Shakai Taishūtō candidates heaped invective on the liberal parties for their continuing association with capitalism.[13]

The Shakai Taishūtō even tried to use rightist terminology in order to gain public support in this campaign, always taking care to give such terms as 'renovation' and 'Shōwa Restoration' a socialist meaning. 'Renovation' was interpreted as signifying the socialist reform of Japan as an alternative to fascism. Shōwa Restoration was similarly portrayed as involving the elimination of the *gunbatsu*, the *kanryōbatsu* (bureaucratic cliques), and the *zaibatsu* for the sake of national salvation and democracy.[14]

The results of the 1937 elections raised the morale of the Shakai Taishūtō immensely. After the ballots were tabulated, the Party emerged in control of 8.2 per cent of the seats in the Diet, having elected thirty-seven of its sixty-six candidates.[15] This made it the third largest political party in the Diet, behind the victorious Minseitō, and the Seiyūkai.[16] In addition, the Shakai Taishūtō had completely eclipsed the national socialist parties in 1937. In contrast to the 1936 elections, when it had captured 58.2 per cent of the proletarian vote, the Shakai Taishūtō share of this vote climbed to 66.8 per cent in 1937.[17] The national socialist parties augmented their showing in 1937 only slightly, from 25.4 per cent of the proletarian vote in 1936 to 27.3 per cent in 1937.[18] The socialist position was even stronger in comparison with the national socialists if one adds to the Shakai Taishūtō vote the 5.5 per cent of the proletarian vote gleaned by the Nihon Musantō (Japan Proletarian Party), led by Katō Kanjū.[19] This Party, founded in February 1937, was composed of former 'legal left' socialists and dissidents who had broken away from the Shaminkei and Nichirōkei in the early 1930s.[20] The remainder of the proletarian vote was divided up by various local socialist parties.

The list of men elected to the Diet on the Shakai Taishūtō ticket in

1937 was a veritable 'who's who' of important socialist politicians: Abe, Katayama Tetsu, Suzuki Bunji, Kamei Kan'ichirō, Nishio Suehiro of the Shaminkei and Asō, Miwa, Asanuma Inejirō, and Kawakami Jōtarō of the Nichirōkei – and many others.[21] Naturally, they were elated over the Party's unprecedented breakthrough. Upon reading the election results, Asō stated confidently that now 'The Party will press forward toward the implementation of domestic renovation and the stabilization of the people's livelihood.'[22]

Various political commentators outside of the Party also interpreted the election as a turning point in the history of Japanese socialism. The journalist Sasa Hirō pointed out in the *Asahi Shūkan* [Asahi Weekly] that the Shakai Taishūtō had finally achieved success in winning the votes of a major cross-section of the population including the proletariat and elements of the middle class – intellectuals, salaried workers, and even some public servants who supported the Shakai Taishūtō as the Party of renovation.[23] Another writer, Kawai Eijirō, noted that this broad base included petty retailers and owners of small and medium-scale enterprises who resented the power of the *zaibatsu*. Kawai said the mobilization of their support constituted an 'Epoch-making event in the annals of Japanese politics'. Kawai predicted that the 'time was not far off' when the Shakai Taishūtō would form a government of its own in Japan.[24]

No less enthusiastic was the prominent political writer and politician, Baba Tsunego. Baba said this election proved that the 'whole-nation' cabinets of men like Saitō, Okada, Hirota, and Hayashi lacked popular support. They would give way to party government again in the near future. Baba wrote that this election showed that the Japanese public was fed up with military interference in national politics. He advised the military to take note of this fact and stick to its proper role, national defense.[25]

Not everyone greeted the results of the 1937 elections so optimistically. Matsuoka Komakichi, who had not run for election that year, felt that the Shakai Taishūtō had simply benefited temporarily from a widespread public revulsion toward the February 26th Incident and the obvious links between the Hirota and Hayashi cabinets and the military. In supporting the Shakai Taishūtō, the public had voted against this situation, not in favor of socialism.[26]

In the light of what happened later, Matsuoka was quite correct in this assessment. Even so, the vitality of the Shakai Taishūtō's performance and the continued vote-getting capacities of the liberal parties in

1937 indicate that at election time, at least, parties in Japan had lost little of their resilience at this stage in Japan's descent into the 'dark valley' of authoritarianism. That intelligent men such as Asō, Kawai Eijirō, and Baba Tsunego could remain hopeful about the future importance of the parties in national politics in the spring of 1937 is evidence of the continuing fluidity and open-endedness of political trends in Japan at the time. This reality seems to have dawned on those elements of the labor movement which had been cool toward politics earlier in the decade. In 1937, the Shaminkei labor organizations in the Zen Nihon Rōdō Sōdōmei and the Kumiai Kaigi were no less energetic in mobilizing the worker vote for Shakai Taishūtō candidates than their counterparts in the Nichirōkei. Nishio Suehiro was one beneficiary of this mobilization; he was elected to the Diet from the Osaka fourth district, this time with the full support of the Osaka labor movement.

However, where the Shaminkei labor movement was concerned, support of Shakai Taishūtō candidates as a protest against anti-labor politics of the government did not necessarily mean that Shaminkei labor as a whole had suddenly rekindled its enthusiasm for socialist ideology as preserved in the Party. Articles in *Rōdō*, for instance, give the impression that Shaminkei labor leaders were more eager to use the Party to defend labor unionism than they were to work through the Shakai Taishūtō to promote socialism. Socialism, per se, was seldom mentioned in labor journals during the election campaign.

The continuing distinction between labor unionism and socialism was an important one. Labor had been aroused by the aftermath of the February 26th Incident from its political lethargy, for it was now seen that the Party presented the unions with the only hope of protection from government intimidation. But the Shaminkei side of the labor movement in the Zen Nihon Rōdō Sōdōmei and Kumiai Kaigi remained becalmed in an ideological sense. Its attention was still fixed on sound unionism rather than socialism. This was true even of Nishio, who, more than anyone else in the Shaminkei labor movement, had been politicized by the trauma of events following the insurrection of 1936.

Thus, the rejuvenation of active labor support for the Shakai Taishūtō in 1937 must be kept in perspective. Apart from the Nichirōkei labor movement in the Zen Nihon Rōdō Sōdōmei and Kumiai Kaigi, which was more responsive to socialist ideology than the Shaminkei, much of the labor movement had not restored the balance between labor unionism and political socialism that had been lost in the early 1930s. This did not deter the Party leaders in their optimism about the future, however. They believed the Shakai Taishūtō could move forward, with increased support from the 'petty bourgeoisie' in particular. But these euphoric expectations were abruptly torpedoed by the outbreak of war on the Asian continent in July. The 'China Incident' also cast a new and profound pall of gloom over the Japanese labor movement and created conditions in which the movement could not survive.

Japanese labor and the China Incident, 1937

Political terrorism in the cause of a Shōwa Restoration had weakened democracy in Japan in the 1930s, even though this goal was never achieved. In the long run, however, war was the more destructive force in the obliteration of democracy. As one historian comments, 'It was war rather than the putschist attempts of the 1930s that suppressed democracy in Japan. Firstly, the Manchurian Incident and its international repercussions created a highly nationalistic atmosphere. Then, the China War, which broke out in 1937, brought about further government controls and a stricter censorship' culminating in the New Order by 1940.[27]

When fighting erupted between Japanese and Chinese troops in the vicinity of the Marco Polo Bridge near Peking on the night of July 7, 1937, the Prime Minister of Japan was Prince Konoe Fumimaro, who had succeeded Hayashi. At the time of his appointment, Konoe had seemed a good bet to restore public confidence in government, for although he had contacts with many well-known ultranationalists in the civilian bureaucracy and the military, he was also thought of as a political moderate.[28] But in foreign policy, Konoe proved to be hawkish. He disregarded counsels of restraint from senior military advisers (who did not want war in China) and committed Japan to a 'war of annihilation' against Nationalist China.[29] The military quickly fell in line behind Konoe but a speedy victory over Chiang Kai-shek was denied Japan as the 'China Incident', really a full-scale war, continued until 1941 when it merged into World War II.

The immediate result of the China conflict in Japan was to quicken the development of a national defense State based on mobilization for total war. This involved the mobilization of the economy for defense production on an unprecedented scale in Japanese history. The cornerstone of this policy was the National Mobilization Law, passed by the

Diet in March 1938. The Law provided the government with emergency powers to manage the economy in whatever ways were judged necessary for defense. It specifically gave the government control over the allocation of labor and materials, price and wage regulation, operation of strategic industries, and it permitted a system of national registration.[30] Military spending soared in the late 1930s as a result, from around 500 million yen (30 per cent of the national budget) in 1931 to 4,000 million yen (70 per cent of the national budget) in 1937 and 1938. Heavy industrial production related to war-preparedness likewise soared to 73 per cent of Japan's total industrial output in the 1937–1942 period.[31]

The China Incident, which was well under way when the Zen Nihon Rōdō Sōdōmei held its annual convention on 17–19 October, 1937, shocked the Federation into passing one resolution after another declaring labor's ardent support for the war. Any other response to the conflict was deemed unthinkable for fear that failure to display patriotic enthusiasm for the nation at war would expose the unions to anti-labor policies from a war-oriented government. Yet, labor's patriotism was not just protective. It was also genuine, for the Incident was perceived by the labor movement as the most serious crisis faced by Japan since the Russo-Japanese War of 1904–1905.

The convention proceedings began with the unanimous passage of a motion entitled '*Kōgun shōshi ni taisuru kansha ketsugi*' or 'Resolution of Appreciation to the Officers and Men of the Imperial Army'. This resolution stated, 'We give our most sincere thanks to the officers and men of the Imperial Army who. . . with the Imperial Navy have done so much to add to the nation's glory throughout China since the Incident began. . .'[32] Declaring that Japan's mission was to oppose the influence of the Comintern in China and to bring stability to the continent, the resolution also promised that the Zen Nihon Rōdō Sōdōmei, by way of registering its appreciation, would 'strive to promote industrial peace [*sangyō heiwa*] and contribute to the strengthening of national unity [*kyokoku itchi*]. . .'[33]

No sooner had the delegates thronging the Federation's Rōdō Kaikan, which was festooned with banners reading '*Kyokoku Itchi!*', passed this patriotic resolution than Nishio Suehiro took the convention floor to proclaim that the most 'sincere' way to back up these sentiments with concrete action was for the Federation to declare publicly that it would renounce the right of labor to strike.[34] At once, the convention passed, again without dissent, a motion to this effect. This was an historic step backward from advocacy of the principle that workers had the right to strike in seeking higher wages or other benefits. In one cutting, swiftly delivered stroke, impelled by a powerful sense of patriotism, the Shaminkei and Nichirōkei organizations within the Zen Nihon Rōdō Sōdōmei had severed themselves from the legacy of the past. In 1937, the days of the Great Noda Strike in 1927 and 1928, and before that the historic strike at the Kawasaki and Mitsubishi Shipyards in Kobe, seemed like ancient history.

The next item on the agenda of the 1937 convention was to launch another 'Home Front Campaign', similar to the one implemented during the Manchurian Incident. But the Home Front Campaign begun in 1937 was pursued far more energetically than before. It involved elaborate funding for donations to families who had sent men to the front and particularly to families whose kin were killed in China. While the emphasis was on aiding working class families, the Campaign was not exclusively restricted to them. Fund-raising activities were carried out from the union local level upward in the Federation's bureaucratic hierarchies.[35] Finally, the convention decided to send a delegation of prominent labor leaders, headed by Matsuoka Komakichi, to the front in order to encourage the soldiers and give them labor's moral support in battle. This mission was justified as a contribution to 'peace in Asia'.[36]

After the 1937 convention, the Zen Nihon Rōdō Sōdōmei attempted to sustain and expand the Home Front Campaign in the spirit of *kyokoku itchi* and *sangyō kyōryoku* by holding a special convention in Tokyo on January 28, 1938, which was advertised in *Rōdō* as the 'Sangyō Kyōryoku Taikai' or 'Industrial Cooperation Convention'.[37] This was convened in the Osaka Building in the Marunouchi section of Tokyo, not far from the Imperial palace. It is not necessary to discuss this convention at length since it was principally a forum for further appeals by Federation leaders for greater financial contributions from the workers to the Federation's special fund referred to above. Similar regional 'Industrial Cooperation Conventions' were staged elsewhere in Japan on January 11, in Osaka, Kobe, and other major cities, thanks to the cooperation of Federation headquarters and local labor leaders around the country.[38]

Later, in the spring of 1938, the Zen Nihon Rōdō Sōdōmei central committee moved to put the Home Front Campaign on a more permanent basis by establishing the club known as the Sankyō Kurabu. The first and second characters in the name of this Club represented 'three' and 'cooperation', respectively. The first referred to labor, management, and government. Evidently Matsuoka, who was the chief architect of the organization, liked to play on words, for the pronunciation of 'Sankyō' in reference to the Club was a pun for the abbreviation of *sangyō kyōryoku* or 'industrial cooperation' which also comes out as 'sankyō' if the elements are combined in a kind of verbal shorthand.

At Matsuoka's behest, a special committee was formed in the Federation to establish the Sankyō Kurabu on March 24, with Matsuoka in the chair.[39] The Sankyō Kurabu was formally created on April 14.[40] Operating as a special body in the Zen Nihon Rōdō Sōdōmei, the Sankyō Kurabu had two central purposes. The first was to coordinate and stimulate the contribution of patriotic donations for the Home Front Campaign. The second was to hold annual meetings to which representatives of management and government would be invited to confer with labor on problems relating to industrial production in wartime.[41] It might be said, too, that the organization of the Kurabu was a public relations device intended to impress management and government with the patriotism of the labor movement. Despite all of the fanfare surrounding its creation, however, the Sankyō Kurabu never amounted to much. Not long after its initiation, it, and the entire labor movement, were to become preoccupied with a newly organized, government-sponsored movement, the Sangyō Hōkoku Undō, or Industrial Patriotic Movement, to be discussed shortly.

Not just the Zen Nihon Rōdō Sōdōmei, but every labor organization associated with the Kumiai Kaigi undertook patriotic initiatives of this sort immediately after the commencement of the China Incident. All traces of anti-fascism in the labor movement apparent in the preceding year had now vanished. So had labor's opposition to the military. Labor's solidarity with the nation at war completely obscured the protests of 1936 and early 1937.

However, despite their patriotism, labor elites found it difficult to put out the fires of worker protest in 1937 in the name of *sangyō kyōryoku* and *kyokoku itchi*. As the figures cited in the last chapter indicate, labor unrest remained significant in 1937, even after the China Incident began. It seems many workers wanted to take advantage of management's concern for increasing production in wartime to secure higher wages. Grievances over wages remained real indeed. While the index of money wages stood at 312 in the 1935–1939 period, the index for real wages was 166 relative to 189 for the cost of living.[42] Inevitably, some unions in the Zen Nihon Rōdō Sōdōmei and other organizations became involved in these protests despite the official policy of labor leaders of opposition to strikes.[43]

In sum, the China Incident broke the short-lived bubble of labor's dissent against fascism and militarism which had arisen in the period between the February 26th Incident and the beginning of the war in China. The Nichirōkei labor movement in the Zen Nihon Rōdō Sōdōmei and Kumiai Kaigi, which had been especially vigorous in opposing fascism and militarism, had suddenly become no less patriotic than the Shaminkei. Indeed, subsequent events revealed that the Nichirōkei labor leaders were even more nationalistic than the Shaminkei. The same surge of patriotism took precedence over everything else in the Shakai Taishūtō, after the eruption of the China War. The Shaminkei and Nichirōkei factions in the Party vied with one another to appear the most patriotic in supporting the nation at war with as much zeal as did their counterparts in the labor movement.

The Shakai Taishūtō first expressed its reaction to the war at its annual convention in November 1937. This convention nearly surpassed the Zen Nihon Rōdō Sōdōmei's, held three months earlier, in professing genuine support for the Japanese offensive in China. Stirring declarations of approval for Konoe's attempt to crush Chiang repeatedly punctuated the proceedings. The Party also altered its platform to meet the crisis of the war. Instead of advocating the 'liberation of the proletarian classes' and the 'overthrow of capitalism', the platform now contained pledges to work for the 'stabilization of the people's livelihood' in wartime and the 'reform' of capitalism to make it stronger for national defense. A new plank was also inserted which stated that the Party stood by to do whatever was necessary to help defend the *kokutai* in the war.[44]

More specifically, the Shakai Taishūtō convention publicized the Party's new mission as the elevation of racial culture. This objective was to be facilitated by serving the '*Nihon kokumin*' (Japanese people) on the basis of the *Kokutai no Hongi* (Basic Principles of National Policy), an ultranationalist tract written by the Ministry of Education in 1937 to clarify the uniqueness of the Japanese Imperial Way. Thus, in one quick stroke, the Party all but abandoned any reference to the *kinrō taishū* as the object of its concern in favor of a broader concept – the entire community of Japanese people, the Japanese race. The Party was still concerned with the interests of the *taishū* (masses) but now this term meant not just the proletariat and allied groups but rather the masses of the entire country, that is, everyone.[45]

Two other developments in the Shakai Taishūtō convention of 1937 assume special significance in view of later events. One was the Party's adoption of the principle that, in the long run, all existing parties in Japan should join hands in a national political front for the sake of solidarity behind the Emperor. The other was the dropping by the Party of its earlier stress on the autonomy of organized labor and its presence as an independent force in the factories. Although it was not yet put into so many words, this step prefigured the idea, which cropped up later in the decade, that all of the unions (like the parties) should merge themselves into a patriotic front.[46]

Soon after this convention, in December, a Shakai Taishūtō delegation headed by Asō paid a visit to the mainland. Like the similar mission from the Zen Nihon Rōdō Sōdōmei, its purpose was to demonstrate the Party's sympathy with the tribulations suffered by Japanese troops in battle. The mission toured Japanese military installations in Manchuria and in north and central China, and conferred on many occasions with commanders and leading civilians in the field. For instance, Asō's team talked with General Tōjō Hideki and Hoshino Naoki, Director of the General Affairs Bureau and the highest-ranking civilian in Manchuria.[47] Asō came away from these discussions confident that Japan's military conquest of China could be completed very quickly. He was convinced that Japan was on the side of right in prosecuting the war.[48]

The full identification of the Shakai Taishūtō with the war made it inevitable that the Party would reject overtures from Kato's Nihon Musantō to form a socialist alliance against the war in 1937. Katō, and Suzuki Mosaburō, another leading figure in the Nihon Musantō, had become desperately anxious to create an anti-fascist popular front. The core of this front, besides the Nihon Musantō itself, was the Nihon Rōdō Kumiai Zenkoku Hyōgikai (National Council of Japanese Labor Unions), or Zempyō, which Katō had organized in 1934 out of elements accompanying him in his earlier withdrawal from the Nichirōkei labor and party movements.[49] But Katō wanted the Shakai Taishūtō and its labor base in the Zen Nihon Rōdō Sōdōmei to join the popular front, realizing that, if they did not, the front would remain perilously small and extremely vulnerable to police repression.

As the only member of the Musantō in the Diet after the elections of 1937, Katō approached the Shakai Taishūtō's parliamentarians on several occasions with a view to enlisting their cooperation in opposing fascism and the war.[50] But neither Abe nor Asō, nor anyone else in the

Shakai Taishūtō, responded favorably, having committed themselves to supporting the war. Thus, the Musantō stood alone in the Japanese party movement in resisting the China Incident. In December, the small popular front formed around the Musantō by Katō was destroyed when the Home Ministry arrested Katō, Suzuki, and others in the Musantō and forced the dissolution of the Party. Zempyō met a similar fate.[51] After this, there was no further protest from the proletariat against the war.

The final submersion of the labor movement, 1938–1940

The final submersion (*chimbotsu*)[52] of the Japanese labor movement in 1940 took place after a series of schisms in both the labor and socialist party movements in the 1938–1940 period. In these last, tortuous years, the alliance of the Shaminkei and Nichirōkei factions in the Zen Nihon Rōdō Sōdōmei and the Shakai Taishūtō came unstuck and the Kumiai Kaigi fell apart at the seams. Since the almost simultaneous fissions in the Zen Nihon Rōdō Sōdōmei and the Shakai Taishūtō were closely interrelated in their causes and effects, they may be discussed together.

Beneath the surface of their external solidarity, the potential for factional fission in these organizations had always been great. The Shaminkei and Nichirōkei had retained their identity within the mergers of the Shakai Taishūtō after 1932, and the Zen Nihon Rōdō Sōdōmei, after 1936. They had shared power in both but they had never trusted one another. Ultimately, the two major issues precipitating their final rupture in the Shakai Taishūtō and the Zen Nihon Rōdō Sōdōmei were the policy of the Konoe administration to create a national political consensus for the prosecution of the China Incident and the related policy of this government to pull all existing labor organizations into a patriotic labor front. For reasons that will become clear later, it is convenient to begin discussing the ways in which these policies wreaked havoc on the labor and socialist party movements with an analysis of the thought and action of the Nichirōkei and, in particular, of Asō Hisashi.

As stated earlier, Asō was enthusiastic about the China Incident. But what distinguished him and his faction from the Shaminkei was their positive view of the Konoe administration and especially of Konoe himself. He appealed to Asō for the same reasons that the army had attracted his attention earlier. Just as Asō had once regarded the army as a progressive political force, so he now perceived Konoe in precisely the same terms.

It is unknown when Asō first met Konoe personally. One speculation is that they were introduced by Kamei Kan'ichirō, which is plausible since Kamei, who was related to nobility, had a social entrée to the Prince.[53] At any rate, Asō and Konoe developed a mutual respect in the course of a secret acquaintance and the Prime Minister enlisted Asō's help in making plans for a new, all-inclusive, national-front party in 1938. Asō had indeed anticipated the usefulness of such a party in 1937, which explains the role he played in supporting the resolution calling for a national-unity party in the Shakai Taishūtō convention of 1937. He calculated that under the umbrella of a national-front party, the influence of the liberal parties and the *zaibatsu* would be neutralized and that the new party might become an agency for both the unification of the nation in wartime and the reconstruction of Japan in a socialist direction.

Asō was further attracted to Konoe because he admired the so-called 'revisionist bureaucrats' upon whom Konoe relied in his administration to make policy. One historian says of these men that they all 'felt a general commitment to change the existing order – political, social, economic, or all three – for the purpose of increasing the nation's spiritual and military power. They advocated either ideological purification, State control of the economy, or both.'[54] In general, they supported the military and its plans for a national defense State geared for total war, opposed capitalism, and worked across ministerial boundaries in the government to these ends.

In other words, Asō pinned his hopes of achieving 'socialism from above' on Konoe and the 'revisionist bureaucrats', many of whom he knew personally. 'Socialism from below', he felt, would take years, if it was ever achieved. But 'socialism from above' seemed to him to be attainable in the near future. Thus, in June 1938 Asō met regularly with one of Konoe's close advisers, Nakamizo Tamakichi, to draw up a proposal for the formation of a new national political front.[55]

Asō did not disclose either his involvement with Konoe or his role in Konoe's plans to form a national-unity party to his colleagues in the Shakai Taishūtō. But he did pressure the Shakai Taishūtō central committee to throw its weight behind the National Mobilization bill presented to the Diet that year by the Konoe administration. One political commentator claimed early in 1939 that Asō and Miwa Jusō had for several years often consulted with the 'revisionist bureaucrats' who drafted this bill and that it was on this account that Asō was so vocal in mobilizing the Shakai Taishūtō's support for the bill.[56]

Asō had no trouble in persuading both factions of the Party to vote for the bill. But it must be emphasized that the Shaminkei wing of the Party backed the National Mobilization bill for reasons that were altogether dissimilar from Asō's. Asō saw this legislation as important in creating a socialist new order in Japan. He anticipated that by giving the government massive power over the economy, the *zaibatsu* would be brought under control and capitalism subordinated to the needs of the State, and, more importantly, to the needs of the masses. However, the Shaminkei endorsed the bill only as a means of helping to win the war in China. The Shaminkei did not see this legislation as the beginning of a process that would lead to a socialist new order under Konoe. Save Kamei Kan'ichirō, no one in the Shaminkei had close ties with Konoe. Nor did these men have contacts with the 'revisionist bureaucrats' around him.

Soon, relations between the Shaminkei and Nichirōkei were strained by the 'Nishio Incident' which took place in the Diet during debate over the National Mobilization bill. Nishio did not oppose the bill; indeed, he wanted it strengthened. He asserted, 'In the world today, individualism is giving way to communalism, liberalism to totalitarianism. The freedom of the individual is being regulated and rationalized as a part of planning the development of the whole. These trends we clearly recognize.' Then, alluding to what he perceived as the clash between the 'have', white nations, and the 'have-not', colored races, the world over, Nishio proclaimed that 'Prime Minister Konoe should lead Japan...like Hitler, Mussolini or Stalin!'[57]

As Gordon Berger states, 'Shocked at the suggestion that Japan might seek inspiration from Stalin, the lower house immediately voted to expel Nishio from its membership.'[58] This move was initiated chiefly by the Minseitō and Seiyūkai but, significantly, Asō Hisashi and others in the Nichirōkei wing of the Shakai Taishūtō's Diet members were also appalled at Nishio's implied admiration for Stalin. Therefore, Asō and Kawakami Jōtarō tried to persuade Nishio to publicly retract his statement. But Nishio refused. When the motion of censure went before a special disciplinary committee in the Diet, Asō tried to persuade Nishio to resign his seat but again Nishio refused, having received support from the liberal politician Ozaki Yukio who had declared that if the Diet was going to expel Nishio, it might as well expel him, Ozaki, as well, since Ozaki regarded the move against Nishio as a threat to freedom of speech.[59] But nevertheless, Nishio was expelled. Shortly before this occurred, the Shakai Taishūtō delegates, led by Abe, staged a walk-out to protest at Nishio's fate. The Nichirōkei joined this demonstration but this was the last time that the two factions in the Shakai Taishūtō would cooperate with one another.[60]

Following the 'Nishio Incident', the Nichirōkei and the Shaminkei diverged sharply in their respective attitudes toward the policies of the Konoe government. But they did not fall out with one another entirely until the Nichirōkei advocated the dissolution of the Shakai Taishūtō in the spring of 1940. That the Nichirōkei would adopt this position was, however, prefigured by various statements made by Nichirōkei members in 1938 and 1939. For instance, Miwa Jusō declared in December 1938 that all of the existing parties ought to rally around Konoe as a symbol of the unity of the people with the government and the Imperial Throne.[61] But Miwa and Asō did not recommend the dissolution of the Shakai Taishūtō at that time. They wanted to wait in taking this crucial step until the plans for Konoe's national-front party were finalized.

The same polarization of opinion regarding the national political front issue arose in the labor movement in 1938 and 1939. Nichirōkei labor leaders like Kono Mitsu and Kikukawa Tadao had agreed with Asō and Kawakami that Nishio's Diet speech, particularly the comparison of Konoe and Stalin, was a most serious indiscretion and a travesty for the Shakai Taishūtō's image in the public eye. In early 1939, they also began to share Asō's enthusiasm for Konoe and the emergent New Order. By contrast, Matsuoka had become increasingly nervous about the possible ramifications of the New Order for the labor movement. He had begun to wonder whether the unions would be pressured into some sort of a massive labor front that would compromise the existence of such autonomous organizations as the Zen Nihon Rōdō Sōdōmei or the Kumiai Kaigi.[62]

The launching by the Konoe cabinet of the Sangyō Hōkoku Undō, or Sampō, in 1938 indicated that precisely this fate lay in store for the labor movement. Preliminary plans for the Industrial Patriotic Movement were first announced in April. It was stated that the general purpose of Sampō was to harmonize labor–management relations to ensure industrial peace and facilitate production for war. The plans envisaged the establishment of *sangyō hōkokukai* (industrial patriotic societies) in every factory to this end. The *hōkokukai* were portrayed as agencies for industrial cooperation that would include all of the workers and management at any given enterprise. According to the rather ambiguous terms of reference which were subsequently formulated for Sampō, the implication was that the *hōkokukai* would merely coexist alongside works councils and labor unions that had taken root in the factories. Ultimately, the plans for Sampō were finalized and approved by Konoe in August, when he instructed the newly established Welfare Ministry and the Home Ministry to put them into immediate operation.[63]

That the *hōkokukai* were to be knit into prefectural Sampō federations supervised by prefectural governors and that Sampō would be administered from a central national headquarters in Tokyo consisting of representatives from the Welfare Ministry, the Home Ministry, the Commerce Ministry, and the Kyōchōkai, made it plain that the *hōkokukai* would in reality be controlled by the government of Japan.[64] Although nothing was said officially to give the impression that Sampō would ultimately replace the unions as a massive labor front into which all the unions would eventually be dissolved, this in truth was what Konoe hoped to accomplish in fostering national unity during the China Incident.

This was also how Matsuoka interpreted Sampō in 1938. He concluded, upon learning of the government's plans, that Sampō was a direct threat to the labor movement.[65] Significantly, business leaders in Zensanren also viewed Sampō with great apprehension. They feared that Sampō would be manipulated by the government to reduce their own authority in the factories. Sampō seemed to them to be an adjunct to the government's increasing power over the economy as manifested in the National Mobilization Law, although officially Sampō had nothing to do with the enforcement of this legislation.[66]

However, neither organized labor nor organized business, both of which were in a weak position in relation to the government, could oppose Sampō. And, in any case, both had painted themselves into the corner of patriotism by professing support for the principle of increased cooperation with the government during the national emergency of the China Incident. The creation by the Zen Nihon Rōdō Sōdōmei of the much-publicized Sankyō Kurabu early in 1938, for example, made it impossible for the Federation to dissent from Sampō since the objectives of the Sankyō Kurabu and Sampō were practically indistinguishable. Consequently, Matsuoka had no choice but to acquiesce when the government asked him to serve on Sampō's board of directors as the representative of organized labor. A similar request was made of Baron

Gō Seinosuke, head of Mitsui, and an important official in Zensanren. His appointment to the board, and Matsuoka's, were the beginning of the co-optation of organized business and organized labor by Sampō.[67]

The new *hōkokukai* proliferated rapidly. By the end of 1938, 1,158 had been established. In April 1939, this number had risen to 3,847. By the end of 1939, there were 19,670 *hōkokukai* in Japan, with roughly 2,989,976 workers in their fold.[68] During this period of growth, the labor unions were exhorted by Sampō headquarters to encourage their members to join the *hōkokukai*. But the unions themselves were not subjected to coercion in this respect. On the contrary, the official policy of Sampō was to praise such organizations as the Zen Nihon Rōdō Sōdōmei for cooperating with Sampō.[69]

Sampō did not coerce the labor movement because it was obvious that coercion was unnecessary. Organized and unorganized workers alike flocked to Sampō on their own volition. At first, this rush into the *hōkokukai* was predominant among rightist labor organizations. For instance, the Aikoku Rōdō Kumiai Zenkoku Kondankai, which had changed its name in November 1938 to the Nihon Kinrō Hōko Renmei (Japan Workers' Patriotic League) dissolved itself voluntarily in October 1939 and called upon all of its members to join the *hōkokukai* in the factories where they worked. Among the Renmei's leaders who took the initiative in making this patriotic gesture was Kaeno Shin'ichi, by now one of the most vigorous supporters of Sampō.[70]

Organizations in the Kumiai Kaigi also rushed into Sampō. In late 1938, the Nihon Kaiin Kumiai, Hamada Kunitarō's organization, and the Nihon Kaiin Kyōkai, pulled out of the Kaigi and formed a new naval federation, the Hōkoku Kaiin Dōmei (Patriotic Naval League) which was pledged to support Sampō.[71] In 1940, this body also dissolved itself, sending all of its members exclusively into Sampō.[72] The loss of these organizations to the Kumiai Kaigi was immeasurable. The Nihon Kaiin Kumiai had been, because of its great size, a major bulwark of the Kaigi. Its defection from the Kaigi weakened the latter considerably. Moreover, it occurred at a bad moment for the Kaigi. At the time of the withdrawal of the Nihon Kaiin Kumiai, the Kaigi was in the midst of its vigorous opposition to the decision of the Konoe government to pull Japan out of the International Labor Organization.[73] The exodus of the Nihon Kaiin Kumiai undermined this protest by provoking an internal crisis in the Kaigi. Matsuoka, who replaced Hamada as head of the Kaigi, found himself presiding over an

organization that was about to lose even more of its member-organiza-
tions to Sampō.

In other words, Sampō had the effect of a magnet, pulling labor
organizations to itself with what seemed to be an increasingly irresistible
attraction. Faced with an obvious erosion of their own capacity to keep
the labor movement intact, the leaders of the Zen Nihon Rōdō Sōdōmei
struggled to find ways to prevent what they feared would be a mass
exodus of their rank and file followers away from the unions into
Sampō. Matsuoka's answer to this dilemma was to support Sampō by
proving that the labor unions under his command could best serve
Sampō by remaining intact as autonomous units outside of the
hōkokukai. He believed it possible for the workers to belong to the
hōkokukai and the unions at the same time, without diminishing their
loyalty to the labor movement.

Matsuoka argued in this vein during the meetings of Sampō's board
of directors. He repeatedly told the board that it was quite unnecessary
for the labor unions to give up their separate identity and autonomy.
They could serve Sampō as its 'flying buttresses', he claimed. He
encouraged the board to see the unions as ready-made allies of the
hōkokukai. He also frequently said that it would not increase the
workers' patriotism to compel them to relinquish their allegiance to
the unions and join Sampō on an exclusive basis since the unions in the
Zen Nihon Rōdō Sōdōmei were already patriotic enough.[74]

To demonstrate his support of Sampō, conditioned by the proviso
that the labor movement should not be displaced by the *hōkokukai,*
Matsuoka actively encouraged the Zen Nihon Rōdō Sōdōmei unions to
form *hōkokukai* in their factories. In fact, they had already begun to do
so. By August 1939, thirty-seven *hōkokukai* had been established by the
Zen Nihon Rōdō Sōdōmei. The Tokyo Iron Workers' Union led the
way by establishing no less than sixteen *hōkokukai* in the factories
where its members were employed.[75]

In many instances, this trend resulted in a rather anomalous situation in which Federation union bosses also served as officers, along with
management, in the *hōkokukai.* In effect, these men, and their fellow
union members, now belonged to two separate kinds of institutions –
the union locals and the *hōkokukai.* As Matsuoka argued, in theory,
this pattern of joint membership was not inimical to the continued
functioning of the unions independently of Sampō. However, in reality
it was inevitable that the focus of such workers would be on the
hōkokukai rather than the unions, not only because the *hōkokukai,*

which were backed by management with the support of the government, were stronger than the unions but also because the emotional pull of the *hōkokukai* on the patriotism of the average worker was extremely strong, much more so than the pull of the Zen Nihon Rōdō Sōdōmei itself. In sum, the formula of dual membership that Matsuoka now advocated to preserve the labor movement was to be a total failure, for Sampō continued to co-opt the loyalty of the workers at the expense of the unions.

As the labor movement grappled with the problems of coping with Sampō, the Shakai Taishūtō decided to give its full backing to Sampō in July 1938. Both the Shaminkei and Nichirōkei factions in the Party agreed that this was necessary. But, whereas the Shaminkei socialists opposed anything which might lead to the dissolution of the unions into Sampō, the Nichirōkei took a different view. For instance, Suzuki Etsujirō began a movement of Nichirōkei unions under his personal influence in the merger to press the Federation's central committee on behalf of dissolving the Zen Nihon Rōdō Sōdōmei so that all of its workers could join the *hōkokukai* without being tied at the same time to labor unions which stood outside of the *hōkokukai*. In early 1939, Suzuki formed a 'Sampō Club' in Osaka to lead the way in this endeavor.[76]

More significant was the view of Nichirōkei labor leaders, including Kono Mitsu and Kikukawa Tadao, on the Sampō question. In late 1938 and early 1939 these men argued quite openly in the Federation for the dissolution of the Federation.[77] They were encouraged by Asō Hisashi in the Shakai Taishūtō.[78] Since Shaminkei labor and Party leaders in the Zen Nihon Rōdō Sōdōmei and the Shakai Taishūtō, respectively, opposed this view, favoring the continuation of the labor movement as an independent force outside of Sampō, it was only a matter of time before both organizations were split apart by factional rivalry over this important issue.

However, this crisis was averted for a brief period because leaders of the Nichirōkei did not want to dissolve the labor movement prematurely. They wanted to wait until it was possible to coordinate the dissolution of the Shakai Taishūtō and the Zen Nihon Rōdō Sōdōmei jointly into the New Order. They referred to this strategy as 'one big dissolution'. This was mainly Asō's idea: he reasoned that if the socialist labor and party movement could swing into line behind the New Order with one dramatic step, then the socialists would have a good chance of impressing Konoe with their support for the New Order and perhaps

influence him to accept some of their policies, to assure that the New
Order would raise the 'people's livelihood' and destroy the privileges
of the elite classes.[79]

Accordingly, Nichirōkei labor leaders tried to restrain Suzuki Etsujirō
from breaking prematurely from the Zen Nihon Rōdō Sōdōmei to join
Sampō. The Shaminkei, led by Matsuoka and Nishio in the labor
movement, wanted to prevent him from doing this for another reason:
they never intended to dissolve the Zen Nihon Rōdō Sōdōmei if they
could help it and they feared that if Suzuki Etsujirō defected, he might
destroy this policy.

Ultimately, however, disagreement concerning Sampō reached the
point where it was no longer possible for the two factions to cooperate
in the Zen Nihon Rōdō Sōdōmei. A crisis occurred during a meeting
of the central committee of the Federation on July 24, 1939, called to
decide upon the long-range strategy of the labor movement. At this
meeting, Kono Mitsu, speaking for the Nichirōkei, said that his faction
was for dissolution, at the appropriate time. He stated that in the past
the mission of the labor movement had been to defend the interests of
the proletariat. The mission was still valid, but it was now important
to subordinate it to the defense of the nation. The two goals were
compatible, Kono argued, because Sampō could be encouraged to
improve the lot of the workers while at the same time serving the
kokutai.[80]

Greatly distressed over this position, the Shaminkei caucused separately and decided to oppose dissolution at all costs. Then, the two
factions met again, at which time Matsuoka informed Kono Mitsu of
the Shaminkei's final decision against dissolution. At once, Kono
declared that the Nichirōkei labor organizations in the Zen Nihon
Rōdō Sōdōmei would leave the Federation immediately, which they
did.[81] On November 3, they coalesced into a Sangyō Hōkoku Kurabu
where they prepared to dissolve into Sampō later at a signal from Asō
Hisashi.[82] Then the Club called a meeting at which the leaders of the
Nichirōkei labor movement took an oath to the Sun Goddess, pledging
to work for the 'spread of the Emperor's benevolent rule throughout
the world'.[83] Matsuoka angrily ridiculed this gesture as an example of
the 'excessive patriotism' that had infected parts of the labor movement; he denounced the Nichirōkei pledge as a 'pious shrine ceremony'.[84]

On July 25, after withdrawal of the Nichirōkei, the Zen Nihon Rōdō
Sōdōmei central committee met in an emergency session to elect

replacements for the departed Nichirōkei officers in Federation head-quarters. Members of the Matsuoka and Nishio factions were duly elevated to important posts on the committee under the domination of Matsuoka, who remained as chairman, and Nishio. Nishio in particular expanded his influence by becoming head of the Federation's political bureau as well as Director. He was also named the Federation's permanent representative on the central committee of the Shakai Taishūtō.[85]

Then, at the Federation's annual national convention, November 3–4 in Osaka, the consequences of the recent split were recognized further by the adoption of a new name for the Federation, which became, simply, the Nihon Rōdō Sōdōmei, with the character for 'Zen', which had referred to the Nichirōkei's participation in the now-defunct labor merger, deleted. The convention reaffirmed its support for the Home Front Campaign and industrial cooperation, called for various laws benefiting the workers, and professed support for the Labor Covenant of the ILO, which made an indirect protest against Japan's severance from that organization in 1938. The only other critical note toward the government's policies struck at the convention was a demand that May Day demonstrations be permitted.[86]

Thus, the problem of how to respond to Sampō destroyed the labor merger of 1936. The Shaminkei and Nichirōkei elements of the labor movement were locked in bitter rivalry once more. Only now, their positions on the spectrum of the labor movement reversed the situation that had prevailed in the 1920s. Whereas, in the past, the Sōdōmei had accused the Nichirōkei labor movement of being pro-communist, now the Nichirōkei's Sangyō Hōkoku Kurabu branded the Sōdōmei as a 'communist organization'.[87] To use the parlance of former times, the centrists had shifted dramatically to the right while the Sōdōmei had shifted to the center, at least on the vital question of whether the unions should dissolve altogether into Sampō.

Inevitably, the 1939 labor split of the Zen Nihon Rōdō Sōdōmei caused a similar rupture in the Kumiai Kaigi. All of the Nichirōkei bloc of labor organizations in the Kaigi withdrew from the Congress and associated themselves with the Sangyō Hōkoku Kurabu. This made the Kaigi little more than a paper organization composed of the tattered remnants of the Sōdōmei's bloc and the reconstituted Sōdōmei itself. Now purely a front organization for the Sōdōmei, the Kaigi was but an empty shell of its former self. But Matsuoka and other Sōdōmei leaders were determined to keep the Kaigi alive, just as they were determined to maintain the General Federation's autonomous existence outside of Sampō.

The labor split in 1939 had also polarized the Shaminkei and Nichirōkei groupings in the Shakai Taishūtō. As the split neared its climax, Asō lent support to his allies in the Zen Nihon Rōdō Sōdōmei and urged that the Party should associate itself with their view in favor of dissolving the Federation into Sampō at an appropriate time in the near future. This was rejected by Abe Isoo and his faction, whose members were anxious to preserve an independent labor base for the Party.[88] But unlike the Zen Nihon Rōdō Sōdōmei, the Shakai Taishūtō did not split in 1939 over the Sampō issue, because neither faction wanted the Party to be ruptured that year.

The Shaminkei socialists in the Party, who were deeply upset by the labor split when it finally occurred, wanted to keep the Party intact in order to provide support for the reconstituted Sōdōmei and to protest against the drift toward the creation of a national-unity political front that would absorb every party in Japan. The Nichirōkei, for its part, wanted to avoid splitting the Party in 1939, not for these ends but in the hopes that the Shakai Taishūtō could be kept intact so that it could undertake a dramatic dissolution at a time when such a demonstration of the Party's support for the New Order would be most likely to impress the government and elicit the government's cooperation in achieving 'socialism from above'.

In Asō's thinking, this time had not yet come. In January 1939, the Konoe cabinet had suddenly fallen, due to the discouragement of the Prince over Japan's failure to decisively attain the upper hand over Chiang Kai-shek in the China Incident, and over the mounting hostility toward Japan in the West.[89] Konoe was replaced by Baron Hiranuma Kiichirō, an ardent conservative nationalist, as Prime Minister. Asō had little admiration for Hiranuma as a national leader and ridiculed him as an unimaginative bureaucrat. Hiranuma was decidedly not the kind of man Asō had envisioned as head of the New Order. Nor did Asō think Hiranuma would be responsive, like Konoe, to socialism in realizing the New Order.[90] So, Asō deliberately delayed in carrying out a 'one big dissolution' of the Shakai Taishūtō and the Sangyō Hōkoku Kurabu until another leader of Konoe's stature, or the Prince himself, should take power again.

As it turned out, Asō did not have to wait very long before recommending 'one big dissolution', although by the time he did so the effect of this strategy would be diminished by the split of the Shakai Taishūtō.

The Hiranuma cabinet had been able to maintain only a marginal grip on national affairs and succumbed to political turmoil soon after Hitler and Stalin signed a Non-Aggression Pact in August 1939. This act called into question the wisdom of Japan's association with Germany in the Anti-Comintern Pact of 1936. Hiranuma's successor as Prime Minister, Admiral Abe Nobuyuki, was in power only four and one-half months before he too was compelled to resign, having failed utterly to obtain the support of the army, the Diet, and the people at large. Yet another cabinet, that of Admiral Yonai Mitsumasa, came and went before Konoe formed his second cabinet on July 22, 1940. Konoe's return to power would soon revive Asō's interest in assisting the New Order and would prompt him to implement his envisaged 'one big dissolution' to that end.[91]

In the confused interim between the first and second Konoe cabinets, Asō contemplated the merger of the Shakai Taishūtō with other political organizations likely to strengthen the cause of 'socialism from above'. Negotiations for this purpose were carried out with Nakano Seigō's Tōhōkai or 'Eastern Association', a nationalist party which, however, supported certain progressive reforms for the workers that were not too dissimilar to those of the socialist movement.[92] However, this merger did not take place, because of disagreements between Asō and Nakano over the leadership of the new party and because of opposition by Shaminkei leaders in the Shakai Taishūtō on the grounds that Nakano's organization was 'fascist'.[93]

The controversy over the Tōhōkai merger question left relations between the Shaminkei and the Nichirōkei more strained than ever in the Shakai Taishūtō. All that was needed to destroy their wobbly alliance was a final crisis between the two factions. Such a crisis, precipitated by the so-called 'Saitō affair', arose on February 2, 1940, when Saitō Takao of the Minseitō stunned the Diet by delivering a broadside attack on the military and the government for persisting in a pointless, stalemate war with China.[94] The Nichirōkei side of the Shakai Taishūtō responded to Saitō's speech by denouncing it as treasonous and calling for his expulsion from the Diet, a demand that was also raised from all quarters of the Diet, including Saitō's own Party.[95] However, the Shaminkei, which was sympathetic to Saitō, refused to join this chorus of pro-expulsion sentiments and on March 7, when it was time for the Diet to vote on a motion to oust the luckless Saitō from its ranks, ten Shaminkei representatives from the Shakai Taishūtō, including Abe, Suzuki Bunji, Katayama Tetsu, Nishio Suehiro, and six others registered their dissent and support for Saitō by staging a dramatic exodus from the proceedings.[96]

This parting of the ways over the Saitō affair led to the final rupture of the Shakai Taishūtō. On March 7, at a special meeting of the Party central committee, Asō Hisashi demanded that all of those who had participated in the pro-Saitō demonstration in the Diet, save for Abe Isoo, be expelled from the Shakai Taishūtō in order to purge the Party of unpatriotic elements.[97] Abe was exempted out of respect for his reputation as the elder statesman of the socialist party movement. After several days of acrimonious debate, the expulsions were carried out on March 10.[98] Eleven days later, Abe retaliated by withdrawing from the Shakai Taishūtō, taking the rest of the Shaminkei faction along with him, whereupon Asō was elected as chairman of the Shakai Taishūtō. In this capacity he exhorted the Party, now under the full control of his own faction, to support the war in China, the Emperor, and the *kokutai*. Asō also accused the Shaminkei of resisting these patriotic goals and thereby undermining the nation.[99]

This climactic rupture of the Shakai Taishūtō caused great anxiety in the Nihon Rōdō Sōdōmei, for now the labor movement was deprived of a political ally which would help protect the unions from the New Order. Consequently, the Sōdōmei began frantic maneuvers to establish a new political party which would counteract the Shakai Taishūtō in preserving the autonomy of the movement. The Sōdōmei signalled its intention to this end on March 30 by formally announcing its withdrawal of support from the Shakai Taishūtō and calling upon Abe Isoo to rally the Shaminkei labor and political elements around a new labor party under his personal leadership.[100]

Losing no time in backing up this position with concrete action, the Sōdōmei hastily organized a conference of labor leaders and influential Shaminkei politicians in Tokyo on March 31 to plan the establishment of a new party. With Suzuki Bunji chairing the proceedings at Matsuoka's request, this conference drew up a list of men who would serve on the party central committee under Abe, the party chairman, and it resolved to call the projected party the Kinrō Kokumintō (Nationalist Labor Party). The choice of title reflected the desire of the conference to emphasize the Shaminkei concept of class (*kinrō*), the labor base of the party, and the nationalistic loyalty of the party to the *kokutai*. The conference ended by setting a date for the inaugural of the Kinrō Kokumintō, May 12.[101]

The various statements issuing from this conference concerning the purpose of the Kinrō Kokumintō suggest that this new party was to be little different from the Shakai Taishūtō in many important respects. Like the Shakai Taishūtō, the Kinrō Kokumintō was seen by its creators as a vehicle for advocating progressive socialist economic programs to benefit the 'people's livelihood'. Similarly, the Kinrō Kokumintō was projected as a party that would support Japan's 'holy war' in Asia, the military strengthening of the country, and the general development of the 'national race' (*kokka minzoku*).[102]

However, the men who laid the basis for the Kinrō Kokumintō differed markedly from their counterparts in the Shakai Taishūtō in the ways in which they viewed the evolution of the New Order. The Shakai Taishūtō was committed to the proposition that all existing political parties and labor organizations in Japan should eventually dissolve themselves into national political and labor fronts. In contrast, the Shaminkei backers of the Kinrō Kokumintō believed that the structure of the New Order should accommodate the diversity and pluralism inherent in interest group politics, and that since the people of Japan were united in their hearts behind the Emperor, it was not necessary to unite them further into national fronts which would obliterate existing political and labor institutions.

Matsuoka Komakichi made plain the vision of the New Order as held by the leaders of the Sōdōmei in an article which he wrote for the April issue of *Rōdō*. Repeating his familiar argument concerning the relationship of the Sōdōmei to Sampō, Matsuoka stated that organizations like the Sōdōmei and the projected Kinrō Kokumintō could serve the nation by mobilizing the people for support of the war in different ways. To unite the people by bringing them into umbrella fronts would not, he said, necessarily increase their identification with the national cause. Matsuoka specifically criticized the Shakai Taishūtō for its intention to support the New Order (Shintaisei) by dissolving itself into the New Order.[103]

Given these contrasting views of the New Order, it might seem plausible to conclude that the Shaminkei's assessment of the Shintaisei was based on a fundamentally democratic perception of politics and society whereas the Nichirōkei's was not. Insofar as the Shaminkei stressed the preservation of pluralism in Japan while the Nichirōkei encouraged the evolution of all-inclusive national fronts, this was partly true. Yet, if one considers the subjective perception of the two factions, this conclusion must be dismissed as being too simplistic. Whatever pluralism that existed in the Shaminkei was implicit at best. It was not based on any ideology that would have clarified the question: pluralism to what ultimate end? Had writers like Matsuoka been enthusiastic about the Kinrō Kokumintō and the Sōdōmei out of a desire to undertake a final struggle for socialism in Japan – as Katō Kanjū had been in mobilizing a popular front – it would be possible to ascribe significant political meaning to their notion of pluralism.

But this was not the case: Matsuoka had long since abandoned any commitment to socialism. His sole ambition in 1940 was to preserve the autonomy of the labor movement as an end in itself. When he backed the Kinrō Kokumintō, he did so in hopes of using the new party to shield the labor movement from Sampō. Although the creators of the Kinrō Kokumintō spoke in vaguely socialist terms of serving the interests of the *kinrō* and advancing the 'people's livelihood', this trace of an earlier notion of 'realist socialism' held little political meaning to Matsuoka. His view of the party, and of pluralism in general, did not transcend the interests of labor unionism. Nor did Matsuoka repudiate the idea of achieving national unity in the New Order. His only quarrel with the New Order was over the necessity of collapsing existing labor and political institutions into national fronts. Accordingly, the Sōdōmei's defense of pluralism did not represent dissent from the spirit of the Shintaisei or the basic goals of the nation.

On the other hand, although Asō Hisashi and others in the Nichirōkei denied pluralism in approaching the New Order, they did not think that in so doing they were necessarily denying democracy. In Asō's thinking, the national fronts of the New Order would be basically democratic in that they would dissolve all existing distinctions between separate groups in society and politics. In exchanging a concept of democracy based on class pluralism for one based on holistic collectivism, Asō was persuaded that the new national fronts would serve the democratic purpose of mediating between the Emperor with his government and the masses by assuring the implementation of progressive social reforms 'from above' that would benefit all strata of society. For Asō, the Shintaisei was not authoritarian. Rather, it was the vehicle of socialist renovation (*kakushin*), the liberation (*kaihō*) of the people from capitalism, and the reconstruction (*kaizō*) of a new Japan.[104]

Although Asō's socialist concept of Shintaisei was not shared by the government, there was sufficient agreement between the Nichirōkei and the government on the need for collective unity to permit the Shakai Taishūtō to escape the kind of repression meted out by the government to the Kinrō Kokumintō. Seeing that the appearance of a new political party ostensibly oriented to class interests would complicate the process of achieving national unity, the Home Ministry served notice on May 7, five days prior to the party's planned inaugural, that the Kinrō Kokumintō would not be tolerated. The Home Ministry's prohibition stated in part,

> A close study of its constituent elements, the ideology and action of its leaders, and the circumstances leading to its organization reveals that the new labor party is nothing but a class party based ideologically on socialism and in organizational setup, the working classes. Because it will instigate class struggle and obstruct the system of national solidarity and because it is liable to be exploited by possibly resurgent Popular Frontists [an allusion to Katō Kanjū's defunct resistance movement], we cannot connive at its organization under the current emergency from the standpoint of peace and order.[105]

The prohibition of the Kinrō Kokumintō even before its formal establishment revealed the depth of the government's determination to remove all obstacles in preparation for the rise of national political and labor fronts, deemed essential to the spirit of unity and consensus in the emergent New Order. However, although the prohibition of the Kinrō Kokumintō was a repressive attempt to ensure the success of the New Order, on balance the government preferred persuasion to intimidation in bringing pluralistic interest groups and parties under the one roof of the New Order. This was because architects of the New Order believed that if the spirit of national unity to be embodied in the Shintaisei was to be genuine, national unity should come about through the freely expressed will of the people, not by coercion.

As a result, the government applied intensive moral pressure on organizations that had yet to indicate full support of the New Order. For instance, in a typical remark made by government officials in the spring of 1940 with respect to the labor movement, a representative of the labor bureau in the Home Ministry told the Diet, 'We hope all of the trade unions will dissolve themselves of their own accord' so that Sampō, which was to be the labor arm of the New Order, would be strengthened.[106] This message was conveyed directly to the Sōdōmei in many similar instances of moral pressure. To illustrate, Matsuoka was visited at his house one evening in March by three officials who served with him on the board of directors of Sampō. They told him they had been sent by Prince Konoe, who was assumed to be the next Prime Minister, to impress upon Matsuoka the importance of supporting Sampō unequivocally by dissolving the Sōdōmei in a demonstration of solidarity with the aims of the Industrial Patriotic Movement. They added that Matsuoka's sincerity in supporting the nation would be in question as long as he stubbornly maintained the existence of the General Federation.

According to one source, Matsuoka is reputed to have replied, 'I cannot agree to dissolve the Sōdōmei...If the government liquidates the Sōdōmei, so be it. But I am far from participating [exclusively] in Sampō. We might win this war but we might all lose [it]. After the war, it may be useful for me to have taken this position.' One of his callers then remarked, 'Well, Matsuoka my friend, do not worry. Losing the war is an impossibility.'[107]

Anxious to ascertain what would happen to the Sōdōmei if it were not voluntarily dissolved, Matsuoka tried many times to see Welfare Minister Yoshida Shigeru for a clarification of government policy toward the labor movement. After refusing to see Matsuoka for many days, Yoshida finally granted him an interview on May 14, at Yoshida's office. On that occasion, Yoshida told the labor leader that the government did not plan to coerce the unions into dissolution. The unions, Yoshida said, were compatible with Sampō. However, he quickly added that it would be ideal from the government's point of view if the unions would undertake 'spontaneous dissolution', acting entirely on their own volition, in order to give full support to Sampō.[108]

This did not quiet Matsuoka's apprehensions; he asked to see Yoshida again on May 17 to discover what the consequences would be if the labor movement did not undertake 'spontaneous dissolution'. Once again, Yoshida assured Matsuoka that the government did not plan to shut down the Sōdōmei. But, rather ambivalently, the Welfare Minister stated that the government was not prepared to let the Sōdōmei go on indefinitely.[109]

The same kind of moral pressure was applied to other interest groups besides the labor movement. From the government's perspective, for example, the existence of business interest groups such as Zensanren did not conform to the spirit of unity envisioned for the New Order any more than did the existence of the unions. In an effort to gauge the intentions of Zensanren regarding the New Order, Yoshida Shigeru at one point asked Fujihara Ginjirō, the former head of Zensanren who was then serving as Minister of Commerce and Industry, whether he thought Zensanren would dissolve itself voluntarily to dramatize business support for the government's control of the economy. Fujihara replied that such business leaders in Zensanren as Gō Seinosuke and Nakagawa Suyekichi (head of the Furukawa Electrical Engineering

Company) would not agree to voluntary dissolution.[110] Indeed, as late as April 23, Zensanren's board of directors had resolved never to close down the organization voluntarily.[111]

However, after intensive efforts by Home and Welfare Ministry officials to persuade Zensanren leaders to reconsider their policy on the matter of voluntary dissolution, Zensanren informed the government on May 4 that it would dissolve itself to comply with the spirit of national unity.[112] This development formed the immediate background of Matsuoka's visits with Yoshida later that month, for the disappearance of Zensanren placed even greater moral pressure on the Sōdōmei to sacrifice its autonomy from Sampō. With Zensanren out of the picture, the Sōdōmei could not argue, as Matsuoka had tried to do, that it should be allowed to continue in existence as long as its powerful business rival was still intact. The voluntary self-destruction of Zensanren therefore weakened the Sōdōmei's already frail position in resisting dissolution.

Still, the central committee of the Nihon Rōdō Sōdōmei stubbornly persisted in passively resisting the implications of Sampō for the future of the labor movement by continuing the policy of nonconformity with the pressures toward voluntary dissolution in the early summer of 1940. Since the government had placed high value on the form by which the New Order would be achieved, emphasizing voluntary compliance with the Shintaisei, the refusal of the Sōdōmei to give in by dissolving itself constituted a symbolic defiance against the form, if not the spiritual content, of the New Order. However, it was impossible for Sōdōmei leaders to sustain their defiance for very long because, much to their anguish, this policy of resistance to dissolution did not have the support of rank and file workers in the Federation, while external pressures on the Sōdōmei to dissolve became overwhelming.

Matsuoka and Nishio were caught unawares by the mass defections of Sōdōmei unions into Sampō, whereby these unions carried out their own version of 'spontaneous dissolution' contrary to the wishes of Sōdōmei headquarters in the spring and summer of 1940. Sōdōmei leaders had been too preoccupied with the external threats to the Federation to appreciate the significance of this erosion of worker support at the grass roots of the labor movement until it was too late to resolve this new and very critical problem within the Sōdōmei itself. In any case, the tide of defection was irreversible since it presented a series of faits accomplis to Sōdōmei headquarters by unions that saw no point in carrying on with the labor movement.

The Sōdōmei was not alone in experiencing this sudden acceleration of 'spontaneous dissolutions' in this period. They occurred throughout the labor movement in all parts of Japan. But the Sōdōmei was hit hard by the self-destruction of some of its strongest unions, particularly in June when, for instance, the Sōdōmei's Tōkyōshi Jūgyōin Kumiai (Tokyo City Employees Union) was closed down by its leaders on the twenty-fourth, to be followed two days later by the dissolution of the large Tōkyō Gasukō Kumiai (Tokyo Gas Workers' Union), and many others including some of the Federation's principal bulwarks in Osaka and Kobe.[113] Indeed, hardly a day passed in June when Sōdōmei leaders in headquarters did not receive word of unions dissolving themselves unilaterally so that their members could belong to the *hōkokukai* exclusively. In some instances, key *kokata* of Matsuoka and Nishio led the way in these desertions, breaking in effect with their *oyakata* in headquarters. Although Sōdōmei records are imprecise, it is doubtful that the Federation had more than 10,000 members at the beginning of July.

Once again, it is worth reiterating that while many workers deserted the labor movement out of patriotism, the majority were also motivated by calculations of self-interest. Since Sampō was backed by the government, it seemed reasonable to expect that they would benefit from the government's desire to upgrade their wages and working conditions in order to improve labor productivity in wartime. For this reason, Sampō was especially attractive to workers in small and medium enterprises who had toiled for low pay in poor conditions.

Similarly, the skilled workers who had benefited from industrial paternalism in large factories could find in Sampō the promise of continued advantages. In addition, having become accustomed to the atmosphere of *jigyō ikka* (enterprise family) engendered by enterprise unionism, they tended to be receptive to the *hōkokukai* which cultivated the same spirit of unity between labor and management for the common good of both. Crossing the line between enterprise unionism and the *hōkokukai* was not considered to be a dramatic step; the *hōkokukai* were in the eyes of many workers more sophisticated versions of the *kigyōbetsu kumiai* model of unionism.

Then, too, the gathering strength of Sampō, in contrast to the dwindling size of the labor movement, created a bandwagon psychological effect on the workers who wished to associate themselves with the trends of the times rather than be left out in the cold. Quite apart from considerations of patriotism and economic advantage, Sampō appealed to them as a collective force which, in exchange for their identification with it, provided psychological gratification in the sense of belonging to an organization that was respectable in the perspective of the government, management, and society at large. Sampō was like a warm reception room where the workers who joined it could feel a sense of security and worth after experiencing anomie in the course of Japan's rapid modernization.

With the Sōdōmei crumbling at their feet, Federation leaders in headquarters began in late June and early July to debate whether to give up a lost cause or go on trying to maintain the existence of the Sōdōmei as long as possible. These discussions were especially gloomy because of mounting external pressures on the central committee to dissolve the Federation. For example, agents of the Kempeitai (Military Police) were known to be circulating among factories where Sōdōmei unions were still intact.[114] This seemed to indicate that the government would, after all, take action against the Sōdōmei if it resisted dissolution much longer. But the greatest pressure on Sōdōmei headquarters came from the decision of the Shakai Taishūtō to dissolve itself on July 3.

As mentioned previously, Asō had been waiting for the right time to dissolve the Shakai Taishūtō. With the certain knowledge that Prince Konoe would soon assemble a second cabinet, Asō closed down the Shakai Taishūtō on July 3 in order to make it the first political party to enter the New Order under Konoe.[115] At the same time, the Sangyō Hōkoku Kurabu was dissolved by Asō's *kokata* in the labor movement in an attempt to coordinate their patriotic gesture with that of the Shakai Taishūtō in carrying out the policy of 'one big dissolution'.[116] Later that month, all of the political parties, with the exception of the Minseitō, also dissolved themselves.[117] The Minseitō did likewise on August 15, by which time Konoe was already back in power. On October 12, these defunct parties were integrated into the well-known Taisei Yokusankai (Imperial Rule Assistance Association), the long-awaited national political front which had Konoe as its titular head.[118] The Taisei Yokusankai was the political equivalent of Sampō in the factories of the New Order.

The dissolution of the Shakai Taishūtō had long been expected in the Sōdōmei. But, even though the Shakai Taishūtō had provided the Federation with no succor, it had been assumed in Sōdōmei headquarters that so long as the parties were in the field, the dissolution of the Federation could somehow be postponed. Now that the Shakai Taishūtō had voluntarily disbanded, the Sōdōmei stood entirely alone (with the Kumiai Kaigi, its paper front) as the last vestige of a once highly ramified social movement. It was in these depressing circumstances that the Sōdōmei central committee decided to dissolve the Federation on July 8.

Several members of the committee, notably Kanemasa Yonekichi, argued vehemently that the Sōdōmei, the oldest labor organization in Japan, should 'go down in martyrdom'. Kanemasa said it was unthinkable that the Federation should dissolve itself voluntarily after so many years of hard struggle to make it a viable organization.[119] But Kanemasa's *oyakata*, Nishio, saw no point in carrying on, now that the rank and file workers of the Sōdōmei were streaming out of the Federation without hesitation.[120] Matsuoka wavered in deciding what to do. He was reluctant to preside over the self-immolation of a labor movement whose mantle he had inherited from Suzuki Bunji, the 'father of the labor movement'. But consoling himself with the thought that maybe the workers would benefit from Sampō, Matsuoka finally agreed to disband the Sōdōmei and the Kumiai Kaigi.[121]

There followed a brief period in which the central committee undertook the business of winding up the Sōdōmei's affairs.[122] Then, on July 21, two days after disbanding the Kaigi, a special national convention of the Sōdōmei was convened in Tokyo to officially close down the Federation. In a final speech, Matsuoka exhorted the delegates to serve Sampō in the spirit of serving Japan. The meeting ended with the delegates on their feet, shouting '*banzai*' at a signal from Suzuki Bunji who was on hand to witness the subsidence of the organization whose predecessor, the Yūaikai, he had founded twenty-eight years before.[123]

In recalling the events leading to the dissolution of the Nihon Rōdō Sōdōmei in 1940, Nishio Suehiro later wrote that he and Matsuoka had been the helpless victims of circumstances beyond their control. Referring to himself and Matsuoka as the 'tragic heroes' of the social democratic movement, he also stated that they had been betrayed by Asō Hisashi and his faction.[124]

In a general sense, Nishio was right. The Nichirōkei 'betrayed' the Shaminkei by leaving the labor and socialist party movements in the lurch as the Nichirōkei set the pace in bringing about their dissolution into the New Order. More significantly, the development of an increasingly authoritarian, war-oriented national defense State in Japan after the February 26th Incident, culminating in the New Order under Konoe in 1940, was such that sectarian interest groups were bound to be consumed sooner or later by the national fronts that emerged in this period; resistance to the 'governmentalization' of interest groups, including the unions, was impossible, for 'governmentalization' was an inexorable function of the government's expanding powers in close cooperation with the military during these years.[125]

But the process of 'governmentalization', wherein interest groups were ultimately absorbed into the New Order, was greatly facilitated by the different elements of the Japanese social democratic movement which, by permitting themselves to succumb to a 'freezing' of their originally progressive commitment to build a new democratic Japan, ended up as docile handmaidens of the New Order.[126] In the case of the Sōdōmei, once labor unionism had been divorced from socialist politics in the course of labor's political becalming, out of a pragmatic desire to adapt to changing circumstances rather than resist them, the unions were rendered vulnerable to co-optation by Sampō, one of the major bastions of the New Order. To re-emphasize an earlier theme, labor unionism without socialist politics inevitably guaranteed the outcome of no labor unionism at all in interwar Japan.

Thus, because of their failure of vision and failure of nerve in adapting organized labor to authoritarian patterns of development in Japan during the 1930s, it is difficult to accept the claim by Nishio that he and Matsuoka were 'tragic heroes'. If they were 'tragic heroes', it was certainly not in the sense of other great heroes in Japanese history who, despite their failures, were ennobled by their courage against overwhelming odds.[127] However much labor leaders tried to rationalize their renunciation of socialist ideals to save the unions, there was nothing noble about their compromises with militarism and authoritarianism in interwar Japan.

Many men who had been prominent in the labor and socialist party movements during the interwar period served in the New Order in the years that followed. Members of the Nichirōkei, whose experience of 'freezing' in relation to original goals in the social democratic movement was due less to an abandonment of socialist objectives than to a perversion of those goals in the form of cooperating with the New Order, were particularly active as officers in the Imperial Rule Assistance Association or in Sampō.[128] But they soon found that the New Order was impervious to 'socialism from above'. As Konoe Fumimaro once said, the New Order was a 'hollow-drum' which 'if you pound it hard, it reverberates loudly; if you hit it gently, it reverberates quietly'.[129] In sum, other than the New Order's profession of 'assistance to Imperial Rule' and the 'fulfillment of our duties as loyal subjects', the

New Order was devoid of political content. It therefore never became an agency for 'renovation' in Japan. After the Imperial Rule Assistance Association and similar fronts were founded, they remained suspended in limbo as bureaucratic organizations that made only a marginal impact on the country.

With regard to Sampō, its impact on industry was not so insignificant. While Sampō did not carry forward all of the institutions of industrial paternalism, it did continue some of them, adding new dimensions to industrial paternalism in the process. For instance, Sampō helped to disseminate in-factory training programs for workers and foremen in both large and small factories where such programs had either been weak or nonexistent in the past. Also, Sampō 'assisted in the administration of workers' health and compulsory savings programs, as established by such laws as the National Health Insurance Law (1938), the Seamen's and Office Workers' Health Insurance Law (1939) and [later] the Workers Pension Insurance Law (1941)'.[130] Moreover, Sampō introduced certain changes into the wage system. Instead of wages based on seniority, with pay pegged low for young workers starting their careers and rising over the years, the formula for wages was re-drawn so as to become ' "family-supporting": a minimum rate for each age bracket, and an extra allowance for each dependent'.[131] And, as Sampō continued into the World War II period, the tendency was toward uniform annual pay increases to all workers, regardless of their length of service to a given firm.[132]

Furthermore, although Sampō did not survive the War, by strengthening the vertical dimensions of labor–management relations that had evolved under industrial paternalism, it demonstrated to the workers the importance of organization within this setting in their respective enterprises. Had the institutions of Sampō 'not been extended throughout the nation from 1938 to 1945, enterprise unions probably would not have been organized as rapidly as they were after the end of the war'.[133] But this was Sampō's legacy to the future. For the purpose of this study, Sampō's significance lay in the fact that it was the final graveyard for the labor movement in 1940.

Conclusion

A balanced assessment suggests that the story of organized labor in interwar Japan was not entirely one of failure. To begin with, although the Japanese labor movement attained only a low overall rate of organization, 7.9 per cent of the total industrial work force at its peak in 1931, this figure is somewhat misleading since the work force consisted of almost as many women and children as male workers; among the latter, nearly twenty per cent were organized in unions in 1932.[1] This was a respectable, albeit unspectacular, achievement in its own right.

Further, it may be that the Japanese labor movement was large enough and assertive enough to register at least a partial impact on wage levels for industrial labor. This hypothesis has been advanced by Koji Taira:

> Trade unions perhaps accentuated the imperfections of the labor market and amplified the fluctuations of wages and wage differentials beyond what one would have expected from the working of the labor market alone. Thus the usual inertia of the labor market would have made money wages sticky downward in any case but in interwar Japan trade unions may have had the effect of making money wages unusually sticky in the face of sustained price decreases over a long period.[2]

If so, it suggests an area in which the labor movement enjoyed a certain degree of success.

Moreover, during the period under review in this book, the Japanese labor movement had the satisfaction of gaining the admission of its representatives to the International Labor Organization; it was afforded more respect overseas than in Japan. Thus the movement was able, up to a point, to invoke the high labor standards of the ILO in its campaign for the improvement of work conditions in Japan.

Finally, on a more general level of analysis, if the 1920s and 1930s are seen as a prefatory period to the history of the Japanese labor movement after 1945, then it might be said that despite its extinction in 1940, the interwar movement bequeathed to its postwar successor both a long experience in trade unionism and an image of struggle upon which the postwar movement could build even though, as we have seen, the theme of struggle was considerably vitiated by the theme of compromise on the part of labor with its environment in the interwar decades. Viewed from this longer perspective, the history of the movement from 1919 to 1940, following earlier attempts to organize workers into unions, was but a middle chapter in a continuing saga which, in the postwar era, has been one of considerable progress.

Nevertheless, organized labor in interwar Japan could neither realize its most important objectives nor save itself from destruction. Its general failure is thrown into relief by comparison with the postwar movement. First, the interwar movement failed to achieve legal sanction for the existence of unions; this right was not enjoyed until the Trade Union Law of 1945 and Article Twenty-Eight of the new Constitution of 1946 were put into effect under the auspices of the Occupation.[3]

Second, the organizational strength of such federations as the Nihon Rōdō Sōdōmei was incomparably weaker than the large national federations dominating the labor movement today. The latter include, for example, the powerful Nihon Rōdō Kumiai Sōhyōgikai (General Council of Trade Unions in Japan) with 4,557,000 workers; Dōmei (Japan Confederation of Labor) numbering 2,210,000 members; Chūritsurōren (Federation of Independent Unions) with 1,330,000 workers; and Shinsanbetsu (National Federation of Industrial Organizations) encompassing 65,000 members. Altogether, these federations together with other organizations have organized 12,437,000 workers into 70,625 unions, which represents an organizational rate of 33.2 per cent of the industrial work force in Japan.[4] Third, the interwar labor movement was weak at the grass roots union level in comparison with the strong enterprise unions which today comprise more than 90 per cent of Japanese unions and provide the present labor movement with a solid mass base.[5]

Fourth, the combination of weakness at both the national federation and the local levels of the interwar movement contributed to the failure of the initiative for collective bargaining in the 1920s and 1930s, whereas today the strength of the big federations and enterprise unions is readily apparent in their success in this activity, especially in the well-known 'spring offensives' (*shuntō*) which began in 1955.[6]

Finally, of central importance to this study, the institutional weakness of the interwar labor movement contributed to a pervasive crisis of confidence and timidity which eroded labor's support of the proletarian parties and their political objectives. The same can hardly be said of postwar labor which was instrumental in supporting the short-lived socialist cabinet of Katayama Tetsu (1947–1948) and which since then has consistently backed the leftist parties in their opposition to the ruling Liberal Democrats, although the persistence of factional rivalries in the labor movement hanging over from the past has contributed to the disunity of the leftist parties, as in the 1920s and 1930s.[7]

These brief contrasts between the interwar labor movement and its postwar successor bring us back to the central question of this book: why did the Japanese labor movement begin the 1920s with such promise and with so many high expectations of helping to remake Japan in a new democratic image, only to falter and die out in the 1930s? The general answer in these pages to this difficult but important historical question, based on an approach that transcends the labor relations and Taishō democracy approaches to Japanese labor history (while at the same time incorporating some of their insights), is that the failure of the Japanese labor movement to cope effectively with the dilemma of political choice that confronts nearly every reform movement was brought about by a combination of external constraints which 'limited the options and controlled the directions of the solutions'[8] available to organized labor on the one hand, and the response of labor leaders and rank and file workers alike to these constraints on the other. It remains for this Conclusion to synthesize these external and internal dynamics which, together, determined the course of labor politics in the 1920s and 1930s. The following observations are accompanied by comparisons with labor history in the West to place Japanese labor history in a wider perspective, which it is hoped will encourage further research in the comparative study of social protest movements.

The timing and nature of industrialization: some implications for Japanese labor politics, 1919–1940

One set of constraints on the Japanese labor movement in the interwar period, discussed in this study under the rubric of industrial paternalism, derived from changes in the nature of industrial labor markets which took place within the context of increasing industrial dualism. As Robert Evans says, 'Unions did not prosper because they failed to provide a meaningful organization consistent with a Japanese pattern of personnel management.'[9] Not only did these constraints impede the quantitative development of the unions; they also obstructed their qualitative capacity to sustain worker protest against the established order. They skewed the unions that existed in large factories in the direction of enterprise unionism, which was under the control of an expanding employer power, and pushed the rest of the labor movement into the small and medium-scale enterprises. Here it languished in impotence without possessing the means to register a significant impact on the economic and political environment.

A useful comparative perspective on the interplay of industrial paternalism and Japanese labor unionism, which may be applied to an assessment of labor politics, is suggested by Solomon Levine and Koji Taira. They point out that labor movements in the West developed 'by accretion' over a long period of industrialization in protest against the exploitation of the workers under 'wage-competitive' labor markets to the point that when the latter were gradually replaced by 'job-competitive' labor markets, unions had sufficiently entrenched themselves to be able to weather this transition without being overwhelmed by it. But in Japan, where industrialization was compressed into a shorter time span, the transition from 'wage-competitive' to 'job-competitive' labor markets occurred 'before Japan's Western-type labor movement had the opportunity to win its place under the "wage-competitive" labor markets'.[10]

Levine and Taira explain as follows,

> Because of Japan's industrialization on the basis of technology borrowed from the West, and because of rapid technological changes in the leading sectors of the Japanese economy, the classic 'wage-competitive' labor markets had not developed extensively or quickly enough to generate the skills needed in large modern manufacturing firms. At a rather early stage, therefore, the Japanese firms worked out the rudiments of 'job-competition' in such characteristics as lines of progression, structure of skills, and clusters of jobs, although these were not fully rationalized or streamlined until after the Second World War...[11]

They add, referring to the large enterprises of the interwar period, '...especially with the shift to heavier and technologically advanced industry and later governmental labor controls, they endeavored to strengthen the system of on-the-job training and seniority-based promotions. The interwar period thus represented a mixture of "wage-competition" and "job-competition" in the large-firm sector of the Japanese labor markets, although the balance was shifting in favor of "job-competition".'[12] Inevitably, as this balance shifted, enterprise unionism in the large firms became an important adjunct to the efforts of employers to gain control over the labor market in order to ensure a stable supply of skilled labor. This trend persisted after World War II by which time the essentials of 'job-competition' had been systematized by the management with the result that postwar unionism generally took the form of enterprise unionism including, for instance, all blue- and white-collar workers in a given enterprise.[13]

Levine and Taira show that a similar transition from 'wage-competitive' to 'job-competitive' labor markets took place in the United States during the interwar period. However, by this time, the American labor movement, which originated with the Knights of Labor in 1869 and the American Federation of Labor, established in 1886, had developed enough staying-power to cope with this transition.[14] Mikio Sumiya notes in this regard, 'With the propagation of labor unions among major corporations in the 1930s, the unions began acting against arbitrary management by employers, establishing the job structure and wage rates in correspondence with individual jobs and creating the seniority rules applicable to promotion and demotion from one job to another, thus leading to the structuring of U.S.-style internal labor markets and the U.S.-style seniority-based system.'[15] Once the Wagner Act, passed in July 1935, gave American workers the right to organize and bargain collectively, thereby confirming the legitimacy and permanence of unionism in the United States, the American labor movement proceeded apace in its historical evolution.[16]

However, in Japan, the timing of industrialization and corresponding changes in the nature of labor markets within a context of increasing industrial dualism pressed in far more heavily against the relatively immature labor movement and dictated that its unions would by necessity evolve along the lines of the enterprise-union pattern. Ronald Dore observes that this trend toward enterprise unionism first arose in the Meiji period:

> The dualism which developed in Japan's sponsored industrialization between the large, bureaucratic capital-intensive firms which benefited from State sponsorship and the small private firms which did not, reflected a difference in capacity to pay which – as soon as trade union organizations started – made enterprise unions, which could push each employer to the limit of his capacity to pay, a natural form of organization. Since the development of lifetime employment patterns preceded the development of effective trade unions in the government-run arsenals of the Meiji period, for example, the enterprise form was the natural one anyway.[17]

As time passed, because of the security of large firms and their ability to undertake long-range planning, they gained control over the labor relations system and the labor market to the extent that they always had the balance of power vis-à-vis organized labor which was still struggling to get on its feet after experiencing initial failure in the Meiji period. Some employers, it is true, were willing to tolerate the de facto if not the de jure existence of moderate unions, like those of the Nihon Rōdō Sōdōmei. But they did so only because they knew they had the advantage over these unions. Dore elaborates,

> By 1922, when employment relations were still in a fluid state, international respectability required Japan to give trade unions an accepted place in the political firmament by allowing them to choose representatives to...the ILO. Japanese employers, therefore, knew that they had to live with unions at an early stage; they were able to adjust to that future prospect by institutionalizing innovations before the unions became so strong that these options were foreclosed – while they still had a large measure of control over the situation.[18]

In point of fact, their own strength and the weakness of organized labor meant that their 'control of the situation' was never in doubt. Although the confidence of big business was eroded by recession and reduced industrial growth in the 'economic muddle of the 1920s', it did not decline radically in its dealings with the unions: 'The cycles of boom and slump were not so lengthy; the troughs were not so deep; their effect in tempering optimism about the prospects of long-term growth not so devastating. Japan, like all follower countries, knew better where she was going. The present of the more advanced countries offered an image of her future.'[19]

Leaders in the Nihon Rōdō Sōdōmei also thought that they could foresee the future success of their endeavors mirrored in the contemporary West, especially in the 1920s. After observing that labor in North America and parts of Europe had shown signs of making headway with this reformist approach, they thus nurtured a measure of optimism in responding politically to the government's policies of 'whip and candy' by emphasizing evolutionary and legal attempts to achieve labor legislation in the Diet. Similarly, they reasoned that the best way to cope with the growing capacity of employers to control the labor markets in the strategic large modern enterprises was to implement the type of collective bargaining campaigns that appeared particularly promising in the contemporary British and American labor movements.

These tactics, sanctioned ideologically by 'realist socialism', seemed sensible in the 1920s. That the government was prepared to undertake labor legislation – at least up to a point – and that it tolerated the existence of moderate proletarian parties after the passage of Universal Manhood Suffrage, augured well for the future of political reformism in this period. Similarly, the transition to 'job-competitive' labor markets did not seem entirely inauspicious for organized labor. As Levine and Taira indicate, 'In comparison with "wage-competitive" labor markets, workers in the "job-competitive" labor markets, even in the absence of labor unions, have considerable, if diffuse and decentralized, bargaining power vis-à-vis management. Their bargaining power arises from the highly sophisticated and tightly structured technology which in order to be effective requires high "morale" and motivation of the entire work force in addition to the usual skill requirements.'[20]

Consequently, the mainstream of the Japanese labor movement placed considerable emphasis on attempts to reach collective bargaining agreements with employers in the 1920s. While pursuing this strategy, it also endeavored to mobilize the skilled worker stratum which seemed ripe for this type of initiative in protesting against the loss of its privileges during the transition from fluid 'wage-competitive' labor markets to the more stable and compartmentalized 'job-competitive' labor markets. And indeed, throughout the history of the interwar labor movement, 'There remained a substantial conservative trade union wing...that had its origins in *oyakata* resistance to management's takeover.'[21]

Even after the political developments which had accompanied the Depression had frightened the labor movement away from its earlier focus on 'realist socialism', collective bargaining continued to be a major emphasis in labor's advocacy of 'sound unionism'. But insofar as collective bargaining in Japan stemmed from an impulse to imitate contemporary trends in the American and British labor movements, it was doomed to fail because the prerequisites for successful collective bargaining in the West – identified by Adolph Sturmthal as the legal existence of unions, a fairly even balance of organizational strength between unions and employers, and a collective bargaining procedure in which the balance of power was such that employers could not always be sure at the outset of negotiations that they would have their own way – simply did not prevail in Japan.[22] Accordingly, the labor movement remained essentially irrelevant to its most immediate context in the factories and ultimately was absorbed by Sampō and the New Order without having made any significant impression on labor–management relations in the interwar period.

So far, the comparative aspects of this discussion have centered on Japan and the United States. But just how disadvantaged the Japanese labor movement was, when one considers the timing of its development in relation to industrialization, can be further illustrated by contrasting the telescoped history of the Japanese labor movement with the more gradual and prolonged evolution of organized labor in Britain and Germany.

In contrast to Japan, in Britain, where industrialization developed over a much longer time span, trade unionism became a permanent and influential fixture relatively early in this process. By 1871 British unions had acquired a legal status which the Japanese movement was not to enjoy until after World War II. Also by 1871 British labor had developed to the point where it could carry out collective bargaining, an activity that the Japanese labor movement was to find perpetually beyond its capacity in the interwar period. Moreover, in the final quarter of the nineteenth century, British labor became increasingly variegated as its momentum accelerated. Alongside the old craft unions which had arisen earlier in the century were the 'new unions' associated with the Trades Union Congress, formed in 1868, the year of the Meiji Restoration in Japan. The TUC was pivotal in lobbying for the Trade Union Act and other labor laws that strengthened labor's hand in the 1870s.

Politically, British unionism assisted the Reform League's struggle for franchise reform in the 1860s and organized labor entered candidates in the 1868 elections. By the 1890s, British labor had elected a small number of representatives to the House of Commons on the Liberal Party ticket. And, although the 'new unions' experienced uneven development, by 1900 they claimed more than 204,000 members, the older unions having organized 1.8 million by the turn of the century.[23]

The success of British trade unionism in entrenching itself early in the industrialization of the country made it possible for British labor to adhere to a pragmatic approach to reform without having to stress political ideology when giving direction to labor's progressive purpose in seeking a better lot for the workers. Harvey Mitchell writes that the British labor movement was therefore characterized by a tendency to 'deny ideology'.[24] He notes, 'The trade unions were able for the most part to determine the shape of independent labor politics and mold them to serve their more limited aims. The prior achievements of the trade unions were sufficient to assure this outcome. The future Labour

Party was never allowed to forget how fragile its foundations were without trade union support.'[25]

The pragmatic reformism of British labor rested, then, on the stable and secure foundations of the unions. British labor could generally afford to soft-pedal over political ideology because reformism with a minimum of ideological content had proved rather successful in advancing labor's interests. But in Japan labor ultimately denied political ideology and stressed pragmatic expedience out of a sense of overwhelming weakness in relation to its environment. Labor retreated from socialism because socialism was too risky: insecurity, not confidence, paralyzed labor's political role in Japan where the labor movement, unlike Britain, arose too late in Japanese industrialization to establish a viable institutional foundation in dealing with business and government.

Germany, like Japan, was a late-comer to industrial development. However, German labor established itself at an earlier point in its course than did organized labor in Japan – just early enough to enable German labor unionism to achieve institutional strength of the sort never attained in interwar Japan. The origins of organized labor in Germany date from 1848, fifty years before the foundation of the first unions in Japan. German labor came of age in the 1860s with the formation of the General German Workers' Association (Allgemeiner Deutscher Arbeiterverein, or ADA) in 1863, under the influence of Ferdinand Lassalle. A second group of unions, which followed August Bebel, arose in the Union of German Workers' Societies (Verband der Deutschen Arbeitervereine). In 1868, the Union dissolved itself to form a new political party, the Social Democratic Workers' Party (Sozialdemokratische Arbeiterpartei, or SAP). Thus, the political orientation of at least part of the German labor movement was already taking form in the same year as the Meiji Restoration.

1868 was also important in German labor history because it was then that the ADA helped spawn the General German Trade Union Federation (Allgemeiner Deutscher Gewerkschaftsverband), known as the Free Unions. This Federation became the pillar of the Social Democratic Party of Germany (Sozialdemokratische Partei Deutschlands), or SDP, which surfaced in 1890, superseding the earlier SAP.[26]

Despite their youth, these organizations were of some size. By 1890 for instance, the Free Unions claimed 227,733 members in fifty-three national unions with 3,150 locals.[27] Thanks in part to their political support, the SDP elected thirty-five of its candidates to the German

Parliament on the strength of 1,427,000 votes or 19.7 per cent of the total votes cast in 1890. In 1912, the Party obtained 110 seats on the strength of 4,250,000 votes or 34.8 per cent of total votes cast.[28]

The progress of the German labor movement was hindered to some extent by political constraints similar to those confronting organized labor in Japan. For example, in 1878, after the attempt on the life of the German Emperor, Chancellor Bismarck engineered the passage of the Anti-Socialist Law. But this legislation was not used so decisively as to block the growth of German unions or prevent them from becoming politically assertive.[29]

In sum, the German labor movement, like the British, established itself early enough in the process of industrialization to be in a position to withstand adverse changes in its environment. The German unions were therefore able to play an important part in the rise of the SDP, just as British labor became the major pillar of the British Labour Party. By contrast, the Japanese labor movement, 'erupting' in a much shorter time span, did not have an opportunity to evolve and develop its trade union institutions before it plunged into political activism, serving in the early 1920s as a surrogate for proletarian parties and later as a bulwark for the socialist parties of the left that emerged after 1925. One may say that the compressed timing of its history forced it to try and do many things all at once without having first achieved the capacity to do much of anything well.

The failure of reformism: worker protest and labor politics in Japan and Germany

A second set of external constraints which 'limited the options and controlled the directions of the solutions' available to Japanese labor politics in the 1920s and 1930s was more directly political in character and included the government's general strategy of repressing the radicals and extending selective concessions to the moderates in the labor movement. This policy of containment, which need not be reiterated at length here, originated in the so-called 'liberal' 1920s but was continued in the 1930s during which time labor's political environment underwent alarming and unpredictable changes as liberal government gave way to bureaucratic politics. The military became increasingly influential in a milieu of resurgent nationalism and crisis, both at home and abroad. Of significance is how the labor movement responded to these developments.

In brief, this study has shown that labor reacted to this political environment by helping to drag the entire social democratic movement into making minimal, compromising responses to 'fascism', militarism, and war. In the 1920s, 'realist socialism' had seemed in the Nihon Rōdō Sōdōmei and its labor bloc the best way to work for labor reforms. Indeed, it had appeared to be the only way to benefit the working class in that period, given the threat to moderate labor from the anarchists and the communists on the radical left.

But when the political climate changed in the 1930s, the leaders of the Sōdōmei continued to perceive socialist reformism largely in terms of promoting and defending the interests of labor unionism, much as they had done in the preceding decade. That is, they failed to adapt their vision of 'realist socialism' to deal with the great new issues facing the socialist movement: the rise of the military in politics, ultranationalism, the demise of liberal party government, and the implications of a powerful and resurgent Japanese imperialism. If 'realist socialism' can be thought of as constituting the symbols as well as the substance of reformism, it is apparent that these symbols lost their vitality in the 1930s as the Sōdōmei and its labor allies gradually abandoned their original, politically progressive objectives of the 1920s, with the consequence that these institutions became becalmed in the face of new and awesome challenges.

This is not to suggest that different strategies, such as Katō Kanjū's abortive efforts to erect a militant proletarian front in order to resist authoritarian trends in the late 1930s, would have preserved more effectively the substance of a genuine socialist alternative. What is pertinent here is that the men who made policy in the Sōdōmei did not dare to make a flexible socialist response to the new conditions of the 1930s. The question is, why did they remain so rigid politically in coping with the new problems facing the social democratic movement in the 1930s? Historians have posed the same question concerning the German socialists who failed to resist Hitler and national socialism during the same period. To compare Japanese socialism with German socialism in this regard may seem awkward; German socialism capitulated to Hitler after the SDP had been in power for significant intervals in the Weimar Republic whereas Japanese socialism collapsed under the weight of the New Order without the consolation of ever having been even remotely near to power.

Nevertheless, despite this contrast, the comparison warrants attention for two reasons. First, comparative research has recently been done on certain 'dilemmas of growth' that attended modernization in Japan and Germany and which intensified in the 1920s and 1930s. So far, the focus has been on the critical areas of political crisis ('fascism'), militarism, foreign policy and imperialism, and to a lesser extent on problems of social and cultural strain. Since the rise of popular social protest movements, including organized labor, manifested a multi-faceted reaction to the process of industrialization in both countries, they too deserve comparative analysis on the part of historians who, in pursuing the 'dilemmas of growth' approach, wish to know more about what went on as well as about 'what went wrong'[30] at the lower level of society in the course of Japanese and German modernization during the interwar period.

Secondly, although the stakes were higher in Germany than in Japan (German socialism had more to lose due to its relatively stronger position in the political sphere), both the German and Japanese socialists grappled with the dilemma of either adapting to the existing order so that they could reform it from within, but at the risk of seeing their democratic principles watered down through the politics of compromise; or staging a revolutionary attack on the status quo, putting the survival of their institutions at risk, but at least maintaining the purity of their ideals. The hypothesis offered here is that organized labor in both countries was instrumental in ensuring that the choice would be made in the direction of adaptation and reform and that the dynamics of labor's political behavior in this respect, as well as the consequences for socialism in Japan and Germany, were fundamentally similar.

The German socialist movement, with organized labor providing much of its mass base, had been active in precipitating the German Revolution of 1918 which brought down the Empire and inaugurated the Weimar Republic. In the first Weimar government the SDP formed part of a coalition with the German Democratic Party (Deutsche Demokratische Partei) and the Catholic Center Party (Zentrum). The coalition of the SDP with these parties kept the SDP in a position of power-sharing from 1919 to 1920, in 1921–1922, 1923, and from 1928 to 1930 (when the coalition was joined by the German People's Party, or Deutsche Volkspartei). The SDP found itself in opposition only during part of 1920 and in the 1924–1928 period. Throughout the Weimar Republic it relied heavily on support from the German labor movement.[31]

However, the 'tragedy' of German socialism in general and of

German labor in particular was that the SDP failed to make use of its opportunities to alter to any significant extent the basically conservative patterns of German politics in the Weimar period. The emphasis of the SDP and its labor support had always been on the gradual development of mass organizations as a basis for acquiring power, and the socialist movement had attained considerable success in the technology of organization-building. It had also augmented its proletarian base by appealing to other strata in society through emphasis on the national, as well as the class, character of the SDP.

The Party's accentuation of moderate parliamentarian tactics had moreover been intensified in the face of challenges from the assertive German communist movement led by Rosa Luxemburg and Karl Liebknecht (the Communist Party of Germany, or Kommunistische Partei Deutschlands – the KDP – had been formed in 1918). Although Luxemburg and Liebknecht were killed in 1919, their challenge to the Majority Socialists who dominated the SDP had forced the latter into an even more moderate political position than before, as was true of the Japanese socialists.[32] Once in power, the leaders of the SDP, including such trade union personalities as Friedrich Ebert of the Free Trade Union movement, also became preoccupied with staving off threats to their power from the conservative centers of power in German politics in the 1920s. This was perhaps a natural reflex on the part of men who, as skillful managers of large-scale socialist organizations, had by then allowed their bureaucratic concern with institution-building to take precedence over any effort to remake the institutions and practices of the existing political system in a democratic mold after the rise of the Republic.

Accordingly, in the words of Richard Hunt, the German socialist movement was characterized from within by 'bossification' (*Verbonzung*), 'ossification' (*Verkalkung*), and 'bourgeoisification' (*Verbürgerlichung*).[33] Hunt observes, 'The task of the party, at least in the eyes of its leaders, was to conserve and consolidate its original gains rather than to press aggressively forward with new demands.'[34] Hunt and others have shown that this stance poorly equipped the SDP for resistance to Hitler before he had become invulnerable in German politics in 1933. The opportunity to do so, like the opportunity to use power earlier in the 1920s to advance the cause of democracy in the Weimar Republic, slipped by the German socialists because they did not see the necessity of moving beyond their conservative instincts.

It should be emphasized that many of these instincts had their origins in the Free Trade Union movement. As Hunt writes, 'The victory of the reformist forces within the party had been in very large measure the victory of the unions and of union ideology...Thus the belief in the tactics of piecemeal reforms, the faith in the stability of the German economy, in steady progress toward evolving socialism, the positive attitude toward the State and nation – these now became articles of faith for the party as they had been previously for the unions.'[35]

Organized labor in Germany had already settled down in a conservative political groove well before the 1918 Revolution. Harvey Mitchell writes that German labor elites before World War I, as elsewhere in Europe, 'were chiefly responsible for the diversion of the working class from their ideology of confrontation to the search for conformity to the ethics of industrial society, the demands of social harmony, and the rules of organized political life'.[36] As to why German labor leaders played this conservative role, Peter Stearns suggests they did so because of pressures from the rank and file workers in the German labor movement. Although the latter 'were in no sense ciphers', they were for the most part quiescent politically. As a result, labor leaders were obliged to play down broad socialist principles and aims in favor of pursuing narrower objectives such as higher wages and better working conditions which were the main concerns of the workers. Stearns agrees with Mitchell that socialism in Germany, and throughout much of Europe during its formative stage from 1890 to 1914, became the vehicle for integrating the labor movement into the capitalist order.[37]

Thus, when it became possible for labor leaders like Ebert to influence the SDP, they were unable to abandon their view of politics as a function of labor union interest. They had a chance to help build a new socialist order but were unsuited to this task. Adolph Sturmthal states, 'Unfortunately for democracy, the decisive Central European labor party, the German Majority Socialists, still clung to the status of a pressure group even after the party acquired power.'[38] The 'tragedy of European labor',[39] exemplified in the failure of the German labor movement to sustain socialist commitment, became part of the greater tragedy of European socialism.

Clearly, the tendencies toward bureaucratic 'bossification' and ideological 'ossification' in the German labor and socialist party movements, which rendered these movements politically conservative, were functions of their success in building up their organizations and attaining power. Nor were these tendencies by any means peculiar to Germany. As has been pointed out often in the theoretical literature on social movements, a good many 'successful' movements in history have taken on the same characteristics, particularly when their struggle for power was intense or if, once in power, challenges to their position created an obsession about the maintenance of this position at all costs, even if it meant putting the brakes on the reform process which had been central to their rise in the first place.[40]

The Japanese labor movement similarly succumbed to the deadening and becalming impact of internal 'bossification' and 'ossification' as it struggled to survive in the 1920s and 1930s. That these tendencies sometimes assert themselves in movements that are failing as well as in those that are succeeding should occasion little surprise. Indeed, one might speculate that the more embattled a social movement becomes, the more likely it is to swing either into a more radical position and wage a do-or-die struggle with its environment – an option that was deliberately ruled out in the Nihon Rōdō Sōdōmei – or to take the opposite course, becoming ever more cautious politically as it endeavors to maintain its existence in strained circumstances over which it has little control.

Like Ebert and other prominent bureaucrats in the German labor movement, Matsuoka Komakichi, Nishio Suehiro, and their *kokata* who occupied middle-level positions of authority in the Sōdōmei hierarchy, were labor bosses par excellence. They placed uppermost emphasis on preserving their own positions of power in the Federation whenever they were threatened by revolts from within the labor movement and whenever they felt threatened by swirling political currents outside the movement that they feared would engulf them. To re-emphasize a point made earlier in this study, because they embraced socialism in the early 1920s long after they had committed themselves to trade unionism, their concept of socialism as a political ideology and a program of action was inevitably colored by their more fundamental fidelity to trade unionism. Although these laboring men recognized during the 1920s the imperative of political action to solve problems besetting the working class that were political in origin, socialism was not the end but the means to the end of making trade unionism secure in Japan. They therefore regarded politics as a function of trade union interest with the same consistency that marked the perception of German labor leaders.

Thus, in subordinating socialism to trade unionism in the Sōdōmei, these men used socialism to rationalize the adaptation of the labor movement to its environment in line with their bureaucratic instincts as cautious custodians of the unions. When, in the 1930s, the link between socialism and trade unionism appeared too risky, they deliberately severed this connection, hoping in vain that trade unionism without socialist politics would have a better chance of survival than would trade unionism closely identified with socialist purpose. Their failure of political vision and nerve left the labor movement becalmed, drifting toward the whirlpool of the New Order.

But if Japanese labor elites became 'bossified' and 'ossified' in their perception of labor politics, it may be suggested that their consequent political behavior also reflected in large measure the conservatism of their rank and file followers. Had they tried to do more to politicize the latter in the interests of socialist principles and objectives, they probably would have encountered the same difficulties as were experienced by European labor leaders who found there were definite limits on how far the ordinary worker would go in identifying with political causes.

Karl Marx, it is well known, believed that 'The development of class antagonism keeps even pace with the development of industry' and that 'there is a steady intensification of the wrath of the working classes' in the course of industrialization.[41] But as Val Lorwin observes, 'These predictions have been contradicted by the experience (thus far) of all the Western nations except France and Italy, nor do France and Italy actually support the prophecy.'[42] Writing about the nature of worker protest in Germany from 1890 to 1914, Stearns states that German workers, as elsewhere in Europe, devoted their energies to the defense of what they had already gained in the past more than fighting for rights not yet attained. He suggests it is wrong to impute ideological political commitment on the part of workers to this kind of defensive action, for rarely did they take action on the basis of political ideology.[43]

Stearns does not argue that socialism was insignificant for European labor. He notes, 'Socialism played a vital role in teaching many workers what political action was and what in socialist terms could be expected from it. In their turn workers. . .taught their parties what they expected and what action they would countenance.'[44] Because the workers 'did not really expect a revolution', they made it clear to their parties that they wanted pragmatic assistance from them in seeking concrete labor reforms above all else: 'Collectively, they were not in a revolutionary mood and revolutionary theory had to bow before this fact.'[45] Stearns' thesis, which can also be applied to Japanese labor in the interwar period, is this: 'In the long run, the politicization of the labor movement helped attach it to the existing order, helped turn it away from revolution; in this sense, even middle-class radicals may have helped tame the working class.'[46]

Stearns might be criticized for going too far in this interpretation. In portraying labor strikes as 'restrained forms of complaint',[47] over issues of security rather than as political acts, he may have ignored the possibility that the motivation of some workers contained a complex mixture of aspirations, including political rage. Moreover, the implication that the workers had no ideology seems questionable. They did not lack ideology but rather it was what Stephen Hill calls the 'ideology of factory consciousness'.[48] These caveats also apply to Japanese workers; only, in Japan, 'factory consciousness' was unusually pronounced due to the success of industrial paternalism and the prevalence of enterprise unionism.

Nonetheless, conceding the difficulty of knowing precisely what individual Japanese workers were thinking when they engaged in industrial protest, it would seem that with the exception of politicized workers in the ideologically radical anarchist and communist labor unions, most Japanese workers were motivated by the same type of nonpolitical concerns for the immediate issues of security that suffused worker protest in Europe. Wages, shorter hours, improved sanitary conditions, better health benefits and the like – these governed their actions more than political concepts based on foreign ideologies that had been recently grafted onto the labor movement, ideologies about which the rank and file workers knew little and perhaps cared less.

That is the picture presented by George Totten when he writes of labor disputes in Japan, 'They often erupted as spontaneous strikes, ignited by some small action but fed on the desiccated discontent of unbearable conditions. Workers reacted simply from a feeling that something had to be done if they were to survive, not from any calculation of what the results of their actions were likely to be.'[49] Like the European workers described by Stearns, most Japanese workers were not in a revolutionary mood, nor did they expect revolution. As long as the labor movement, through its emphasis on trade unionism, served their immediate interests, some of them remained loyal to it. But when it became apparent that the movement could do little for them in this regard, they abandoned it altogether and rushed into Sampō without a second thought.

Thus, labor's political becalming cannot be attributed solely to the thought and action of labor elites. It also occurred because the organized rank and file workers welcomed an emphasis on 'sound unionism' over socialist politics, as in Germany. Japan's labor leaders, as 'managers of discontent',[50] followed in the footsteps of their German counterparts in regarding themselves as realists while they attuned their priorities to the desires of their followers. Like many intellectuals in their midst, Matsuoka and Nishio rejected the 'restrictive ideologies' of anarchism and communism for the porous formulation of 'realist socialism' which they believed would serve trade unionism. But as they did so, they exemplified the failure, as Seki Yoshihiko puts it, of Japanese socialists in general to think through 'the relationship between democracy, socialism, and nationalism' in the interwar period.[51]

Masujima Hiroshi's comment on Asō Hisashi also describes these men, and perhaps German labor leaders as well: 'In the reality of militarism and reactionary trends, Asō fervently advocated realism. That was a theory of situationalism that buried one in the circumstances of the moment. As it did not resist the raging stream, it finally became a theory which was swept along by the raging stream.'[52]

The problem of class consciousness and labor politics in Japan and Germany

That an incipient working class consciousness had begun to take form in the early years of Taishō is undeniable; without it, the rise of the labor movement in the World War I period and immediately thereafter is difficult to explain. But a third constraint on Japanese labor politics was a social system and patterns of behavior that militated against the further development of the worker's class consciousness in the 1920s and 1930s.

Of course, if one looks with only a casual glance at much of the rhetoric emanating from the labor and proletarian party movements in this period, a different impression might be formed, namely, that these movements were pervaded by a genuine class consciousness of the proletariat. The anarchists, communists, and far left of the socialist movement were eloquent in consistently proclaiming the imperative of militant class struggle against the bourgeoisie, capitalism, the Emperor system, and a host of other enemies which confronted the working class. The socialists of a more moderate political persuasion rejected this militancy. But they too used a vocabulary rich in allusions to 'class', whether to stress the need for strictly legal initiatives on the part of the working class or whether to advocate the wisdom of allying with the petty bourgeoisie or what they perceived to be an emergent 'new middle class' of white-collar salaried workers.

However, the reality of interwar Japan was that, aside from an ideologically articulate minority in the social protest movements of the 1920s and 1930s, class consciousness remained generally weak. A number of explanations have been suggested for this phenomenon. For example, in propounding her theory of a 'vertical society', the anthropologist Chie Nakane argues that the elitist character of the Meiji Restoration left undisturbed the basic modes of social organization that existed in the feudal past and that subsequent developments in Japanese society since the Restoration revolved around vertical 'frames', with 'frame' referring to a locality or an institution in which the modern Japanese operates according to the same hierarchical principles that were valid for his feudal predecessors. In her view, recruitment into, and position within, the 'frame' is invariably decided by personal ties between *oyakata* and *kokata*, whether it is in a political party, a business corporation, an academic body, an underworld gang, or a military unit. Once formed, the 'frame' and personal relations within it remain highly durable. Because of its fixed nature, this mode of social organization obstructs horizontal alignments, including those of class, that transcend the 'frame'.[53]

Another explanation for the general weakness of class consciousness in Japan, which is perhaps more cultural in orientation, resides implicitly in Takeshi Ishida's suggestion that in situations of stress the Japanese have tended to 'depend and presume upon another's benevolence' (*amaeru*). He states that in interwar Japan, where anxiety reflected the fear of losing 'the vested interests an individual had in the old system', it was usually resolved by being 'reorganized and institutionalized into a sense of dependence' on national symbols of authority 'using as a medium of transformation the artificially stirred-up sense of crisis that threats were being posed from without the country'.[54]

Ishida continues, 'In dealing with anxiety' the leaders of Japan 'chose to transform anxiety directly and indirectly into a sense of dependence. Theirs was an attempt to wipe out anxiety through institutionalization of dependence but not one to devise a solution to the anxiety itself', and as a result the New Order did little to inspire the people of Japan once it was erected.[55] Insofar as *amae* (dependence) suffuses all types of social relations in which subordinates identify with superiors in a pattern of personal dependence, so reinforcing the hierarchical nature of their interaction, the relations of dependence serve to weaken class relations in which the individual might be expected to act upon his anxiety by identifying horizontally with others who share similar stress.

Yet, explanations of this type are at best controversial and cannot be regarded as conclusive in analyzing the weakness of class consciousness in interwar Japan. Instead of relying on broad generalizations about the deterministic effects of an alleged vertical principle inherent in the social structure or the equally deterministic effects of alleged cultural or psychological tendencies to act in accordance with *amaeru*, it may be more useful to consider other explanations of an historical nature, for as Dore states, 'There are good historical reasons why class consciousness should be more blurred and consciousness of class membership less distinct in Japan than in, say, England. . . '[56]

First, the Meiji Restoration, which was more of a 'national revolution'[57] than a class upheaval, set in motion a succession of reforms that dismantled the rigid class distinctions of the Tokugawa social order by creating a new, more open society. This was characterized by considerable upward social mobility through such channels as a modern educational system, and service in the bureaucracy, the military, and in industry where acquired skills based on achievement opened the door to new opportunities for people who demonstrated a capacity to assist Japan's surge to 'wealth and power'. Regardless of whether in fact these channels were always fluid, they were 'sufficient to prevent the class divisions from seeming rigid predetermined barriers which the individual can never hope to cross and this has weakened any sense of the injustice of the social system which is an essential precondition of militant working class consciousness'.[58] A related observation by James Scoville, concerning the effect of social mobility on labor movements, applies to Japan: 'Social mobility. . .reduces the clarity and permanence of class lines, thereby mitigating the grievances of labor as a group, as well perhaps as those of a middle class collaborating group.'[59]

Second, because of upward social mobility, 'The Japanese upper class has been less culturally homogenous and the cultural gulf between it and the middle and lower classes has not been as great as in England.'[60] This fact, and the 'relatively weak development of the middle class' in interwar Japan likewise contributed to the blurring of class distinctions and of class consciousness.[61] Third, as Dore and

Reinhard Bendix have observed, the prevalence of strong kinship ties has also diminished class consciousness in Japan.[62] Dore comments: 'In the Japan of the last century, in which the maintenance of family ties has been given high moral priority, it is the rigidity of class distinctions and the strength of class solidarity which has suffered...'[63] Yet a fourth impediment to class consciousness has been a similar prevalence of strong regional ties wherein, for example, workers, many of whom came into the factories from rural peasant communities, retained their links with the village and often returned there after completing work contracts or being dismissed from work. As long as they could depend upon the village for support, their need to rely on the working class community was not very great.[64]

Given these factors, together with others such as the negative impact of enterprise consciousness on class consciousness in large industrial firms and the existence of many smaller firms that were 'strongholds of the paternalistic relations which serve more to foster the feudal attitudes of status consciousness than class consciousness in the usual sense',[65] class consciousness in Japan was mostly confined to those radical elements of the labor movement who, in describing a situation of class conflict, were in fact describing their own minority outlook and what they wanted to see occur rather than the actual mentality of the workers and what was actually likely to occur in the interwar period.

Perhaps status consciousness, not class consciousness, generally characterized social relations in Japan, including those of the labor movement. As Thomas Smith writes, 'Status consciousness is relatively strong in Japan in part because there was no revolutionary struggle against inequality but for that reason class consciousness is relatively weak. These attitudes are by no means contradictory. The nervous concern of Japanese for status is quite consonant with their relatively weak feeling about classes – higher ups to some extent being looked on as superior extensions of the self.'[66] Another way of expressing Smith's point about the primacy of status consciousness in Japan is suggested by George Lichtheim's observations concerning class consciousness in Britain, which would seem equally applicable to Japanese labor:

> The British working class, ever since its birth during the prolonged and painful crisis of the early industrial revolution, consistently displayed a profound sense of separateness from the other classes of society. But this consciousness was of the 'corporate' variety...The Social Democratic mass movement...was socialist in name only. The great majority of the British...working class was instinctively 'laborist' in the sense of empha-

sizing its corporate separateness rather than desiring to remodel society in its own image.[67]

Given the likelihood that status rather than class consciousness prevailed in Japan, the task of recruiting workers into unions and the task, insofar as it was carried out, of politicizing them, were inevitably difficult to fulfill. This was another important factor behind the failure of the labor movement to expand its numbers, much less commit the movement to sustained socialist politics which rested implicitly on class interest. Indeed, since mainstream labor leaders such as Matsuoka and Nishio interpreted class struggle in the meekest of terms, viewing the 'working class' in such broad terms as to make this conceptual category practically meaningless, it was likewise inevitable that the most they would do would be to cultivate a 'laborist' corporate sense of separateness among the workers rather than the kind of class consciousness envisioned by the radical left. Thus, the political becalming of the labor movement followed from the social as well as the economic and political conditions of the interwar period.

In Germany, on the other hand, one finds a rather different relationship between class consciousness and the growth of unions. The relative rigidity of class distinctions that survived the 1918 Revolution, coupled with the historic and continuing impact of the French Revolution, led to a situation in which acceptance of inequality 'was destroyed, and hence inferiors who had always been status conscious also became class conscious'.[68] The impressive development of German trade unionism owed much to this working class revolt against inequality, and the unions prospered accordingly.

However, the depth of working class consciousness in Germany ought not to be exaggerated, particularly in the case of German labor leaders. Many of these men, who had been skilled workers before rising up the ranks of the labor movement, succumbed to 'bourgeoisification' which, as Carl Schorske says, made theirs 'a quest not for power but for "*Gleichberechtigung*" (equal rights)', being 'bound up with the desire for status and recognition within the existing order'.[69] This tendency toward 'bourgeoisification', including an 'acceptance of middle class values and tastes in matters of dress, housing, education, etc. – in short...the adoption of a middle class style of life',[70] was brought about by the participation of middle class intellectuals in the labor movement, the entry of men with working class backgrounds into the established political process through their roles in the SDP, and the emphasis of the German labor movement and the SDP on appealing for support to the petty bourgeoisie as well as to the workers.[71] The more 'bourgeoisification' took root, the more conservative German socialism became.

Moreover, 'bourgeoisification' predated the Weimar Republic. Asking why German socialism became rigidly reformist prior to World War I, Harry Marks contends that the skilled labor aristocracy of the labor movement, which exerted influence in the SDP, aspired to middle class status and hence interpreted socialism to make it a 'respectable ideology'. Marks states, 'Representing the point of view of these "middle class" workers, reformism repudiated the theory and practice of revolution' in Germany.[72] 'Those upper strata of the working class... were inclined to view the world through middle class spectacles.'[73]

Marks concludes, 'The reformists, as spokesmen for the labor aristocracy, whose wages were rising nicely as a result of business expansion, adopted the position of a humanitarian, liberal–capitalist opposition to colonialism' that evaporated during World War I into support for the defense of the Fatherland.[74] Indeed, the significance of 'bourgeoisification' was often noted by contemporary observers including Hans Speier whom Hunt quotes as saying,

> The interest of the proletarian cause requires that functionaries adapt themselves to bourgeois forms and conventions. They yield... to the spirit of the institution in which they meet with their bourgeois opponents; this spirit however is distinctly not proletarian. When in 1913 the first Social Democrat entered the Reichstag presidium, Bebel asked him first of all whether he had formal clothes... The high functionaries of different classes resemble one another, in the rule, far more than the classes they are supposed to represent.[75]

Other contemporary writers noted the same process of 'bourgeoisification' amidst the rank and file workers, too, albeit to a lesser extent. According to Henrik deMan, 'The proletariat – even the class conscious proletariat – is succumbing more and more to the inclination to imitate, in the nonpolitical areas of daily living, the bourgeois or petty bourgeois style of life.'[76] This writer summed up the 'ossifying' consequences of this tendency as follows:

> The social position of the workers makes them amenable to socialist sentiments; these sentiments become the primary motive force of attempts to improve the material and moral position of the working class; but such improvements as are effected tend to bring the workers more and more under the cultural influence of the bourgeois and capitalist environment, and this counteracts the tendency towards the formation of a socialist mentality.[77]

However, the corrosive influence of 'bourgeoisification' on German labor politics at the lower echelons of the labor movement was checked considerably by the presence in Germany of a highly ramified socialist subculture that put a brake on the weakening of class consciousness among the workers. This subculture had developed significant proportions by the late nineteenth century. Peter Lösche describes it as a 'counter world...which permeated the daily life of the workers in all of its aspects. Organizationally, this was expressed in all kinds of workers' sports clubs, the theatre organization Freie Volksbühne, consumer cooperatives, special organizations for children, teenagers, and women, the free-thinkers organizations (Freidenkerverband) which provided the funeral services of their members', and so on.[78] 'From birth to death the party member was surrounded and absorbed by the organizations of the labor movement. The internationalism of the SDP and of other Socialist parties of the Second International was the extroverted face of this subculture.'[79]

The sense of class consciousness which this socialist subculture had nurtured earlier was sustained after the 1918 Revolution which, by failing to end the dominance of the Junkers, assured that class divisions would prevail and that the inequalities they manifested would continue to elicit protest from the working class even though this protest was increasingly expressed in only a conservative fashion. Lichtheim remarks that 'Marxism...equipped the workers' movement with an ideology that was both a defensive armature and a "false consciousness". The ideology immunized the workers to conservative or liberal ideas and to that extent articulated a kind of corporate political awareness. At the same time it enabled the movement to settle down within the existing order.... This passivity went with a pronounced class consciousness of a nonrevolutionary kind.'[80]

In view of the relative plasticity of class distinctions in Japan, it is doubtful whether one can speak in terms of the 'bourgeoisification' of Japanese labor elites, at least in the same sense as in Germany. On the other hand, there is reason to think that something resembling this process occurred in the careers of men like Matsuoka and Nishio, although on a lesser scale. Certainly their endeavor to make labor unionism 'respectable' might be said to have deproletarianized their identification with the working class from whose ranks they had come. In part this was the result of their close contacts with middle class intellectuals like Suzuki Bunji who liked to dress in three-piece business suits as he consulted with political and business leaders in the execution

of his duties in the Sōdōmei. His respectability was further enhanced
when Suzuki represented Japanese labor at the ILO or when he
delivered a speech on the floor of the Diet. Suzuki was a compelling
model for the skilled worker elites of the Sōdōmei who aspired to
respectability.

Nishio and Matsuoka also enjoyed associating with Japan's political
elites; Nishio courted respectability in the Diet; and both men basked
in the glow of their importance as envoys to the ILO. Nishio for
example recalls in his memoirs how he liked playing mahjong with
Japanese business and government representatives on the deck of the
ship carrying them to the ILO meetings in Europe in 1929 and how he
equally enjoyed eating and drinking with these men at the hotel where
they all stayed in Geneva.[91] Matsuoka, in turn, liked to play golf with
others in the Japanese delegation to the ILO, whenever time permitted,
even though on one occasion a government representative asked
Matsuoka in feigned mockery whether this was 'suitable behavior' for
a worker.[82]

Other examples of 'bourgeois' or 'unproletarian' behavior can be
cited in the lifestyles of these worker-leaders. Nishio describes with
pride his purchase in 1933 of a new house in Tokyo, bought with some
of his savings, which amounted to 2,500 yen, that he had accumulated
through thrift over the years from various sources, including money left
over from his trips to ILO meetings, given him by the Sōdōmei, and
money he had received for performing various duties in the Federation.[83] A similar pride is discernible when Nishio recorded the fact that
his eldest daughter married a physician,[84] or of how he, Nishio, a
worker, had married the daughter of an elementary school principal
many years earlier.[85] And, there is the account by Matsuoka's bio-
grapher of how Matsuoka was criticized in the labor movement as a
'labor movement activist' who had become rather like a 'banker'
because of such things as his purchase and enjoyment of a motorcycle
complete with side-car, using the residue of money given him for his
ILO expenses, as Nishio did.[86]

We need to know more about the social history of class relations in
interwar Japan before we can refer confidently to the 'bourgeoisification' of social movements but, assuming that middle class ways infiltrated the labor movement at least to some extent, Harry Harootunian's
comments on middle class intellectuals – some of whom were significant
in the labor movement – are worth considering in relation to Japanese
labor politics. He writes,

Middle class intellectuals, on whom the idea of *bunka* [culture] and *kyōyō* [self-refinement] conferred aristocratic values and elite status, pitted culture and refinement against the threatening claims of mass culture – consumption and consumerism, and the feared 'secularization' and democratization of cultural life itself which the emergence of new classes in the Taishō period had promised to promote. The high-minded cultural aspiration of Taishō intellectuals was to defend *bunka* before the onslaught of debasement which the masses promised to bring in their wake and to translate this conviction into a common set of pieties and a shared posture promoting the rejection of politics as the surest defense of culture.[87]

Harootunian adds,

Ironically, this belief in the fundamental incompatibility of culture and democracy seeped into the ideological pronouncements of social reformers and supporters of democratism and explains why so many Taishō ideologues...were able to dramatize the social problem but failed to link it to the broadening of political consciousness.[88]

Matsuoka and Nishio, taking their cue from middle class intellectuals in the labor movement, surely dramatized the problem of worker deprivation, but without significantly contributing to the 'broadening of political consciousness' in the labor movement. They may have inadvertently introduced into the movement the disjunction between politics and culture and the 'rejection of politics', notably during their retreat from socialism in the 1930s, that Harootunian finds in the behavior of middle class intellectuals.

Their failure to encourage the development of the kind of socialist subculture in the Japanese labor movement that existed in Germany, which might have stimulated class consciousness among the workers, supports this view. Needless to say, the relative weakness of a socialist subculture in interwar Japan was not entirely the responsibility of these labor elites. As Lösche notes, not all labor movements develop subcultures comparable to that of Germany. He suggests that a socialist subculture will arise only if the movement experiences a fairly long and continuous evolution and if it thus cultivates its own tradition of struggle to achieve emancipation; the longer the movement is involved in this struggle, the greater the chances are that it will build a subculture which will support this struggle.[89]

A similar subculture might have crystallized in Japan had the labor movement been given more time to develop its institutions. But the history of the Japanese labor movement was too choppy, too much pockmarked by stops and starts, to provide the institutional continuity required for the growth of a viable subculture. Elements of such a subculture existed, it is true, including labor newspapers, labor halls, cooperatives, welfare societies, recreational associations, worker schools, worker songs, union badges and flags, and so forth. But these existed only in embryonic form and never amounted to much.

The only exception to this was the Sōdōmei's workers' schools, some of which were quite substantial. But they did little to encourage class consciousness. The major portion of their curricula, consisting of training in ethics, was intended to raise the cultural tone of the workers and instill an appreciation of self-refinement. In this, they may have reinforced among the workers the values of *bunka* and *kyōyō*, prized by the middle class. These schools reinforced the emphasis found in the national school system on the 'importance of conformity to the social order', not in the sense that students were conditioned to resist change but in the sense that they were taught to conform to the 'changing situation' around them.[90] This was scarcely a promising recipe for socialist labor politics. Only the far left of the labor movement, for example, men like Watanabe Masanosuke with his 'spirit of Nankatsu' tried to arouse class consciousness among the workers. But the suppression of radical politics and the radical subculture of the communist movement dictated that this endeavor would be still-born.

To reiterate an earlier theme, even had the mainstream of the labor movement gone to greater lengths to construct a viable socialist subculture as a means of politicizing the workers, this endeavor would have probably met with futility because the skilled workers who comprised the nucleus of the movement already possessed a powerful enterprise consciousness that militated against their class consciousness. Everything about what Hiroshi Hazama calls their 'enterprise life style' taught them to conform to the enterprise rather than to identify with the working class.[91] The worker who lived in company housing, played baseball on company fields, and who organized his budget to plan for the expenses of daily life in the way employers encouraged him to do could not help but think of himself as belonging to a working class only in the most abstract and weakest of terms. His enthusiasm for participating in a labor subculture was bound to be less than his enthusiasm for being part of the enterprise.

In retrospect, the fate of attempts to carve out a viable socialist subculture that might have strengthened labor politics in Japan resembled the British experience in this area more than the German. Gareth Stedman-Jones' study of worker culture in Victorian London, the tradition of music hall, indicates that it fostered the acceptance by the workers of the mainstream values of Victorian culture around them.

He states, 'Working class music hall was conservative in the sense that it accepted class divisions and the distribution of wealth as part of the natural order of things. Out of music hall came fatalism, political skepticism, evasion of tragedy or anger, and a stance of cosmic stoicism.'[92]

English workers, influenced by the music hall, ceased believing that 'they could shape society in their own image. Capitalism had become an immoveable horizon.'[93] This subculture spawned 'an enclosed defensive conservatism' that persisted beneath the continuing program of unionism and the foundation of the British Labour Party. Partly because of this, British workers eschewed intense commitment to socialism and concentrated on the 'abolition of poverty' as the main objective. Unions, cooperatives, friendly societies all manifested a 'de facto recognition of the existing order as the inevitable framework of action. The same can be said of music hall. It was a culture of consolation.'[94]

So, too, did labor's subculture in Japan produce, as far as it went, an acceptance of things as they were instead of a powerful, deep-seated desire to change the status quo in any significant political sense. It did little to stimulate class consciousness in the labor movement. It was not a culture of liberation but, as in Victorian London, a 'culture of consolation'.

The degree of class consciousness in Japanese labor politics today is probably much greater than it was in the past. But as Robert Cole says, 'The political slogans are seen by the workers as symbols of a willingness to oppose management in the shop...the left-wing leader is not elected for his political beliefs per se but for their symbolic value.'[95] Cole expands this point further: 'In short, workers are not class conscious in the Marxian sense of recognizing their exploitation, identifying their oppressors as capitalists, and taking collective action to build a new society.'[96] Socialism and communism appeal to them more as symbols of protest, as a kind of 'moral armor' for the advocacy of their interests in the shop.

That the problem of expanding a sense of class consciousness remains today even in the more ramified subculture of the Japanese left, and even amidst the more politically active labor movement of the present, is suggested by the following remarks of a Japanese worker,

> We like to sing here [in a bar where the clientele enjoys revolutionary songs] and march in demonstrations because it gives us a release from the tensions that build up while working a sixty-hour week. And by doing **this**

we can go back and put in a hard day's work on Monday again...We don't need a union at our shoe factory because our boss is a guy you can talk with and besides, we will never make it into a big successful company if we have a union.[97]

The carnivalism, political indifference, and 'factory consciousness' evoked by this man gives the historian of the Japanese labor movement a feeling of déjà vu as he surveys the contemporary scene. It seems true that 'in spite of the wartime hiatus in political party and labor union activities, the postwar movement has', in some respects at least, 'been an intellectual extension or sequel to the prewar movement'.[98]

Appendix

Nihon Rōdō Sōdōmei reported membership figures
(selected years)

1919:	30,000
1924:	27,901
1925:	37,000 (pre-split)
1926:	19,460
1927:	37,855
1929:	37,517
1930:	44,219
1932:	47,986
1933:	51,165
1935:	50,512
1936:	96,926 (after establishment of Zen Nihon Rōdō Sōdōmei)

Source: Sōdōmei 50-shūnen kinnen iinkai, eds., *Yūaikai-Sōdōmei 50nen shi Nempyō* (Tokyo, 1962), pp. 292–3.

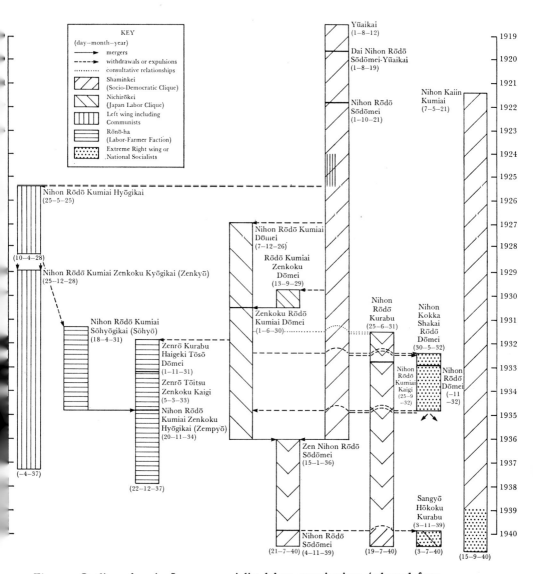

Fig. 1. Outline of main Japanese socialist labor organizations (adapted from George Totten, 'Lineages of Japanese Labor Unions', *Social Democratic Movement in Prewar Japan* (New Haven, 1966), p. 407). For translations see p. 263.

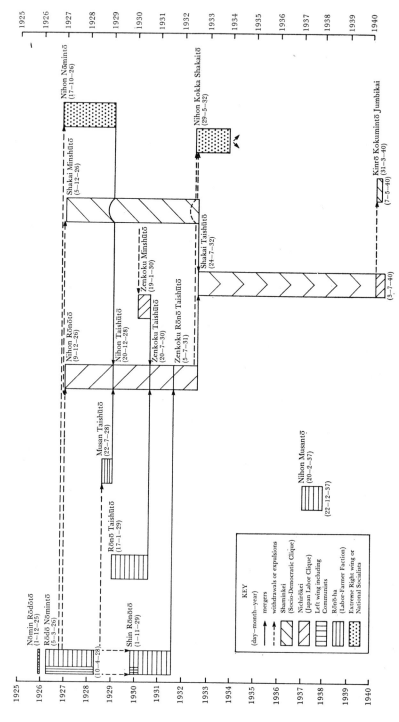

Fig. 2. Outline of main Japanese socialist parties (adapted from George Totten, 'Lineages of Japanese Social Democrat Parties', *Social Democratic Movement in Prewar Japan* (New Haven, 1966), p. 406). For translations see p. 263.

KEY

(day–month–year)

→ mergers

⇢ withdrawals or expulsions

Shaminkei (Socio-Democratic Clique)

Nichirōkei (Japan Labor Clique)

Left wing including Communists

Rōnō-ha (Labor-Farmer Faction)

Extreme Right wing or National Socialists

Nōmin Rōdōtō (1–12–25)

Rōdō Nōmintō (5–3–26)

(10–4–28)

Shin Rōnōtō (1–11–29)

Nihon Nōmintō (17–10–26)

Shakai Minshūtō (5–12–26)

Nihon Kokka Shakaitō (29–5–32)

Nihon Rōnōtō (9–12–26)

Musan Taishūtō (22–7–28)

Nihon Taishūtō (20–12–28)

Zenkoku Taishūtō (20–7–30)

Zenkoku Minshūtō (19–1–30)

Zenkoku Rōnō Taishūtō (5–7–31)

Shakai Taishūtō (24–7–32)

Rōnō Taishūtō (17–1–29)

Kinrō Kokumintō Jumbikai (31–3–40)

(7–5–40)

Nihon Musantō (20–2–37)

(22–12–37)

(3–7–40)

Translations of names appearing in Figs. 1 and 2

1. Main Japanese socialist labor organizations

Dai Nihon Rōdō Sōdōmei-Yūaikai   Friendly Society Greater Japan General Federation of Labor
Nihon Kaiin Kumiai   Japan Seamen's Union
Nihon Kokka Shakai Rōdō Dōmei   Japan State Socialist Labor Federation
Nihon Rōdō Dōmei   Japan Labor Federation
Nihon Rōdō Kumiai Dōmei   Federation of Japanese Labor Unions
Nihon Rōdō Kumiai Hyōgikai   Council of Japanese Labor Unions
Nihon Rōdō Kumiai Kaigi   Congress of Japanese Labor Unions
Nihon Rōdō Kumiai Sōhyōgikai   General Council of Japanese Labor Unions
Nihon Rōdō Kumiai Zenkoku Hyōgikai   National Council of Japanese Labor Unions
Nihon Rōdō Kumiai Zenkoku Kyōgikai   National Conference of Japanese Labor Unions
Nihon Rōdō Kurabu   Japan Labor Club
Nihon Rōdō Sōdōmei   Japan General Federation of Labor
Rōdō Kumiai Zenkoku Dōmei   National Federation of Labor Unions
Sangyō Hōkoku Kurabu   Industrial Patriotic Club
Yūaikai   Friendly Society
Zen Nihon Rōdō Sōdōmei   All-Japan General Federation of Labor
Zenkoku Rōdō Kumiai Dōmei   National Labor Union Federation
Zenrō Kurabu Haigeki Tōsō Dōmei   National Labor Struggle Combination to Boycott the Japan Labor Club
Zenrō Tōitsu Zenkoku Kaigi   National Congress for the Unification of the National Labor Union Federation

2. Main socialist parties

Kinrō Kokumintō Jumbikai   Preparatory Committee for the Nationalist Labor Party
Musan Taishūtō   Proletarian Masses' Party
Nihon Kokka Shakaitō   Japan State Socialist Party
Nihon Musantō   Japan Proletarian Party
Nihon Nōmintō   Japan Farmers' Party
Nihon Rōnōtō   Japan Labor-Farmer Party
Nihon Taishūtō   Japan Masses' Party
Nōmin Rōdōtō   Farmer Labor Party
Rōdō Nōmintō   Labor–Farmer Party
Rōnō Taishūtō   Labor–Farmer Masses' Party
Shakai Minshūtō   Social Democratic Party
Shakai Taishūtō   Social Masses' Party
Shin Rōnōto (Shin Rōdō Nōmintō)   New Labor Farmer Party
Zenkoku Rōnō Taishūtō   National Labor–Farmer Masses' Party
Zenkoku Minshūtō   National Democratic Party
Zenkoku Taishūtō   National Masses' Party

Notes

The following abbreviations are used in the notes:
NMS   Nihon minshū shimbun
NRUS   Nihon rōdō undō shiryō
R   Rōdō
SGS   Sōdōmei gojūnen shi

Introduction

1. Takeshi Ishida, 'The Development of Interest Groups and the Pattern of Political Modernization in Japan', in Robert E. Ward, ed., *Political Development in Modern Japan* (Princeton, 1968), pp. 294–6.
2. Mayer Zald and Roberta Ash, 'Social Movement Organizations: Growth, Decay, and Change', in Joseph Gusfield, ed., *Protest, Reform, and Revolution* (New York, 1970), p. 518.
3. Examples of scholarly works which stress the labor relations approach include: Hazama Hiroshi, *Nihon rōmu kanrishi kenkyū* (Tokyo, 1964); Masumi Tsuda, 'The Basic Structure of Japanese Labor Relations', *Musashi daigaku ronshū* (May 1964), pp. 1–104; Eitarō Kishimoto, 'The Characteristics of Labor-Management Relations in Japan and their Historical Formation', *Kyoto University Economic Review* (October 1965), pp. 33–5, and (April 1966) pp. 17–38; Kazuo Ōkōchi, 'Traditionalism of Industrial Relations in Japan', in *The Changing Patterns of Industrial Relations: Proceedings of the International Conference on Industrial Relations* (Tokyo, 1965), pp. 126–41; Kazuo Ōkōchi, Bernard Karsh, and Solomon Levine, eds., *Workers and Employers in Japan: The Japanese Employment Relations System* (Tokyo, 1973); Ronald Dore, *British Factory–Japanese Factory: The Origins of National Diversity in Industrial Relations* (London, 1973); Robert Evans, 'Evolution of the Japanese System of Employer–Employee Relations, 1868–1945', *Business History Review* (Spring 1970), pp. 110–25; Koji Taira, *Economic Development and the Labor Market in Japan* (New York, 1970); Michael Yoshino, *Japan's Managerial System: Tradition and Innovation* (Cambridge, Mass., 1968); and Robert Cole, 'The Theory of Institutionalization: Permanent Employment and Tradition in Japan', *Economic Development and Cultural Change*, xx: 1 (1971), pp. 47–70.
4. Gaston Rimlinger, 'The Legitimation of Protest: A Comparative Study in Labor History', in Gusfield, *Protest, Reform, and Revolution*, p. 363.
5. Although the reign of the Taishō Emperor extended from 1912 to 1926, most scholars use the term, 'Taishō democracy', to refer to a broader time span, going back as far as 1905, and extending to the early 1930s. For

example, cf. Takayoshi Matsuo, 'The Development of Democracy in Japan', *Developing Economies* (December 1966), pp. 612–37, and Harry Harootunian, 'Introduction: A Sense of an Ending and the Problem of Taishō', in Bernard Silberman and Harry Harootunian, eds., *Japan in Crisis: Essays on Taishō Democracy* (Princeton, 1974), pp. 3–28.

The 'Taishō democracy' interpretation can be found, with different degrees of emphasis, in the following works: Shinobu Seizaburō, *Taishō seiji shi* (Tokyo, 1968); and *Taishō demokurashi shi*, Volumes I and II (Tokyo, 1965) and Volume III (Tokyo, 1968); Matsuo Hiroshi, *Nihon rōdō undō shi* (Tokyo, 1965); Nimura Kazuo, 'Senzen ni okeru rōdō undō no honkakuteki hatten to haiboku', in Rōdō undō shi kenkyūkai, eds., *Nihon rōdō undō no rekishi to kadai* (Tokyo, 1970), pp. 46–73; and in a source that is important for this book, Sōdōmei gojūnen shi kankō iinkai, eds., *Sōdōmei gojūnen shi*, Volume I (Tokyo, 1965) and Volume II (Tokyo, 1967) – hereafter referred to as *SGS*. Western writers who emphasize 'Taishō democracy' include Edwin Reischauer, *Japan: The Story of a Nation* (New York, 1970) and George Totten, *The Social Democratic Movement in Prewar Japan* (New Haven, 1966).

6. The *jiyū minken undō* of the 1870s and 1880s expressed the desire of certain samurai and other disaffected strata in Meiji Japan for a political system of greater power-sharing, as opposed to the authoritarian rule of the Meiji oligarchs.

7. Peter Gay, *The Dilemma of Democratic Socialism: Eduard Bernstein's Challenge to Marx* (New York, 1952), p. ix.

8. The theoretical basis for this book's discussion of bureaucratization and oligarchization in the Sōdōmei is Robert Michels, *Political Parties* (New York, 1962). It is recognized, however, that Michels' well-known 'iron law of oligarchy' does not always apply to the history of social movements. For a critique of Michels, cf. Zald and Ash, pp. 533–4.

9. Rudolf Heberle, *Social Movements: An Introduction to Political Sociology* (New York, 1951), p. 162.

10. Ted Gurr, *Why Men Rebel* (Princeton, 1970), p. 24.

11. James Geschwender, 'Explorations in the Theory of Social Movements and Revolution', *Social Forces* (December 1968), p. 129.

12. Yoshio Sugimoto, 'Economic Fluctuations and Popular Disorders in Prewar Japan', unpublished paper presented to the Forty-Sixth Australia–New Zealand Association for the Advancement of Science Congress, Canberra, January 1975.

13. Arthur Kornhauser, 'Human Motivations Underlying Industrial Conflict', in Arthur Kornhauser, Robert Dubin, and Arthur Ross, *Industrial Conflict* (New York, 1956), p. 81.

14. Adolph Sturmthal, 'Economic Development and the Labour Movement', in Arthur Ross, ed., *Industrial Relations and Economic Development* (London, 1966), pp. 165–81.

15. Eric Hobsbawm, 'Labor History and Ideology', *Journal of Social History*, 7:4 (Summer 1974), pp. 379–80.

1 Labor's image of the past in 1919–1920

1. Bell suggested this schema in comments on Irving Bernstein's article, 'Union Growth and Structural Cycles', in Walter Galenson and Seymour Martin Lipset, eds., *Labor and Trade Unionism: An Interdisciplinary Reader* (New York, 1960), p. 90.
2. This phrase is taken from Robert Scalapino, 'Labor and Politics in Postwar Japan', in William Lockwood, ed., *The State and Economic Enterprise in Japan* (Princeton, 1965), p. 671.
3. Robert Scalapino, *Democracy and the Party Movement in Prewar Japan: The Failure of the First Attempt* (Berkeley, 1962), p. 249.
4. Totten, *Social Democratic Movement*, p. 20.
5. Rōdō undō shiryō iinkai, eds., *Nihon rōdō undō shiryō*, Volume x (Tokyo, 1968), Table vi–17, p. 440. Hereafter cited as *NRUS*.
6. The use of the American Federation of Labor as a model for these early Japanese labor organizations is discussed in Ōshima Kiyoshi, 'Rōdō kumiai no tanjō: Takano Fusatarō no shōgai', *Hōsei* (October 1968), pp. 26–31. Also, cf. Iwao Ayusawa, *A History of Labor in Modern Japan* (Honolulu, 1966), Chapter ii.
7. These unions are discussed in Ōkōchi Kazuo and Matsuo Hiroshi, *Nihon rōdō kumiai monogatari: Meiji* (Tokyo, 1965), pp. 63–74. For information on Katayama and Takano, cf. Hyman Kublin, *Asian Revolutionary: The Life of Sen Katayama* (Princeton, 1964). Note that the Kappankō Kumiai (Printers' Union) and the Nitetsu Kyōseikai (Japan Railways Improvement Society), organized by the Kiseikai in 1898 and 1899 respectively, each numbered around 2,000 workers.
8. An excellent source on wages and working conditions affecting workers in the Meiji period and later is Mori Kiichi, *Nihon rōdōsha kaikyū jōtai shi*, two volumes (Tokyo, 1974).
9. William Lockwood notes, 'In 1896, for example, 261,000 out of 435,000 operatives in private plants employing ten or more workers were women.' Cf. William Lockwood, *The Economic Development of Japan: Growth and Structural Change* (Princeton, 1954), p. 485. For a study of female labor in the textile industry, cf. Gary Saxonhouse, 'Country Girls and Communication Among Competitors in the Japanese Cotton-Spinning Industry', in Hugh Patrick, ed., *Japanese Industrialization and Its Social Consequences* (Berkeley, 1976), pp. 97–125.
10. The poor conditions suffered by Japanese workers were first surveyed by the government in a five-volume study entitled *Shokkō jijō*, published by the Ministry of Agriculture and Commerce in 1903. For a description of these conditions based on this study, see Kazuo Ōkōchi, *Labor in Modern Japan* (Tokyo, 1958).
11. Quoted from Jon Halliday, *A Political History of Japanese Capitalism* (New York, 1975), p. 62.
12. Mikio Sumiya, 'The Emergence of Modern Japan', in Ōkōchi, Karsh, and Levine, pp. 32–4. Also cf. Koji Taira, 'Factory Legislation and Management Modernization During Japan's Industrialization, 1886–1916', *Business History Review* (Spring 1970), pp. 85–6.
13. Ōkōchi, 'Traditionalism', pp. 131–3, and Chapter 13 in Ōkōchi, Karsh, and Levine, pp. 487–8.

14. *Oyakata* means 'father figure' or 'parent figure'; *kokata*, 'child figure'. The role of the *oyakata* in recruiting and training other workers is discussed in Dore, *British Factory–Japanese Factory*, Chapter 14, 'The Origins of the Japanese Employment System'.
15. Ibid., p. 384, and Ōkōchi, Karsh, and Levine, pp. 487–8.
16. See Chapter 4.
17. Quoted from Byron Marshall, *Capitalism and Nationalism in Prewar Japan: The Ideology of the Business Elite, 1868–1941* (Stanford, 1967), p. 58.
18. Ibid., p. 82.
19. Several good examples are discussed in Taira, 'Factory Legislation and Management Modernization', pp. 95–109.
20. This is a main theme of Marshall, *Capitalism and Nationalism*; cf. Chapters 4 and 5 in particular.
21. The Japanese text of Article Seventeen may be found in Sumiya Mikio, *Nihon rōdō undō shi* (Tokyo, 1966), p. 59. For English translations of Articles Seventeen and Thirty, cf. Stephen Large, *The Rise of Labor in Japan: The Yūaikai, 1912–1919* (Tokyo, 1972), p. 3.
22. Ōkōchi and Matsuo (Meiji), pp. 89–100.
23. This phrase is suggested by Bernard Karsh, 'The Development of a Strike', in Gusfield, p. 313.
24. These organizations are discussed in Totten, *Social Democratic Movement*, pp. 23–6. Note that the Shakaishugi Kenkyūkai was later succeeded by the Shakaishugi Kyōkai. Cf. Totten, p. 26.
25. An authoritative source on Kōtoku is Fred Notehelfer, *Kōtoku Shūsui: Portrait of a Japanese Radical* (Cambridge, 1971).
26. The founding of the Yūaikai is discussed in my book, *The Rise of Labor in Japan*, pp. 11–12. A briefer study of the Yūaikai is available in my article, 'The Japanese Labor Movement, 1912–1919: Suzuki Bunji and the Yūaikai', *Journal of Asian Studies*, xxix:3 (May 1970), pp. 559–79. Also refer to Suzuki Bunji, *Rōdō undō nijūnen* (Tokyo, 1931).
27. An analysis of the Yūaikai's growth is given in Watanabe Tōru, 'Yūaikai no soshiki no jittai', *Jimbun gakuhō* (October 1963), pp. 1–70.
28. Large, *Rise of Labor*, pp. 16–28.
29. Kozo Yamamura, 'The Japanese Economy, 1911–1930; Concentration, Conflicts, and Crises', in Silberman and Harootunian, *Japan in Crisis*, p. 301.
30. Ibid., p. 302.
31. Ōkōchi, *Labor in Modern Japan*, p. 39. For a break-down of workers by occupations in 1920, cf. Shūichi Harada, *Labor Conditions in Japan* (New York, 1928), pp. 109–11.
32. Yamamura, 'Japanese Economy', pp. 306–7.
33. Ibid., p. 306.
34. This remark is attributed to Kagawa Toyohiko by Kondō Eizō in an article written by the latter entitled, 'Kaisan! Dogō! Konran! Kansai kōenkai no ki', *Shakaishugi* (November 1920), p. 1.
35. *NRUS*, x, Table vi–17, pp. 440–1. Information on the duration of these disputes, which tended to last up to ten days for the most part, and on the types of workers involved may be found on p. 488 and on pp. 446–7.
36. Ibid., p. 424. The estimate of 100,000 workers in unions in 1919 is made by Taira in *Economic Development and the Labor Market*, p. 144.

37. Large, *Rise of Labor*, pp. 35–7, passim.
38. The Shin'yūkai was established in April 1917 as a successor to the defunct Ōyūkai (Europe Friends' Society), an organization that had first arisen in 1907 with Japanese type-setters employed by European language publications as its nucleus. Most workers in the Shin'yūkai were printers or metal workers. Printing workers employed in Tokyo newspapers also formed the backbone of the Seishinkai, founded in December 1919. For a brief analysis of both groups, cf. Komatsu Ryūji, *Nihon anākizumu undō shi* (Tokyo, 1972), pp. 93–9. Historical documents relating to the Shin'yūkai are available in *NRUS*, III (Tokyo, 1968), pp. 554–8.
39. Ōkōchi, 'Traditionalism', p. 132.
40. Ibid.
41. The emergence of Matsuoka and Nishio as leaders in the Yūaikai is discussed at length in Large, *Rise of Labor*. Also, cf. Nakamura Kikuo, *Matsuoka Komakichi den* (Tokyo, 1964), and Nishio Suehiro, *Taishū to tomo ni* (Tokyo, 1952). For a study of Nishio's role in Japanese socialism, see my article, 'Nishio Suehiro and the Japanese Social Democratic Movement, 1920–1940', *Journal of Asian Studies*, XXXVI:1 (November 1976), pp. 37–56.
42. Two good sources on Yoshino's thought are Bernard Silberman, 'The Political Thought of Yoshino Sakuzō', *Journal of Modern History*, XXXI:4 (December 1959), pp. 310–24, and Tetsuo Najita, 'Some Reflections on Idealism in the Political Thought of Yoshino Sakuzō', in Silberman and Harootunian, *Japan in Crisis*, pp. 29–66.
43. The development of the parties, particularly the Seiyūkai, is described in Tetsuo Najita, *Hara Kei in the Politics of Compromise* (Cambridge, Mass., 1967). Prior to the formation of the Hara administration, Japan had been ruled in the Taishō period by the cabinets of Prime Ministers Admiral Yamamoto Gombei (February 1913–April 1914), Ōkuma Shigenobu (April 1914–October 1916), and General Terauchi Masatake (October 1916–September 1918). Each of these administrations, especially those of Yamamoto and Terauchi, had been beholden to the most powerful remaining Meiji oligarch, Yamagata Aritomo who as *genrō* had exercised influence in politics by recommending prime ministers to the Emperor.
44. Cf. Large, *Rise of Labor*, Chapters 5 and 7, passim, concerning the development of radicalism in the context of the Russian Revolution and the Rice Riots in World War I Japan.
45. Ibid., p. 58.
46. Ibid., pp. 137–8.
47. Ibid., p. 140. The Factory Law of 1911, which came into force in 1916, was deficient in many respects. It did not cover workers in enterprises employing five or fewer workers and the machinery to implement its enforcement was defective. For instance, the Law provided for 199 inspectors to inspect over 20,000 factories. Cf. ibid., pp. 73–4; Ayusawa, *A History of Labor*, pp. 182–95; and Yamamura, 'Japanese Economy', pp. 308–9. Yamamura states, 'as late as in 1925, only about 50 per cent of the labor force came under the protection of the law' (p. 309).
48. On Kagawa, see George Bikle, *The New Jerusalem: Aspects of Utopianism in the Thought of Kagawa Toyohiko* (Tuscon, 1976); a good study of

Kawakami is available in Gail Bernstein, *Japanese Marxist: A Portrait of Kawakami Hajime, 1879–1946* (Cambridge, Mass., 1976). Kagawa's role in the Yūaikai is discussed in Large, *Rise of Labor*.

49. A good source on the Shinjinkai is Henry Smith, *Japan's First Student Radicals* (Cambridge, Mass., 1972). The impact of the Shinjinkai on the Yūaikai is traced in Large, *Rise of Labor*, pp. 146–58.

50. Asō Hisashi, 'Rōdō undō no shin'igi', *Rōdō oyobi sangyō* (July 1919), p. 9.

51. The goals of the anarchists, as expressed in their publications, are studied in Komatsu, *Nihon anākizumu*, pp. 99–103, passim.

52. Large, *Rise of Labor*, p. 157.

53. For a study of Watanabe, cf. my article, 'Revolutionary Worker: Watanabe Masanosuke and the Japanese Communist Party, 1922–1928', *Asian Profile* (August 1975), pp. 371–90.

54. Large, *Rise of Labor*, pp. 158–66.

55. The formation of the Kyōchōkai and Suzuki's attitude toward this organization are analyzed in ibid., pp. 172–7.

56. Cf. ibid., pp. 178–85, for an account of the convention.

57. Quoted in translation from Ōkōchi Kazuo and Matsuo Hiroshi, *Nihon rōdō kumiai monogatari: Taishō* (Tokyo, 1965), p. 144.

58. *SGS*, I, p. 278.

59. Ōkōchi and Matsuo (*Taishō*), pp. 144–5.

60. Large, *Rise of Labor*, p. 187.

61. For a full list of groups in the Alliance, see Ayusawa, *A History of Labor*, pp. 137–8.

62. Ibid., pp. 138–9.

63. Watanabe Tōru, '1919nen yori 21nen ni itaru rōdō undō shisō no sui-i', in Inoue Kiyoshi, ed., *Taishōki no seiji to shakai* (Tokyo, 1969), p. 217. Also, cf. Peter Duus, *Party Rivalry and Political Change in Taishō Japan* (Cambridge, Mass., 1968), pp. 140–2.

64. Ōhara shakai mondai kenkyūjo, eds., *Nihon rōdō nenkan* (Tokyo, 1922), p. 105.

65. *SGS*, I, pp. 379–83. For a list of members in the Shakaishugi Dōmei, see Katō Kanjū, 'Dantai no shōsoku', *Shakaishugi* (September 1920), and Sakai Toshihiko, 'Nihon shakai undō no hitobito', *Kaizō* (January 1921), pp. 1–13. The Dōmei, it should be stressed, was not exclusively anarchist politically. Its members included anarchists, socialists of various types, and 'bolsheviks'. Cf. Totten, *Social Democratic Movement*, p. 33.

66. For instance, cf. 'Shihon senseishugi o haisu', *Rōdō* (June 1920), pp. 1–2. *Rōdō* replaced the former Yūaikai organ, *Rōdō oyobi sangyō*, in 1919. Hereafter, it is cited as *R*.

67. *Nihon rōdō nenkan* (1922), p. 105. This figure applied to data as of October that year. Industrial unemployment also worsened in the early 1920s due to the reduction of naval development imposed upon Japan by the naval disarmament agreements in the 1921 Washington Conference and due to the earthquake in the Kantō area in September 1923. Cf. Ayusawa, *A History of Labor*, pp. 204–5 for details.

68. *NRUS*, X, Table VI-18, p. 442.

69. Suzuki Bunji, 'Kanryōshugi ka mimponshugi ka', *Rōdō oyobi sangyō* (November 1919), p. 1.

70. Katsuji Katō, 'The Labor Movement in Japan', *Japan Review* (October 1921), p. 219.
71. *SGS*, I, p. 483.

2 Anarchism, socialism, and communism in the labor movement, 1920–1923

1. Robert Scalapino, *The Japanese Communist Movement, 1920–1966* (Berkeley, 1967), p. 11.
2. Ōzawa Masamichi, *Ōsugi Sakae kenkyū* (Tokyo, 1968); Bradford Simcock, 'The Anarcho-Syndicalist Thought and Action of Ōsugi Sakae', *Papers on Japan*, I (Cambridge, Mass., 1970), pp. 31–54; Tatsuo Arima, *The Failure of Freedom: A Portrait of Modern Japanese Intellectuals* (Cambridge, Mass., 1969), Chapter III; and Stephen Large, 'The Romance of Revolution in Japanese Anarchism and Communism During the Taishō Period', *Modern Asian Studies*, II:3 (1977), pp. 441–67.
3. The amount was stipulated as fifteen *sen* in the 1919 convention. Cf. *SGS*, I, p. 1074.
4. Large, *Rise of Labor*, p. 100.
5. Sōdōmei gojūnen shi kankō iinkai, eds., *Kanemasa Yonekichi tsuisōroku* (Tokyo, 1969), p. 66. Toyotomi Hideyoshi was one of Japan's great warlords in the sixteenth century who, along with Oda Nobunaga and Tokugawa Ieyasu, unified the country through conquest. His power lay in Western and Central (*chūgoku*) Japan, hence this reference to Kanemasa who was a pillar of the labor movement in Osaka. Information on Nishio's clique is found throughout his autobiography, *Taishū to tomo ni*; Matsuoka's clique is often mentioned in Nakamura, *Matsuoka Komakichi den*.
6. Asō's clique is discussed in Large, *Rise of Labor*, pp. 146–53, and in Kawakami Jōtarō, *Asō Hisashi den* (Tokyo, 1958).
7. Cf. note 5, above. For a time, Oda was lord to Hideyoshi.
8. Matsuoka's opinions on intellectuals in the labor movement were expressed most clearly in his article, 'Chishiki kaikyū ni kibō su', *Demokurashī* (April 1919), p. 11.
9. Matsuo Hiroshi, 'Yūaikai, Sōdōmei no rōdō kumiaika, sentōka katei to sampa no hassei', *Rōdō undō shi kenkyū* (January 1963), pp. 28–31. In an interview on May 27, 1969 at Matsumoto City, Tanahashi Kotora told me that Asō, despite his willingness to work with Matsuoka in transforming the Yūaikai into the Sōdōmei, had deep reservations about Matsuoka's political views which Asō thought were too conservative for the labor movement.
10. Information on *Shin Kōbe* is available in the introduction of the reprinted edition of *Shin Kōbe–Rōdōsha Shimbun* (Kobe, 1970), written by Professor Ōmae Gorō who supervised the publication of the re-edition.
11. This problem of regionalism was inherited from the Yūaikai; cf. Large, *Rise of Labor*, Chapter 7, 'Political Activism in the Labor Movement', and Chapter 8, 'Plans for a New Yūaikai', passim.
12. Ibid., p. 54 and p. 130. For an analysis of these large unions in the Sōdōmei, see Ikeda Makoto and Ōmae Gorō, *Nihon rōdō undō shi ron* (Tokyo, 1967), and Ikeda Makoto, *Nihon kikaikō kumiai seiritsu shi ron* (Tokyo, 1970).
13. A full list of Sōdōmei unions as of 1925 is provided in Kyōchōkai, eds.,

Saikin no shakai undō (Tokyo, 1929), p. 231. A similar list of Sōdōmei unions as of 1928 is given in George Totten, 'Japanese Social Democracy: An Analysis of the Background, Leadership, and Organized Support of the Social Democratic Movement in Prewar Japan', Ph.D. dissertation, Yale University, 1954, Publication No. 11,212, University Microfilms, Ann Arbor, Michigan, pp. 217–18; Totten also supplies membership figures for each union.

14. I could find no instance in which a worker aspiring to join the Sōdōmei was refused membership.

15. An indispensable source on Takata is 'Takata Waitsu', *Rōdō undō shi kenkyū* [published by the Saitama Prefecture Labor Movement History Research Society] (March 1967), pp. 10–50. Also, cf. Takata Waitsu, *Nazo no rōdō fungi: Shibaura jiken no shinso* (Tokyo, 1920).

16. Yamamoto was a skilled metal worker at the Shibaura Manufacturing Company.

17. 'Yūaikai jidai o kataru', *Rōdō undō shi kenkyū* (September 1962), p. 24.

18. To wit, in his account of the 1919 convention, Suzuki Bunji did not mention the 'anarchist problem' at all. Suzuki, *Rōdō undō nijūnen*, pp. 179–86.

19. *SGS*, I, p. 357.

20. The events leading to the formation of the Tokyo *rengōkai* are analyzed in ibid., pp. 358–9.

21. Ibid., pp. 359–60.

22. Ibid., pp. 363–4.

23. Kamijō Aiichi, 'Ni, san no rimen shi', *Rōdō undō shi kenkyū* (March 1962), p. 17.

24. Ōkōchi and Matsuo, (*Taishō*), p. 204.

25. Kondō Eizō, 'Kumiai ronsha ni', *Rōdō undō* (March 1921), in Tanaka Sōgorō, ed., *Taishō, shakai undō shi: shiryō*, Volume I (Tokyo, 1970), p. 384.

26. Ōkōchi and Matsuo, (*Taishō*), p. 204.

27. Ibid.

28. The debates over the control of strikes are treated in *SGS*, I, pp. 373–4.

29. Mizunuma Yoshio, 'Rōdō Kumiai Dōmeikai no bunretsu', *Rōdō undō* (June 25, 1921), in Tanaka, *Taishō shakai undō shi*, Volume I, pp. 412–13.

30. Large, 'Revolutionary Worker', p. 372.

31. Tanahashi Kotora, 'Rōdō kumiai e kaere', *R* (January 1921), p. 13.

32. Tanahashi Kotora, 'Yūaikai o omoide', *Rōdō undō shi kenkyū* (March 1962), p. 13.

33. Anarchist attacks against Kagawa were bitter because of his opposition to anarchism. Cf. Bikle, *New Jerusalem*, p. 108.

34. Ōkōchi and Matsuo, (*Taishō*), pp. 201–2.

35. Totten, *Social Democratic Movement*, pp. 33–4.

36. For instance, cf. Watanabe Tōru et al., eds., *Nihon shakaishugi undō shi ron* (Tokyo, 1973), pp. 108–16. A good English-language account of the JCP is George Beckmann and Genji Okubo, *The Japanese Communist Party, 1922–1945* (Stanford, 1969).

37. George Beckmann, 'The Radical Left and the Failure of Communism', in James Morley, ed., *Dilemmas of Growth in Prewar Japan* (Princeton, 1971), p. 144.

38. Ibid., p. 147.
39. Cf. Beckmann and Okubo, 'Bibliography', for a comprehensive list of sources on intellectuals such as Yamakawa and Sakai who became communists. The book also includes valuable, albeit brief, biographical sketches of key men in the communist movement, pp. 362–89.
40. Tanno Setsu, *Tanno Setsu: kakumei undō ni ikiru* (Tokyo, 1970), pp. 51–2.
41. Quoted from Beckmann and Okubo, p. 51.
42. Yamakawa meant here that it was not enough for the proletariat to simply reject bourgeois politics, for this negative course by itself would breed passivity. As Yamakawa said, 'If the proletariat truly rejects bourgeois politics, it must not be simply passive...It must put up proletarian politics against bourgeois politics.' Ibid., p. 52.
43. The full text of Yamakawa's article is found in Tanaka, *Taishō shakai undō shi*, pp. 537–40.
44. Tanno, pp. 46–8, 180.
45. See biographical notes in Beckmann and Okubo for information on these men.
46. *SGS*, I, p. 635.
47. Perhaps because of his later battles with the communists, Nishio Suehiro played down these early contacts with them in his memoirs, *Taishū to tomo ni*, pp. 160–5. But Kanemasa, who was also interested in communism during this period, and who developed an admiration for Lenin, gives the impression that Nishio was in fact more involved in communist ideology than is conveyed in Nishio's book. *Kanemasa Yonekichi*, pp. 87–8.
48. Beckmann and Okubo mention Akamatsu among the early JCP members, p. 50.
49. This strategy was recommended to the JCP by the Comintern. Ibid., p. 37.
50. The main organizations in the Dōmeikai are listed in *SGS*, I, p. 412.
51. Ibid., pp. 634–50.
52. Nabeyama and Nakamura Yoshiaki had quickly established a communist power base in the Osaka Electric Industry Workers' Union of the Sōdōmei. Nabeyama's recollections of the interwar labor movement are contained in his book, *Shakai minshūshugi to no tōsō* (Tokyo, 1932).
53. For example, Matsuoka Komakichi, 'Jiyū rengō ronsha ni ataeru', *R* (December 1922), p. 3, and Yamakawa Hitoshi, 'Anākisuto no kokusai taikai', *Zen'ei* (August 1922), in Tanaka, *Taishō shakai undō shi*, I, pp. 541–2.
54. See *SGS*, I, pp. 571–80, for a detailed account of this convention.
55. Ōzawa, *Ōsugi*, pp. 329ff.
56. Ivan Morris has suggested that the Japanese pay special respect to 'tragic heroes' who are overcome by circumstances despite great courage. This would apply to Ōsugi, although Morris did not include him in his book, *The Nobility of Failure: Tragic Heroes in the History of Japan* (London, 1975).
57. 'Rōdō kaikyū no hanseiji', *R* (April 1921), pp. 2–3.
58. Yamamoto Kenzō, 'Rōdōsha no tachiba kara', *R* (January 1922), p. 5.

3 The communist offensive and the 1925 labor split

1. *NRUS*, x, Table vi–1, p. 424.
2. Ibid., pp. 426–7; cf. Table vi–5 and Table vi–6.
3. Ibid., Table vi–8, p. 427.
4. Kondō, 'Kaisan! Dogō! Konran!', in Tanaka, *Taishō shakai undō shi*, p. 346.
5. *Kanemasa Yonekichi*, p. 61.
6. Beckmann and Okubo, p. 68.
7. Cf. Tsunekawa Nobuyuki, *Nihon Kyōsantō to Watanabe Masanosuke* (Tokyo, 1971), pp. 127–9. Tsunekawa lists those Nankatsu members who were killed. Hirazawa Keishichi was also killed.
8. Totten, *Social Democratic Movement*, p. 44.
9. These events are described in Arahata Kanson, *Hantaisei o ikite* (Tokyo, 1972), pp. 148–51, and Beckmann and Okubo, pp. 76–7, 83.
10. *SGS*, i, pp. 686–8.
11. Beckmann and Okubo, p. 76.
12. A detailed analysis of the Health Insurance Law is provided in Harada, pp. 263–70, and in Ayusawa, *A History of Labor*, pp. 209–14.
13. Amendments to the Factory Law are discussed in Harada, pp. 251–6.
14. These laws and others are listed, with summaries of their contents, in John Orchard, *Japan's Economic Position: The Progress of Industrialization* (New York, 1930), pp. 406–7.
15. Harada and Ayusawa offer critiques of these laws. Also see Takeshi Takahashi, 'Social Security for Workers', in Ōkōchi, Karsh, and Levine, pp. 443–4, passim.
16. Totten, *Social Democratic Movement*, p. 46.
17. *SGS*, i, p. 695.
18. Totten, *Social Democratic Movement*, p. 55.
19. *SGS*, i, pp. 694–6.
20. 'Musan seitō mondai', *R* (September 1924), p. 3.
21. 'Seiji to rōdō kumiai-in', *R* (September 1924), p. 3.
22. Suzuki, Nishio, and Matsuoka represented Japan the most often at the ILO. To ascertain who went to Geneva on behalf of Japanese labor in any given year, cf. the chronological tables for the history of the Sōdōmei in *SGS*, i, pp. 1,278–308, and *SGS*, ii, pp. 1,011–126.
23. Ayusawa, *A History of Labor*, p. 132.
24. Totten, *Social Democratic Movement*, p. 46.
25. Akamatsu Katsumaro, *Shakai minshūshugi no hata no shita ni* (Tokyo, 1930), p. 67.
26. This translation is from David Lu, *Sources of Japanese History*, Volume 2 (New York, 1974), pp. 113–14.
27. Nishio, p. 169.
28. Yamakawa Hitoshi, 'Futsū senkyo to musan kaikyūteki senjutsu', *Zen'ei* (March 1922) in Tanaka, *Taishō shakai undō shi*, Volume i, pp. 486–7.
29. Lu, p. 114.
30. Ibid.
31. Ibid.
32. Quoted from Smith, p. 58.

33. Takagi Ikurō, 'Musan seitō no shisō', in Sumiya Etsuji et al., eds., *Shōwa no hantaisei shisō* (Tokyo, 1968), pp. 173–4.
34. Ibid., pp. 167–9, passim.
35. Akamatsu Katsumaro, *Tenkanki no nihon shakai undō* (Tokyo, 1926), p. 23.
36. Akamatsu employed this phrase often in his writing. A good explanation of what he meant by it is given in his article, 'Kagakuteki nihonshugi kara shuppan shite', *Kaizō* (December 1931), pp. 72–7.
37. Ibid.
38. Takagi, p. 169.
39. Ibid., p. 177.
40. Ibid., p. 168.
41. Akamatsu, *Tenkanki*, pp. 37–40.
42. Beckmann and Okubo, pp. 59–62.
43. Murayama Kazunori, 'Nihon Rōdō Sōdōmei ni kamei shita roku kumiai ni tsuite', *Shakai undō kenkyū* (December 1961), pp. 1–21, passim.
44. There were the Kantō Insatsu Rōdō Kumiai (Kantō Printers' Labor Union), the Tokeikō Kumiai (Watchmakers' Union), the Kantō Kikaikō Kumiai (Kantō Machinists' Union), the Yokohama Gōdō Rōdō Kumiai (Yokohama Amalgamated Labor Union) and the Kōgaku Gikōkai (Optics Craftsmen's Society), all of which are mentioned at length in ibid.
45. *SGS*, I, p. 698.
46. Ōkōchi and Matsuo, (*Taishō*), pp. 317–20.
47. Uchida Tōshichi, 'Tekkō rōdōsha to shite', *Rōdō undō shi kenkyū* (March 1962), p. 16. For other accounts of the Dōmeikai convention, see *SGS*, I, pp. 701–6, and 'Sōdōmei dai-ichiji bunretsu o megutte–zadankai', *Rōdō undō shi kenkyū* (January 1963), pp. 45–6.
48. 'Sōdōmei dai-ichiji bunretsu', p. 45.
49. In Japanese, '*kotetsusei no kikansha*'. *SGS*, I, p. 701.
50. Nakamura, *Matsuoka Komakichi den*, p. 107.
51. 'Sōdōmei dai-ichiji bunretsu', p. 42.
52. *SGS*, I, p. 707.
53. Ibid., pp. 719–21; also, Ōkōchi and Matsuo, (*Taishō*), pp. 335–8.
54. Nishio, p. 204.
55. Ibid., pp. 205–6.
56. Nishio portrays the Kantō insurgents as 'irrational' in their refusal to accept his plan. Ibid., p. 207.
57. Ibid., p. 205.
58. *SGS*, I, p. 1,187.
59. Ibid., and Kyōchōkai, p. 554.
60. Kyōchōkai, p. 555.
61. Ōkōchi and Matsuo, (*Taishō*), p. 354.
62. Kyōchōkai, p. 554.
63. Ibid.
64. Quoted from David Lu, *Sources of Japanese History*, Volume II (New York, 1974), p. 117.
65. *SGS*, I, p. 1,179.
66. Ibid., pp. 729–30.
67. The full name of the 'rally' was Nihon Rōdō Sōdōmei Kakushin Dōmei,

or Rally for the Renovation of the Japan General Federation of Labor.
Ibid., pp. 730–1 and Ōkōchi and Matsuo, (*Taishō*), pp. 360–3.
68. *SGS*, I, pp. 743–4.
69. Ibid., p. 743.
70. Ibid., pp. 748–9. Another recommended source on the May 16 decision is *Kanemasa Yonekichi*, pp. 95–6.
71. *SGS*, I, p. 749.
72. Kyōchōkai, p. 231. Communist sources state that the Sōdōmei numbered 13,110 members, the Hyōgikai, 12,505, after the split. Cf. Taniguchi Zentarō, *Nihon Rōdō Kumiai Hyōgikai shi*, Volume I (Tokyo, 1949), p. 93.
73. Yamamoto Kenzō, 'Warera no tachiba', *Kaizō* (June 1925), pp. 145–8.
74. Yamakawa Hitoshi, 'Nihon Rōdō Sōdōmei to bunretsu no kiki', *Kaizō* (June 1925), pp. 148–52. Similar interpretations are found in Taniguchi, and two books by Noda Ritsuta, *Rōdō undō jissen ki* (Tokyo, 1937) and *Hyōgikai tōsō shi* (Tokyo, 1932).
75. Matsuoko Komakichi, 'Sōdōmei funjō no shinsō o semmei su', *Kaizō* (June 1925), pp. 139–43.
76. Beckmann and Okubo, p. 89.
77. Ibid., pp. 305–6.
78. This was Arahata Kanson's view. Cf. his *Kanson jiden* (Tokyo, 1960), p. 472 and his *Hantaisei*, p. 155. Tokuda Kyūichi, however, had not opposed splitting the Sōdōmei. He argued for building a new communist federation. It may be surmised that the disagreements in the communist ranks over policy toward the Sōdōmei reflected the collapse of communist discipline following the destruction of the Party in 1924. It is possible that had the JCP not been dissolved and had discipline been maintained, Watanabe might not have been so free to escalate his boring-from-within strategy to the point where it created a massive counter-reaction from the Sōdōmei leadership resulting in the labor split.

4 Industrial paternalism and Sōdōmei–Hyōgikai rivalry in the factories

1. Lockwood, *Economic Development of Japan*, Table 15, p. 202.
2. Ibid.
3. Ibid., p. 205.
4. Yamamura, 'Japanese Economy', p. 312.
5. Ibid., p. 310.
6. Ōkōchi, Karsh, and Levine, p. 489.
7. Ibid.
8. Michael Yoshino uses the term 'industrial paternalism' in *Japan's Managerial System*, p. 66. 'Corporate paternalism' is suggested by Dore, *British Factory–Japanese Factory*, p. 400.
9. Two general sources on the evolving role of the *rōmu* section in Japanese factories are Hazama, *Nihon rōmu kanrishi kenkyū*, and Johannes Hirschmeier and Tsunehiko Yui, *The Development of Japanese Business*, *1600–1973* (London, 1975), pp. 188–200.
10. This analysis is based on Shōjirō Ujihara, 'Japan's Laboring Class: Changes in the Postwar Period', *Journal of Social and Political Ideas in Japan*, III:3

(December 1965), pp. 60-7, and Hideaki Okamoto, 'Management and Their Organizations', in Ōkōchi, Karsh, and Levine, pp. 182-200, passim.

11. Cf. sources cited above in note 10, and Totten, 'Japanese Social Democracy', p. 76.

12. Ikeda Makoto, 'Dai-ichiji taisen ni okeru rōdō kumiai undō no tokushitsu', *Nihon rōdō kyokai zasshi* (February 1968), p. 20. Also see Ikeda's book, *Nihon kikaikō kumiai*, Chapter II.

13. Cf. works cited in note 3, Introduction.

14. Robert Cole, *Japanese Blue Collar: The Changing Tradition* (Berkeley, 1971), Chapters III and IV, passim.

15. Ōkōchi, Karsh, and Levine, pp. 491-2.

16. Ibid., p. 492.

17. Naomichi Funahashi, 'The Industrial Reward System: Wages and Benefits', ibid., p. 383, and Hirschmeier and Yui, pp. 198-9.

18. Funahashi, p. 379.

19. An excellent study of permanent employment in Japanese factories is Cole, 'Theory of Institutionalization'.

20. Kishimoto, 'The Characteristics of Labor–Management Relations' (April 1966), pp. 27-9.

21. Funahashi, p. 383. Ōkōchi discusses the idea of *jigyō ikka* in his essay, 'Traditionalism', p. 140.

22. Hazama, *Nihon rōmu kanrishi kenkyū*, and Dore, *British Factory–Japanese Factory*, pp. 380-5.

23. Dore, *British Factory–Japanese Factory*, p. 396.

24. Cole, 'Theory of Institutionalization', p. 57.

25. Ōkōchi, 'Traditionalism', pp. 134-5.

26. Mikio Sumiya, 'The Emergence of Modern Japan', in Ōkōchi, Karsh, and Levine, pp. 46-7.

27. Kazuo Ōkōchi, 'The Characteristics of Labor–Management Relations in Japan', *Journal of Social and Political Ideas in Japan*, III:3 (December 1965), p. 47. Also see Solomon Levine, 'Labor Markets and Collective Bargaining in Japan', in William Lockwood, *The State and Economic Enterprise in Japan*, pp. 633-67.

28. Ōkōchi, 'Traditionalism', pp. 136-9, passim.

29. Ibid., p. 139, and Ōkōchi, Karsh, and Levine, pp. 493-5, 505-6.

30. Sumiya, 'Emergence', p. 46.

31. *NRUS*, X, Table VI-2, p. 424.

32. Ibid.

33. Ibid.

34. Ibid.

35. George Totten, 'Collective Bargaining and Works Councils as Innovations in Industrial Relations in Japan During the 1920s', in R. P. Dore, ed., *Aspects of Social Change in Modern Japan* (Princeton, 1967), p. 210.

36. Ibid., 217, and Kishimoto, 'The Characteristics of Labor–Management Relations' (April 1966), p. 25.

37. Kishimoto, 'The Characteristics of Labor–Management Relations' (April 1966), p. 30.

38. Orchard, p. 300.

39. Harada, p. 237.

40. This account of business organizations is based on Ishida, 'The Development of Interest Groups', pp. 301–5.
41. Ayusawa, *A History of Labor*, p. 172.
42. Tōru Ariizumi, 'The Legal Framework: Past and Present' in Ōkōchi, Karsh, and Levine, pp. 100–1.
43. Cf. Harada, pp. 259–61 for examples.
44. *NRUS*, x, Table vi–7, p. 426.
45. Totten, *Social Democratic Movement*, p. 319; also, see his dissertation, 'Japanese Social Democracy', Table i, pp. 217–18.
46. Totten, 'Japanese Social Democracy', Table iii, pp. 228–30.
47. Taira, *Economic Development and the Labor Market*, p. 148.
48. Ibid.
49. Cole, 'Theory of Institutionalization', pp. 56–7.
50. Ibid., p. 57.
51. Ōkōchi, Karsh, and Levine, p. 490.
52. Cf. Shimada Haruo, 'Nenkōsei no shiteki keisei ni tsuite', in Keiō Gijuku Daigaku Sangyō Kenkyūjo, eds., *Sangyō kenkyūjo shiriizu*, No. 227 (1968–1969), pp. 39–75, passim, for observations concerning the *shokucho*.
53. Totten, *Social Democratic Movement*, p. 324.
54. Noda was not a communist at the time of the 1925 labor split but became one later.
55. In addition to biographical information given on these men in Beckmann and Okubo, cf. Noguchi Gimei, *Musan undō sōtōshi* (Tokyo, 1931), for brief accounts of their careers.
56. Tanno, pp. 63–5. Also, cf. Watanabe Masanosuke, *Sayoku rōdō kumiai no soshiki to seisaku* (Tokyo, 1930), p. 25. Note this latter book was published posthumously, its editors unidentified.
57. Noda, *Hyōgikai tōsō shi*, pp. 99–100.
58. Ibid., p. 100.
59. Totten presents a full list of the Councils, in 'Japanese Social Democracy', pp. 228–30.
60. Noda, *Hyōgikai tōsō shi*, p. 101.
61. Ibid., p. 100.
62. Ayusawa, *A History of Labor*, Table 15, p. 155.
63. Beckmann and Okubo, p. 92.
64. Some of the most significant strikes involving the Hyōgikai are reviewed in Noda, *Hyōgikai tōsō shi*, pp. 273–372, and Taniguchi, i, pp. 196–206 and Taniguchi, ii, pp. 252–6.
65. Strikes in which the Sōdōmei participated are surveyed in *SGS*, i, pp. 846–859 and *SGS*, ii, pp. 27–41.
66. Quoted from Harada, pp. 197–8.
67. This account of the Numazu local is based on Tada Shin'ichi, *Numazu shibu rōdō jūnen shi* (Shizuoka, 1937). Totten found that the Sōdōmei had more women workers in its fold than other labor organizations: 'In 1928 organized women workers, 11,848 in all, represented only 3.9 per cent of organized labor. Of these 6,884, or 58.1 per cent, most of whom were engaged in the textile industry, belonged to the General Federation and accounted for about one fourth of its membership.' *Social Democratic Movement*, p. 320.

68. The Noda strike is discussed in the next chapter.
69. These schools are analyzed in *SGS*, I, pp. 498–502.
70. Kamijō, 'Ni, san no rimen shi', p. 20.
71. Large, *Rise of Labor*, pp. 14, 23, 34–5.
72. Large, 'Romance of Revolution', discusses this communist subculture in relation to Watanabe Masanosuke.
73. Examples of Sōdōmei leaflets expounding this type of propaganda are found in Tada, pp. 131–2.
74. For instance, cf. Sōdōmei criticism of the Hyōgikai in Nishio Suehiro, 'Sōdōmei to Hyōgikai no seisaku', *R* (April 1926), p. 3. Hyogikai attacks on the 'realism' of the Sōdōmei were numerous, as in 'Dakyō ka tōsō ka: iwayuru genjitsu seisaku ni tsuite', *Rōdō shimbun* (June 5, 1926), in Tanaka, *Taishō shakai undō shi*, II, p. 983.
75. Quoted from Harada, pp. 204–5.
76. Totten, *Social Democratic Movement*, pp. 320–1.
77. Kawamura founded the Kangyō Rōdō Sōdōmei in 1922 but his career as a labor organizer began earlier, in 1919, when he established the Kōjōkai (Advancement Society), a union of army arsenal workers in Tokyo. Cf. Noguchi, pp. 96–7.
78. These are approximate figures, due to the unreliability of statistics kept by these organizations.
79. The Dōmei bloc is surveyed in Totten, *Social Democratic Movement*, pp. 323–4.
80. Komatsu Ryūji, *Kigyōbetsu kumiai no seisei* (Tokyo, 1971).
81. Ibid., pp. 107–12.
82. Ibid., pp. 112–13.
83. Ibid., pp. 158–9.
84. Ibid., p. 159.
85. Ibid., pp. 294–5.
86. Ibid., pp. 317, 340–1.
87. Ibid., p. 195.
88. Ibid., p. 210.
89. Ibid., p. 213.
90. Ibid., p. 224.
91. Ibid., pp. 225–6.
92. Ibid., p. 242.
93. A thorough account of the convention and these resolutions is given in Taniguchi, II, pp. 349–99. For an English translation of the more important resolutions, see Harada, p. 202.
94. Fukumoto's impact on the Japanese communist movement is discussed in Beckmann and Okubo.
95. Nishio Suehiro, 'Hyōgikai no shinhōkō tenkan to kono eikyō', *R* (August 1927), pp. 4–5.
96. The March arrests are treated in Beckmann and Okubo, p. 154.
97. Totten, *Social Democratic Movement*, p. 64. The Shinjinkai was dissolved by university authorities, rather than by the police directly, after the March 1928 arrests. Cf. Smith, pp. 207–8, passim.
98. Concerning Watanabe's death and its impact on the communist movement, cf. Large, 'Revolutionary Worker', pp. 387–9.

5   Labor and the socialist party movement, 1925–1928

1. The economic background to these trends in rural Japan is summarized cogently by Yamamura, 'Japanese Economy', pp. 303–5. Also, cf. Totten, *Social Democratic Movement*, pp. 35–8.
2. Totten sketches Sugiyama's background, *Social Democratic Movement*, pp. 145–6.
3. The full name of the Suiheisha was Zenkoku Suiheisha, or National Levelling Society. The origins and purposes of the Suiheisha, and the *eta* pariah class, organized into special villages or *buraku*, are discussed in Ayusawa, *A History of Labor*, pp. 166–70.
4. Cf. Smith, pp. 209–10.
5. For a list of all organizations invited by the Nōmin Kumiai to participate in discussions leading to a party, see *SGS*, I, p. 794.
6. There are a number of accounts of these meetings. Two, which reflect Sōdōmei perspectives, are Asō Hisashi, 'Rodo Sōdōmei no dattai ni itaru made', *Kaizō* (January 1926), pp. 31–5, and Nishio, pp. 218–22. For a communist view, cf. Nakamura Yoshiaki, 'Sodōmei no dattai to Hyōgikai no dattai', *Kaizō* (January 1926), pp. 48–52.
7. Totten, *Social Democratic Movement*, p. 56.
8. Tsunekawa, pp. 194–5.
9. Nishio, p. 220.
10. Ibid., pp. 221–2.
11. Akamatsu Katsumaro, *Nihon shakai undō shi* (Tokyo, 1968), pp. 222–5. This book was originally published in 1953.
12. Takano, a Professor at Tokyo Imperial University, had been an ally of Suzuki Bunji in the Yūaikai. Concerning his career in Japanese social movements, see Large, *Rise of Labor*, and Ōshima Kiyoshi, *Takano Iwasaburō den* (Tokyo, 1968).
13. Ono Setsuko, et al., *Musan seitō no kenkyū* (Tokyo, 1969), p. 3.
14. Kono Mitsu, *Nihon shakai seitō shi* (Tokyo, 1960), p. 66.
15. Nishio, p. 224.
16. Ibid., pp. 226–7.
17. Totten, *Social Democratic Movement*, p. 60.
18. Nishio, p. 229.
19. An excellent analysis of the rise of this Party is presented in Nakamura Katsunori, 'Shakai Minshūtō no sōritsu', *Hōgaku kenkyū* (October 1970), pp. 101–17. Also see Abe Isoo, Horie Kiichi, Yoshino Sakuzō, 'Seimesho', *Nihon minshū shimbun* (November 15, 1926), p. 1. (Hereafter, this reference is cited as *NMS*.) This declaration was dated November 4 and proclaimed the intention of these men to form the Party. The involvement of the Sōdōmei in this effort is clear from an article, 'Jūnigatsu gonichi kettō no genjitsuteki musan seitō', *R* (December 1926), pp. 6–7.
20. 'Shakai Minshūtō seiritsu su', *NMS* (December 15, 1926), p. 1.
21. 'Shakai Minshūtō dai-ikkai taikai kiji', *R* (January 1928), p. 20.
22. 'Shakai Minshūtō seiritsu su', p. 1. The character for *shū* in Shakai Minshūtō refers to the general populace and is the same as in Shūgi-in (House of Representatives); rather than *shu*, referring to 'master' or 'lord', as in *shujin*. The latter character was used for the Shakai Minshūtō of 1901

and indicated at that time a socialist party dedicated to mastership of the people. The character for the 1926 Party, by contrast, 'implied a socialist party for and by the masses, or the people, without implying disrespect for the emperor or accusation thereof'. Kenneth Colegrove, 'Labor Parties in Japan', *American Political Science Review*, XXIII:2 (May 1929), footnote 37, p. 346. Also, cf. *SGS*, II, p. 58.

23. Yamakawa Hitoshi, 'Musan kaikyū seiji sensen no konran', *Kaizō* (January 1927), p. 50.

24. 'Jūnigatsu gonichi', p. 7.

25. In 1919, Yoshino had expressed reservations about socialism. He wrote, 'I am not at all opposed to socialism...but some socialists feel that the workers can do nothing and many socialists feel that humanism and philanthropism have been historically served by capitalism...I am opposed to capitalism...But as far as reconstructing a society which has faults and building a new society, I am opposed to destroying the capitalists'. Humanism, not socialism, was the key to reconstruction, he declared. Cf. 'Rōdō mondai to jindōshugi', *Rōdō oyobi sangyō* (September 1919), pp. 9–13. But by the mid-1920s, Yoshino thought of himself as being a socialist, of the 'realist' variety. Cf. Takagi, pp. 160–2.

26. These conversations are mentioned by Nakamura, 'Shakai Minshūtō no sōritsu', p. 103; Kawakami, pp. 267–9; and in Miwa Jusō denki kankōkai, eds., *Miwa Jusō no shōgai* (Tokyo, 1966), p. 307.

27. Judging from available sources, the participants in these discussions concerning a third party seem not to have considered the possibility that their plans would lead to another split of the Sōdōmei. On the contrary, it was assumed that the third party could rely on support from within the Sōdōmei and other proletarian organizations without causing their disruption. Cf. Kawakami, p. 267, and *Miwa Jusō*, pp. 311–12.

28. Nakamura, 'Shakai Minshūtō no sōritsu', p. 103.

29. Nishio, p. 241.

30. 'Rōdō Sōdōmei no jinyō junka su', *R* (April 1927), p. 9.

31. Ibid., p. 5 supplies a good account of the decision to expel Asō and his followers.

32. Cf. Nishio, p. 243 for a list of defecting unions.

33. The Nihon Rōnōtō central committee is listed in Kono, *Nihon shakai seitō shi*, p. 85.

34. *Miwa Jusō*, p. 311, and Kawakami, p. 217.

35. The '*Minshū Shimbun*' affair is recounted in *Miwa Jusō*, p. 311, and by Nakamura, 'Shakai Minshūtō no sōritsu', p. 107. Also, cf. Kawakami, p. 268.

36. Nishio, p. 243.

37. Interview with Okada Sōji on February 25, 1972, in Tokyo.

38. Kikukawa Tadao tsuitō shuppan iinkai, eds., *Kikukawa Tadao: sono shisō to jissen* (Tokyo, 1956), p. 2.

39. Interview with Iwauchi Zensaku on February 2, 1972, in Tokyo.

40. Totten, *Social Democratic Movement*, p. 323.

41. Akamatsu Katsumaro, 'Niko no shidō seishin', *Kaizō* (April 1926), p. 68.

42. Akamatsu Katsumaro, 'Fusen dai-ichisen to rōdō kumiai no tachiba', *R* (November 1927), p. 25.

43. Suzuki Bunji, 'Warera no zento', *R* (January 1926), p. 1.
44. Yamakawa Hitoshi, 'Rōdō Sōdōmei no uyoku renmei e no shinshutsu', *Kaizō* (November 1926), pp. 52–7.
45. A good example among many is the unknown author of 'Rōdō Sōdōmei no jinyō junka su', *R* (April 1927), p. 7. Also cf. Ōyama Ikuo, 'Musan seitō sensenjo ni okeru shoha no tairitsu kankei', *Kaizō* (January 1927), pp. 61–9, and Nishio Suehiro, 'Jikkō wa konnan da', *R* (April 1927), p. 9.
46. Totten, *Social Democratic Movement*, pp. 112–13, 398.
47. Ibid., pp. 112–13.
48. Ibid., p. 181.
49. Ibid., p. 182.
50. Nishio, pp. 251–3.
51. Takagi, pp. 174–5.
52. Totten, *Social Democratic Movement*, pp. 182–3.
53. Ibid., p. 190.
54. Takagi, pp. 182–3.
55. A good source on the Rōnōha is Koyama Kōken, 'Rōnōha marukusushugi', in Sumiya Etsuji et al., eds., *Shōwa no hantaisei shisō*, pp. 278–334. In English, cf. Totten, *Social Democratic Movement*, pp. 151–75. In Totten's classification of Japanese social democrats, the Rōnōha was the most important group of several associated with the legal left. Elements of the legal left included those who had broken off from the communist movement but who remained opposed to the government; they were called the legal left to distinguish them from the illegal communists.
56. Quoted from Harada, p. 208. The Japanese text is available in Kono, *Nihon shakai seitō shi*, p. 67.
57. Quoted from Harada, p. 212; Kono, *Nihon shakai seitō shi*, pp. 75–6.
58. Harada, p. 217.
59. Cf. Totten, *Social Democratic Movement*, pp. 212–26, for a thorough comparison of the parties' platforms and policies on the labor and agrarian fronts.
60. Ibid., pp. 227ff.
61. Ibid., pp. 250–4.
62. Ibid., pp. 255–8.
63. Ibid., pp. 269–74.
64. Ibid., p. 274.
65. Ibid., pp. 273–5.
66. Ibid., pp. 282ff.
67. Totten explains the politicization of the local as a result of close links between the founder of the local and such Sōdōmei leaders as Suzuki and Matsuoka. Cf. George Totten, 'Japanese Industrial Relations at the Crossroads: The Great Noda Strike of 1927–1928', in Silberman and Harootunian, eds., *Japan in Crisis*, p. 411. The Noda local (Nihon Rōdō Sōdōmei Noda shibu) was founded in December 1921. By 1927, it constituted the largest element in the Sōdōmei's Kantō Brewery Union; of the Union's 3,245 members, the Noda local had 1,547. The Union was itself affiliated with the Kantō Rōdō Dōmeikai, which depended heavily on the Union for financial support. Cf. p. 413.

68. Ibid., p. 416.
69. Ibid., p. 418.
70. Ibid.
71. Matsuoka's role in the strike is discussed in Nakamura, *Matsuoka Komakichi den*, pp. 165–76. Note that Matsuoka wrote his own account of the strike, *Noda dai rōdō sōgi*, which is cited extensively in Totten's study.
72. 'Shakai Minshūtō dai-ikkai taikai kiji', *R* (January 1928), pp. 20–1.
73. Totten, 'Japanese Industrial Relations', p. 419.
74. Ibid.
75. Ibid., p. 406.
76. Ibid., p. 415.
77. Taira, *Economic Development and the Labor Market*, pp. 150–1.
78. Ibid., pp. 149–50.
79. Ibid., p. 163.
80. A contrary view is expressed in Takahashi, p. 447.
81. *SGS*, I, p. 1,182.
82. Ibid.
83. Ibid., p. 791.
84. Nakamura Katsunori, 'Shakai Minshūtō no dai-ichinen', *Hōgaku kenkyū* (June 1971), p. 1.
85. 'Shibu setsuritsu no dai-ichi koe', *NMS* (December 15, 1926), p. 1. Other Sōdōmei-based Party branches are discussed in 'Shakai Minshūtō ni koō su', *R* (February 1927), p. 5.
86. The bylaws and regulations of the Shakai Minshūtō which governed the operations of the Party at all levels were published in *NMS*. Cf. 'Shakai Minshūtō tōsōku', *NMS* (December 15, 1926), p. 1, and 'Shakai Minshūtō shibu kiyaku junsoku', p. 2 of the same issue.
87. *SGS*, I, pp. 1,181–9, and *SGS*, II, pp. 61–2.
88. Kyōchōkai, p. 599.
89. Ibid.
90. Ibid.
91. Ibid., p. 610. Also, cf. 'Hisshō o kiseru Shakai Minshūtō no kyodan', *Shakai Minshū Shimbun* (January 20, 1928), p. 1, and 'Sōsenkyo taisakusen no kōsei', *R* (February 1928), pp. 4–5.
92. Harold Quigley, *Japanese Government and Politics* (New York, 1932), p. 261.
93. Wakabayashi Ankō, 'Suzuki Bunji to senkyo', in Nakamura Katsunori, ed., *Suzuki Bunji kenkyū nōto* (Tokyo, 1966), pp. 87–90.
94. Ibid., p. 87.
95. Kyōchōkai, p. 611.
96. Katayama Tetsu, *Kaiko to tembō* (Tokyo, 1967), p. 156.
97. Colegrove, p. 335.
98. Wakabayashi, 'Suzuki Bunji to senkyo', pp. 89–90.
99. Totten, 'Japanese Social Democracy', p. 189.
100. Totten, *Social Democratic Movement*, p. 300.
101. For a list of candidates, including winners and losers from all proletarian parties in 1928, cf. ibid., pp. 414–16.
102. The Seiyūkai emerged with 217 seats in the lower house, the Minseitō, with 216. For a complete analysis of voting patterns in this election, see

Robert Scalapino, 'Elections and Political Modernization in Prewar Japan', in Ward, pp. 276–7.

103. Colegrove, p. 334.
104. Katayama, *Kaiko to tembō*, p. 156.
105. Quigley, p. 260.
106. Colegrove, p. 333.
107. Ibid., p. 335.
108. Ibid.
109. Ibid.
110. Ibid., p. 337.
111. Maurice Duverger, *Political Parties: Their Organization and Activity in the Modern State* (New York, 1967), pp. 291–4, 297–8.
112. Kono, *Nihon shakai seitō shi*, p. 119.
113. Totten, *Social Democratic Movement*, pp. 344–5. The main leaders of this organization included Suzuki Bunji, Katayama Tetsu, Akamatsu Katsumaro, and Miyazaki Ryūsuke.
114. Ibid., p. 346.
115. Suzuki Bunji, 'Seisen no ato', *R* (March 1928), p. 3.
116. This view was most strongly advanced by Suzuki; cf. ibid.
117. Colegrove, pp. 362–3.
118. Totten, 'Japanese Industrial Relations', p. 434.

6 Labor's retreat from socialist politics, 1929–1932

1. Takeshi Ishida, 'Movements to Protect Constitutional Government – A Structural-Functional Analysis', in George Totten, ed., *Democracy in Prewar Japan: Groundwork or Facade?* (Boston, 1965), p. 85.
2. Ibid., p. 75.
3. Cf. Najita, *Hara Kei*, and Duus.
4. This phrase is from Hugh Patrick, 'The Economic Muddle of the 1920s', in Morley, pp. 211–66.
5. Good sources on the economic problems of the 1920s include ibid.; Yamamura, 'Japanese Economy'; and Lockwood, *Economic Development*, Chapter II, passim.
6. Scalapino, *Democracy and the Party Movement*, p. 272.
7. Ibid., p. 293.
8. For instance, cf. Masao Maruyama, 'The Theory and Psychology of Ultranationalism in Japan', in his book, *Thought and Behaviour in Modern Japanese Politics* (London, 1963), pp. 1–24.
9. The Chang Tso-lin affair is discussed in Akira Iriye, *After Imperialism: The Search for a New Order in the Far East, 1921–1931* (Cambridge, Mass., 1965), pp. 192, 214.
10. Patrick, 'Economic Muddle', p. 255.
11. Ibid.
12. Lockwood, *Economic Development*, p. 63.
13. G. C. Allen, *A Short Economic History of Modern Japan* (New York, 1966), p. 104.
14. Ibid.
15. Ibid., p. 105.

16. Lockwood, *Economic Development*, pp. 72–3, passim.
17. Ōkōchi Kazuo and Matsuo Hiroshi, *Nihon rōdō kumiai monogatari: Shōwa* (Tokyo, 1965), p. 168.
18. Lockwood, *Economic Development*, p. 459, and Koji Taira, 'Labor Markets, Unions, and Employers in Inter-war Japan', in Adolph Sturmthal and James Scoville, eds., *The International Labor Movement in Transition* (Urbana, 1973), p. 158.
19. Lockwood, *Economic Development*, p. 567.
20. Ibid., pp. 70–1, passim.
21. Taira, 'Labor Markets', p. 159.
22. Lockwood, *Economic Development*, pp. 567–71 outlines cooperation between business and government in rationalization during and after the Depression.
23. Patrick, 'Economic Muddle', pp. 222–3.
24. Ibid., and Taira, 'Labor Markets', p. 157.
25. Patrick, 'Economic Muddle', p. 222.
26. Taira, 'Labor Markets', p. 157.
27. Ibid.
28. Ōkōchi, *Labor in Modern Japan*, pp. 56–7. He notes that government figures did not take into account hidden unemployment in the small and medium enterprises.
29. Ibid., p. 56.
30. Ibid.
31. Ibid.
32. Ibid., p. 66.
33. Ōkōchi and Matsuo (*Shōwa*), p. 172.
34. Ibid., pp. 181–3.
35. Ibid., p. 190.
36. *SGS*, II, p. 270.
37. These strikes are discussed in Ōkōchi and Matsuo (*Shōwa*), pp. 169–208.
38. *SGS*, II, p. 220.
39. Interview with Uchida Sakurō on December 6, 1971, in Tokyo and with Okada Sōji on February 25, 1972, also in Tokyo.
40. 'Rōdō kumiai no honrui ni kaere', *R* (August 1930), pp. 2–3; 'Chūshō kōgyō to rōdō kumiai', *R* (September 1930), pp. 2–3; and 'Shakai Minshūtō taikai', *NMS* (December 15, 1930), p. 1.
41. 'Nishio-shi no funtō', *NMS* (May 12, 1930), p. 1.
42. For good examples of this kind of reasoning, cf. Satō Ken'ichi, 'Seiji kōdō to keizai kōdō no kondo', *R* (March 1929), pp. 14–15; 'Musan kaikyū undō ni okeru kakuha sensen no bunya', *R* (September 1929), pp. 14–15; and 'Sayoku, uyoku oyobi chūkanha', *R* (June 1930), pp. 12–13.
43. Cf. 'Shakai Minshūtō taikai', p. 1.
44. *SGS*, II, pp. 145–51.
45. A description of these upheavals is presented in Richard Storry, *Double Patriots* (London, 1957).
46. A good account of the thought and action of Tachibana and Gondō is found in Thomas Havens, *Farm and Nation in Japan: Agrarian Nationalism, 1870–1940* (Princeton, 1974).
47. Kita and Ōkawa are discussed in Maruyama, *Thought and Behaviour*.

pp. 37–8, passim. Also cf. George Wilson, *Radical Nationalist in Japan: Kita Ikki, 1883–1937* (Cambridge, Mass., 1969).

48. Cf. George Wilson, 'Restoration History and Shōwa Politics', in George Wilson, ed., *Crisis Politics in Prewar Japan* (Tokyo, 1970), pp. 71–8.

49. Masao Maruyama, 'Patterns of Individuation and the Case of Japan: A Conceptual Scheme', in Marius Jansen, ed., *Changing Japanese Attitudes Toward Modernization* (Princeton, 1965), p. 496.

50. Shūichi Katō, 'Japanese Writers and Modernization', in ibid., p. 441.

51. This phrase was suggested to the author in this context by Professor Matsuzawa Hiroaki.

52. Cf. Stephen Pelz, *Race to Pearl Harbor* (Cambridge, Mass., 1974).

53. Sadako Ogata, *Defiance in Manchuria* (Berkeley, 1964).

54. Komatsu, *Kigyōbetsu kumiai*, p. 231.

55. Ibid.

56. Ibid., p. 232.

57. Ibid.

58. Ibid.

59. Ibid.

60. Ibid.

61. Quoted from Beckmann and Okubo, p. 174.

62. Totten, *Social Democratic Movement*, p. 325.

63. Beckmann, 'The Radical Left and the Failure of Communism', pp. 160–76.

64. Nishio, p. 258; *Kanemasa Yonekichi*, p. 102. Biographical information on the Yamanouchi faction is given in Noguchi.

65. *SGS*, II, pp. 85–93 summarizes the events of the 1929 split; a list of expelled unions is given on pp. 91–3. Other good sources are 'Sayoku no jomei', *R* (October 1929), pp. 4–6, and 'Kinkyū chūō iinkai', *R* (September 1929), p. 8.

66. Totten, *Social Democratic Movement*, p. 328.

67. The circumstances leading to the formation of the Nihon Taishūtō and the history of this Party are treated in detail in Ono, *Musan seitō*, pp. 238–43. For a briefer discussion, cf. Totten, *Social Democratic Movement*, pp. 192–4. The journal, *Chūō Kōron*, published a series of articles on the Nihon Taishūtō in its February 1929 issue under the general title, 'Nihon Taishūtō kessei hihan', pp. 33–48.

68. The history of the Zenkoku Taishūtō is discussed in Ono, pp. 344–64.

69. Totten, *Social Democratic Movement*, p. 163.

70. Ibid., p. 164.

71. The Zenkoku Minshūtō was formed January 19, 1930. Ibid., p. 303.

72. Ibid., p. 162. The structure, composition, and history of this Party are discussed in Ono, pp. 365–435.

73. Totten, *Social Democratic Movement*, pp. 326–7. Most of Sōhyō's leaders were also leaders of the Shin Rōdō Nōmintō.

74. 'Kakuchi ni hisshō o kishite Shakai Minshūtō jumbi zenji', *R* (February 1930), pp. 6–7.

75. 'Gikyo no Matsuoka-shi tatsu', *NMS* (January 21, 1930), p. 1.

76. 'Kakuchi ni hisshō', p. 7.

77. 'Gikyo no Matsuoka-shi', p. 1.

78. Nakamura, *Matsuoka Komakichi den*, pp. 196–202.

79. Katayama, *Kaiko to tembō*, p. 160.
80. Cf. the photograph in ibid., p. 161.
81. Ibid., p. 162.
82. Ibid., p. 158.
83. Totten, *Social Democratic Movement*, pp. 416–17.
84. Scalapino, 'Elections and Political Modernization', p. 278.
85. 'Sōsenkyo daizanpai', *NMS* (February 24, 1930), p. 1.
86. Ōkōchi, *Labor in Modern Japan*, p. 54.
87. The announcement confirmed to some extent high hopes expressed earlier in the Sōdōmei regarding the progressive potential of the Hamaguchi cabinet. Cf. 'Hamaguchi naikaku to rōdō kumiai undō', *R* (August 1929), pp. 4–5.
88. Nakamura, *Matsuoka Komakichi den*, p. 206.
89. Nakamura Mototada, *Nihon Kōgyō Kurabu ni jūgonen shi* (Tokyo, 1943), Volume 2, p. 702.
90. Ibid., p. 712.
91. The official decision to organize Zensanren was made in a meeting of Club officials at the headquarters of the Tokyo Chamber of Commerce on February 27, 1931. The actual inauguration of Zensanren occurred on April 21. Ibid., pp. 736–7. For a list of officers and organizations in Zensanren, see 'Zenkoku Sangyō Dantai Rengōkai no seiritsu', *R* (June, 1931), pp. 2–3.
92. Cf. Appendix, Volume 2 of Nakamura, *Nihon Kōgyō Kurabu*.
93. *SGS*, ii, p. 220, and Nakamura, *Matsuoka Komakichi den*, p. 207.
94. Nakamura, *Matsuoka Komakichi den*, p. 214.
95. Matsuoka Komakichi, 'Rōdō kumiaihō ni taisuru shihonka no byūsetsu', *R* (February 1931), pp. 2–3.
96. Ibid.
97. Nishio, p. 274.
98. Nakamura, *Nihon Kōgyō Kurabu*, Volume 2, pp. 734–5.
99. 'Kaiin Kumiai teishō no Nihon Rōdō Kurabu nara', *NMS* (July 15, 1931), p. 1.
100. Ibid.
101. Ibid.
102. Ōkōchi and Matsuo (*Shōwa*), p. 205. The events leading to the rise of the Nihon Rōdō Kurabu are also presented in *SGS*, ii, pp. 474–9. See page 477 for a list of member organizations. Another valuable source on the formation of the Kurabu is *NRUS*, Volume vii (Tokyo, 1964), pp. 353–452, which contains primary documents relating to the organization.
103. The committee members are listed in 'Kaiin Kumiai teishō', p. 1.
104. Shirai Taishirō, 'Senzen ni okeru rōdō kumiaishugi no hyōka ni tsuite', *Nihon rōdō kyōkai zasshi* (February 1961), p. 23.
105. Ōkōchi and Matsuo (*Shōwa*), p. 204.
106. *SGS*, ii, p. 477.
107. Quoted from Totten, *Social Democratic Movement*, p. 76.
108. Ibid. Also, see Shirai, p. 23.
109. Totten, *Social Democratic Movement*, pp. 76–7.
110. Indispensable sources on the formation of the Kumiai Kaigi include *SGS*, ii, pp. 480–5; Shirai, p. 24ff; and *NRUS*, vii, pp. 452–90. Participating

organizations, with their respective memberships, are listed in *SGS*, II, p. 482.

111. *SGS*, II, p. 485.
112. Shirai, 'Senzen ni okeru', pp. 30–4.
113. The official Sōdōmei record of this convention is found in *SGS*, II, pp. 830–51.
114. 'Hijō jidai ni okeru rōdō kumiai undō', *R* (February 1932), pp. 2–3.
115. Quoted from Totten, *Social Democratic Movement*, p. 259. The original text is found in the July issue of *Rōdō* in 1932.
116. 'Kakuchi ni kagayakeru tokubetsu iinkai jin'yō', *R* (January 1932), pp. 6–8.
117. 'Shina shihonshūgi bokkō de mammō ni nihon no eihaku shi', *NMS* (August 1931), p. 1.
118. 'Shakai Minshūtō no surogan', *NMS* (September 15, 1931), p. 1.
119. For instance, cf. 'Puroretaria no chi de mamoreta manshū no futatabi burujoa no kuimono ni sarasu nai', *NMS* (January 15, 1932), p. 1. Also, cf. Totten, *Social Democratic Movement*, pp. 260–5.
120. For a general analysis of the election, see Scalapino, 'Elections and Political Modernization', p. 279; Totten, *Social Democratic Movement*, pp. 305, 418–19.
121. Nishio, pp. 280–2; Nakamura, *Matsuoka Komakichi den*, pp. 197–8. Nishio's defeat was regarded as a serious setback for the Shakai Minshūtō, for he was considered one of the most able politicians in the Shaminkei. Cf. Katayama, *Kaiko to tembō*, pp. 157–8.
122. Akamatsu's views are discussed at length in 'Shakai Minshūtō bunretsu no kiki kuru', *NMS* (April 15, 1932), p. 1, and 'Hatashite dattai ni ishiki ari ya', *NMS* (May 1, 1932), pp. 22–3.
123. Totten, *Social Democratic Movement*, pp. 77–80.
124. Ibid., p. 80.
125. 'Hatashite dattai ni ishiki', p. 22.
126. Ibid., and 'Shakai Minshūtō no bunretsu to Rōdō Sōdōmei no taidō', *R* (May 1932), pp. 2–3.
127. Totten, *Social Democratic Movement*, p. 80.
128. Ibid., pp. 80–1. Space does not permit an in-depth analysis of rightist labor groups in this study. A recommended source, however, is *NRUS*, VII, pp. 598–712.
129. Kono, *Nihon shakai seitō shi*, p. 129. A thorough analysis of the new Party is provided in Ono, pp. 436ff.
130. Kono, *Nihon shakai seitō shi*, p. 127.
131. The Party's policies are discussed in Ono, pp. 439–49, and in Totten, *Social Democratic Movement*, Chapters 9 and 10, passim.
132. Totten, *Social Democratic Movement*, pp. 181–3.
133. Cf. 'Suzuki kaichō jinin happyō ni itaru made no temmatsu hōkoku sho', *R* (January 1931), pp. 6–7; *SGS*, II, pp. 105–8.
134. 'Matsuoka Komakichi Sōdōmei shuji tokanbu o jishi', *NMS* (August 15, 1932), p. 2, and Nakamura, *Matsuoka Komakichi den*, p. 227.
135. *SGS*, II, p. 227.
136. Ibid., p. 233.
137. Ibid.
138. Ibid., pp. 231–3.

139. Ibid., p. 234.
140. Taira, *Economic Development and the Labor Market*, p. 144.
141. Zald and Ash, pp. 525, 527.
142. Cf. ibid. for a good summary of the theories of Max Weber and Robert Michels, pp. 517–18, and John Wilson, *Introduction to Social Movements* (New York, 1973), Chapters VI and X, passim.
143. 'Mobilization', 'articulation', and 'integration' are terms used by Joseph Gusfield in analyzing types of social movement leadership. Cf. Zald and Ash, p. 535.
144. James Scoville, 'Some Determinants of the Structure of Labor Movements', in Sturmthal and Scoville, p. 74.
145. Joel Seidman, 'The Labor Union as an Organization', in Kornhauser, Dubin, and Ross, pp. 119–20.

7 Labor becalmed, 1932–1936

1. The text of Kikukawa's 1931 book is found in *Kikukawa Tadao*, Part Two. Cf. p. 2 for this quotation.
2. Ibid., pp. 18–19.
3. Kikukawa's bias in favor of the Zenkoku Rōdō Kumiai Dōmei is prevalent throughout his book. In particular, cf. pp. 64–75.
4. James Crowley, *Japan's Quest for Autonomy* (Princeton, 1966), Chapters III, IV, passim.
5. Quoted from Akira Iriye, 'The Failure of Military Expansionism', in Morley, p. 111.
6. 'Naishō no kunji to rōdō seisaku', *R* (June 1934), p. 3.
7. Cf. Crowley, *Japan's Quest for Autonomy*, Chapter V.
8. Ibid., pp. 262–7.
9. Cf. Maruyama, *Thought and Behaviour*, pp. 54–5, 318–19.
10. A good source in English on Minobe is Frank Miller, *Minobe Tatsukichi: Interpreter of Constitutionalism in Japan* (Berkeley, 1965).
11. This theme of self-fulfilling prophecy is discussed in Iriye, 'Failure of Military Expansionism', and Edwin Reischauer, 'What Went Wrong?', in Morley.
12. Taira, 'Labor Markets', p. 158.
13. Two of the important new combines that emerged in the 1930s were Nakajima (aircraft) and Nissan, which was active in the economic development of Manchuria.
14. Lockwood, *Economic Development*, p. 65.
15. Ibid., p. 66.
16. Ibid., pp. 67–8. Lockwood says these fears of Japanese 'dumping' were not justified.
17. Ibid., p. 70.
18. Ibid., p. 71.
19. Taira, *Economic Development and the Labor Market*, Table 17, p. 146. On p. 157, Taira offers data showing that for skilled workers in large firms, who were generally beyond the unions' reach, the average length of service in their respective factories notably increased in this period.
20. Iwao Ayusawa, 'Japan', in H. Marquand et al., eds., *Organized Labor in*

Four Continents (London, 1939), p. 489. Also, see p. 228 of Ayusawa, *A History of Labor*, for figures on union growth.

21. Ayusawa, *A History of Labor*, p. 228.
22. Ibid.
23. Ibid.
24. Ibid.
25. 'Rōdō kumiai', *R* (May 1933), pp. 22–3.
26. Nakamura, *Matsuoka Komakichi den*, p. 236. Also, cf. Beckmann, 'The Radical Left and the Failure of Communism', pp. 164–76, and Sano Manabu, 'Iwayuru tenkō ni tsuite', *Chūō Kōron* (May 1934), pp. 62–71, regarding the Sano–Nabeyama statement.
27. Totten, *Social Democratic Movement*, p. 330.
28. Ibid., p. 80.
29. Ibid., p. 81.
30. 'Wazawai o tenjite fuku to nase', *R* (March 1933), pp. 2–3.
31. Matsuoka Komakichi, 'Iwayuru "infure keiki" o mai ni shite kumiai shokun ni tsugu', *R* (February 1933), pp. 2–3.
32. *SGS*, ii, pp. 257–61 deals with the details of the campaign including its administration, strategies, and results.
33. Taira, *Economic Development and the Labor Market*, p. 147.
34. Ibid.
35. Ibid.
36. Matsuoka Komakichi, 'Sangyō kyōryoku no tettei ni maishin seyo', *R* (April 1933), pp. 2–3.
37. 'Wagakuni ni okeru dantai kyōyaku no genjō', *R* (June 1933), pp. 2–3.
38. 'Zadankai: Sōdōmei no dantai kyōyaku wa ikani unyō sareru ka?', ibid., pp. 8–11.
39. 'Zadankai: Kyōsantō sennyū shudan to nihonshugi rōdō kumiai no yakuwari', *R* (October 1933), pp. 8–12.
40. Ibid. Data on works councils are from Taira, *Economic Development and the Labor Market*, p. 148.
41. 'Zadankai' (June 1933), pp. 8–9. Also, cf. 'Zadankai: shibu kanbu no kushin o monogatari', *R* (July 1935), p. 10.
42. Matsuoka Komakichi, 'Sangyō kyōryoku undō wa kokumin undō', *R* (March 1934), p. 10.
43. Kikukawa Tadao, 'Genka rōdō kumiai undō no jōsei', *Kaizō* (May 1933), pp. 110–20.
44. *SGS*, ii, p. 244.
45. Satō Ken'ichi, 'Nihonhin no boikotto', *R* (April 1934), pp. 12–13, and 'Sangyō to rōdō tōsei no hanashi', *R* (August 1934), pp. 12–13.
46. 'Sangyō tōsei kondankai', *R* (February 1934), pp. 20–1.
47. It should be noted that the government did enact labor laws in the 1930s, especially in connection with war-mobilization late in the decade. But these laws did nothing for unions per se. Several of the laws were the Workmen's Accident Compensation Insurance Law (1931), the Retirement Provident Fund Law (1936), the National Health Insurance Law (1938), the Seamen's and Office Workers' Health Insurance Law (1939), and so on. Cf. Takahashi, pp. 444–5; Ayusawa, *A History of Labor*, pp. 230–1; and Makoto Sakurabayashi and Robert Ballon, 'Labor–Management Relations in

Modern Japan: A Historical Survey of Personnel Administration', in
Joseph Roggendorf, ed., *Studies in Japanese Culture: Tradition and
Experiment* (Tokyo, 1965), pp. 260–1.

48. Nishio, p. 289.
49. Kishimoto, 'The Characteristics of Labor–Management Relations' (April
1966), pp. 27–34.
50. *SGS*, II, pp. 468–73 deals with the *toppa* campaigns.
51. Ibid., p. 538.
52. This conscious effort to rationalize union affairs was intended to parallel
industrial rationalization undertaken by business in this period. Cf. ibid.,
pp. 384–92.
53. Ibid., p. 380.
54. These programs are analyzed in ibid., pp. 359–76. Besides consumer
cooperatives and clinics, the Sōdōmei maintained fire and unemployment
insurance schemes, financed emergency strike funds, and so on. This was
done at the union local level under the supervision of Federation headquarters which conducted regular audits of union records pertaining to
these programs.
55. Ibid., pp. 337–47 provides information on the construction program.
56. Ibid., p. 382.
57. Ibid., pp. 390–1.
58. Ibid., p. 380.
59. Ibid.
60. Ibid., p. 381.
61. Ibid., p. 1,122.
62. Ibid., pp. 1,047–8.
63. Ibid., pp. 1,050–1.
64. Ibid., p. 1,014.
65. Events leading to the formation of the Congress are presented in ibid.,
pp. 500–5.
66. During its existence the Congress passed various resolutions against Western
capitalism and imperialism in Asia and was also critical of the ILO for not
doing enough to assist Asian workers in colonialized areas. The Congress also
condemned Western racial prejudice against Asians. Cf. ibid., pp. 506–7,
and Totten, *Social Democratic Movement*, p. 275. *SGS*, II, pp. 510–19
sketches the history of the Congress after 1934.
67. Good sources on the Sōdōmei's expectations of the merger are Nishio,
pp. 300–1; 'Sensen tōitsu to warera no taidō', *R* (July 1935), p. 3; and
Matsuoka Komakichi, 'Gōdō narite', *R* (December 1935), p. 3. For
Nichirōkei thoughts on the merger, cf. Kikukawa, 'Genka rōdō kumiai undō
no jōsei', *Kaizō* (May 1933), pp. 114–19. Kikukawa argued here that the
Nichirōkei could use the merger to push the Sōdōmei toward political
struggle. This view was also expressed by Yamakawa Hitoshi in an article,
'Hijō ni aegu rōdō kumiai undō', *Kaizō* (June 1934), pp. 118–27.
68. An excellent account of the negotiations is given in *SGS*, II, pp. 534–6.
The merger had the support of Shaminkei and Nichirōkei political leaders
in the Shakai Taishūtō; cf. p. 529, passim.
69. Information on the inaugural convention of the Zen Nihon Rōdō Sōdōmei
is provided in ibid., pp. 537–40. Cf. pp. 541–3 for a list of unions, with their

respective memberships, of both the Sōdōmei and the Dōmei which comprised the merger. A list of formal policy statements and the platform of the merger are also found in this account.

70. Ibid., p. 536.
71. Ibid., pp. 538–40. Related primary documents which shed light on the formation of the Zen Nihon Rōdō Sōdōmei and its political character are found in *NRUS*, vii, pp. 712–30.
72. Nishio refers to this problem in connection with lingering Sōdōmei–Dōmei rivalry in Osaka. Cf. *Taishū to tomo ni*, p. 303.
73. Abe's position, in relation to Shaminkei labor leaders, was not much different from Suzuki Bunji's after 1919 in the sense that both men were regarded as valuable for their symbolic leadership and prestige more than as power-holders in the labor movement per se.
74. An indispensable source on Asō in this period is William Wray, 'Asō Hisashi and the Search for Renovation in the 1930's', *Papers on Japan*, v (Cambridge, Mass., 1970). Cf. pp. 59 60 regarding Asō's fervent anti capitalism in the early phase of the Depression.
75. Ibid., p. 63 discusses Asō's contacts with Ōkawa.
76. Ibid., pp. 61–2. Asō's interest in cooperating with the army stemmed in part from his fascination with an army pamphlet written by Nagata Tetsuzan, *Kokubō no hongi to sono kyōka no teimei* (1934) in which Nagata stressed sweeping reforms to strengthen defense and correct social injustices produced by liberalism and capitalism in Japan. Asō's reaction to this document is discussed by Wray and by Kawakami, pp. 455–9. Also, cf. Totten, *Social Democratic Movement*, pp. 92–3.
77. Quoted from Kawakami, p. 457.
78. Reactions in the Party to Asō's position on cooperating with the army are described in Ōkōchi and Matsuo (*Shōwa*), pp. 295–7.
79. *Miwa Jusō*, pp. 354–5.
80. Ōkōchi and Matsuo (*Shōwa*), p. 297.
81. Totten, *Social Democratic Movement*, Chapter 9, passim.
82. Cf. ibid., Chapter 10, passim.
83. Ibid., p. 306.
84. Totten, 'Japanese Social Democracy', p. 182.
85. *Miwa Jusō*, p. 328.
86. Ono, p. 465.
87. Ibid., pp. 465–6.
88. Ibid., p. 467.
89. Scalapino, 'Elections and Political Modernization', pp. 280–1.
90. Totten, *Social Democratic Movement*, pp. 419–20.

8 Toward dissolution, 1936–1940

1. Nakamura, *Matsuoka Komakichi den*, p. 244.
2. *SGS*, ii, p. 558.
3. Ibid.
4. Ibid.
5. Ibid., p. 563.
6. Nakamura, *Matsuoka Komakichi den*, p. 254.

7. For instance, cf. Matsuoka Komakichi, 'Kangyō Rōdō no kin'en o nan zu', *R* (October 1936), p. 1, and 'Shōwa jūichinen o okuru', *R* (December 1936), p. 1.

8. Asō Hisashi continued to be very active in the Party in the attack on Hirota. Cf. Asō Hisashi, 'Kakushinteki taishū seiryoku no sōzōteki hatten', *R* (January 1937) for a typical statement of his views of Hirota.

9. Scalapino, *Democracy and the Party Movement*, p. 385.

10. Ibid.

11. Kawakami, pp. 465, 468.

12. Wray, 'Asō Hisashi and the Search for Renovation', pp. 70–3.

13. *Miwa Jusō*, pp. 352–4.

14. Kawakami, p. 469.

15. Totten, *Social Democratic Movement*, Table 8, p. 308.

16. Scalapino, 'Elections and Political Modernization', p. 282.

17. Totten, *Social Democratic Movement*, p. 308.

18. Ibid.

19. Ibid.

20. Ibid., p. 98.

21. Ibid., pp. 420–1.

22. Quoted from Kawakami, p. 471.

23. Sasa Hirō, 'High Voters' Abstention Does Not Mean Denial of Political Parties', translated from *Asahi Shūkan* (May 16, 1937) in *Contemporary Opinions on Current Topics* (Tokyo Information Bureau), No. 176 (January–June 1937), pp. 1–3.

24. Kawai Eijirō, 'Social Mass Party Made Outstanding Showing in Recent Elections', translated from *Kaizō* (June 1937) in ibid., No. 179 (January–June 1937), pp. 1–4.

25. Baba Tsunego, 'Political Parties Likely to be Power in Not Remote Future', translated from *Kaizō* (April 1937) in ibid., No. 171 (January–June 1937), pp. 9–11.

26. Nakamura, *Matsuoka Komakichi den*, p. 248.

27. Ben-Ami Shillony, 'Myth and Reality in Japan of the 1930's', in W. G. Beasley, ed., *Modern Japan: Aspects of History, Literature, and Society* (London, 1975), p. 84.

28. An analysis of Konoe is found in Richard Storry, 'Konoye Fumimaro, "The Last of the Fujiwara"', St Anthony's Papers, VII, in G. F. Hudson, ed., *Far Eastern Affairs*, No. 2 (London, 1960), pp. 9–23.

29. An authoritative source on the outbreak of the war in 1937 is James Crowley, *Japan's Quest for Autonomy* (Princeton, 1966), Chapter VI, passim.

30. For a concise discussion of this legislation, cf. W. G. Beasley, *Modern History of Japan* (New York, 1963), pp. 253–4.

31. Ibid., p. 254.

32. *SGS*, II, pp. 901–2.

33. Ibid., p. 902.

34. Ibid., p. 901.

35. Information on the 'Home Front Campaign' (*jūgo undō*) is given in ibid., pp. 622–38.

36. Nakamura, *Matsuoka Komakichi den*, p. 255.

37. *SGS*, II, p. 638.
38. Ibid.
39. Ibid., pp. 641–2.
40. Ibid., p. 642.
41. Ibid., pp. 642–3.
42. Lockwood, *Economic Development*, p. 144.
43. For a discussion of these strikes, see *SGS*, II, pp. 580–91.
44. Wray, 'Asō Hisashi and the Search for Renovation', pp. 73–4, and Ono, p. 32.
45. Wray, 'Asō Hisashi and the Search for Renovation', p. 74.
46. The Party also supported in principle Japan's leadership over a new 'League of Asiatic Races'.
47. Wray, 'Asō Hisashi and the Search for Renovation', p. 74.
48. Ibid.
49. Totten, *Social Democratic Movement*, pp. 100, 332. Zempyō had roughly 12,000 members.
50. For a critique of Katō's views on the Sino-Japanese War, cf. ibid., p. 172.
51. Ōkōchi and Matsuo (*Shōwa*), p. 333. Cf. William Wray, 'The Japanese Popular Front Movement, July, 1936–February, 1938', *Papers on Japan*, VI (Cambridge, Mass., 1972) on the history of the popular front.
52. This is another metaphor that is sometimes used by Japanese writers to refer to the final eclipse of the labor and proletarian party movements in this period. It also sometimes refers to the repression of the socialist movement in the late Meiji period.
53. Totten, *Social Democratic Movement*, p. 102, note 53.
54. Robert Spaulding, 'The Bureaucracy as a Political Force, 1920–1945', in Morley, p. 62.
55. Totten, *Social Democratic Movement*, p. 103. Nakamizo, with Konoe's approval, also organized a gang of roughnecks known as the Bōkyō Gokokudan, or Anti-Communist Protect the Country Corps, to attack the headquarters of the Seiyūkai and the Minseitō, to frighten these parties into dissolution. Whether Asō knew of this initiative on Nakamizo's part is uncertain.
56. Kashiwagi Saburō, 'Social Mass Party Forced to Turn to Totalitarianism', translated from *Konnichi no Mondai* (February 1939) in *Contemporary Opinions on Current Topics*, No. 266 (January–June 1939), pp. 4–5.
57. The text of Nishio's remarks is found in Katayama, *Kaiko to tembō*, pp. 189–90. Also, cf. Nishio, pp. 319–22.
58. Gordon Berger, *Parties Out of Power in Japan, 1931–1941* (Princeton, 1977), p. 156.
59. Nishio, p. 323.
60. Ibid. Nishio returned to the Diet one year later.
61. *Miwa Jusō*, pp. 371–2.
62. Matsuoka's concern was reflected in his article, 'Shinko no kyokoku itchi to sono kyōka', *R* (August 1937), p. 1. The text is reproduced in *SGS*, II, pp. 573–4.
63. *SGS*, II, pp. 647–9.
64. Ibid., p. 648. The organizations comprising Sampō were all part of the Sangyō Hōkoku Renmei (Industrial Patriotic League), as it is known. In

November 1940 the name of the Renmei was changed into Dai-Nippon Sangyō Hōkokukai (Japan Association for Service to the State Through Industry). Most accounts, however, use the term Sampō to refer to the League and in particular to the *hōkokukai* in the factories. This is the practice followed in this book.

65. Nakamura, *Matsuoka Komakichi den*, p. 263.
66. *SGS*, II, p. 646. Even so, Zensanren was obliged to officially support Sampō, which it did. Cf. Nakamura, *Nihon Kōgyō Kurabu*, II, p. 1051.
67. The full list of the board is available in Ōkōchi and Matsuo (*Shōwa*), p. 347. Matsuoka's name does not appear inasmuch as technically he was an 'adviser' to the board. It should be noted that Miwa Jusō was on the board.
68. Ibid., p. 349.
69. Ibid.
70. *SGS*, II, p. 653.
71. Ōkōchi and Matsuo (*Shōwa*), p. 350.
72. Ibid., p. 363.
73. *SGS*, II, pp. 688–701 deals with Japan's withdrawal from the ILO, which took place officially on November 3, 1938, and the Kaigi's opposition to the withdrawal.
74. Ibid., p. 655.
75. Ibid., p. 678.
76. *Kanemasa Yonekichi*, pp. 167–9, and *SGS*, II, p. 669.
77. *Kanemasa Yonekichi*, pp. 166–7.
78. Ibid., p. 166.
79. Interview with Uchida Sakurō on December 6, 1971.
80. There are several good accounts of this meeting. Cf. *SGS*, II, pp. 671–4; Nishio, pp. 331–2; and Nakamura, *Matsuoka Komakichi den*, p. 266. Also, cf. Ōkōchi and Matsuo (*Shōwa*), pp. 354–7.
81. Both sides issued final statements summarizing their positions at the time of separation. The Shaminkei reasserted that it wanted to maintain the autonomy of the labor movement from Sampō and regretted that Kono Mitsu and others in the Nichirōkei wished to see the movement dissolved. In reply, the Nichirōkei stressed that patriotic duty to the nation compelled full compliance with Sampō, including dissolution of the independent labor movement. The documents in question are found in *SGS*, II, pp. 671–3.
82. Ibid., p. 673.
83. Totten, *Social Democratic Movement*, p. 334.
84. *SGS*, II, p. 673.
85. Ibid.
86. The complete official record of this convention is available in ibid., pp. 906–12.
87. Ibid., p. 673.
88. *Miwa Jusō*, pp. 340–1.
89. Robert Butow, *Tōjō and the Coming of the War* (Princeton, 1961), p. 134.
90. Kawakami, p. 478.
91. The Abe and Yonai cabinets are discussed briefly in Butow, *Tōjō*, pp. 138–40. Pp. 140–3 deal with the selection of Konoe as Yonai's successor and some of the men, including Tōjō Hideki, who were appointed to Konoe's second cabinet.

92. An excellent analysis of Nakano is Tetsuo Najita, 'Nakano Seigō and the Spirit of the Meiji Restoration in Twentieth-Century Japan', in Morley, pp. 375–421.
93. As Najita says, 'The plans broke down at the very last stage because neither side could be convinced as to which would "absorb" the other'. Ibid., p. 410. Other sources on the merger talks and their ultimate failure include *Miwa Jusō*, pp. 331–6; Kawakami, pp. 479–82; and Nishio, p. 333. Another good source, which includes primary documents concerning the aborted merger with the Tōhōkai is Kono, *Nihon shakai seitō shi*, pp. 162–5.
94. Kono, *Nihon shakai seitō shi*, p. 169 presents the key parts of Saitō's critique.
95. Katayama, *Kaiko to tembō*, pp. 191–5.
96. Ibid., p. 195, and Kono, *Nihon shakai seitō shi*, pp. 170–1.
97. Nishio, pp. 335–6.
98. Ōkōchi and Matsuo (*Shōwa*), p. 359.
99. *Miwa Jusō*, pp. 342–3.
100. *SGS*, II, p. 709.
101. Ibid., p. 712.
102. Cf. ibid., pp. 712–13 for policy statements of the Party.
103. The text of Matsuoka's article is reproduced in ibid., pp. 714–15.
104. The continuity of Asō's socialist idealism is emphasized by Wray, 'Asō Hisashi and the Search for Renovation', p. 77.
105. Quoted from Kitamura Saburō, "Service-to-the-Nation-Through-Industry-Movement in Japan", translated from *Genchi Hōkoku* (June 10, 1940), in *Contemporary Opinions on Current Topics*, No. 333, January–June, 1940, p. 10.
106. Ibid.
107. Quoted from *SGS*, II, pp. 717–18.
108. Kitamura, 'Service-to-the-Nation', p. 10.
109. Nakamura, *Matsuoka Komakichi den*, p. 167.
110. Kitamura, 'Service-to-the-Nation', p. 11.
111. Ibid., p. 12.
112. Nakamura, *Matsuoka Komakichi den*, p. 269.
113. *SGS*, II, p. 719.
114. Ibid., pp. 678, 717, and *Kanemasa Yonekichi*, p. 171.
115. *Miwa Jusō*, pp. 343–4 discusses the dissolution of the Party. A series of documents reflecting Miwa's enthusiasm for the New Order are reproduced on pp. 382–90.
116. This marked the end of the centrist labor movement. Many of the movement's leaders subsequently became officials in Sampō.
117. Scalapino, *Democracy and the Party Movement*, p. 388.
118. For a thoughtful assessment of the IRAA, cf. Gordon Berger, *Parties Out of Power in Japan, 1931–1941* (Princeton, 1977), Chapters VII and VIII, passim.
119. *Kanemasa Yonekichi*, p. 172.
120. Nishio, pp. 339–40.
121. *Kanemasa Yonekichi*, p. 172. The final decision to close down the Sōdōmei was not unanimous: Kanemasa opposed it to the end. Also, cf. Ōkōchi and Matsuo (*Shōwa*), p. 363.

122 The dismantling of the Sōdōmei proved to be a rather complicated and somewhat prolonged procedure. In part, this was due to the fact that the central committee was not permitted by the Home Ministry to publish its formal declaration to disband which was drawn up on July 7. According to *SGS*, II (p. 723), this made it necessary for the committee to communicate its decision informally to those unions still in existence. Then, too, arrangements had to be made to close down the bureaucratic offices of individual unions and regional federations, turn their funds over to Sampō and dispose of such things as Sōdōmei flags, badges, and publications. All of the labor halls, including the main one in Tokyo, likewise were turned over to Sampō. These problems are discussed in *SGS*, II, pp. 727ff.

123. Ibid., pp. 725–7.

124. Nishio, p. 230.

125. Ishida, 'The Development of Interest Groups', p. 297.

126. Ibid. Ishida explains that 'The "freezing" of an organization means a functional paralysis making further development difficult.' Cf. note 3, p. 297. The concept of 'freezing' is similar to that of 'becalming', discussed earlier in this study in reference to the theories of Zald and Ash. Relating 'governmentalization' to 'freezing', Ishida writes of the former: 'In this process the specific purposes of interest groups become fused with governmental purposes and thus accelerate the freezing process.'

127. Cf. Morris, *Nobility of Failure*.

128. For instance, Miwa Jusō became Chief of the Liaison Section of the IRAA's Organization Board; Kawakami Jōtarō became a member of the IRAA Secretariat; Kono Mitsu served as Vice-Chief of the Lower House Screening Section of the IRAA's Diet Board; and Kikukawa Tadao served on the Secretariat of Sampō. Had he lived long enough, Asō Hisashi would have also served on the IRAA Secretariat, at Konoe's request, but Asō died in September 1940, after a long illness. Cf. Kawakami, p. 295. *SGS*, II, pp. 728–9 remarks on the subsequent careers of the above-mentioned men in the New Order.

129. Quoted from Takeshi Ishida, 'Elements of Tradition and "Renovation" in Japan During the "Era of Fascism" ', *Annals of the Institute of Social Science* (University of Tokyo), No. 17 (1976), p. 120.

130. Sakurabayashi and Ballon, p. 260.

131. Ibid.

132. Ibid.

133. Ōkōchi, Karsh, and Levine, p. 496.

Conclusion

1. Taira, 'Labor Markets', p. 168.

2. Ibid., p. 169.

3. Cf. Ariizumi, pp. 91–4. Article Twenty-Eight of the new Constitution states, 'The right of workers to organize and to bargain and act collectively is guaranteed'.

4. These figures are as of June 1977. *Japan Labor Bulletin* (Japan Institute of Labor), 17:3 (March 1, 1978), pp. 4–5.

5. An excellent short survey of the postwar Japanese labor movement is

found in Hisashi Kawada and Ryūji Komatsu, 'Post-war Labor Movements in Japan', in Sturmthal and Scoville, pp. 123–48. Also, cf. Solomon Levine, 'Postwar Trade Unionism, Collective Bargaining, and Japanese Social Structure', in Dore, ed., *Aspects of Social Change*, pp. 245–85; Scalapino, 'Labor and Politics in Postwar Japan', pp. 669–720; Solomon Levine, *Industrial Relations in Postwar Japan* (Urbana, 1958); Shiota Shōbei, *Gendai rōdō kumiai undō ron* (Tokyo, 1969); and Yamazaki Gorō, *Nihon rōdō undō shi* (Tokyo, 1966).

6. On the importance of the 'spring offensives', cf. Taishirō Shirai, 'Collective Bargaining' and Wakao Fujita, 'Labor Disputes', in Ōkōchi, Karsh, and Levine, passim.

7. Cf. George Totten et al., *Socialist Parties in Postwar Japan* (New Haven, 1966), and Scalapino, 'Labor and Politics in Postwar Japan'.

8. Cole, 'Theory of Institutionalization', p. 57.

9. Evans, p. 125.

10. Solomon Levine and Koji Taira, 'Labor Markets, Trade Unions, and Social Justice: Japanese Failures?', *Japanese Economic Studies*, v:3 (Spring 1977), p. 75.

11. Ibid.

12. Ibid., p. 76.

13. Ibid., p. 81.

14. Cf. James McBrearty, *American Labor History and Comparative Labor Movements: A Selected Bibliography* (Tucson, 1973) for sources on American labor history.

15. Mikio Sumiya, 'Japanese Industrial Relations Revisited: A Discussion of the *Nenkō* System', *Japanese Economic Studies*, v:3 (Spring 1977), p.37.

16. Cf. R. W. Fleming, 'The Significance of the Wagner Act', in Milton Derber and Edwin Young, eds., *Labor and the New Deal* (Madison, 1957), p. 149.

17. Dore, *British Factory–Japanese Factory*, p. 415.

18. Ibid., p. 410.

19. Ibid., p. 413.

20. Levine and Taira, p. 81.

21. Levine, 'Labor Markets and Collective Bargaining', p. 646.

22. Adolph Sturmthal, 'Industrial Relations Strategies', in Sturmthal and Scoville, pp. 9–11.

23. This discussion of the British labor movement is based on Harvey Mitchell, 'Labor and the Origins of Social Democracy in Britain, France, and Germany, 1890–1914', in Harvey Mitchell and Peter Stearns, *Workers and Protest: The European Labor Movement, the Working Classes, and the Origins of Social Democracy, 1890–1914* (Itasca, Illinois, 1971), pp. 27–35.

24. Ibid., p. 25.

25. Ibid., pp. 31–2.

26. This brief summary of German labor history is based on Richard Hunt, *German Social Democracy, 1918–1933* (New Haven, 1964), Chapters 1, 2 and 5, and Helga Grebing, *The History of the German Labour Movement: A Survey* (London, 1966), Chapters 1–3.

27. Hunt, p. 152.

28. Grebing, p. 71.

29. Ibid., pp. 54–8 deals with the impact of the Law on German labor.
30. This phrase is from Edwin Reischauer, 'What Went Wrong?', pp. 489–510. Some of the literature which compares Japan and Germany includes Maruyama, *Thought and Behaviour*, passim; Kentarō Hayashi, 'Japan and Germany in the Interwar Period', in Morley, pp. 461–88; David Landes, 'Japan and Europe: Contrasts in Industrialization', in Lockwood, ed., *State and Economic Enterprise*, pp. 93–182; and Reinhard Bendix, 'Preconditions of Development: A Comparison of Japan and Germany', in Dore, ed., *Aspects of Social Change*, pp. 27–68.
31. Cf. Grebing, Chapter 6.
32. Ibid., p. 101.
33. Cf. Hunt, 'Conclusion: The Middle-Aged Party', pp. 241–60.
34. Ibid., p. 254.
35. Ibid., p. 178.
36. Mitchell in Mitchell and Stearns, p. 223.
37. This is the main theme in Peter Stearns, 'The European Labor Movement and the Working Classes, 1890–1914', in Mitchell and Stearns, pp. 118–221.
38. Adolph Sturmthal, *The Tragedy of European Labor* (London, 1970), p. 53.
39. This is Sturmthal's phrase; cf. ibid.
40. Cf. Ralph Turner and Lewis Killian, *Collective Behavior* (Englewood Cliffs, New Jersey, 1957), p. 320, and Wilson, *Introduction to Social Movements*, pp. 340–43, 353–6, 359.
41. Quoted from Val Lorwin, 'Working-Class Politics and Economic Development in Western Europe', *American Historical Review*, No. 2 (January 1958), p. 342.
42. Ibid.
43. Stearns in Mitchell and Stearns, p. 124.
44. Ibid., p. 201.
45. Ibid., p. 213.
46. Ibid., p. 151.
47. Ibid., p. 168.
48. Stephen Hill, 'Norms, Groups, and Power: The Sociology of Workplace Industrial Relations', *British Journal of Industrial Relations*, XII:2 (July 1974), p. 221.
49. Totten, 'Collective Bargaining and Works Councils', p. 205.
50. This phrase is from Karsh, 'Development of a Strike', in Gusfield, p. 315.
51. Quoted from Wray, 'Asō Hisashi and the Search for Renovation', p. 80.
52. Quoted from ibid., p. 64.
53. Chie Nakane, *Japanese Society* (London, 1974), pp. 1–8, passim.
54. Ishida, 'Elements of Tradition', p. 133.
55. Ibid., p. 136.
56. Ronald Dore, *City Life in Japan: A Study of a Tokyo Ward* (Berkeley, 1967), p. 216.
57. W. G. Beasley, *The Meiji Restoration* (Stanford, 1972), p. 424.
58. Dore, *City Life*, pp. 219–20.
59. Scoville, 'Some Determinants', p. 68.
60. Dore, *City Life*, p. 216.
61. Bendix, 'Preconditions', p. 30.
62. Ibid., p. 54, and Dore, *City Life*, p. 218.

63. Dore, *City Life*, p. 219.
64. Ibid.
65. Ibid., p. 220.
66. Quoted from Bendix, 'Preconditions', p. 53.
67. George Lichtheim, *A Short History of Socialism* (London, 1970), p. 205.
68. Bendix, 'Preconditions', p. 54.
69. Quoted from Hunt, p. 145.
70. Ibid., p. 143.
71. Ibid., pp. 142–3.
72. Harry Marks, 'The Sources of Reformism in the Social Democratic Party of Germany, 1890–1914', *Journal of Modern History*, No. 3 (September 1939), p. 343.
73. Ibid., p. 350.
74. Ibid., p. 343.
75. Hunt, p. 143.
76. Quoted from ibid., p. 146.
77. Ibid., p. 147.
78. Peter Lösche, 'Stages in the Evolution of the German Labor Movement', in Sturmthal and Scoville, p. 109.
79. Ibid., p. 110.
80. Lichtheim, pp. 234–5.
81. Nishio, p. 282.
82. Nakamura, *Matsuoka Komakichi den*, p. 187.
83. Nishio, p. 299.
84. Ibid.
85. Ibid., p. 14.
86. Nakamura, *Matsuoka Komakichi den*, pp. 373–5.
87. Harootunian, 'Introduction: A Sense of an Ending', pp. 16–17.
88. Ibid.
89. Lösche, p. 110.
90. Takeshi Ishida, *Japanese Society* (New York, 1971), p. 37.
91. Hiroshi Hazama, 'Historical Changes in the Life Style of Industrial Workers', in Patrick, ed., *Japanese Industrialization and Its Social Consequences*, p. 41, passim.
92. Gareth Stedman-Jones, 'Working-Class Culture and Working-Class Politics in London, 1870–1900: Notes on the Remaking of a Working Class', *Journal of Social History*, 7:4 (Summer 1974), p. 478.
93. Ibid., p. 499.
94. Ibid.
95. Robert Cole, 'Japanese Workers, Unions, and the Marxist Appeal', *Japan Interpreter*, vi:2 (Summer 1970), p. 125.
96. Ibid., p. 126.
97. Quoted from ibid., p. 123.
98. Fukuo Noda, 'Introduction' [to a study of the left-wing movement in Japan], *Journal of Social and Political Ideas in Japan*, iii:i (April 1965), p. 2.

Glossary

anākizumu   anarchism
bunka   culture
bunretsu   split
   dai-ichiji bunretsu   'first great split'
   dai-niji bunretsu   'second great split'
   dai-sanji bunretsu   'third great split'
chokusetsu kōdō   direct action
chūritsuteki   centrist
genjitsuteki na shakaishugi   'realist socialism'
genrō   elder statesmen
gikaishugi   parliamentarianism
gōdō rengō   amalgamated federation; centralization
goyō kumiai   company union
gunbatsu   military cliques
hanbatsu   ruling cliques
hōkō no tenkan   change of direction
jigyō ikka   'enterprise family'
jiyū rengō   free federation; decentralization
jōkyū shokuin   top-grade employees
jōyō-kō   regular or permanent workers
kaihō   liberation
kaizō   reconstruction
kakushin   renovation; reform
kakyū shokuin   low-grade employees
kanryōbatsu   bureaucratic cliques
kenjitsuteki na kumiaishugi   'sound unionism'
kigyōbetsu kumiai   enterprise unions
kinrō kaikyū   'devotedly laboring class'
kinrō taishū   'masses of working people'
kisei seitō   'established parties'
kōchō   workshop foremen
kōin   factory workers
kōjō iinkai   works councils
kokata   'child figure'; follower
kokutai   'national polity'
kumichō   workbench foremen
kyokoku itchi   national unity
kyōyō   self-refinement

minarikō   apprentice workers
musan kaikyū   'propertyless class'; proletariat
nenkō seido   'length of service system'
Nichirōkei   'Japan Labor Clique'
onjōshugi   paternalism
oyakata   'father figure' or 'parent figure'; leader
puroretariāto (or *puroretaria*)   proletariat
rengōkai   federation
rinji-kō   temporary workers
rōdō   labor
rōdō gakkō   labor schools
rōdō kizoku   'labor aristocracy'
rōdō kumiai   labor unions
rōdōsha   workers
rōmu   labor management
sangyō gōrika   industrial rationalization
sangyō heiwa   industrial peace
sangyō hōkokukai   industrial patriotic societies
sangyō kyōryoku   industrial cooperation
sayoku   left wing
shain   company officials
shakaishugi   socialism
Shaminkei   'Socio-Democratic Clique'
shokuchō   foremen
shuji   director
shūjū kankei   hierarchical relations
shūshin koyō   lifetime employment
teikokushugi   imperialism
toppa   'breakthrough' (campaign)
uyoku   right wing
zadankai   roundtable discussions
zaibatsu   financial combines

Bibliography
Selected works

I. PRIMARY SOURCES IN JAPANESE

Periodicals

Chūō kōron
Demokurashī
Kaihō
Kaizō
Marukusushugi
Nihon minshū shimbun
Nihon rōdō nenkan
Rōdō
Rōdō kumiai
Rōdō oyobi sangyō
Rōdō shimbun
Rōdō undō
Rōdōsha shimbun
Rōnō
Shakaishugi
Shin Kōbe
Zen'ei

Selected books and articles

Abe Isoo, *Seiji dōtoku ron*. Tokyo, 1930.
　Shitsugyō mondai. Tokyo, 1929.
Akamatsu Katsumaro, *Atarashii yabanshugi*. Tokyo, 1939.
　Kaihō undō no shidō riron. Tokyo, 1929.
　Kokuminshugi to shakaishugi. Tokyo, 1931.
　Nihon rōdō undō hattatsu shi. Tokyo, 1925.
　Nihon shakai undō shi. Tokyo, 1968.
　Shakai minshūshugi no hata no shita ni. Tokyo, 1930.
　Shakai undō ni okeru genjitsushugi. Tokyo, 1928.
　Shin kokumin undō no kichō. Tokyo, 1932.
Arahata Kanson, *Hantaisei o ikite*. Tokyo, 1972.
　Kanson jiden. Tokyo, 1960.
Kamijō Aiichi, 'Ni, san no rimen shi'. *Rōdō undō shi kenkyū* (March, 1962),
　pp. 17–26.
　Rōdō undō yawa. Tokyo, 1950.
Katayama Tetsu, *Kaiko to tembō*. Tokyo, 1967.
　Seijiteki jiyū no kakutoku. Tokyo, 1928.
Kikukawa Tadao, *Rōdō kumiai soshiki ron*. Tokyo, 1931.

Kono Mitsu, *Nihon rōdō undō shoshi.* Tokyo, 1947.
  Nihon shakai seitō shi. Tokyo, 1960.
  Waga kuni ni okeru rōdō mondai. Tokyo, 1931.
Koyama Hisao, *Shitsugyō mondai.* Tokyo, 1929.
Matsuoka Komakichi, *Noda dai rōdō sōgi.* Tokyo, 1928.
  Rōdō kumiai ron. Tokyo, 1929.
Nabeyama Sadachika, *Shakai minshūshugi to no tōsō.* Tokyo, 1932.
Nihon Kyōsantō chūō iinkai shuppanbu, editors, *Watanabe Masanosuke chosa-kushū,* Tokyo, 1967.
Nishio Suehiro, *Taishū to tomo ni.* Tokyo, 1952.
Noda Ritsuta, *Hyōgikai tōsō shi.* Tokyo, 1932.
  Rōdō undō jissen ki. Tokyo, 1937.
Ōsugi Sakae, *Ōsugi Sakae zenshū.* Eight volumes, Tokyo, 1926.
Ōzawa Masamichi, editor, *Ōsugi Sakae sen: rōdō undō ronshū.* Tokyo, 1970.
Rōdō undō shiryō iinkai, editors, *Nihon rōdō undō shiryō.* Volume VII, Tokyo, 1964; Volume X, Tokyo, 1968.
Sōdōmei dai-ichiji bunretsu o megutte–zadankai'. *Rōdō undō shi kenkyū* (January 1963), pp. 40–8; (March 1963), pp. 34–9.
Suzuki Bunji, *Rōdō rippō ron.* Tokyo, 1929.
  Rōdō undō nijūnen. Tokyo, 1931,
Takata Waitsu, *Nazo no rōdō fungi: Shibaura jiken no shinso.* Tokyo, 1920.
Tanahashi Kotora, 'Yūaikai o omoide'. *Rōdō undō shi kenkyū* (March 1962), pp. 1–13, 23–6.
Tanaka Sōgorō, editor, *Taishō shakai undō shi: shiryō.* Two volumes, Tokyo, 1970.
Taniguchi Zentarō, *Nihon Rōdō Kumiai Hyōgikai shi.* Two volumes, Tokyo, 1949.
Tanno Setsu, *Tanno Setsu: kakumei undō ni ikiru.* Tokyo, 1970.
Uchida Tōshichi, 'Tekkō rōdōsha to shite'. *Rōdō undō shi kenkyū* (March 1962), pp. 14–16.
Watanabe Masanosuke, *Sayoku rōdō kumiai no soshiki to seisaku.* Tokyo, 1930.
Yamakawa Hitoshi, *Shakaishugi seitō no hanashi.* Tokyo, 1949.
Yoshino Sakuzō, *Kindai seiji no kompon mondai.* Tokyo, 1929.
  Nihon musan seitō ron. Tokyo, 1929.
'Yūaikai jidai o kataru'. *Rōdō undō shi kenkyū* (September 1962).

II. SECONDARY SOURCES IN ENGLISH AND JAPANESE

Abegglen, James, *The Japanese Factory.* Glencoe, 1958.
Allen, G. C., *A Short Economic History of Modern Japan.* New York, 1966.
Ariizumi Tōru, 'The Legal Framework: Past and Present'. In *Workers and Employers in Japan: The Japanese Employment Relations System,* edited by Kazuo Ōkōchi, Bernard Karsh, and Solomon Levine, pp. 89–132. Tokyo, 1973.
Arima Tatsuo, *The Failure of Freedom: A Portrait of Modern Japanese Intellectuals.* Cambridge, Mass., 1969.
Ayusawa, Iwao, *A History of Labor in Modern Japan.* Honolulu, 1966.
  'Japan'. In *Organized Labor in Four Continents,* edited by H. Marquand et al., pp. 481–510. London, 1939.
Beckmann, George, 'The Radical Left and the Failure of Communism'. In

Dilemmas of Growth in Prewar Japan, edited by James Morley, pp. 139–78. Princeton, 1971.

Beckmann, George, and Genji Okubo, *The Japanese Communist Party 1922–1945*. Stanford, 1969.

Bendix, Reinhard, 'Preconditions of Development: A Comparison of Japan and Germany'. In *Aspects of Social Change in Modern Japan*, edited by R. Dore, pp. 27–68. Princeton, 1967.

Bernstein, Gail, *Japanese Marxist: A Portrait of Kawakami Hajime, 1879–1946*. Cambridge, Mass., 1976.

Bernstein, Irving, 'Union Growth and Structural Cycles'. In *Labor and Trade Unionism: An Interdisciplinary Reader*, edited by Walter Galenson and Seymour Martin Lipset, pp. 73–101. New York, 1960.

Bikle, George, *The New Jerusalem: Aspects of Utopianism in the Thought of Kagawa Toyohiko*. Tucson, 1976.

Changing Patterns (The) of Industrial Relations: Proceedings of the International Conference on Industrial Relations. Tokyo, 1965.

Cole, G. D. H., *British Working Class Politics, 1832–1914*. London, 1941.

Cole, Robert E., *Japanese Blue Collar: The Changing Tradition*. Berkeley, 1971.
    'Japanese Workers, Unions, and the Marxist Appeal'. *Japan Interpreter*, VI:2 (Summer 1970), pp. 114–34.
    'The Theory of Institutionalization: Permanent Employment and Tradition in Japan'. *Economic Development and Cultural Change*, XX:1 (1971), pp. 47–70.

Colegrove, Kenneth, 'Labor Parties in Japan'. *American Political Science Review*, XXIII:2 (May 1929), pp. 329–63.

Dahrendorf, Ralf, *Class and Class Conflict in Industrial Society*. Stanford, 1959.

Dore, Ronald, editor, *Aspects of Social Change in Modern Japan*. Princeton, 1967.
    British Factory–Japanese Factory: The Origins of National Diversity in Industrial Relations. London, 1973.
    City Life in Japan: A Study of a Tokyo Ward. Berkeley, 1967.

Duus, Peter, *Party Rivalry and Political Change in Taishō Japan*. Cambridge, Mass., 1968.

Duverger, Maurice. *Political Parties: Their Organization and Activity in the Modern State*. New York, 1967.

Evans, Robert, 'Evolution of the Japanese System of Employer–Employee Relations, 1863–1945'. *Business History Review*, XLIV:1 (Spring 1970), pp. 110–25.

Eyck, Erich, *A History of the Weimar Republic*. Two volumes, New York, 1967.

Fujita Wakao, 'Labor Disputes'. In *Workers and Employers in Japan: The Japanese Employment Relations System*, edited by Kazuo Ōkōchi, Bernard Karsh, and Solomon Levine, pp. 309–60. Tokyo, 1973.

Funahashi Naomichi, 'The Industrial Reward System: Wages and Benefits'. In *Workers and Employers in Japan: The Japanese Employment Relations System*, edited by Kazuo Ōkōchi, Bernard Karsh, and Solomon Levine, pp. 361–97. Tokyo, 1973.

Galenson, Walter and Seymour Martin Lipset, editors, *Labor and Trade Unionism: An Interdisciplinary Reader*. New York, 1960.

Gay, Peter, *The Dilemma of Democratic Socialism: Eduard Bernstein's Challenge to Marx*. New York, 1952.

Geschwender, James, 'Explorations in the Theory of Social Movements and Revolutions'. *Social Forces* (December 1968), pp. 127–35.

Grebing, Helga, *The History of the German Labour Movement: A Survey.* London, 1966.

Gurr, Ted, *Why Men Rebel.* Princeton, 1970.

Gusfield, Joseph, editor, *Protest, Reform, and Revolution.* New York, 1970.

Halliday, Jon, *A Political History of Japanese Capitalism.* New York, 1975.

Harada Shūichi, *Labor Conditions in Japan.* New York, 1928.

Harootunian, Harry, 'Between Politics and Culture: Authority and the Ambiguities of Intellectual Choice in Imperial Japan'. In *Japan in Crisis: Essays on Taishō Democracy*, edited by Bernard Silberman and Harry Harootunian, pp. 110–55. Princeton, 1974.

'Introduction: A Sense of an Ending and the Problem of Taishō'. In *Japan in Crisis: Essays on Taishō Democracy*, edited by Bernard Silberman and Harry Harootunian, pp. 3–28. Princeton, 1974.

Hayashi Kentarō, 'Japan and Germany in the Interwar Period'. In *Dilemmas of Growth in Prewar Japan*, edited by James Morley, pp. 461–88. Princeton, 1971.

Hazama Hiroshi, 'Historical Changes in the Life Style of Industrial Workers'. In *Japanese Industrialization and Its Social Consequences*, edited by Hugh Patrick, pp. 21–51. Berkeley, 1976.

Nihon rōmu kanrishi kenkyū. Tokyo, 1964.

Heberle, Rudolf, *Social Movements: An Introduction to Political Sociology.* New York, 1951.

Hill, Stephen, 'Norms, Groups and Power: The Sociology of Workplace Industrial Relations'. *British Journal of Industrial Relations*, XII:2 (July 1974), pp. 213–35.

Hirschmeier, Johannes and Tsunehiko Yui, *The Development of Japanese Business, 1600–1973.* London, 1975.

Hobsbawm, Eric J., 'Labor History and Ideology'. *Journal of Social History*, 7:4 (Summer 1974), pp. 371–81.

Hunt, Richard, *German Social Democracy, 1918–1933.* New Haven, 1964.

Ichikawa Shōichi, *Nihon Kyōsantō tōsō shoshi.* Tokyo, 1954.

Iida Kanae, 'Rōdō undō shi kenkyū no tame ichi-tōron – Ōkōchi Kazuo kyoju no rōdō undō ron ni yoseru'. *Nihon rōdō kyōkai zasshi* (February 1963), pp. 13–20.

Ikeda Makoto, 'Dai-ichiji taisen ni okeru rōdō kumiai undō no tokushitsu'. *Nihon rōdō kyōkai zasshi* (February 1968), pp. 11–21.

Nihon kikaikō kumiai seiritsu shi ron. Tokyo, 1970.

Ikeda Makoto and Ōmae Gorō, *Nihon rōdō undō shi ron.* Tokyo, 1967.

Inoue Kiyoshi and Watanabe Tōru, *Taishōki no kyūshinteki jiyūshugi.* Tokyo, 1972.

Iriye Akira, 'The Failure of Economic Expansion: 1918–1931'. In *Japan in Crisis: Essays on Taishō Democracy*, edited by Bernard Silberman and Harry Harootunian, pp. 237–69. Princeton, 1974.

'The Failure of Military Expansionism'. In *Dilemmas of Growth in Prewar Japan*, edited by James Morley, pp. 107–38. Princeton, 1971.

Ishida Takeshi, 'The Development of Interest Groups and the Pattern of Political Modernization in Japan'. In *Political Development in Modern Japan*, edited by Robert E. Ward, pp. 293–336. Princeton, 1968.

'Elements of Tradition and "Renovation" in Japan During the "Era of

Fascism" '. *Annals of the Institute of Social Science* (University of Tokyo), No. 17 (1976), pp. 111–40.

Japanese Society. New York, 1971.

'Movements to Protect Constitutional Government – A Structural-Functional Analysis'. In *Democracy in Prewar Japan: Groundwork or Facade?*, edited by George Totten, pp. 75–89. Boston, 1965.

Itō Takashi, *Taishōki 'kakushin' ha no seiritsu.* Tokyo, 1978.

Jansen, Marius, editor, *Changing Japanese Attitudes Towards Modernization.* Princeton, 1965.

Joll, James, *The Anarchists.* New York, 1965.

Kajinishi Mitsuhaya et al., *Seishi rōdōsha no rekishi.* Tokyo, 1955.

Kamijō Aiichi, editor, *Yamana Yoshitsuru no kiroku.* Tokyo, 1968.

Kanemasa Yonekichi. See first Sōdōmei entry on p. 310.

Katō Shūichi, 'Japanese Writers and Modernization'. In *Changing Japanese Attitudes Toward Modernization*, edited by Marius Jansen, pp. 425–46. Princeton, 1965.

'Taishō Democracy as the Pre-Stage for Japanese Militarism'. In *Japan in Crisis: Essays on Taishō Democracy*, edited by Bernard Silberman and Harry Harootunian, pp. 217–36. Princeton, 1974.

Kawada Hisashi and Komatsu Ryūji. 'Post-war Labor Movements in Japan'. In *The International Labor Movement in Transition*, edited by Adolph Sturmthal and James Scoville, pp. 123–48. Urbana, 1973.

Kawakami Jōtarō, *Asō Hisashi den.* Tokyo, 1958.

Kerr, Clark, John Dunlop, Frederick Harbison and Charles Myers, *Industrialism and Industrial Man: The Problems of Labor and Management in Economic Growth.* New York, 1964.

Kikukawa Tadao tsuitō shuppan iinkai, editors, *Kikukawa Tadao: sono shisō to jissen.* Tokyo, 1956.

Kishimoto Eitarō, 'The Characteristics of Labor-Management Relations in Japan and their Historical Formation'. *Kyoto University Economic Review* (October 1965), pp. 33–5; (April 1966), pp. 17–38.

Nihon rōdō undō shi. Tokyo, 1950.

Kobayashi Jun'ichirō kankō iinkai, editor, *Kobayashi Jun'ichirō.* Tokyo, 1964.

Koga Susumu, *Saikin nihon no rōdō undō.* Tokyo, 1924.

Komatsu Ryūji, *Kigyōbetsu kumiai no seisei.* Tokyo, 1971.

Nihon anākizumu undō shi. Tokyo, 1972.

'Taishō-Shōwa shoki ni okeru jiyū rengōshugi rōdō undō to kikanshi shi'. *Rōdō undō shi kenkyū* (September 1962), pp. 1–14.

Kornhauser, Arthur, 'Human Motivations Underlying Industrial Conflict'. In *Industrial Conflict*, edited by Arthur Kornhauser, Robert Dubin, and Arthur Ross, pp. 62–85. New York, 1956.

Kornhauser, Arthur, Robert Dubin, and Arthur Ross, editors, *Industrial Conflict.* New York, 1956.

Koyama Kōken, 'Nihon marukusushugi no keisei'. In *Shōwa no hantaisei shisō*, edited by Sumiya Etsuji et al., pp. 68–146. Tokyo, 1968.

Kublin, Hyman, *Asian Revolutionary: The Life of Sen Katayama.* Princeton, 1964.

Kyōchōkai, editors, *Saikin no shakai undō.* Tokyo, 1929.

Labor Relations in the Asian Countries: Proceedings of the Second International Conference on Industrial Relations. Tokyo, 1967.

Landes, David, 'Japan and Europe: Contrasts in Industrialization'. In *The State and Economic Enterprise in Japan*, edited by William Lockwood, pp. 93–182. Princeton, 1965.

Large, Stephen, 'The Japanese Labor Movement, 1912–1919: Suzuki Bunji and the Yūaikai'. *Journal of Asian Studies*, XXIX:3 (May 1970), pp. 559–79.

'Nishio Suehiro and the Japanese Social Democratic Movement, 1920–1940'. *Journal of Asian Studies*, XXXVI:1 (November 1976), pp. 37–56.

'Perspectives on the Failure of the Labor Movement in Prewar Japan'. *Labor History*, No. 37 (November 1979), pp. 15–27.

'Revolutionary Worker: Watanabe Masanosuke and the Japanese Communist Party, 1922–1928'. *Asian Profile*, 3:4 (August 1975), pp. 371–90.

The Rise of Labor in Japan: The Yūaikai, 1912–1919. Tokyo, 1972.

'The Romance of Revolution in Japanese Anarchism and Communism During the Taishō Period'. *Modern Asian Studies*, II:3 (1977), pp. 441–67.

Lebra, Takie Sugiyama, *Japanese Patterns of Behavior*. Honolulu, 1976.

Levine, Solomon, *Industrial Relations in Postwar Japan*. Urbana, 1958.

'Labor Markets and Collective Bargaining in Japan'. In *The State and Economic Enterprise in Japan*, edited by William Lockwood, pp. 633–67. Princeton, 1965.

Levine, Solomon, and Koji Taira, 'Labor Markets, Trade Unions and Social Justice: Japanese Failures?'. *Japanese Economic Studies*, V:3 (Spring 1977), pp. 66–95.

Lichtheim, George, *A Short History of Socialism*. London, 1970.

Lipset, Seymour Martin, 'The Political Process in Trade Unions: A Theoretical Statement'. In *Labor and Trade Unionism: An Interdisciplinary Reader*, edited by Walter Galenson and Seymour Martin Lipset, pp. 216–242. New York, 1960.

Lockwood, William, *The Economic Development of Japan: Growth and Structural Change*. Princeton, 1954.

editor, *The State and Economic Enterprise in Japan*. Princeton, 1965.

Lorwin, Val, 'Working-Class Politics and Economic Development in Western Europe'. *American Historical Review*, No. 2 (January 1958), pp. 338–51.

Lösche, Peter, 'Stages in the Evolution of the German Labor Movement'. In *The International Labor Movement in Transition*, edited by Adolph Sturmthal and James Scoville, pp. 101–22. Urbana, 1973.

Marks, Harry, 'The Sources of Reformism in the Social Democratic Party of Germany, 1890–1914'. *Journal of Modern History*, No. 3 (September 1939), pp. 334–56.

Marshall, Byron, *Capitalism and Nationalism in Prewar Japan: The Ideology of the Business Elite, 1868–1941*. Stanford, 1967.

Maruyama Masao, *Nihon no shisō*. Tokyo, 1975.

'Patterns of Individuation and the Case of Japan: A Conceptual Scheme'. In *Changing Japanese Attitudes Toward Modernization*, edited by Marius Jansen, pp. 489–531. Princeton, 1965.

Thought and Behaviour in Modern Japanese Politics. London, 1963.

Matsuo Hiroshi, 'Manshū jihen zen'ya no rōdō sōgi, rōdō kumiai'. *Rōdō undō shi kenkyū* (June 1966), pp. 10–16.

Nihon rōdō undō shi. Tokyo, 1965.

'Yūaikai, Sōdōmei no rōdō kumiaika, sentōka katei to sampa no hassei'. *Rōdō undō shi kenkyū* (January 1963), pp. 23–35.

Matsuo Takayoshi, 'The Development of Democracy in Japan'. *Developing Economies*, IV:4 (December 1966), pp. 612–37.

Taishō demokurashī no kenkyū. Tokyo, 1966.

Matsuzawa Hiroaki, *Nihon shakaishugi no shisō.* Tokyo, 1973.

McBriar, A. M., *Fabian Socialism and English Politics.* Cambridge, 1962.

Michels, Robert, *Political Parties.* New York, 1962.

Mitchell, Harvey and Peter Stearns, *Workers and Protest: The European Labor Movement, the Working Classes, and the Origins of Social Democracy, 1890–1914.* Itasca, Ill., 1971.

Mitchell, Richard, *Thought Control in Prewar Japan.* Ithaca, 1976.

Miwa Jusō denki kankōkai, editors, *Miwa Jusō no shōgai.* Tokyo, 1966.

Mizuno Hironori, *Musan kaikyū to kokubō mondai.* Tokyo, 1929.

Mori Kiichi, *Nihon rōdōsha kaikyū jōtai shi.* Two volumes, Tokyo, 1974.

Morley, James, editor, *Dilemmas of Growth in Prewar Japan.* Princeton, 1971.

Morris, Ivan, *The Nobility of Failure: Tragic Heroes in the History of Japan.* London, 1975.

Murayama Kazunori, 'Nihon Rōdō Sōdōmei ni kamei shita roku kumiai ni tsuite'. *Shakai undō kenkyū* (December 1961), pp. 1–21.

Najita Tetsuo, *Hara Kei in the Politics of Compromise.* Cambridge, Mass., 1967.

'Some Reflections on Idealism in the Political Thought of Yoshino Sakuzō'. In *Japan in Crisis: Essays on Taishō Democracy,* edited by Bernard Silberman and Harry Harootunian, pp. 29–66. Princeton, 1974.

Naka Masao, *Senkusha no keifu.* Tokyo, 1949.

Nakamura Katsunori, 'Shakai Minshūtō no dai-ichinen'. *Hōgaku kenkyū* (June 1971), pp. 1–19.

'Shakai Minshūtō no seishin'. *Hōgaku kenkyū* (February 1971), pp. 37–53.

'Shakai Minshūtō no sōritsu'. *Hōgaku kenkyū* (October 1970), pp. 101–17.

editor, *Suzuki Bunji kenkyū nōto.* Tokyo, 1966.

Nakamura Kikuo, *Matsuoka Komakichi den.* Tokyo, 1964.

Nakamura Mototada, *Nihon Kōgyō Kurabu ni jūgonen shi.* Two volumes, Tokyo, 1943.

Nakane Chie, *Japanese Society.* London, 1974.

Nimura Kazuo, 'Senzen ni okeru rōdō undō no honkakuteki hatten to haiboku'. In *Nihon rōdō undō no rekishi to kadai,* edited by Rōdō undō shi kenkyūkai, pp. 46–73. Tokyo, 1970.

Noda Fukuo, 'Introduction'. *Journal of Social and Political Ideas in Japan,* iii:1 (April 1965), pp. 2–17.

Noguchi Gimei, *Musan undō sōtōshi.* Tokyo, 1931.

Nōshōmu shō, shōkō kyoku, *Shokkō jijō.* Tokyo, 1903.

Notehelfer, Fred G., *Kōtoku Shūsui: Portrait of a Japanese Radical.* Cambridge, 1971.

Okamoto Hideaki, 'Management and Their Organizations'. In *Workers and Employers in Japan: The Japanese Employment Relations System,* edited by Kazuo Ōkōchi, Bernard Karsh, and Solomon Levine, pp. 163–215. Tokyo, 1973.

Ōkōchi Kazuo, 'The Characteristics of Labor–Management Relations in Japan'. *Journal of Social and Political Ideas in Japan,* iii:3 (December 1965), pp. 44–9.

Kurai tanima no rōdō undō. Tokyo, 1970.

Labor in Modern Japan. Tokyo, 1958.

'Traditionalism of Industrial Relations in Japan'. In *The Changing Patterns of Industrial Relations: Proceedings of the International Conference on Industrial Relations,* pp. 126–41. Tokyo, 1965.

Ōkōchi Kazuo, Bernard Karsh, and Solomon Levine, editors, *Workers and Employers in Japan: The Japanese Employment Relations System*. Tokyo, 1973.

Ōkōchi Kazuo and Matsuo Hiroshi, *Nihon rōdō kumiai monogatari: Meiji*. Tokyo, 1965.

Nihon rōdō kumiai monogatari: Shōwa. Tokyo, 1965.

Nihon rōdō kumiai monogatari: Taishō. Tokyo, 1965.

Ono Setsuko et al., *Musan seitō no kenkyū*. Tokyo, 1969.

Orchard, John, *Japan's Economic Position: The Progress of Industrialization*. New York, 1930.

Ōshima Kiyoshi, 'Rōdō kumiai no tanjō: Takano Fusatarō no shōgai'. *Hōsei* (October 1968), pp. 26–31.

Takano Iwasaburō den. Tokyo, 1968.

Ōyama Nobuyoshi, 'Nihon no rōshi kankei to kyōdōtai chitsujo'. *Nihon rōdō kyōkai zasshi* (October 1970), pp. 10–27.

Ōzawa Masamichi, *Ōsugi Sakae kenkyū*. Tokyo, 1968.

Patrick, Hugh, 'The Economic Muddle of the 1920s'. In *Dilemmas of Growth in Prewar Japan*, edited by James Morley, pp. 211–66. Princeton, 1971.

editor, *Japanese Industrialization and Its Social Consequences*. Berkeley, 1976.

Pelling, Henry, *A History of British Trade Unionism*. Baltimore, 1963.

The Origins of the Labour Party. London, 1954.

Piovesana, Gino, 'Men and Social Ideas of the Early Taishō Period'. *Monumenta Nipponica*, Volume xxx (1964), pp. 111–29.

Quigley, Harold, *Japanese Government and Politics*. New York, 1932.

Reischauer, Edwin, 'What Went Wrong?' In *Dilemmas of Growth in Prewar Japan*, edited by James Morley, pp. 489–510. Princeton, 1971.

Reynolds, Lloyd, *Labor Economics and Labor Relations*. New York, 1953.

Rimlinger, Gaston, 'The Legitimation of Protest: A Comparative Study in Labor History'. In *Protest, Reform, and Revolution*, edited by Joseph Gusfield, pp. 363–76. New York, 1970.

Roth, Guenther, *The Social Democrats in Imperial Germany: A Study in Working Class Isolation and Integration*. Totawa, New Jersey, 1963.

Sakurabayashi Makoto and Robert Ballon, 'Labor–Management Relations in Modern Japan: A Historical Survey of Personnel Administration'. In *Studies in Japanese Culture: Tradition and Experiment*, edited by Joseph Roggendorf, pp. 245–66. Tokyo, 1965.

Saxonhouse, Gary, 'Country Girls and Communication Among Competitors in the Japanese Cotton-Spinning Industry'. In *Japanese Industrialization and Its Social Consequences*, edited by Hugh Patrick, pp. 97–125. Berkeley, 1976.

Scalapino, Robert, *Democracy and the Party Movement in Prewar Japan: The Failure of the First Attempt*. Berkeley, 1962.

'Elections and Political Modernization in Prewar Japan'. In *Political Development in Modern Japan*, edited by Robert E. Ward, pp. 249–91.

'Japan: Between Traditionalism and Democracy'. In *Modern Political Parties: Approaches to Comparative Politics*, edited by Sigmund Neumann, pp. 305–53. Chicago, 1956.

The Japanese Communist Movement, 1920–1966. Berkeley, 1967.

'Labor and Politics in Postwar Japan'. In *The State and Economic Enterprise in Japan*, edited by William Lockwood, pp. 669–720. Princeton, 1965.

Schorske, Carl, *German Social Democracy, 1905–1917*. Cambridge, Mass., 1955.

Scoville, James, 'Some Determinants of the Structure of Labor Movements'. In *The International Labor Movement in Transition*, edited by Adolph Sturmthal and James Scoville, pp. 58–78. Urbana, 1973.

Seidman, Joel, 'The Labor Union as an Organization'. In *Industrial Conflict*, edited by Arthur Kornhauser, Robert Dubin, and Arthur Ross, pp. 109–20. New York, 1956.

Shiga Yoshio, *Nihon kakumei undō shi no hitobito*. Tokyo, 1948.

Shillony, Ben-Ami, 'The February 26 Affair: Politics of a Military Insurrection'. In *Crisis Politics in Prewar Japan*, edited by George Wilson, pp. 25–50. Tokyo, 1970.

'Myth and Reality in Japan of the 1930's'. In *Modern Japan: Aspects of History, Literature, and Society*, edited by W. G. Beasley, pp. 81–8. London, 1975.

Revolt in Japan: The Young Officers and the February 26, 1936 Incident. Princeton, 1973.

Shimada Haruo, 'Nenkōsei no shiteki keisei ni tsuite'. *Sangyō kenkyūjo shiriizu*, edited by Keiō Gijuku Daigaku Sangyō Kenkyūjo, No. 227 (1968–1969), pp. 39–75.

Shinabu Seizaburō, *Taishō demokurashi shi:* Volumes I and II, Tokyo, 1965, and Volume III, Tokyo, 1968.

Taishō seiji shi. Tokyo, 1968.

Shiota Shōbei, *Gendai rōdō kumiai undō ron.* Tokyo, 1969.

'Sensō zen'ya to undō shi kadai'. *Rōdō undō shi kenkyū* (June 1966), p. 2.

'1929–39nen ni okeru nihon no keizai kiki to rōdō undō'. *Rōdō undō shi kenkyū* (January 1960), pp. 1–10.

Shirai Taishirō, 'Senzen ni okeru rōdō kumiaishugi no hyōka ni tsuite'. *Nihon rōdō kyōkai zasshi* (February 1961), pp. 20–35.

Shisō no kagaku kenkyūkai, editor, *Tenkō.* Volume I, Tokyo, 1968.

Silberman, Bernard, 'The Political Thought of Yoshino Sakuzō'. *Journal of Modern History*, XXXI:4 (December 1959), pp. 310–24.

Silberman, Bernard, and Harry Harootunian, editors, *Japan in Crisis: Essays on Taishō Democracy.* Princeton, 1974.

Simcock, Bradford, 'The Anarcho-Syndicalist Thought and Action of Ōsugi Sakae'. *Papers on Japan*, Volume I (Cambridge, Mass., 1970), pp. 31–54.

Smith, Henry, *Japan's First Student Radicals.* Cambridge, Mass., 1972.

Sōdōmei gojūnen shi konkō iinkai, editors, *Kanamasa Yonekichi tsuisōroku.* Tokyo, 1969.

Sōdōmei gojūnen shi kankō iinkai, editors, *Sōdōmei gojūnen shi.* Volume I, Tokyo, 1965, and Volume II, Tokyo, 1967.

Spaulding, Robert, 'The Bureaucracy as a Political Force, 1920–1945'. In *Dilemmas of Growth in Prewar Japan*, edited by James Morley, pp. 33–80. Princeton, 1971.

Stedman-Jones, Gareth, 'Working-Class Culture and Working-Class Politics in London, 1870–1900: Notes on the Remaking of a Working Class'. *Journal of Social History*, 7:4 (Summer 1974), pp. 460–508.

Storry, Richard, *Double Patriots.* London, 1957.

'Konoye Fumimaro, "The Last of the Fujiwara"'. St Anthony's Papers, No. VII. *Far Eastern Affairs*, No. 2, edited by G. F. Hudson, London, 1960, pp. 9–23.

Sturmthal, Adolph, *Comparative Labor Movements: Ideological Roots and Institutional Development.* Belmont, California, 1972.

The Tragedy of European Labor. London, 1970.

Unity and Diversity in European Labor, 1953.

Sturmthal, Adolph, and James Scoville, editors, *The International Labor Movement in Transition.* Urbana, 1973.

Suehiro Izutarō, *Nihon rōdō kumiai undō shi.* Tokyo, 1950.

Sugimoto Yoshio, 'Economic Fluctuations and Popular Disorders in Prewar Japan'. Unpublished paper presented to the Forty-Sixth Australia–New Zealand Association for the Advancement of Science Congress in Canberra, January 1975.

'Surplus Value, Unemployment and Industrial Turbulence: A Statistical Application of the Marxian Model to Postwar Japan'. *Journal of Conflict Resolution* (March 1975), pp. 25–47.

Sumiya Etsuji et al., editors, *Shōwa no hantaisei shisō.* Tokyo, 1968.

Taishō demokurashī no shisō. Tokyo, 1967.

Sumiya Mikio, 'The Emergence of Modern Japan'. In *Workers and Employers in Japan: The Japanese Employment Relations System,* edited by Kazuo Okōchi, Bernard Karsh, and Solomon Levine, pp. 15–48. Tokyo, 1973.

'Japanese Industrial Relations Revisited: A Discussion of the *Nenkō* System'. *Japanese Economic Studies,* v:3 (Spring 1977), pp. 3–47.

Nihon no shakai shisō Tokyo, 1968.

Nihon rōdō undō shi. Tokyo, 1966.

Suzuki Jirō, *Uyoku no rekishi.* Tokyo, 1967.

Tada Shin'ichi, *Numazu shibu rōdō undō jūnen shi.* Shizuoka, 1937.

Taira Koji, *Economic Development and the Labor Market in Japan.* New York, 1970.

'Factory Legislation and Management Modernization During Japan's Industrialization, 1886–1916'. *Business History Review,* XLIV:1 (Spring 1970), pp. 84–109.

'Labor Markets, Unions, and Employers in Inter-war Japan'. In *The International Labor Movement in Transition,* edited by Adolph Sturmthal and James Scoville, pp. 149–77. Urbana, 1973.

Takagi Ikurō, 'Musan seitō no shisō'. In *Shōwa no hantaisei shisō,* edited by Sumiya Etsuji et al., pp. 147–204. Tokyo, 1968.

Takahashi Takeshi, 'Social Security for Workers'. In *Workers and Employers in Japan: The Japanese Employment Relations System,* edited by Kazuo Ōkōchi, Bernard Karsh, and Solomon Levine, pp. 441–84. Tokyo, 1974.

'Takata Waitsu'. *Rōdō undō shi kenkyū* [published by the Saitama Prefecture Labor Movement History Research Society] (March 1967), pp. 10–50.

Tanaka Sōgorō, *Yoshino Sakuzō.* Tokyo, 1958.

Tatewaki Sadayo, 'Rōdō fujin undō no senzen to sengo'. *Rōdō undō shi kenkyū* (March 1960), pp. 24–41.

Totten, George, 'Collective Bargaining and Works Councils as Innovations in Industrial Relations in Japan During the 1920s'. In *Aspects of Social Change in Modern Japan,* edited by R. P. Dore, pp. 203–43. Princeton, 1967.

editor, *Democracy in Prewar Japan: Groundwork or Facade?* Boston, 1965.

'Japanese Industrial Relations at the Crossroads: The Great Noda Strike of 1927–1928'. In *Japan in Crisis: Essays on Taishō Democracy,* edited by Bernard Silberman and Harry Harootunian, pp. 398–436. Princeton, 1974.

'Japanese Social Democracy: An Analysis of the Background, Leadership, and Organized Support of the Social Democratic Movement in Prewar Japan'.

Ph.D. dissertation, Yale University, 1954; Publication No. 11,212, University Microfilms, Ann Arbor, Michigan.

'Labor and Agrarian Disputes in Japan Following World War I'. *Economic Development and Cultural Change*, IX:1, part II (October 1960), pp. 187–212.

The Social Democratic Movement in Prewar Japan. New Haven, 1966.

Totten, George, et al., *Socialist Parties in Postwar Japan*. New Haven, 1966.

Tsuda Masumi, 'The Basic Structure of Japanese Labor Relations'. *Musashi daigaku ronshū* (May 1964), pp. 1–104.

Tsunekawa Nobuyuki, *Nihon Kyōsantō to Watanabe Masanosuke*. Tokyo, 1971.

Turner, Ralph and Lewis Killian, *Collective Behavior*. Englewood Cliffs, New Jersey, 1957.

Ujihara Shōjirō, 'Japan's Laboring Class: Changes in the Postwar Period'. *Journal of Social and Political Ideas in Japan*, III:3 (December 1965), pp. 60–7.

Uyehara, Cecil, *Left-Wing Social Movements in Japan: An Annotated Bibliography*. Tokyo and Rutland, Vermont, 1959.

Ward, Robert E., editor, *Political Development in Modern Japan*. Princeton, 1968.

Watanabe Tōru, *Nihon rōdō kumiai undō shi*. Tokyo, 1954.

'Taishō 8nen ni okeru rōdō kumiai ron no kentō'. *Jimbun gakuhō*, Volume 20 (1964), pp. 233–46.

'Yūaikai no soshiki no jittai'. *Jimbun gakuhō* (October 1963), pp. 1–70.

'1919nen yori 21nen ni itaru rōdō undō shisō no sui-i'. In *Taishōki no seiji to shakai*, edited by Inoue Kiyoshi, pp. 205–50. Tokyo, 1969.

et al., editors, *Nihon shakaishugi undō shi ron*. Tokyo, 1973.

Webb, Sidney and Beatrice, *History of Trade Unionism*. London, 1920.

Wilson, George, editor, *Crisis Politics in Prewar Japan*. Tokyo, 1970.

Radical Nationalist in Japan: Kita Ikki, 1883–1937. Cambridge, Mass., 1969.

'Restoration History and Shōwa Politics'. In *Crisis Politics in Prewar Japan*, edited by George Wilson, pp. 71–8. Tokyo, 1970.

Wilson, John, *Introduction to Social Movements*. New York, 1973.

Wray, William, 'Asō Hisashi and the Search for Renovation in the 1930s'. *Papers on Japan*, V (Cambridge, Mass., 1970), pp. 55–98.

'The Japanese Popular Front Movement, July, 1936–February, 1938'. *Papers on Japan*, VI (Cambridge, Mass., 1972).

Yamamura Kozo, 'The Japanese Economy, 1911–1930: Concentration, Conflicts, and Crises'. In *Japan in Crisis: Essays on Taishō Democracy*, edited by Bernard Silberman and Harry Harootunian, pp. 299–328. Princeton, 1974.

Yoshino, Michael, *Japan's Managerial System: Tradition and Innovation*. Cambridge, Mass., 1968.

Zald, Mayer and Roberta Ash, 'Social Movement Organizations: Growth, Decay, and Change'. In *Protest, Reform, and Revolution*, edited by Joseph Gusfield, pp. 327–40. New York, 1970.

Index